PRECERAMIC SUBSISTENCE IN TWO ROCK SHELTERS IN FRESNAL CANYON, SOUTH CENTRAL NEW MEXICO

Vorsila L. Bohrer

Arizona State Museum
THE UNIVERSITY OF ARIZONA.

Arizona State Museum Archaeological Series 199

Arizona State Museum
The University of Arizona
Tucson, Arizona 85721-0026

ISBN (paper): 978-1-88-974781-1

Library of Congress Control Number: 2007936125

ARIZONA STATE MUSEUM ARCHAEOLOGICAL SERIES

General Editors: E. Charles Adams and Richard C. Lange
Technical Editors: Melanie A. Dedecker and Richard C. Lange

The *Archaeological Series* of the Arizona State Museum, The University of Arizona, publishes the results of research in archaeology and related disciplines conducted in the Southwest U.S. and Northwest Mexico. Original, monograph-length manuscripts are considered for publication, provided they deal with appropriate subject matter. Information regarding procedures or manuscript submission and review may be obtained from the General Editor, *Archaeological Series*, Arizona State Museum, P.O. Box 210026, The University of Arizona, Tucson, Arizona, 85721-0026; Email: ecadams@u.arizona.edu or langer@email.arizona.edu

Publication of this volume was made possible by generous grants from the Arizona State Museum and Eastern New Mexico University.
Distributed by The University of Arizona Press, 355 S. Euclid Ave., Suite 103, Tucson, Arizona 85719

CONTENTS

Contents   iii

List of Figures   vi

List of Tables   vi

Acknowledgments   viii

Chapter 1. Introduction   1

Chapter 2. Environmental and Cultural   5

    Part I. The Environment of the Tularosa Basin and the
    Sacramento Mountains   5
      The Tularosa Basin   5
      The Chihuahuan Desert   7
      Modern Fresnal Canyon Vegetation   12
      Location of Suitable Areas for Farming   13
      Physiography   13
    Part II. Sources of Evidence of Post Pleistocene Climate and Vegetation   14
      Wood Rat Middens   14
      Geomorphological Studies   14
      Stalagmite Studies   15
      Modern Climate   15
      Rock Shelter Species in Relation to Post Pleistocene Vegetation   16
    Part III. Cultural Activity in the Tularosa Basin and the Sacramento Mountains   17
      Prehistory   17
      History of the Tularosa Basin   23

Chapter 3. Nature of the Rockshelter Deposits, Related Problems and Ethnobotanical Procedures   25

    Part I. Influences on Site Formation, Preservation, Stratigraphy and Dating   25
    Overview of the Two Rock Shelters   25
      Abiotic Influences   25
      Biotic Factors   29
      Fresnal Shelter Features, Stratigraphy and Dating   31
      High Rolls Cave Stratigraphy, Features and Dating   37
    Part II. Ethnobotanical Procedures in the Two Rock Shelters   38
      Fresnal Shelter Ethnobotanical Analysis   38
      High Rolls Cave Ethnobotanical Analysis   46

Chapter 4. Distribution of Plant Taxa in the Rock Shelters with Notes Pertaining to their Nature and
    Potential Significance to Humans and Rodents   49

    The Subsistence Scoring System for Fresnal Shelter   49

Interpreting Plant Remains at High Rolls Cave from a Later Time Perspective   51
Cone Bearing Evergreens or Gymnosperms   52
    Cupressaceae (Cypress Family)   52
    Pinaceae (Pine Family)   54
Monocotyledonous Flowering Plants   57
    Agavaceae (Agave Family)   57
    Cyperaceae (Sedge Family)   61
    Liliaceae (Lily Family)   61
    Poaceae (GrassFamily)   62
    Typhaceae (Cattail Family)   72
Dicotyledonous Flowering Plants   73
    Aizoaceae (Carpetweed Family)   73
    Amaranthaceae (Amaranth Family)   73
    Anacardiaceae (Sumac Family)   76
    Apiaceae (Parsley Family)   78
    Apocynaceae (Dogbane Family)   78
    Asteraceae (Sunflower Family)   79
    Berberidaceae (Barberry Family)   83
    Boraginaceae (Borage Family)   83
    Brassicaceae (Mustard Family)   83
    Cactaceae (Cactus Family)   83
    Capparidaceae (Caper Family)   86
    Chenopodiaceae (Goosefoot Family)   86
    Convolvulaceae (Morning Glory Family)   88
    Cucurbitaceae (Squash Family)   89
    Ericaceae (Heather Family)   90
    Fabaceae (Pea or Legume Family)   91
    Fagaceae (Beech Family)   94
    Fouquieriaceae (Ocotillo Family)   94
    Garryaceace (Silk Tassel Family)   95
    Lamiaceae (Mint Family)   95
    Malvaceae (Mallow Family)   96
    Nyctaginaceae (Four O'Clock Family)   96
    Oleaceae (Olive Family)   97
    Portulaceaceae (Purslane Family)   97
    Ranunculaceae (Crowfoot Family)   98
    Rosaceae (Rose Family)   98
    Rutaceae (Rue Family)   99
    Solanaceae (Potato Family)   99
    Ulmaceae (Elm Family)   101
    Zygophyllaceae (Caltrop Family)   101
    Unidentified quids   102
Termite fecal pellets from Fresnal Shelter   102

Chapter 5. Fresnal Shelter   103

Comparing Natural Stratigraphic Unit Flotation and Screened Samples   103
Comparing Flotation from Natural Stratigraphic Units and Seven Pits from
   Square D 27 with Screened Levels   104
Identification of Common Dietary Components   105
Medicinal Ceremonial Plants   109
Seasonality   109

Size, Number and Nature of Large Pits in Relation to Winter Occupancy   112

Estimated Size and Nature of Collecting Territory   113

     Maximum Distance Traveled to Higher Elevations   115

     Maximum. Distance Traveled to Lower Elevations   115

     Summary of Travel   116

Risk Minimization or Maximizing the Reliability of Food Procurement   116

A Ranked Comparison of Screened Levels with and without Maize   116

The Role of Fresnal Shelter from Earliest Dated Maize to the Start of a

    Very Moist Period (2945 ± 55 B.P. to 2770 ± 70 B.P.)   118

     Dietary Arguments for a Short-term Winter Base Camp   119

     Geographic Arguments for a Short Term Winter Base Camp   119

     Cultural Arguments for a Short-term Winter Base Camp   119

     Role Either As a Residential Base Camp or Temporary Field

     Camp or Both   120

     Role As a Temporary Logistical Camp for Butchering Deer   120

The Role of Fresnal Shelter from Earliest Introduction of Beans Until

    Abandonment (2,085 ± 60 B.P. to 1,550 B.P.)   121

Who Were These People   121

Chapter 6. High Rolls Cave   125

Identification of Dietary Components   125

     Vertebrate Bone Remains   125

     Plant Remains   126

Seasonality in Stratum 2 and 3   131

Role of High Rolls Cave Stratum 2 and 3   132

Stratum 1 Notes on Subsistence   133

Travel Between the Tularosa Basin and High Rolls Cave   133

Medicinal or Ceremonial   133

Chapter 7. Behavioral Ecology, Optimal Foraging, and the Diet Breadth Model   135

Favorable Aspects of Optimal Foraging Strategy at the Rock Shelters   139

     I. A widely diverse diet results from low availability of high

     ranked resources   139

     II. As high ranked prey fluctuates, optimal diet bread shrinks or

     expands   139

     III. Inclusion of a prey type should depend on the availability of

     higher ranked prey types, not on its own availability   141

     IV. Prey or resource types should be added or dropped from the

     diet in rank order of handling efficiency, kcal per unit of time   141

     V. If travel to obtain food at a distance is a factor, only selected

     items will be obtained   142

     VI. Collectors relied on logistical mobility   142

Troublesome Aspects of Optimal Foraging Strategy at the Rock Shelters   142

Uniquely Human Aspects of Optimal Foraging Strategy   144

Chapter 8. Fresnal Shelter and High Rolls Cave   145

Comparisons and Contrasts   145

     Plant Dietary Use   145

     Resolution of Dietary Differences   146

Partitioning of Plant Resources   147
Cultigen Radiocarbon Dates and the Climatic Record   148
Some Reasons for the Addition of Maize Agriculture   149
Sedentary and Semi-sedentary   150
Dietary Elements from Fresnal Canyon Archaic in Pueblo Food Traditions   151

Appendix A. Fresnal Shelter: Content of Excavation Units and Features   153

A.1 Fresnal Shelter Feathers Identified by Charmion McKusick Sept. 1, 1971   154
A.2. Modern Plant Voucher Specimens from the Fresnal Canyon Vicinity
      of the Sacramento Mountains of New Mexico   156
A.3. Distribution of Plant Remains in Screened Squares by Level   161
A.4. Identification of Ten Natural Strata with Original Volume of Floated Matrix Sampled   165
A.5. Condition and Distribution of Plant Parts in Ten Natural Stratigraphic Units   166
A.6. Condition and Distribution of Plant Remains in Seven Pits in Square D 27   169

Appendix B. High Rolls Cave: Content of Excavation Units and Features   171

B.1. Content of Excavation Units and Features   171
      B.1.1 List of Flotation Samples from High Rolls Cave Arranged by
           Field Sample Number   203
      B.1.2 Six Flotation Samples Analyzed by Teresa M. Fresquez   204
      B.1.3 Carbonized Flotation Samples Analyzed by Vorsila L. Bohrer   205
B.2. Taxonomic Notes   207
      B.2.1 Comparison of corollas of *N. Trigonophylla*, *N. rustica*, and
           corolla FS 742a   217
      B.2.2 Typical measurements of rodent fecal pellets   217
B.3. Chronology   219
      B.3.1 Chronology of Radiocarbon Dated Charred Material
           Associated with Flotation from Features   220
      B.3.2 Chronology of Radiocarbon Dated Charred Material Associated
           with Fotation from Excavation Units and Undated Interpolated Samples   220
      B.3.3 Radiocarbon Dated Cultigens from Excavation Units in Stratum 2   221
B.4. Pollen Concentration of Insect and Non-Arboreal Wind Pollinated Plants from
      High Rolls Cave, Their Relations to Flotation, and Their Significance   223
      B.4.1 Pollen samples with low concentration values from High Rolls Cave   229
      B.4.2 Pollen concentration distribution of non-arboreal wind and
           insect pollinated plants from High Rolls Cave excavation units   230

References Cited   233

Figures

Figure 2.1   Tularosa Basin with location of places mentioned in Chapter 2   6
Figure 2.2   Physiography and vegetation of Tularosa Basin near Fresnal Shelter   20
Figure 3.1   Fresnal Shelter grid plan with the location of grids screened for plant
                material   26

Figure 3.2   Diagrammatic profile of excavation levels in Squares C28 to C31, Fresnal Shelter   27
Figure 3.3   Plan view of seven pits in Square D27 in Fresnal Shelter   36
Figure 3.4   High Rolls Cave with expanded view of features and activity clusters
               at the top of Stratum 2   36
Figure 3.5   High Rolls Cave Feature 11   39

Tables

1.1   Fresnal Shelter history of excavation   3
1.2   High Rolls Cave history of excavation   4
1.3   Comparison of Fresnal Shelter and High Rolls Cave   4
2.1   Vegetation Types on the White Sands Missile Range in the Tularosa Basin, New Mexico   8
2.2   Content of three Holocene wood rat middens at 1,555 m   14
2.3   Stalagmites and the climatic record   16
2.4   Perishable artifacts from the Tularosa Basin margin   19
2.5   Chronology of climatic clues and cultural events, Tularosa Basin and margin   21
2.6   Estimated age of selected stylized bifaces with associated radiocarbon sample   23
3.1   Effect of rodents on cave vegetal content and stratigraphic position   30
3.2   Description of large storage cists   32
3.3   Square C29 levels and dating   33
3.4   Size and nature of seven pits in Square D27   34
3.5   Summary of plant material separated by a ¼ inch screen in six strata   42
3.6   Number of plant parts in two 20 ml samples from 01.B29.E6   44
3.7   Number of plant parts from two 100 ml samples from Pit 7, Square D27   44
3.8   A comparison of quantity of taxa between halves of Units A and D in Square B28   45
3.9   Differences in the number of taxa in the same strata between Squares B28 and B29   46
3.10   Index to geographic grouping of flotation samples within High Rolls Cave   48
4.1   Scoring system used to recognize prehistoric subsistence items in Fresnal Shelter   50
4.2   Distribution of ponderosa pine and ocotillo bark in grid squares by weight (g)   56
4.3   *Amaranthus* identifications from Fresnal Shelter   74
4.4   Distribution of types of common beans in grid squares   93
5.1   Comparison of plant parts in flotation by screen size   105
5.2   Ranked subsistence scores of plant material from Fresnal Shelter   106
5.3   Plants whose reproductive parts best document seasonal procurement   111
5.4   Location, composition, and distance of food patches from Fresnal Shelter   114
5.5   Ranked comparison of content of screened levels with and without maize   117
6.1   High Rolls plant foods arranged chronologically from oldest to youngest by
          carbon-14 dated features   127
6.2   High Rolls excavation unit plant foods arranged chronologically from oldest
          to youngest stratigraphic unit by field sample number   128
6.3   Frequency and ranking of dietary components in all excavation units and features   129
6.4   Plants from High Rolls Cave whose reproductive parts best document seasonal procurement   132
7.1   Comparison of kilocalories per kilogram of selected animal and plant food
          sources ranked by (net) kilocalories per hour   140
8.1   Earliest cultigen dates from High Rolls Cave and Fresnal Shelter   149

Acknowledgments

Grants secured by Cynthia Irwin-Williams while at Eastern New Mexico University allowed summer excavations of Fresnal Shelter and winter sorting of screen and flotation samples between 1969 and 1972 at University of Massachusetts at Boston (Table 1.1). Later, Eastern New Mexico University Department of Anthropology provided access to Fresnal Shelter field notes and collections. Funding provided by the New Mexico State Highway and Transportation Department provided for the excavation of High Rolls Cave and production of a site report (Lentz 2006) through the Office of Archaeological Studies of the Museum of New Mexico. Publication of this monograph was made possible by a generous grant from the Arizona State Museum and Eastern New Mexico University.

A series of skilled taxonomists brought their expertise to bear on varied aspects of plant classification at Fresnal Shelter. Dr. Lyman Benson, while chairman of the Department of Botany and Director of the Herbarium, Pomona College, identified key cacti. Ms. Caryl S. Busman, while an herbarium research assistant at the University of Arizona in Tucson, provided identifications of modern plant specimens that proved difficult. Dr. Walton C. Galinat, when Professor in the Department of Environmental Sciences of the University of Massachusetts at Waltham, assessed significant characteristics of maize during the early stages of excavation at Fresnal Shelter. Dr. Charles B. Heiser, while Professor of Botany at Indiana University, kindly provided identifications of modern *Helianthus* and *Viguiera*. Dr. Lawrence Kaplan, Professor of Biology of the University of Massachusetts Harbor Campus, classified the cultivated beans. Dr. Jonathan Sauer, as Professor of Geography and Director of the Herbarium at the University of California at Los Angeles, provided identifications of both the wild and cultivated species of *Amaranthus* from Fresnal Shelter.

Numerous individuals played vital roles in aspects of Fresnal Shelter research. Dr. Cynthia Irwin-Williams contacted the author while employed by University of Massachusetts at Boston to analyze plant remains upon recommendation of Dr. Richard I. Ford of the University of Michigan Ethnobotanical Laboratory. Dr. Austin Long of the Department of Geosciences at the University of Arizona furnished the first direct dates of maize. Ms. Teresa Mesman provided computerized versions of the illustrations. Dr. John F. Montgomery of Eastern New Mexico University was instrumental in securing proper curation of material from Fresnal Shelter and providing access to the archaeological collections. Dr. Phillip Shelley of Eastern New Mexico University encouraged a series of graduate students in anthropology over an extended period of time to study material from Fresnal Shelter. Dr. James Schoenwetter, Anthropology Department at Arizona State University, introduced me to the mid-range theory of hunter-gatherers propounded by David Hurst Thomas (1983a). Dr. Patricia M. Spoerl, while an archaeologist with the Lincoln National Forest, supplied background concerning historic forest grazing. Students at the University of Massachusetts at Boston who assisted with various aspects of sorting Fresnal Shelter plant material included Marlene Beggelman, Elaine Bodnaruk, Ann Henderson, Richard Smigielski, and David Winthrop. Marlene Beggelman and Elaine Bodnaruk undertook problem-oriented plant collecting in Fresnal Canyon. Emily McClung deTapia, while a student at Brandeis University, also provided help.

At High Rolls Cave the experienced excavation crew led by Stephen C. Lentz of the Office of Archaeological Studies of the Museum of New Mexico included Dorothy Zamora, who obtained flotation samples that preserved cultivated amaranth. The identification of compressed vegetal layers and the study of six additional flotation samples by Teresa M. Fresquez, the analysis of maize cobs by Mollie Toll, pollen by Dr. Richard Holloway of Quaternary Services in Flagstaff, Arizona, and the timely sharing of radiocarbon data by Stephen Lentz were appreciated components of initial work. Dr. Kelly W. Allred of the Department of Animal and Range Sciences at New Mexico State University identified *Eragrostis erosa* from High Rolls Cave. The report on faunal analysis by Nancy J. Akins of the Office of Archaeological Studies proved vital in balancing biological sources of information in regard to seasonality of site occupation.

The reviewers of the manuscript deserve sincere thanks in redirecting my writing: Dr. Karen R. Adams, Archaeobotanical Consultant, Tucson; Dr. Linda S. Cordell, Director, University of Colorado Museum at Boulder; and Dr. Robert J. Hard, University of Texas Center for Archaeological Studies in San Antonio.

So many teachers guided my understanding of prehistory that it would be a disservice to name some and inadvertently omit others. Many are no longer here to read these lines. But I feel fortunate and grateful for their generosity of time, skill, and interest. I owe a great debt to those who came before and regret that the people who lived during the preceramic times in Fresnal Canyon cannot protest the inevitable omissions and distortions of this investigation.

Chapter 1
Introduction

Many plant fragments recovered from two pre-ceramic rock shelters occupied some 3000 or more years ago look no different from modern plants. When plant material preserves so well, the contribution of ethnobotany to archaeological research can be enormous. Volney Jones (1941: 220) defined ethnobotany as the study of the interrelationship of pre-industrial people and plants. In archaeological sites ethnobotanists, through attention to taxonomic peculiarities, can identify plant fragments primarily at the generic level, but also to races and varieties in some cultivated plants. Existing traditions of utilization, the context of recovery (such as a burned seed in a hearth), and other indirect lines of evidence serve to categorize plant remains according to use: foods, fuels, basketry, sandals, cordage, medicinal, or ceremonial items. This study attempts to identify and interpret food usage when cultivated crops were initially available in south-central New Mexico.

Because people typically concentrate culturally utilized plants in habitation areas, proportions of plants recovered seldom reflect their true relative abundance in the natural world. Food plants from most non-urban archeological sites are assumed to have yielded sufficient nutrients to have made the labor of harvest worthwhile. If the dietary components have suffered only minor modern or historic displacement, one can determine the probable resource exploitation locales and subsequently calculate the minimum distance needed to obtain the native plants that formed a regular part of diet. Estimates of the seasonal availability of foods tend to further clarify the natural rhythm of food procurement.

Other information about formerly extant plants may have been inadvertently incorporated into a site through the indiscriminant gathering of a variety of grasses for bedding or roofing, by the foraging of rodents, and by the wind transport of pollen, leaves, or seeds. In such a fortuitous manner the inventory of plants growing near the site becomes augmented, allowing the assessment of the nature of the former environment.

Although the preceding enumeration of possible interpretations of ethnobotanical remains lacks unifying theory, ethnobotanical data can test or support models concerning the nature of human adaptation, foraging, subsistence, and social and religious behavior. Such themes, posed by archaeologists, biologists, or ethnobotanists, may find corroboration in the individual interpretations within each category of plant remains recovered or within their collective consideration and provide the basis for understanding the human condition far beyond the limits of a single archaeological site. When the year 2000 began, I wished to publish my analysis of the Late Archaic plant remains from Fresnal Shelter in the Sacramento Mountains of south central New Mexico, part of a project promoted by Mark L. Wimberly and initiated in l969 by Cynthia Irwin-Williams (1936-1990).

Mark Wimberly and Peter Eidenbach kept three summer seasons of excavation efforts organized and moving, while creating Human Systems Research (1972), stimulating ancillary research, and analyzing artifacts (Wimberly and Eidenbach 1981).

During the first year of excavation of Fresnal Shelter, Cynthia Irwin-Williams requested my help in handling the ethnobotanical aspects of research (Table 1.1). At the time I was based at the University of Massachusetts at Boston, but in the fall of 1973, when lack of funding terminated excavation, I came to Eastern New Mexico University in Portales to investigate vegetative reconstruction on Cynthia Irwin-Williams's Puerco Valley Project west of Cuba. Subsequently the plant remains from the Salmon Ruin Project in Farmington, New Mexico abrogated my time. Except for a brief period preceding 1980 when I organized Fresnal results into a preliminary manuscript, my Fresnal research remained dormant. Meanwhile, injuries from a helicopter accident in the Sacramento Mountains claimed Mark Wimberly's life in 1981. Afterwards, excavated material and records became part of Eastern New Mexico University. With the encouragement of Phillip Shelley, Fresnal Shelter became a focus for graduate study (R. Jones 1990; McNally 1996; Merchant 2002a and b; Moots 1990;). Cynthia Irwin-Williams' interest in the Archaic inspired a new generation of archaeologists while I remained eager to update my own research (Bohrer 1981a, 1981b) on the plant remains.

In 2001, Stephen C. Lentz of the Museum of New Mexico advised me of plans to excavate the Late Archaic site of High Rolls Cave in the same canyon as Fresnal Shelter (Table 1.2). Because site testing revealed well-preserved plant remains, I initially thought that my previous identification of Fresnal Shelter plant remains would simplify work. But as my ethnobotanical analysis progressed at High Rolls Cave, I realized the site contrasted in many ways with Fresnal Shelter (Table 1.3). To present a balanced view of preceramic plant foraging and farming in Fresnal Canyon, I would need to consider both sites.

In the following pages, Chapter 2 provides background regarding the natural and cultural environment of the Tularosa Basin and Sacramento Mountains. Chapter 3 presents factors that influenced site deposition and preservation in each rock shelter as well as dating problems and procedures that affected ethnobotanical interpretation.

The 104 plant taxa recovered in Fresnal Shelter required the use of objective criteria for recognition of human plant use and reference to local modern plant species distribution for each taxon, presented in Chapter 4. Similar information for High Rolls Cave is subsumed under each taxon when appropriate. The discussion of Fresnal Shelter (Chapter 5) precedes that of High Rolls Cave (Chapter 6). However, I have deferred my discussion of Optimal Foraging Theory, which focuses my interpretation of subsistence activities at both rock shelters, for Chapter 7. The final chapter compares aspects of diet at both rock shelters, climate, ecology, and cultigen dates. It examines Pueblo traditions of food uses in relation to dietary elements from the Fresnal Canyon Archaic. The abbreviations for field sample (FS), meters below datum (mbd), centimeters below datum (cmbd), and centimeters below surface (cmbs) can be found throughout the publication.

I wrote this monograph with the full realization that others may find new ways to interpret the data, just as my own viewpoint has changed with time. For that reason, the content of the appendixes may provide other insights or become the basis for testing new theories.

Table 1.1. Fresnal Shelter History of Excavation

Excavation Year	Funding Source	Accomplishments
1969	Eastern New Mexico University Sigma Xi	Trench 2 m wide opened along grid lines 26 and 27. Depths of 5 or10 cm used in area beneath overhang in C and D, 28 to 31, the location of well-preserved deposits. Screens suspended from tripods. Duplicate field record initiated for botanical analysis.
1970	Eastern New Mexico University Wenner Gren Foundation National Endowment for the Humanities	Excavators began a l5 cm wide strip (B 28 to B 31) by natural stratigraphic units. A flotation plan was begun to recognize error in different methods of recovery. Modern plant collecting and prehistoric plant identification initiated.*
1971	National Endowment for the Humanities	Natural stratigraphic units excavated in E to G, 22 through 24 and F to G, 14 through 20, revealing burned lenses of *Stipa* grass. Completed B 28 to B 31, including infant burial. Screening continued and screen loss samples taken. Modern plant collecting continued. Root of desert four o'clock recognized as shelter food.
1972	Human Systems Research	Funding request rejected. Final season of excavation and modern plant collecting. Relict stand of *Stipa neomexicana* grass located.

*Plants were identified primarily during the academic years from l970 through 1972. See Chapter 3, Part II for method of naming excavation grids; also see Figure 3.1.

Table 1.2. High Rolls Cave History of Excavation

Year	Accomplishments
Prior to 2000	Erosion and unauthorized excavation. Site placed within the Archaeological Site Stabilization and Protection Project by State Highway and Transportation Department and funding initiated.
Fall 2000	Data recovery began preliminary to installation of metal grate for site protection. Sampling for pollen began in test trenches. A 25 m by 2 m trench was excavated across the mouth of the cave and divided into 50 1 m by 1 m excavation units. Excavation began in arbitrary 10 cm intervals down to culturally sterile soil or bedrock. After a stratigraphic profile was established, excavation proceeded by natural levels.
Winter 2001	Excavation of remainder of cave approved by Lincoln National Forest and New Mexico State Highway and Transportation Department.
Spring and Summer 2001	Crew under direction of Stephen C. Lentz, Museum of New Mexico, Office of Archaeological Studies. Excavated in natural stratigraphic units.
Late Fall 2001	Excavation completed by Stephen C. Lentz

Table 1.3. Comparison of Fresnal Shelter and High Rolls Cave

Attribute	Fresnal Shelter (LA 10101)	High Rolls Cave (LA 114103)
Elevation	1922 m	1906 m
Exposure	South facing	North facing
Size	33 m by 10 m	36 m by 13 m
Major factors affecting preservation	Dry conditions	Percolating water Cave opening blasted to build modern highway
Stratigraphy	Human bioturbation, wood rats, mice Abundant rock fall	Wood rats, carnivores mice in Strata 2 and 3 Limited rock fall
Number of plant taxa recovered	104	34
Perishable artifacts	Numerous	Rare
Large storage pits	5	1
Occupation		
Earliest	7310 BP	3460 BP to 3250 BP (Stratum 3)
Middle	2945 BP to 2770 BP	3260 BP to 2890 BP (Stratum 2)
Latest	2085 BP to 1550 BP	2300 BP to 1610 BP (Stratum 1)

Chapter 2
Environmental and Cultural Background

PART I. THE ENVIRONMENT OF THE TULAROSA BASIN AND THE SACRAMENTO MOUNTAINS

In Fresnal Canyon, two rock shelters at the base of limestone cliffs in the Sacramento Mountains of south-central New Mexico formed long before people were present. Fresnal Canyon drains the western face of the Sacramento Mountains and empties northwestward into La Luz Canyon where it reaches the margin of the Tularosa Basin near the community of La Luz, about 16 km north of Alamogordo. Fresnal Canyon lies within the Basin-and-Range-Physiographic Province that extends for 1,717,000 square km (MacMahon 1988, Table 8.1). Relatively large basins are bounded by mostly north-to-south trending mountain ranges. The basins are dotted with temporary lakes or playas formed by the accumulation of run-off from the mountains. As the standing water evaporates, salts high in sodium and calcium form, including gypsum. On the downwind side dune fields can develop as a result of wind erosion of the playa sediments. The mountain flanks accumulate detrital material that gradually slopes more gently toward the basin interior. Alluvial fans emanate from the mountain canyons and spread into the valley plains and playa floor or basin.

The Tularosa Basin

The Tularosa Basin internally drains an area about 64 km east-to-west and 241 km north-to-south, or 15,424 square km (Meinzer and Hare 1915: 11). The Basin ranges in elevation from 1,189 m to 1,464 m. The eastern perimeter has gentle slopes (2 to 5 percent average) punctuated occasionally by low mesas and hills slashed by arroyos that spread their sediment in alluvial fans at the mouth of the canyons originating from the Sacramento Mountains. The slopes on the arroyo sides near the mountains commonly exceed 10 percent (Maker and others 1972: 28). Between La Luz and Alamogordo the land lies between 1,357 m and 1,464 m elevation. Beginning about 24 km south of Alamogordo and extending to the southwest, sandy soils form extensive dune landscapes (Maker and others 1972). In the central part of the basin, extensive deposits of gypsum have eroded into spectacular dune fields that form part of White Sands National Monument; immediately north, fields of wind-deposited quartz sand impinge in turn on lava outcrops (Fig. 2.1). Soils develop in gypsiferous earth or saline valley fill intruded by admixtures of strongly calcareous sediments from the bordering mountains. The Sacramento Mountains along with the San Andres Mountains on the western side of the Tularosa Basin form two of the most conspicuous features in southern New Mexico.

The Sacramento and Sierra Blanca mountains that skirt the Tularosa Basin on its eastern side ascend so abruptly from the

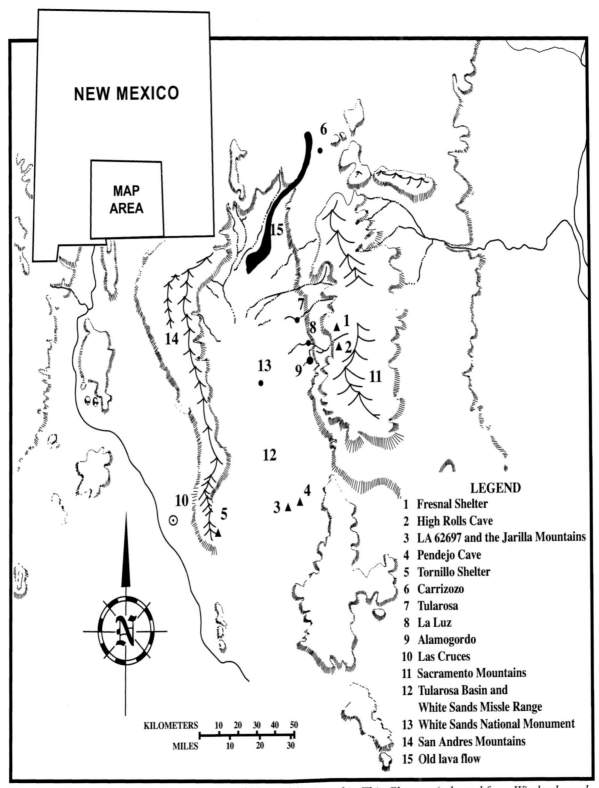

Figure 2.1. Tularosa Basin with Locations of Places Mentioned in This Chapter (adapted from Wimberly and Eidenbach 1977)

Basin's rim that the crest is only 11 km to 21 km distant. Most foothills quickly rise 152 m or more above the floors of the canyons that dissect them (Maker and others 1974: 44). For example, in the last 2 km where La Luz Canyon opens to the Tularosa Basin, escarpments rise over 305 m. Although Fresnal Shelter lies in one of the widest portions of the mountain range, it is only 9.6 km down canyon to the Tularosa Basin and about the same distance up to the crest. La Luz canyon, to which Fresnal Canyon is tributary, broadens briefly before it repeats the pattern of other canyons by continuing to narrow and steepen. Many canyons rise to the level of the long, relatively flat ridge tops that start to enclose them at elevations of approximately 1,982 m. It is close to this topographic transition that Fresnal Shelter and High Rolls Cave are located. An upland area of rolling ridge tops and low hills emerges between 2,135 m and 2,745 m.

The Chihuahuan Desert

A large tongue of the Chihuahuan Desert extends north into the Tularosa Basin and laps against the lower xeric slopes of the mountains that edge it. The Tularosa Basin belongs to the northern third of the Chihuahuan Desert, termed the Trans-Pecos Region, and includes all of that desert in Texas and New Mexico and more than half the desert areas of Chihuahua, Mexico. The middle third, known as the Mapimian, resembles the northern third with its Basin-and-Range limestone topography and playas. It includes parts of eastern Chihuahua, Coahuila, and some of Durango (MacMahon 1988: 248). The lower third and most southern region includes Zacatecas and San Luis Potosi.

In contrast to the Sonoran Desert, the higher elevation Chihuahuan Desert has a significant grass component (MacMahon 1988: 248). Much of the northern Chihuahuan Desert grades into grasslands (MacMahon 1988: 256). Visualizing the Tularosa Basin up to about 1,830 m as a mosaic of desert grassland and desert scrub whose proportions may have varied during the Holocene provides a long term ecological perspective. Many areas in the Rio Grande Valley and elsewhere in southern New Mexico known as grasslands historically have become Chihuahuan desert scrub (Buffington and Herbel 1965; Gardner 1951; York and Dick-Peddie 1969). Desert shrubs have invaded much of the desert grassland in southern Arizona as well. Plateau grasslands above 1,000 m elevation once had a short bunch-grass appearance with the desert scrub restricted to ravines, knolls, and sites where soils were particularly poor, thus limiting the more productive grasses (Sims 1988: 280; York and Dick-Peddie 1969).

Since a vegetation survey of the White Sands Missile Range by the Natural Resources Conservation Service (USDA 1976) covered over half (8,651 square km) of the Tularosa Basin, most descriptions are likely to be representative of the whole basin. Although the vegetation in the Tularosa Basin relates more to the soil conditions and past grazing pressure than it does to elevation, the vegetation groups in Table 2.1 are listed from what likely is to be encountered from the lowest elevation to the highest, beginning with the largest playa lake, Lake Lucero. Such an approach has some historical validity, for there have been changes in ground water levels that affect vegetation. Around 1915, 388.5 square km to 518 square km of the Tularosa Basin was occupied by ground water rising to the surface by capillary action (Meinzer 1927: 36). This would foster the spread of iodine bush as indicated in Table 2.1. The two most widespread vegetation categories on the White Sands Missile Range are those from (1) grassland and dunes derived from gypsum soil accounting for 1,532 square km and (2) sand grasslands and dunes that make up

Table 2.1. Vegetation Types on the White Sands Missile Range in the Tularosa Basin, New Mexico*

Nature of Soil	Species Composition
1. Intermittent lakes (playas), salt flats	1. Scattered iodine bush (Where more alkaline, sparse clumps of four-wing saltbush, iodine bush, and alkali sacaton)
2. Saline soil a. Low to moderately saline soil	a. Alkali sacaton, four-wing saltbush
b. Strongly saline soil	b. Four-wing saltbush, iodine bush, alkali sacaton in sparse clumps
3. Soils derived from gypsum dunes a. Shallow soil	a. Sparse cover of coldenia, gyp grass, ephedra, alkali sacaton, and lichens
b. Deep soil	b. Alkali sacaton, four-wing saltbush, ephedra, gyp grama
c. Interdunal areas only	c. Giant dropseed, spike dropseed, Indian rice grass, little blue stem, rubber rabbitbrush, and four-wing saltbush
d. Unique community	d. Ephedra, sandhill muhly dominates over four-wing saltbush, tall rabbitbrush, Indian rice grass, gyp grama, little bluestem, and mesquite
4. Sand grasslands a. Dunes	a. Dunes with mesquite, almost no grasses
b. Level to gently undulating deep sand	b. Giant dropseed, mesa dropseed, spike dropseed, and sand sagebrush; formerly Indian rice grass
c. Sandy loam soils	c. Mesa dropseed, spike dropseed, tobosa, black grama, yucca
d. Saline, sandy loam variant	d. Four-wing saltbush, alkali sacaton
5. Clay or clay loam grasslands a. On flood plains and nearly level alluvial fans	a. Vine mesquite grass dominates sacaton and tobosa
b. Uplands	b. Alkali sacaton, tobosa, fluffgrass, four-wing saltbush

Table 2.1. Vegetation Types on the White Sands Missile Range in the Tularosa Basin, New Mexico, cont'd*

Nature of Soil	Species Composition
6. Gravelly, very limy soils just below footslope grasslands	
a. Soils nearly always eroded	a. Creosote bush dominates, but mesquite, tarbush, and mariola also present
b. Soils in good condition	b. Areas dominated by black grama with creosote bush reduced 20 percent by weight
7. Footslope grasslands	
a. On lower mountain slope	a. Black grama, blue grama, side-oats grama
b. Alluvial fans with gravelly to sandy loams Below 1982 m about half bare rock	b. Add to "a:" bush muhly, sand sagebrush, four-wing saltbush, yucca, and snakeweed. Mariola and formerly, New Mexico feather grass.
8. Lava flows with pockets of soil.	8. Four-wing saltbush, creosote bush dominates over black grama, alkali sacaton, mariola
9. Semi-desert hills and rockland	9. Black grama, creosote bush, fluff grass, ocotillo

*Adapted from U.S.D.A. 1976. Chapter 4 has all but the following scientific names: bush muhly (*Muhlenberia porteri*), fluffgrass (*Dasyochloa pulchella =Tridens pulchella*), iodine bush (*Allenrolfea occidentalis*), gyp grass, gyp grama (*Bouteloua breviseta*), little bluestem *(Schizachrium scoparium =Andropogon scoparius)*, mesa dropseed (*Sporobous flexulosus*), rubber rabbitbrush (*Ericameria nauseosa*), sand sagebrush (*Artemesia filifolia*), snakeweed (*Gutierrezia sarothrae)*, spike dropseed (*Sporobolus contractus*), tarbush (*Flourensia cernua*), and vine mesquite grass (*Panicum obtusum*).

1,471 square km. Each group represents about 17 percent of the missile range. As in other parts of the Chihuahuan Desert, the gypsum dune community carries a variety of endemic plant species (MacMahon l988: 248).

Species dominance and composition of vegetation types has been altered by grazing. Creosote bush (*Larrea tridentata*) dominates gravelly, very limy soils just below footslope grasslands as semi-desert shrub land (1,090 square km or 12 % of the missile range) except where this vegetation type has suffered least from grazing. In such locations, black grama grass (*Bouteloua eriopoda*) dominates, and creosote bush is reduced to about 20 percent by weight. Black grama has been conspicuous enough to mark its presence in five of nine vegetation groups (Table 2.1). Indian rice grass (*Oryzopsis hymenoides*) is limited to interdunal areas derived from gypsum in the Tularosa Basin today (Table 2.1). Bush muhly grass (*Muhlenbergia porteri*) is abundant enough to report it in the footslope grassland vegetation group. A 1975 grazing management text indicates all three grass species as well as curly mesquite grass (*Hilaria belangeri*) were once the important species in desert grasslands because of their forage value or coverage of vast areas of land or both (Sims 1980: 280). Combined heavy grazing and drought near the turn of the century nearly eliminated Arizona cottontop (*Digitaria californica*) from the Tularosa Basin. The degree of recovery of Arizona cottontop after a dry year is strongly linked to the average level of grazing use (Cable 1979: 17-18). Its apparent absence from the White Mountains (Hutchins 1974) and from modern Fresnal Canyon testifies to some intense years of grazing prior to becoming part of Lincoln National Forest. The species has survived in the nearby Carrizozo lava flow even after a series of drought years (Shields 1956: 62) and has been reported as part of flora of the Jornada Experimental Range, just west of the San Andres Mountains (Little and Campbell 1943: 657). If curly mesquite grass were present formerly, it would have been part of sandy grasslands and semi-desert hills (Gould 1951: 159). In all, 52 species of grasses have been reported on the missile range (USDA 1976).

The former distribution of species of prehistoric economic importance like mesquite (*Prosopis* sp.), alkali sacaton grass (*Sporobolus airoides*), and Indian rice grass is of interest. Mesquite is found in gravelly, very limy soils just below the footslope grasslands (Table 2.1). The east slope of the Tularosa Basin near Alamogordo once had a north-to-south band of mesquite about 4 km wide and 48 km long (Fig. 2.1). The former prevalence of mesquite near Alamogordo has been attributed in large measure to floodwaters (Meinzer 1927: 48) that have since been diverted. On alluvium with low salinity in the Chihuahuan Desert, vast stands of mesquite (*Prosopis glandulosa*) can be found along with saltbush (*Atriplex canescens*) and *Lycium* (boxthorn) species (MacMahon 1988: 252). Mesquite is present in the gypsum grassland and occupies more than half of the sandy grassland area (Table 2.1). However,

coppice dunes with mesquite are not believed to be part of the former Holocene landscape (Blair and others 1990: 750).

Alkali sacaton and four-wing saltbush co-occur in four vegetation groups: clay grasslands, salt flats, sand grasslands and dunes, and lava flows (Table 2.1). Many species of dropseed (*Sporobolus* spp.) dominate the sandy grassland and dune vegetation group. At the base of the Sacramento mountains on sloping alluvial land one might expect footslope grasslands on gravelly or sandy loams. While this is a fairly stable grama grass community today, under disturbed, agrading conditions, stands of alkali sacaton might be expected along with saltbush. Alkali sacaton is unusually well adapted to burial by sediments (Hubbell and Gardner 1944: 42).

Though seldom noted in the Tularosa Basin, Indian rice grass has been described as a conspicuous component of sandy plant communities in the Chihuahuan Desert (MacMahon 1988: 251). It very likely once played a similar role in the Tularosa Basin. Indian rice grass multiplies with a minimum of competition from other grasses. For example, it has become established following the installment of water spreading devices on the Navajo Reservation (Hubbell and Gardner 1944: 42) and has successfully colonized abandoned sandy roadbeds (Jaynes and Harper 1978: 409). It is at least moderately tolerant of alkaline conditions (USDA 1937: G88).

Although Indian rice grass can grow from 1,068 m to 1,981 m (Gould 1951: 256) on dry southerly slopes, it may live as high as 3,050 m (USDA 1937: G88). It typically grows in sandy, well-drained soil (Hubbell and Gardner 1944: 42; USDA 1937: G88) and has been reported growing on the Jornada Experimental Range west of the San Andres Mountains, which is mostly a plain between 1,220 m and 1,403 m elevation in Doña Ana County (Little and Campbell 1943: 667).

Within the Tularosa Basin, records indicate Indian rice grass grew on the lava flow west of Carrizozo (Shields 1956: 62) and as part of the sparse community in the interdunal areas of gypsum sands both on the White Sands Missile Range and at White Sands National Monument (Emerson 1935: 233; Shields 1956: 54; Wooton and Standley 1915: 73). Its survival in gypsum dunes and on former lava flows may be due to relatively low grazing pressure compared with sandy or loamy soils near the eastern perimeter of the Tularosa Basin. Populations rapidly decline with too much grazing in winter and spring (Robertson 1977: 25).

One must travel from Fresnal Shelter about 24 km to reach White Sands National Monument where Indian rice grass grows today. Dense stands might have been formerly exploited in low sand dune areas about 24 km south of Alamogordo where it could have colonized the wind disturbed soils. It might also have grown in the sandy soils northwest of Tularosa, New Mexico (Fig. 2.1). The grass typically matures in late spring before New Mexico feather grass.

New Mexico feather grass (*Stipa neomexicana*) survives in less grazed locations in the Sacramento Mountains today on steep slopes, hill crowns, or ridges between 1,525 m and 1,982 m. It is capable of growing in desert shrub, juniper, or scrub-oak associations as low as 1,068 m and up to 1,982 m (Gould 1951: 247). Because the present city of Alamogordo lies on the margin of the Tularosa Basin at 1,312 m, former vistas of this cool season grass might have extended at least from there all the way up to Fresnal Shelter and High Rolls Cave.

In 1912, Wooton and Standley described New Mexico feather grass as growing on dry hills east of Alamogordo. The authors predicted its gradual disappearance from rangelands along with needle-and-thread grass (*Stipa comata*).

They are relished by stock and considered very good food by stockmen: they are of especial importance because they appear at a time when most of the other grasses are dead and dry. Apparently they do not reproduce readily and since they are now rarely allowed to go to seed, they are probably being gradually exterminated wherever stock can get to them. (Wooton and Standley 1912: 58)

Certain cacti have a patchy distribution. The cane cholla *(Opuntia imbricata)* and prickly pear (*Opuntia* sp.) may be only locally abundant (Brown 1982: 177), but the stands can be dense. Turk's head barrel cactus (*Echinocactus horizonthalonius*) can also be common locally (MacMahon 1988: 252).

Marshes may have been more extensive at one time. An 1859 to 1867 map of the Tularosa Basin and adjacent country (Meinzer and Hare 1915, Plate V) characterizes the Tularosa Basin as a sand belt with salt marshes and lakes. The Spanish name *tularosa* signifies reddish reeds or willows (Pearce 1965: 171). In 1870, seasonal salt marshes were described around the margins of an extensive area of white gypsum sand in a letter by a general living at Fort Stanton (Meinzer and Hare 1915). Malapais Spring, on the eastern edge of the Tularosa Basin, overflows onto an area 1.6 km long and about 274 m wide supporting a growth of cattail (*Typha latifolia*), bulrush (*Scirpus americana),* and other marsh species (Shields 1956). The Spanish name of *Carrizo,* or reed grass, was incorporated into the name of the early settlement of Carrizozo. Arroyo mouth ponds, located in aeolian depressions near the piedmont, were common features throughout the Holocene (Blair and others 1990: 758)

With higher effective moisture, Fresnal Canyon might have supported temporary pools or more extensive marsh vegetation along its route or near its mouth. Woodhouse toad remains were recovered in Fresnal Shelter, but today the toads are restricted to major river drainages (Applegarth 1979: 162). The presence of the toad suggests a slightly wetter climate and locally marshy conditions (Applegarth 1979: 163). Because a salt-tolerant cattail grows lower in Fresnal Canyon and only pollen of a cattail more typical of fresh water is in High Rolls Cave (Appendix B.4), it seems likely that a marsh existed at the same elevation or higher. Willow pollen is more concentrated near the opening than the cave interior (Holloway 2002). One wonders if locally high ground water levels in the community of High Rolls were once high enough to create a marsh.

Modern Fresnal Canyon Vegetation

The vegetation group described as semi-desert hills and rock land in Table 2.1 characterizes the south-facing canyon slopes where Fresnal Shelter is located at 1,922 m. Wright's silk tassel (*Garrya wrightii*) is common in addition to creosote bush, mariola *(Parthenium incanum)*, and a thin scatter of mesquite (*Prosopis glandulosa*). The distribution of many plants occupying a 7.6 m wide transect has been plotted (HSR 1973: 410-420). The sotol (*Dasylirion wheeleri*), agave (*Agave parryi*), and yucca (*Yucca carnerosana*) that grow there are characteristic of semi-desert grassland (Brown 1982: 127) as well as the presence of black grama grass (*Bouteloua eriopoda*) and bush muhly. Additional grasses in the understory are of species that now are common in Plains grassland and are said to be typical of desert grassland at higher elevations (Brown 1982: 127): blue grama (*Bouteloua gracilis*), plains lovegrass (*Eragrostis intermedia*), wolftail (*Lycurus phleoides*), and plains bristle grass (*Setaria macrostachya*).

The pinyon-juniper woodland begins on the north slope of Fresnal Canyon opposite the shelter at 1,922 m. It is intermixed with oak, broad-leaved yucca, mountain mahogany (*Cercocarpus*), and three-leaved sumac (*Rhus trilobata*). Less frequently one encounters beargrass (*Nolina microcarpa*), Mormon tea (*Ephedra*), flowering ash (*Fraxinus cuspidata*), and false mock orange (*Fendlera rupicola*).

Pinyon-juniper communities commonly accompanied by shrub oaks and mountain mahogany continue on open mountain slopes until around 2,134 m, where temperatures are milder and rainfall higher. Depending on the fire history, pinyon communities may blend into ones dominated by ponderosa pine or be replaced by ponderosa pine. Similarly, mixed conifer communities at higher elevations may be replaced in part by ponderosa pine (Lambert 1980). For example, at higher elevations along crests of the Sacramento Mountains one may encounter ponderosa pine, but north- and east-facing slopes may have spruce (*Picea* sp.), white fir (*Abies concolor*), Douglas fir (*Pseudotsuga* sp.) (Maker and others 1972: 16), white pine (*P. strobiformis* and *P. flexilis*), and some aspen (*Populus* sp.).

Most of the canyons on the western side of the Sacramento Mountains foster at least some riparian vegetation due to permanent springs in La Luz Canyon to the north and Fresnal Canyon itself, as well as in Dry, Marble, Caballero, and Alamo canyons, which cut through the western face of the mountains for about 11 km south of Fresnal Canyon.

For as long as people can remember, Fresnal Canyon has had perennial flowing water. The canyon itself bears the Spanish name for ash trees (Pearce 1965: 60) that grow there. Below Fresnal Shelter, the stream in the canyon bottom cuts through travertine and creates pools up to 3 m in depth. The relict alluvial bottom has been recently entrenched and only a small portion of the original alluvium remains. Gambel oak (*Quercus gambellii*), velvet ash

(*Fraxinus velutina*), grape (*Vitis arizonica*), chokecherry (*Prunus serotina*), algerita (*Berberis fremontii*), and *Brickelia*, along with other herbs and grasses flourish in the moisture and partial shade (HSR 1973).

Location of Suitable Areas for Farming

A climatic evaluation of Mountain Park, 1.6 km east of Fresnal Shelter at 2,050 m, suggests it would be possible to raise corn at this elevation and lower (HSR 1973). In any location, variability in rainfall is high. Based on almost 40 years of observation, rainfall ranges from about 7.6 cm to 55.9 cm annually in Alamogordo and from 12.7 cm to 73.7 cm annually in Mountain Park (HSR 1973).

A survey and evaluation of arable land in and near Fresnal Canyon was made in 1972 with the help of the Natural Resources Conservation Service while Fresnal Shelter was under excavation (HSR 1973: 428-443). Three areas were thought to have potential for agriculture. Within the community of High Rolls, land under cultivation at 2,129 m was thought to have potential for raising maize. The investigators noted that the high water table would be detrimental to deep-rooted plants, but would be fine for raising maize. The growing season was adequate with 140 to 180 days. A second area was lower in Fresnal Canyon at 1,586 m on a first alluvial terrace. A third area was the Randy Berger farm at 1,470 m near La Luz, north of Alamogordo. The last two locations with typic torriorthent soils have excellent qualities for past agricultural use. The silty loam soils have moderate to slow permeability but are of high water holding capacity (Maker and others 1972, Table 4). The soils are classed as part of the Largo series, which, along with deep alluvial soils, is the only land classed as suitable for irrigation (Maker and others 1972: 19) and is found in small and widely distributed tracts.

Physiography

The modern highway climbs the Sacramento Mountains through Dry Canyon, and close to 1,830 m it begins to skirt high along the south side of Fresnal Canyon and briefly expands to a parking area just before entering the tunnel as the road ascends to Cloudcroft. The first-time viewer sees a wild, remote, and seemingly inaccessible western landscape. The dramatic backdrop of blue sky is abruptly slashed by sheer canyon walls of limestone whose distant, narrow sloping ledges support a scatter of what seems like miniature prickly pear. The shadow of a limestone overhang discretely covers Fresnal Shelter. Lush trees and other riparian growth in the canyon bottom visually flatten into a homogenous ribbon of green that flows westward toward the Tularosa Basin.

Leslie Marmon Silko (1987: 94) captures the essence of living in the immensity of Southwestern landscapes in the Hopi country:

> The bare vastness of the Hopi landscape emphasizes the visual impact of every plant, every rock, every arroyo. Nothing is overlooked or taken for granted. Each ant, each lizard, each lark is imbued with great value simply because the creature is there, simply because the creature is alive in a place where any life at all is precious. Stand on the mesa edge at Walpi and look west over the bare distances toward the pale blue outlines of the San Francisco Peaks where the ka'tsina spirits reside. So little lies between you and the sky. So little lies between you and the earth. One look and you know that simply to survive is a great triumph, that every possible resource is needed, every possibly ally--even the most humble insect or reptile. You realize you will be speaking with all of them if you intend to last out the year. Thus it is that the Hopi elders are grateful to the landscape for aiding them in their quest as a spiritual people.

When standing on the overlook to Fresnal Canyon and gazing west toward the pale blue outlines of the San Andres Mountains fronted by the shimmering white sands, one can be overcome by similar feelings.

PART II. SOURCES OF EVIDENCE OF POST-PLEISTOCENE CLIMATE

Wood Rat Middens

Part of our understanding of post-Pleistocene vegetation and climate depends on the analysis of wood rat middens preserved in mountain canyons and on geological studies in the Tularosa Basin. Because wood rats tend to forage within 30 m to 50 m of their nests, the plants used to construct the nest may be presumed to come from a limited area (Van Devender and others l984: 345). The organic content of old wood rat (*Neotoma*) nests preserved in dry rock shelters of Big Boy and Marble canyons less than 8 km (about 5 miles) to the south of Fresnal Canyon have been analyzed and radiocarbon dated (Table 2.2).

Through the wood rat midden studies we are able to perceive the increasing aridity beginning in the early Holocene times by the upslope migration of vegetation. The three middens at one elevation that exemplify the early to late Holocene plant record also show a number of species persisted throughout the Holocene. They include shrubs such as three-leaved sumac (*Rhus trilobata*) and four-winged saltbush (*Atriplex canescens*), as well as succulents such as prickly pear cactus and hedgehog cactus (*Echinocereus* sp.).

A porcupine midden in Marble Canyon at 1,580 m that dated 5430 B.P. (middle Holocene) contained nine grass species that presently grow in desert grassland habitats. The characterization of the location was that of desert grassland mixed with remnant woodland and some Chihuahuan Desert elements (Van Devender and others l984: 355).

Geomorphological Studies

An ancient Holocene soil horizon known as "Q2" in the southern Tularosa Basin dates about 15,000 to 9000 B.P. based on correlation with a project on the western side of the San Andres Mountains that has a single radiocarbon date

---

Table 2.2. Content of Three Holocene Wood Rat Middens at l555 m*

Time Period	Plant Content
18,000 to 16,000 BP	Douglas fir, Rocky Mountain juniper, piñon, one-seeded juniper
11,000 to 8000 BP	One-seeded juniper
8000 to 4000 BP	Piñon, mountain mahogany, mesquite
4000 BP to present	Creosote bush, New Mexican agave, golden eye, Apache plume

*Marble and Big Boy Canyon, Sacramento Mountains

(Blair and others 1990). The Q2 soil horizon has been extensively stripped by wind erosion from an onslaught of aridity until it is nearly absent in some areas (Doleman and others 1992: 112). The desiccation surely gave creosote bush, sotol (*Dasylirion wheeleri*), mesquite, and other desert scrub species their reproductive advantage in the Tularosa Basin. It made the survival of pinyon and mountain mahogany at 1,555 m impossible. The combined loss of moisture and soil cover through wind erosion vastly altered the habitats for growing plants, making it possible for Chihuahuan Desert plant species to successfully compete in the altered environment.

It is upon the eroded or absent Q2 soil surface that the Q3 soil began development in the mid-Holocene in the Tularosa Basin. A weak A horizon gives way to Bw and Bk horizons. Its depositional duration is estimated from 7300 to 150 B.P. (Blair and others 1990). This soil horizon is the source of almost all archaeological remains in the Tularosa Basin with dates ranging from 3995 to 440 B.P., or 2045 B.C. to A.D. 1510 (Doleman and others 1992: 112). A single radiocarbon date on the humate fraction of soil indicates stable desert grassland vegetation at 160 B.P. or A.D. 1790 (Doleman and others 1992: 112).

The previously cited wood rat studies recognize desert grassland as well, but emphasize the Chihuahua Desert flora on south-facing slopes with limy soil. Indeed, the steep, erodable limestone slopes may be far more sensitive to throbs of aridity than the Tularosa Basin proper. The recent erosional cycle, about 150 years in age, began with the breakup of the stable Q3 grassland that was either caused or exacerbated by late nineteenth century grazing in the area (Doleman and others 1992: 112). The spread of mesquite through the digestive system of cattle contributed to the steep coppice dune formations of mesquite that are apparently unique to

recent times (Blair and others 1990).

Stalagmite Studies

During the late Pleistocene massive stalagmites were produced in caves in the Guadalupe Mountains of southern New Mexico, but virtually none formed following that period. However, growth of the small columnar stalagmites during the late Holocene, though minute by comparison, resumed about 4000 B.P., marking the beginning of increased precipitation (Polyak and Asmerom 2001). Small, columnar stalagmites from Carlsbad Caverns and Hidden Cave in the Guadalupe Mountains have variations in annual band thickness, mineralogy, and growth versus no-growth records. When these differences are studied in conjunction with high precision uranium series dating of stalagmite deposits, a record of climatic variation emerges. In this semi-arid region stalagmite growth is moisture-limited, and unlike other settings, produces annual bands that reveal climate. Layers of clear calcite alternate with inclusion-rich calcite to form annual bands. The former are due to seasonal periods of increased drip rates. The thickness of annual bands on one stalagmite were measured and dated. The degree of thickness represented the growth rate. Thicker bands are relative indicators of increased precipitation. Four additional stalagmites were used for corroboration (Table 2.3).

Modern Climate

The present day climate in the Tularosa Basin is of the arid continental type. Mild winters and warm summers prevail with little rainfall (20 cm to 25 cm annually). In Tularosa (1,384 m), the annual pattern of precipitation is representative of basin elevations (Maker and others 1972: 9). On average, 50 percent (12 cm) of precipitation comes between September and March. Snow falls each winter but usually

		Table 2.3 Stalagmites and the Climatic Record*		
Age Before Present	Age	Stalagmite Interpretation
4000 to 3000	2050 to 1050 BC	Intervals of slightly greater effective moisture than at present
3000 to 1700	1050 BC to AD 250	Significantly greater annual moisture than at present
2800 to 2600	850 to 650 BC	Wettest interval for the late Holocene
2000	50 BC	Sizable effective moisture
1700 to 1300	AD 250 to 650	Similar to today but slightly wetter
800 to 700	AD 1150 to 1250	Three of five stalagmites stop growth

* Polyak and Asmeron 2001

disappears within a day. At lower elevations snowfall ranges from 5 cm to 15 cm. At 1,830 m average annual snowfall is about 61 cm (Maker and others 1972: 7). Rains during this period are associated with the cyclonic storms accompanying large air-mass movements from the Pacific Ocean.

The regional storms are of moderate to low intensity. Spring (April and May) rainfall is low, forming only 10 percent (2 cm) of the annual total. Around 40 percent of the precipitation (10 cm) comes from June to the end of August, where it takes the form of brief but occasionally heavy local thunderstorms. During this period, as the summer progresses, the probability of rainfall increases. In any location, variability in rainfall is high.

Winds are light to moderate most of the year (average 16 km per hour) but may be strong in spring. The freeze-free period in most lower elevations, like Alamogordo (1,326 m), is April to November, about 213 days (Maker and others 1972: 9). In mountain areas, the freeze-free period decreases by about two months, lasting from May through September. In Fresnal Canyon at Mountain Park (2,048 m elevation), the average frost-free period is 179 days, April 29 to October 25 (Maker and others 1972: 9). Annual temperatures decrease about 2.2°C for each 305 m increase in elevation (Maker and others 1972: 7).

Rock Shelter Species in Relation to Post-Pleistocene Vegetation

Many plant species deposited during the occupation of Fresnal Shelter by humans and wood rats duplicate the ones recovered from the middle to late Holocene wood rat nests in Marble and Big Boy canyons that are equivalent in age (Table 2.2).

One-seeded juniper, broad-leaved yucca (*Yucca baccata*), agave (*Agave* sp.), ocotillo (*Fouquieria splendens*), creosote bush, side-oats grama (*Bouteloua curtipendula*), black grama, mesquite, Apache plume (*Fallugia paradoxa*), mariola, sotol, hedgehog cactus, prickly pear, trailing four o'clock (*Allionia incarnata*) and, *Kallstroemia* were all part of wood rat nests (Van Devender and others 1984). All were identified from Fresnal Shelter except black grama, which was recovered in High Rolls Cave. The presence of mesquite in the Marble Canyon wood rat nests casts doubt on speculation that the species was established on the slopes of Fresnal Shelter with human help, for it may have grown there earlier.

The south-facing slopes at Fresnal Shelter today, but for the lack of one-seeded juniper and herbs subject to grazing pressure such as *Kallstroemia* and *Allionia incarnata*, have many of the same species, including black grama (see Table A.2) as the late Holocene wood rat middens described by Van Devender and others (1984).

Because the prehistoric plants compare so well to modern plants, Fresnal Shelter plant identifications and interpretations based on modern species composition and distribution in floras appear appropriate in most cases. A similar observation applies to High Rolls Cave because it was occupied at a comparable time.

PART III. CULTURAL ACTIVITIES IN THE TULAROSA BASIN AND SACRAMENTO MOUNTAINS

Prehistory

The Tularosa Basin belongs to the western Trans-Pecos culture area (south-central New Mexico, western Texas, and northeastern Chihuahua, Mexico) where hundreds of open-air sites with thermal features lack any evidence of maize (Miller and Kenmatsu 2004: 228). Archaeology within the Tularosa Basin struggles with regional problems of defining

sedentism and mobility. The problems are linked to judging the importance of agriculture through time against a backdrop of collecting wild plants when little direct evidence of either exists. Many assume a steady progression towards a settled life while others envision a prehistory with a series of peaks and deeply etched valleys. Still others concede the possibility of co-existence of both sedentary and more mobile life styles. Surveys exist in abundance, yet problems persist in defining a site or the extent of a lithic scatter, recognizing seasonal versus permanent settlements, and understanding dune deflation and erosion as it affects artifact distribution and chronological control.

In 1971, a transect survey was made between 1,525 m and 2,135 m in the Sacramento Mountains that revealed four apparent site types (1) small hearth sites on ridge saddles, (2) large open sites on ridge sides usually associated with open meadows, (3) large roasting pits and associated hearths and (4) caves lower on the mountain slope. Many of the sites appeared to be roughly contemporaneous with Fresnal Shelter (HSR 1972: 23, 30). What may be a late Paleoindian or an Early Archaic visitation at Fresnal Shelter preserves in wood charcoal radiocarbon dated 7310 ± 75 B.P. (Tagg 1996: 316).

In 1981, a series of archaeological surveys within the Lincoln National Forest began about 1,830 m and extended from the southern beginnings of the Sacramento Mountains northward as far as the Mescalero Apache Reservation (Spoerl 1981). Three small ephemeral lithic scatters were above 2,897 m on open areas of canyon slopes of typically southern exposure. Sixty-two of the 78 lithic scatters (79 %) were between 1,830 m and 2,074 m elevation. Thirty-nine, or half the lithic scatters, were on broad ridge tops on the western side of the Sacramento Mountains. Other lithic scatters were in canyon bottoms on benches above the drainage or near the base of canyon sides.

During the early Holocene (about 11,000 to 8000 B.P.) Paleoindian hunters made at least occasional use of the Tularosa Basin. Sites include Moody Tank, just north of the Jarilla Mountains in the central Tularosa Basin (Russell 1968); the Lone Butte Folsom Site at 1,185 m in the north; and the Holloman Cody Site on a ridge at 1,220 m elevation (HSR 1973: 223).

Although the extensive Archaic occupation of the Tularosa Basin proper dates from the middle Holocene (8000 to 4000 B.P.), the majority of the recovered Archaic points date to the late Holocene (4000 B.P. to present), or Middle and Late Archaic periods, as does the radiocarbon record (Doleman and others 1992: 191).

Throughout the western Trans-Pecos in the Late Archaic (1200 B.C. to A.D. 200/900) sites, features, and associated material culture dramatically increase. Central basin landforms undergo either a peak in intensity of use or population judging from more than 550 radiocarbon dates of more than 300 features from the western Trans-Pecos (Miller and Komatsu 2004: 226). A study of perishable artifacts from the margins of the Tularosa Basin dating between 4500 and 2000 years B.P. (Hyland and Adovasio 2000) reveals both a disjuncture and an innovation in perishable forms. After ruling out several possible scenarios, the authors hypothesize a migration of southern origin followed by amalgamation (Table 2.4 and Fig. 2.2).

Despite extensive radiocarbon dating and related archaeological activity near Las Cruces and El Paso in recent years (Miller and Kenmatsu 2004: 210), few Archaic sites in the Tularosa Basin proper have been excavated, and even fewer have been radiocarbon dated (Doleman and others 1992: 186), though Doleman and his associates have done much to remedy the situation. The Middle-to-Late Archaic is represented by 10 radiocarbon dates ranging from 4075 to 2040 B.P., or 2115 to 90 B.C. (Swift, Morrison and Doleman 1991: 185).

Specifics of the nature of settlement and subsistence during the Tularosa Basin Archaic are now apparent. Information on settlement has developed through a careful unraveling of the interface between geomorphological and archaeological aspects of sites (Doleman and Swift 1991). Using an experimental approach with fire-cracked rock, researchers Richard Duncan and William Doleman tentatively concluded that the fracture pattern on monzonite, an igneous rock recovered in the White Sands Missile Range, evidently reflects thermal shock resulting from use in stone boiling rather than gradual heating and cooling associated with stones in roasting pits (Doleman and others 1992: 193).

The patterning of distribution of thermal features with fire-cracked rock in the southern Tularosa Basin reveals an apparently functional distinction between sites with boiling stones and those sites lacking them. Activities producing boiling stones were more common in the transition from the bajada and in the basin floor compared to the bajada itself where lithic raw materials originated (Doleman and others 1992: 232). A strong positive relationship exists between boiling stones and sand mounds in the extreme 53 km southwest of Alamagordo. Even though bajada zones were much closer to sources of monzonite for stone boiling, it was apparently easier to move the rock to sand mound locations on the basin floor or in the transition zone to the basin floor. Implied here is a short-term residence that included stone boiling of local grains and other small seeds. The category "sand grasslands and dunes" in Table 2.1 enumerates some potential plant resources.

A dated Archaic site from the Jarilla Mountain piedmont may prove typical of oth-

Table 2.4. Perishable Artifacts from the Tularosa Basin Margin

Older Pendejo Cave Forms from Before 4450 BP Retained	Added Innovative Forms from 4450 BP to 1700 BP*
Sandals: present; include two-warp scuffer toe (F)	Two-warp sandals predominate (F) Four-warp sandal appear (F)
Cordage: usual two-ply, S-spun, Z twist (F)	Proliferation of cordage types (F, S) Feather-wrapped cordage (F) Increase in final S-twist cordage but Z-twist remains dominant pattern
Netting: knots of sheet bend or weaver type	
Twined mats (F), bags	Plaited mats (F) and containers Checkerweave mats of untrimmed sotol (F)
Coiled basketry: two-rod and bundle non-interlocked stitch (F)	Bundle with rod core foundation and interlocked stitch (F,S)
Single rod, stacked and bunched foundations with non-interlocked stitch	Bundle foundation with non-interlocked stitch, close coiling (F,S)

* Pendejo Cave, Tornillo Rockshelter, Fresnal Shelter, and Chavez Cave (Hyland and Adovasio 2000)
(F) Present at Fresnal Shelter (HSR 1973, Merchant 2002, Moots 1990)
(S) No record of earlier innovation to north, but extensive antiquity to south

ers in a similar setting. The drainage near LA 62697 fostered the existence of a large ephemeral pond to the west and a smaller depression to the northeast (Swift and others 1991). Slab metates were the most common type of ground stone and debitage flakes were dominant. There were 52 definite boiling stones amidst three radiocarbon-dated hearths (3995 ± 105 B.P., 4075 ± 20 B.P., and 3300 ± 105 B.P.) suggesting a Middle-to-Late Archaic occupation. The environmental setting of LA 62697 duplicates physiographically similar areas. Low reddish sand dunes extend a number of kilometers north, west, and east of the Jarilla Mountains and south to the Texas border. A large part of the area has numerous small arroyos that maintain themselves for only short distances among the drifting sand and end in shallow depressions often called "lakes" (Meinzer and Hare 1915).

The Late Archaic is often the primary time period represented in rock shelters (Miller and Kenmatsu 2004: 226). Both Fresnal Shelter and High Rolls Cave were occupied during the late Archaic. The relationship between previously discussed climatic clues and cultural markers is summarized in Table 2.5. A pronounced increase in radiocarbon dated features and contexts begins between 1200 and 1000 B.C., about the time cultigens appear (Miller and

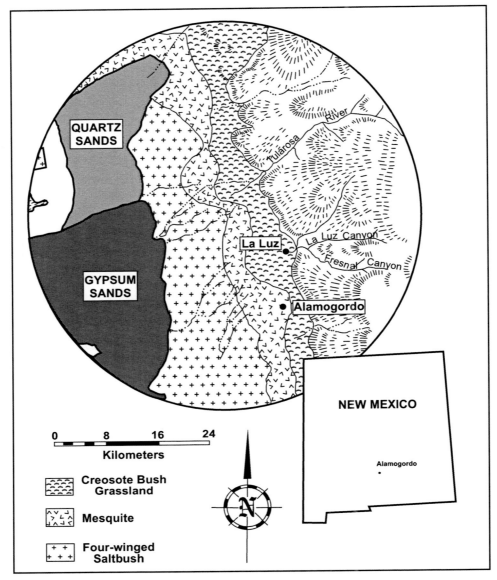

Figure 2.2. Physiography and Vegetation of Tularosa Basin near Fresnal Shelter (adapted by V. Gnabasik from Shields 1956)

Kenmatsu 2004: 231). The earliest dated maize in Fresnal Shelter and the well-represented Stratum 2 at High Rolls Cave belong to this trend, as does the renewed activity in Stratum 1, typical elsewhere between 200 B.C. and A.D. 1 (Miller and Kenmatsu 2004: 231).

The gemstone site of the Middle and Late Archaic is Fresnal Shelter, perched in Fresnal Canyon in the Sacramento Mountains, which frame the eastward margin of the Tularosa

Basin. Nowhere else in the western Trans-Pecos is the perishable component of the Archaic so well preserved.

Of the 28,000 bone fragments, 869 represented remains of large and medium size mammals. Twenty-nine animals were identified with certainty: 26 mule deer and one each of pronghorn, buffalo, and bighorn sheep (Wimberly and Eidenbach 1981: 23). Cameron (1973) examined 1,264 elements of small vertebrates

Table 2.5. Chronology of Climatic Clues and Cultural Events, Tularosa Basin and Margin

Age BP	Nature of Evidence	Climatic Clues*	Cultural Event
18,000		Douglas fir	
		Rocky Mountain juniper	
17,000	Wood rat midden	Piñon, one-seeded juniper	
16,000			
15,000	Soil horizon Q2	Soil extensively stripped by wind	
14,000	in Tularosa Basin		
13,000			PaleoIndians
12,000			in Tularosa Basin
11,000	Wood rat midden	One-seeded juniper present at l555 m	
10,000			
9000			
8000	Wood rat midden	Piñon, mountain mahogany, mesquite at 1155 m	
7000	Soil horizon Q3	Modern soil horizon	F.S. hearth
6000		established in Tularosa Basin	7310 BP (Tagg 1996: 316)
5000			
4000	Wood rat midden	Modern creosote bush, New Mexican agave, golden eye, Apache plume at 1155 m	
4000	Stalagmites	Area has intervals of slightly more effective annual moisture to 3000 BP	LA 62692 occupied in in Tularosa Basin
3900			
3800			
3600			
3500			
3450			
3300			H.R.C. Strat 3
3000	Stalagmites	Significantly greater annual moisture begins in area	H.R.C. Strat 2
2950			
2945			maize at F.S & H.R.C.
2800		Wet interval increases	
2770		Wet interval continues	
2600		Wet interval declines	F.S. unoccupied?
2500			
2400			
2300			H.R.C. Strat 1
2200			
2085			
2000	Stalagmites	Period of sizable effective moisture	H.R.C.
1900			
1800			F.S.
1700	Stalagmites	A dry period begins; but is slightly wetter than today; it ends in 1300 BP	
1625			
1550			

F.S. = Fresnal Shelter; H.R.C. = High Rolls Cave
*Climatic clues derived from Doleman and others l992, Polyak and Asmerom 2001, Van Devender and others 1984.

from five hearth areas, and found 58 percent of them sowed signs of burning. Wood rat, deer mice, other rodents, amphibians, birds, and rabbits were subsumed under the term *small vertebrates*. A turkey feather that had heat applied to it and a cache of turkey feathers (Table A.1) indicate cultural use.

Coiled basketry included a pitch-covered piece indicating the inhabitants had a way of carrying and storing water. Both twilled and twined matting were recovered (HSR 1972). The sandals (N=152) were all of plain weave with two warps most common, although as many as four were used. The heels of the sandals are commonly closed with the fishtail treatment, but sometimes with a rounded heel (Merchant 2002). Simple two-ply cordage of plant fibers predominates in deposits, with no general trend for spin or twist (Moots l990), though results differed in a later study (McBrinn 2005). Irwin-Williams (1979, Fig. 12) illustrates a string and feather ornament from Fresnal Shelter. Feather-wrapped cordage was rare, though Moots identified rabbit fur cordage.

Wooden foreshafts, points, digging sticks, tool hafts, fire-boards, and hair pins form part of the assemblage. The slotted foreshaft of an atlatl dart, bone awl, and bone gaming pieces have been illustrated (Irwin-Williams l979, Fig.

12). Deer antler tines showing wear on their tips were considered curated tools. Eight metates and 30 manos were present (HSR 1972).

Three sources of stylistic influences upon the crafting of bifaces recovered at Fresnal Shelter are recognized by R. Jones (1990), although the styles all share Mexico in their southern distribution. The earliest influence began with the Cochise culture in the Augustin type biface. The San Pedro and Bat Cave Type 4 have a stylistic influence suggestive of southern Arizona, southwestern New Mexico, and Northern Mexico. The San Pedro represents a transition stage between late Cochise and early Mogollon (R. Jones 1990: 71). Stylistic influence from northern Mexico can be seen in the Cahuila or Fresnal type biface. It has been associated with the Cahuila complex, which covers most of the Archaic in Southwestern prehistory (R. Jones 1990: 74). The Trans Pecos-Rio Grande style is typified by a variety of bifaces with the Perdernales type representing the earliest. Also present were the Palmillas and Shumla type bifaces (R. Jones 1990: 104), which have a stylistic influence from the Trans-Pecos area southward into Mexico (R. Jones 1990: 78). The Oshara Tradition, suggesting a northern influence, is represented by the Bajada, En Medio, and San Jose types. Table 2.6 has dates assigned by Jones for the common biface styles that were associated with a radiocarbon sample. McBrinn (2005: 86) notes that though there is heterogeneity within a point type, there is little or no regional variation.

At High Rolls Cave, En Medio type projectiles came from Stratum 1 and Hueco points predominate in Stratum 2. A cache of projectile points included Hueco and Pendejo points and single San Pedro, Augustin, Fresnal, and Shumla points. The latter was made from heat-treated Alibates chert. No milling stones were recovered, and there was only one small piece of both ground stone and abalone shell. Perishable artifacts were limited primarily to

cordage segments and sandals. Five of the six two-warp sandals were small enough to be worn by children. Two sandals had heels finished with a fishtail and four had rounded heels (Merchant 2002b). The four date from 1400 to 1020 B.C.

The close of the Archaic signaled a pronounced shift in regional dynamics. Existing similarities in basketry and weaving between the Trans-Pecos and northern Mexico and the primary restriction of obsidian resources to within the Chihuahuan Desert, both north-to-south trends, give way to ones more oriented east-to-west or toward the Mogollon of western New Mexico (Miller and Kenmatsu 2004: 236). Cultural remains become more typical of the Jornada Branch of the Mogollon Culture Area.

The remaining periods of the Tularosa Basin prehistory are subsumed under the heading "Formative" with three temporal phases (Mesilla, Doña Ana, and El Paso) first outlined by Lehmer (1948). The culture locally present is known as the El Paso expression. Many surveys that cover the temporal phases indicate a change in settlement patterns from more or less dispersed small residential sites on the basin floor and mountain periphery to more aggregated settlements on the alluvial fans at the edge of the basin, particularly in the El Paso Phase. It is only in the El Paso Phase that maize is commonly recovered (see reviews by Doleman and Eidenbach [1992] and Miller and Kenmatsu [2004]).

Three sites relating to Formative development have been reported both near and within the city of Alamogordo. Site 3, within the city limits, consists of surface rooms and pit rooms with associated ceramics indicative of a late Doña Ana phase. El Paso phase Site 1 is located 3.2 km (2 miles) north of Alamogordo, and Site 2, 3.2 km (two miles) southeast (Marshall 1973: 91). Rooms are arranged around a central plaza and in discrete lines. Alamogordo Site 1 has a

Table 2.6. Estimated Age of Selected Stylized Bifaces with Associated Radiocarbon Sample*

Biface Name	Estimated Age	Fresnal Location	C14 Lab and Number	Location of C14	Age BP (Tagg 1996)
Trans-Pecos					
Palmillas	<915 BC	C 29.81 129 cmbd	ISGS 969	C 29.65 126 cmbd	2770 +/- 70
	to AD 113	B 27.42 132 cmbd B 27.100 153 cmbd B 27.121 174 cmbd	Beta36738	B 27.421 132 cmbd	1890 +/- 60
Shumla	<915 BC	C 29.65? 126 cmbd	ISGS 969	C 29.65 126 cmbd	2770 +/- 70
	to 833 BC	? E 28.43 140 cmbd	ISGS 897	C 29.122 136 cmbd	2690 +/- 60
Cochise or Mogollon					
San Pedro	<915 BC	E 28. 43 140 cmbd	ISGS 969	C 29.65 126 cmbd	2770 +/- 70
Type 4	<915 BC	C 29.62 126 cmbd	ISGS 969	C 29.65 126 cmbd	2770 +/- 70
Augustin	<3951 BC	C25.249 141 cmbd	Beta 36739	C 29.264 120-125 cmbd	5090 +/- 60
Coahuila or Fresnal	1428 BC	D 27.201 162 cmbd	ISGS 888	D 27.11 170-178 cmbd	3150 +/- 70
	to 915 BC	C 29.173 141 cmbd	ISGS 969	C 29.65B 126 cmbd	2770 +/- 70
Rio Grande					
En Medio	1314 BC	D 28.19 98 cmbd	Beta 36745	D 28.143 148-151 cmbd	3040 +/- 70

*from Jones 1990, text, Table 1, and Tagg 1996, Table 1

room with two contiguous square adobe bins. The manner in which the bins had been roofed lead Stanley Stubbs to believe they had been turkey pens (Marshall 1973: 106). At the two El Paso Phase Alamogordo sites as well as at the Bradfield Site just east of the Organ Mountains, maize with a slender cob and relatively low row number (Lehmer 1948: 95) exhibit traits that characterize maize in the much older deposits from Fresnal Shelter.

History of the Tularosa Basin

Areas of the Pecos drainage, the Sacramento Mountains, the Tularosa Basin, the San Andres Mountains, and the Organ Mountains became the adopted territory of many groups. The Lipan and Mescalero Apache, the Mansos, and the Suma are known to have lived in the region as well (Stuart and Gauthier 1981: 212). Other travelers included two missionaries on their way to northern New Mexico who baptized a number of Indians in 1719 and built a chapel called *Nuestra Señor de La Luz* near the present town of La Luz (Pearce 1965: 83). At the time of and prior to the withdrawal of the Mexican government in 1846, a wagon road led from El Paso over the desert east of the Franklin, Organ, and San Andres mountains to the alkali flats and apparently northward to Manzano in the Estancia Valley. Salt found on the alkali flats and at Malapais Spring on Salt Creek was a valued natural resource from the Tularosa Basin (Meinzer and Hare 1915: 16).

After New Mexico became a United States Territory, attempts to create permanent settlements increased in number. Parties of Spanish and Mexican immigrants from the Mesilla Valley established Tularosa in 1860 and again in 1862 due to Apache interference (Writers Program 1940: 372). La Luz Canyon, just a few kilometers above modern La Luz, was settled in 1864 (Pearce 1965: 83). The community of Fresnal, above High Rolls in Fresnal Canyon, began in the 1870s about the time the Mescalero Apache Reservation was organized as an area separate from Fort Stanton (Pearce 1965: 60).

Ranching operations expanded quickly into country recently vacated by the Apache. Its promoters were quick to see the arrival of the railroad (at Alamogordo in 1898) as a ready means to reach eastern markets. Stock-raising reached lofty proportions up and through World War I when the market bottomed out (Writers Program 1940: 85). Timber and mining industries were also established in this boom period.

The number of domestic livestock foraging on unfenced rangeland in a volatile economic period can only be estimated, much less the number that might have treaded through Fresnal Canyon. The canyon was a major access route to and from the mountains for the communities of La Luz (1,464 m) and those living near High Rolls and Mountain Park (2,013 m). When the Alamo National Forest was established in 1907, an estimated 10,000 sheep, 40,000 goats, and 17,000 head of cattle and horses utilized the newly established National Forest in what are now the Cloudcroft and Mayhill districts. Many of the goats and sheep must have bedded in Fresnal Shelter in order to form the thick layer of dung that capped the prehistoric deposits. By 1911, grazing for the Alamo National Forest (now the Guadalupe District of the present National Forest) decreased to 12,000 sheep and goats (USFS files). By that time all grazing in the Tularosa Basin had been reduced due to drought.

The economy of the Tularosa Basin began to swing upward again in 1939 when the military facilities of Holloman Air Force Base and later the White Sands Missile Range were established. Today a great percentage of the population depends on the military for income. Only limited numbers are engaged in ranching, agriculture, and timber, which depend directly on the productivity of the land.

Chapter 3
Nature of the Rock Shelter Deposits, Related Problems, and Ethnobotanical Procedures

Overview of the Two Rock Shelters

The uppermost layers of Fresnal Shelter were formed from historic animal dung enriched by limestone breakdown from the shelter wall. The next two layers of grey-brown soil were heavily disturbed by rodent activity. The fill beneath, which reached some 2 m in places, consisted primarily of vegetal material amended with fine silts of aeolian origin. Heavy rock fall, which was most frequent at the outer limits of the shelter, provided irregular spaces for human activity while rock fissures and crevices furnished living areas for rodents. Vegetal material 1 cm to 2 cm long plugged rock crevices, rodent burrows, and declivities in an extremely compact manner. In some places vegetal material seemed cemented in a hard matrix of charcoal and ash whereas in other places, it was less consolidated. Although no evidence was seen of prepared floors or purposeful structures, pits were common. Consequently, stratigraphic units that united more than several grid squares were rare.

Comparative analysis of plant remains was restricted to the portion of Fresnal Shelter protected from moisture by the cliff overhang where plant remains were better preserved than elsewhere (Fig. 3.1) and far better than at High Rolls Cave. When one examines the screened content of the eight grid squares that run parallel to the shelter wall beneath the overhang (C28, C29, C30, and C31, and D 28, D29, D30, and D31), the similarity in botanical content between squares is even more apparent (see Table A.3 and Figure 3.2).

High Rolls Cave exhibited stratigraphy that carried the promise of segregating two different periods of Archaic occupation. The organic deposits appear condensed by decay, but preservation of uncarbonized plant material, though uneven, was evident. Short segments of grassy stems, like the ones that plugged rock crevices in Fresnal Shelter, were part of flotation samples (Appendix B.1). Similarly, several of the firepits (Features 18, 19, and 23) had a highly compacted agglomeration of ash, gypsum, and limestone. Flotation samples came from hearths, shallow pits, and occupational surfaces.

Abiotic Influences

At Fresnal Shelter the wind deposited fine silts, a scatter of oak and silk tassel leaves, chaff from winnowed grass grain, and ashes into the far recesses of the shelter. In High Rolls Cave a similar mix of oak and silk tassel leaves preserved in flotation. At High Rolls Cave, wind served as an initial major distributor of most pollen, for a gradient of concentration can be demonstrated from the front to the rear of the

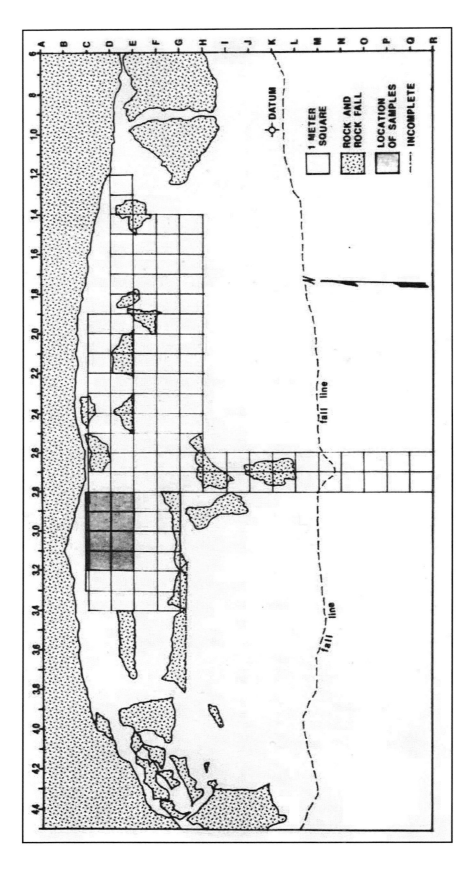

Figure 3.1. Fresnal Shelter Grid Plan with the Location of Grids Screened for Plant Material.

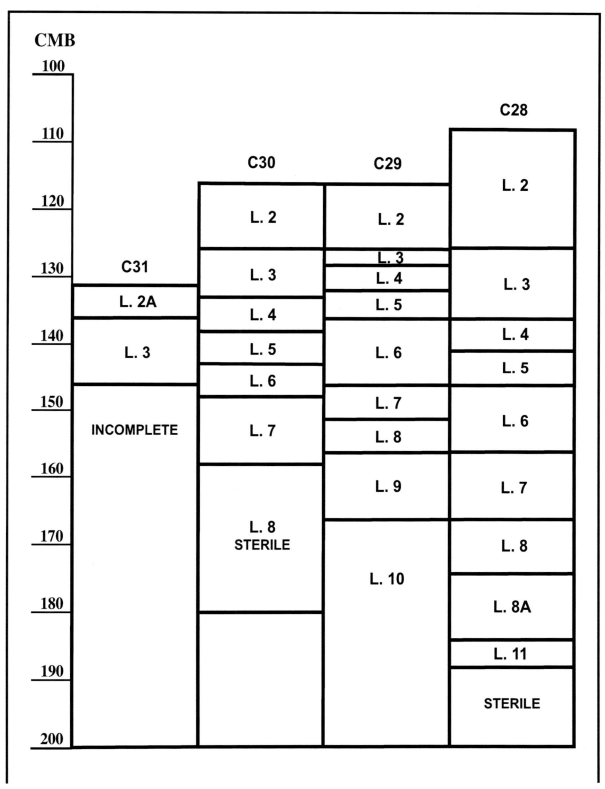

Figure 3.2. Diagrammatic Profile of Excavation Levels in Squares C 28 to C 31, Fresnal Shelter.

cave (Holloway 2002).

Freezing and thawing of the intermittently-damp limestone walls doubtless led to accelerated rock fall and spall formation in both rock shelters, but was much more evident in Fresnal Shelter, which had a southern exposure. However, rock fall was less in the central section of the shelter, which was protected by about 4 m of cliff overhang.

Fresnal Shelter deposits may have been subject to size-sorting through the dynamic movement of granular material. Lithic debitage as well as minced, dry plant remains can be displaced differentially by human trampling as well as by other factors. Granular movement may begin by small vibrations (Jaeger and Nagel 1997) generated through trampling, rock fall, or by the gradual settling of deposits as decay from the damp bottom of the cave reduces the organic material that contacts it. The vibrations can foster vertical movements both downward and upward. The move upward of large diameter pieces bears no relation to the object's density. This process has been called "the Brazil Nut effect" from the phenomenon seen in mixtures of nuts prepared for commerce. The conformation of the container (for example, the local deposit formed by rock fall and concentrations of consolidated ash) influences the direction of movement. In addition, what are known as convection rolls can generate vertical circular movements of various sized small-grained material. People who study the physics of granular materials are not sure what causes the latter movements (Jaeger and Nagel 1997: 545). Experiments in displacement of lithic debitage through trampling in silty loam indicate horizontal movements of artifacts, while in unconsolidated sandy soil debitage can move downward as much as 8 cm as well as down slope (Gifford-Gonzales and others 1985).

My own experience in separating threshed seeds from their chaff by jiggling an open, flat basket or one more concave in nature reminds me that the size-sorting that takes place in preparation for winnowing replicates on a small-scale the physical forces at work within dry cave deposits. When the living surface of High Rolls Cave was dry and in use, trampling must have been responsible for movement of some vegetal material.

Both shelters have evidence of former moisture. However, when R. Jones (1990: 33) studied the stylized bifaces from Fresnal Shelter, he noted that groundwater infiltration had caused a heavy carbonate layer on artifacts. Moisture accumulated at the rear of the shelter because only a portion of the bones of an infant burial remained (G. Hall 1973: 386) and another portion of the rear of the cave contains water deposited rock (Square B 32 W, unit Q). Excavators noted dampness in the lowest levels of the shelter beneath the overhang (B 27, C 27, and C 29). It seems likely that the earliest organic material in contact with damp soil has degraded. Moreover, the decay of organic material must contribute to the settling of the overlying strata, including slumpage over tilted rock faces. The shelter floor consists of gravel topped by a sterile yellow to tannish-yellow silt. Mixed with the silts are scale and breakdown from the limestone wall.

At High Rolls Cave, the best-preserved flotation samples have plant parts that show degradation due to moisture. A single flotation sample may show great variation in preservation as, for example, one with a yucca leaf that is a bundle of fibers only partly covered by epidermis, a leaf of leathery texture, and a delicate tubular flower. Even though mice and wood rat fecal pellets were common in flotation samples, excavators had great difficulty detecting their tunnels. I can only suppose that the moisture that initiated decay promoted stratigraphic compaction, during which rodent tunnels might have collapsed.

Percolating water as well as sediment

compaction may have contributed to high pollen concentrations at High Rolls Cave. Almost all of the types of non-arboreal pollen are present in concentrations at least as high as 31,000 grains per gram, though concentrations reach as high as 158,760 grams per grain (Appendix B. 4). Pollen concentration values are reminiscent of canal sediment samples from the middle Gila River of Arizona. One of two canal samples considered of a highly organic content contained the maximum pollen concentration recovered, 162,419 grains per cc, and the next highest were from canal sediments that match the interpretation of slow, low-energy flows with 52,885 grains per cc and 45,509 grains per cc (Adams and others 2002: 41). Some of the High Rolls Cave pollen samples contain a diversity of insect-pollinated floral types that suggest human use (Appendix B. 4).

Biotic Factors

Wood rats (*Neotoma* sp.) and deer mice (*Peromyscus* sp.), two rodents that easily tolerate the presence of humans, lived within the rock shelters. They, like humans, have the capacity to control the availability of food in space and time through storage. Inevitably, both rodent and human inhabitants of each rock shelter may wish to store the same food item and come into conflict in regards to finite resources. In High Rolls Cave approximately half the flotation samples in East Clusters A and B contained fecal pellets of rodents. Moreover, the shredded condition of much material in Fresnal Shelter and in uncarbonized flotation samples in High Rolls Cave serves as an added reminder of their activity (Appendix B.1, sample prefaces). Even in thermal areas at High Rolls Cave, periods of disuse by humans provided an opportunity for rodents to introduce three-leaved sumac into hearths prior to its next use. Excavators at High Rolls Cave reported small groups of pinyon

nuts that probably represent rodent caches. We cannot always recognize rodent transport, but many vegetal items have moved around since their original deposit in both rock shelters.

Deer mice store food items in small, scattered subsurface caches as well as in larger caches below ground in storage chambers. Fresnal Shelter retained numerous examples of small sub-surface caches of maize as well as larger ones, while High Rolls Cave preserved an example of a large, diverse cache of foodstuff. For a scattered, subsurface cache the mouse digs a hole from 2.5 cm to 10 cm deep and expels the contents of the internal cheek pouches into the hole and covers it with soil and litter (VanderWall 1990).

During the first year of excavation of Fresnal Shelter, an inventory of maize for potential radiocarbon dating was compiled for Square C 29. Of the 59 entries for kernels, 70 percent were recorded in clusters from two to five kernels. If 10 kernels of wheat can be carried in cheek pouches by a single deer mouse (VanderWall 1990: 259), then two to five grains of maize might be carried as easily, depending on their size. The very act of burial in a subsurface cache could transfer maize kernels as much as one or two 5 cm arbitrary excavation levels. More than likely, most kernels were lost one by one, only to be recovered by mice and cached together. Rodent reburial of maize kernels may explain dating discrepancies with associated dated charcoal. None of the Tandem Accelerator Mass Spectrometer (TAMS) radiocarbon dated maize from Square C 29 (Tagg 1996) derived from the solitary recovery of a kernel in a grid Level. In two instances, large caches of 238 (C29.201) and 239 maize kernels (C 29.65A) were dated by selection of a single kernel (Tagg 1996: 317).

Mice apparently scavenged human food items, human discards, and flowering portions of plants (Table 3.1). The last category may

Table 3.1. Effect of Rodents on Cave Vegetal Content and Stratigraphic Position

Animal	Activity in Rock Shelters*
Rodents Introduce dietary items from nearby. Shred plant material.	F.S.: sedge seed into pits, acorns, *Kallstroemia*, poison ivy, hackberry seeds from vicinity H.R.C.: piñon, juniper seeds, acorns
Tunnels conduct percolating water.	
Wood Rats Remove material from primary site of deposition to secondary ones, often upon the same living surface.	F.S.: corn cobs, sandals, lithics can plug tunnels to nests beneath rocks.
Scavenge from outside the cave.	Transport pinyon nuts, juniper berries, hackberries, mesquite pods, cholla, and prickly pear fruits to nest chambers and introduce dietary items (VanderWall 1990: 262).
Introduce dietary items.	Prickly pear and cholla fruits (Spencer and Spencer 1941: 281)
Mice Scavenge food gathered by humans for caching, including grass grains and maize kernels.	F.S.: maize kernels cached below habitation surface, 2.5 to 10 cm. H.R.C.: buffalo gourd, giant dropseed grass.
Scavenge human food waste products for consumption.	H.R.C.: seeds of prickly pear, hedgehog cactus, juniper, yucca seeds, and mesquite endocarps
Introduce seeds of disturbed ground plant species some of which may be humanly consumed as well	F.S.: *Helianthus* or *Viguiera* achenes H.R.C.: cheno-ams, goosefoot, buckwheat, stickseed, purslane, sunflower, *Salvia,* and *Helianthus* or *Viguiera* achenes
Introduce seeds of nearby trees. Introduce floral parts from nearby habitats.	H.R.C.: piñon, juniper, acorns H.R.C.: emerging pine needles, pine pollen-bearing cones, flowers of three-leaf sumac, flowers of the sunflower family

*F.S. = Fresnal Shelter; H.R.C. = High Rolls Cave

affect pollen deposition while the introduction of maize kernels or disturbed ground plants may inadvertently enrich the flotation record. Many of the rodent-introduced taxa prsented in Table 3.1 are discussed in greater detail in the next chapter. At High Rolls Cave, a flotation sample characterized by large numbers of mouse feces and diverse plant content was recovered from Stratum 3 (FS 67), though selected items could also be found in Stratum 2 where, presumably, the mouse first located them.

Wood rats continually carry small objects about and often drop one in favor of another more to their liking. The most attractive items are carried to the nest vicinity. The net result for archaeologists is that the wood rat removes items from the primary site of deposition. Wood rats are not known to scatter-hoard seeds and nuts as is the habit of mice (VanderWall 1990: 262). Their nests are built to protect against predators and may be in rock crevices or under boulders. When constructed near rock outcrops, tunnels may extend to inaccessible natural cavities (VanderWall 1990: 260), at least until exposed by the archaeologist's trowel. In Fresnal Shelter, maize cobs, utilized flakes, and sandals were recovered from either wood rat tunnels or nests or both, often in otherwise inaccessible locations. Because of subsurface wood rat nest locations in Fresnal Shelter, many vegetal items might have been removed by wood rats from a living surface to a deeper level.

Since there is less rock fall in High Rolls Cave, rummaging and transport may have been limited to living surfaces. However, one cannot easily dismiss 10 stratigraphically-misplaced corn cobs. Some strata have considerable evidence of carnivore gnawing, punctures, and crushing. A fresh looking partial hind foot of a coyote is in Stratum 2 (Akins 2002).

Fresnal Shelter Features, Stratigraphy, and Dating

Hearths could be bowl shaped or outlined with fire-cracked limestone fragments (HSR 1972). Two hearths in the lowest cultural horizon have been dated 7310 ± 75 B.P. and 7110 ± 75 B.P. (Tagg 1996: 316). Hearths interrupted stratigraphy beneath the overhang, except possibly in Square C 30, which might have been a continuous repository of plant refuse.

Pits dug into earlier strata or into former pits also disrupt the stratigraphy beneath the rock overhang. More ephemeral pit excavations were sometimes signaled by a change in orientation of vegetal material rather than by a change in soil color or composition as in Square B 29, Unit D. Square C 29 has three superimposed storage pits that belong to a total of five storage cists that represent major features in the shelter (Table 3.2). These pits retain a vegetal lining and average a meter in diameter and from 17 cm to 24 cm in depth. When excavated, all the storage pits contained discarded cultural material, indicating a loss in function.

Square C 29 has stratigraphic problems. Maize kernels recovered in small concentrations in almost all levels of Square C 29 suggest rodent caches, while cobs within the same grid square equal only one or two per Level (Table A.3). It is only in Level 5 (132-136 cmbd) that one gains the impression that maize might be in its original depositional context. Cornhusks and stalks were numerous, tassel fragments were present, and a series of 30 white chert flakes were in association. The radiocarbon date on a Level 5 husk (2015 ± 60 B.P) and kernel (1935 ± 65 B.P.) are in substantial agreement (Table 3.3). The date for the husk in Square C 29 coincides with the date on the bean recovered in Square D 27 Pit 1 (2015 ± 65 B.P., or 87 B.C. to A.D. 65). Evidently the protection afforded by the cliff overhang was important at that time. The maize kernel in Level 3 is younger than

			Table 3.2. Description of Large Storage Cists
Excavation Square	Pit Diameter (m)	Pit Depth (cm)	Remarks
C 23	1	17	Extends from 1.22 to 1.39 mbd. Pit may have been 10 cm deeper as another pit was superimposed on it. First grass, then basketry and matting fragments rest on rock floor. Lining is grass.
C 26, C 27, D 26, D 27	0.9 x 1	24	Pit encountered from 1.66 to 1.90 mbd. Mixture of grass, juniper bark, and pine bark lining. Bottom had checkerweave mat fragments. Many mesquite seeds were interspersed among the grass lined walls.
C29	0.7 x 0.7	17	At 1.66 mbd grass on side of cist but not on bottom. Some pine bark around edges. Bottom tilts on west from 1.76 mbd to 1.83 mbd and has a close coiled basket fragment with non-interlocking stitches (01.C29.313) at base.
C 29	1 x 1.4	23	Basal pit begins at 1.75 mbd in moist brown matrix. Lined first with ponderosa pine bark, then with dried grass. A folded checker weave matting fragment extends from 1.75 to1.97 mbd. Bottom at 1.98 mbd, level 10. Within grass lining were two fist-sized balls of shredded grass whose interior had been lined with soft heads of *Chloris crinita* grass. A stick of saltbush penetrated one nest.
C 29	unknown	unknown	Beneath the above example were remnants of another possible cist marked by the presence of juniper bark mixed with ash and charcoal.

Table 3.3. Square C 29 Levels and Dating

Level	Dated Maize BP*	Other Dated Material BP	Other Material in Same Level**
1			
2			
3	1690 +/- 55 k	2770 +/- 70	Bean, cholla, and eastern prickly pear fruit
	In cache of 239	Charcoal	San Pedro, Type 4, Coahuila, and Shumla Bifaces
4	1720 +/- 65 k		Bean
5	2015 +/- 55 h	2690 +/- 80	Pinto bean, 30 flakes of chert, pine bark
		Charcoal	
	1935 +/- 65 k		
6			Bean
7	1665 +/- 65 k	1995 + /- 55	3 beans
	In cache of 238	Bean	
		2890 +/- 70	
		Charcoal	
8			3 beans
9			4 beans
10		3590 +/- 70	22 beans
		Charcoal in cist	
11		2740 +/- 60	Mouse nest in cist
		Charcoal in cist	

* k = kernel, h = husk
** Also see Table 2.6

the dated maize husk in Level 5 (Table 3.3). If the scenario is correct, then the wood charcoal in Level 3 (2770 ± 70 B.P.) was moved upward by the more recent disturbance.

However, below Level 5 younger and older material form a depositional puzzle. For example, a radiocarbon date on charcoal directly beneath the Level 5 corn stalks and husk dated 2690 ± 80 B.P. (ISGS 897, Tagg l996) and a bean below it in Level 7 dated 1955 ± 55 B.P. along with more wood charcoal 2890 ± 70 B.P. Level 7 has the youngest maize, dated from a kernel that was part of a cache of 328 kernels (1665 ± 66 B.P.). Conceivably, the kernel cache might have been transported from Level 3! The downward dribble of seemingly young common beans extends from Level 3 to Level 10 and adds to the confusing nature of deposition and re-deposition. At the bottom of Square C 29, the charcoal sample (01. C29.311 at 1.93 to 1.95 mbd), which rests on a checkerweave matting fragment, dates 2740

± 60 B.P., which is younger than the charcoal from the storage cist above it (01.C29.312 at 1.75 to 1.76 mbd) that dates 3590 ± 70 B.P. or shredded grass lined with even softer grass heads, presumably a mouse nest, resting on the lowermost cist (Table 3.2).

In Square C 29, thanks to radiocarbon dating, we know maize has undergone vertical movement and that some levels have been enriched with corn by the activities of the later occupants, human or otherwise. Dated cultigens disrupted the column as far as Level 7, almost as deep as the nested storage pits that are in Levels 10 and 11. If all the beans in the column are late introductions into Levels 8, 9, and 10, then the disturbance goes as far as the nested storage pits in Levels 10 and 11. Dates on charcoal in the deepest levels appear out of sequence. The percentage of screened levels with maize is apt to be inflated, and can only be regarded as an approximation. The dating of artifacts (R. Jones 1990; Merchant 2002;

Table 3.4. Size and Nature of Seven Pits in Square D 27

Feature Number	Cat. no.*	Diameter (cm)	Depth (cm)	Remarks on construction, fill, radiocarbon dates**, and disturbance
1	.125	36-38	9	Pit 7 overlaps Pit 1. Fill is of loose brown soil with vegetal material, seeds, charcoal. Contained 169 beans and 11 maize kernels. Date on one bean 2015 +/- 65 and another bean 2085 +/- 65 BP. Early (1982) date on maize kernel 1990 +/- 320 BP. Rodent coprolites and mariola achenes present.
2	.126	15-18	3	Pit seems formed in wet soil and ash as faint striations can be seen on wall and floor. Pit 2 was apparently the last pit dug among pits 2, 3 and 4. Fill has much charcoal and some seeds. A sedge achene and half of a *Helianthus* achene may indicate rodent activity.
3	.127	17	10-11	Charcoal dated 3150 +/- 70 BP. Maize cob half dated 2540 +/- 200 BP in 1982. In 1991, remaining half dated 2945 +/- 55 BP. Cultivated *Amaranthus cruentus* in pit. No signs of rodent disturbance recognized.
4	.128	17-19	7	Maize cob dates 2880 +/- 60 BP. Rodent coprolites, mariola achenes, and *Helianthus* achene strips indicate rodent activity.
5	.129	24	19	Pit tapers to 14 cm diameter at base. It extends to Square D 26, which lacks other pits. Bottom penetrates weathered limestone gravel. Loose fill is mixed with much grass, some stone, charcoal and seed. Rodent disturbance indicated by coprolites, sedge achene, poison ivy stone, mariola achenes, and *Helianthus* achene strips.

Table 3.4. Size and Nature of Seven Pits in Square D 27, cont'd

Feature Number	Cat. no.*	Diameter (cm)	Depth (cm)	Remarks on construction, fill, radiocarbon dates**, and disturbance
6	.130	16-20	5	Pit perimeter irregular and rough. Fill composed of hard ashes and charcoal. Flotation revealed an *Allionia* fruit, *Helianthus* achene strips, and a beeweed seed that may indicate rodent disturbance.
7	.131	31	17	Grey-brown hard sediments form walls and floor, which contain impressions of grass. Fill of loose brown organic soil with charcoal, stones, seed and abundant grass. Pit 7 was probably dug later than Pit 1. Rodent disturbance indicated by coprolites, 27 sedge achenes, poison ivy stone, mariola achenes, *Helianthus* achene strips and half.

* Catalog number prefix is 01.D27
** Tagg 1996

Moots 1990) through association with possibly displaced radiocarbon-dated charcoal in Square C 29 deserves review (Table 2.6).

The cluster of seven cylindrical pits encountered in Square D 27 was typical of some 30 small pits in the shelter (see Table 3.4 and Figure 3.3). They served as a repository for food waste, charcoal, ash and fragile chaff, a few maize kernels, and beans (Appendix A.6). The beans have accumulated in Pit 1. One of the C 11 type beans (01.D27.103A) radiocarbon dated at 2015 ± 65 B.P (Tagg 1996), similar to the corn husks in Square C 29. If people were seeking a dry spot in Fresnal Shelter in which to store cultigens at that time, they might act similarly during an even a wetter interval from 2800 to 2600 B.P. (850 to 650 B.C.). The wide bands measured in stalagmites from the Guadalupe Mountains indicate what is apparently the wettest interval for the late Holocene for the region (Polyak and Asmerom 2001). Perhaps people were making no use of Fresnal Shelter; perhaps they did not raise maize. We have not dated whatever plant residue they may have left behind. Charcoal, maize, mesquite, juniper, nor pinyon has been dated. Two dates on wood charcoal at Fresnal Shelter fall at the beginning of the wet interval, 2770 ± 70 B.P. and 2740 ± 60 B.P. (Tagg 1996: 316). The next date, on a bean, follows the wettest interval 2085 ± 60 B.P. (Tagg 1996).

Pit 3 contains the oldest directly dated maize from the shelter and the earliest radiocarbon date on charcoal associated with maize (Table 3.4). In 1982, when half of the maize cob (D27.108) was dated with the early TAMS technology, the dating (1990 ± 320 B.P.) was imperfectly developed compared to in

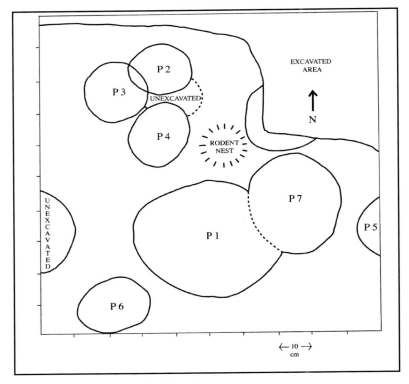

Figure 3.3. Plan view of seven pits in Square D 27 in Fresnal Shelter.

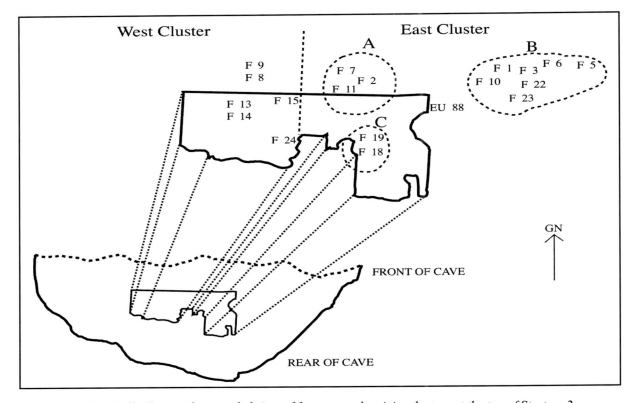

Figure 3.4. High Rolls Cave with expanded view of features and activity clusters at the top of Stratum 2.

1991 when the remaining cob half was dated at 2945 ± 55 B.P. Differences in the methods used in the early years of TAMS dating compared to recent ones apparently have affected results. A maize kernel from Pit 1, also TAMS dated in 1982, may not be trustworthy for similar reasons.

High Rolls Stratigraphy, Features, and Dating

Three major strata are evident. Stratum 1 delineates the final Late Archaic occupation, with En Medio-like projectiles but no associated features, and spanned between 2300 B.P. and 1610 B..P. Stratum 1 existed on the east side of the cave only, and parts of it were disturbed. Beneath it are remnants of a culturally sterile layer followed by Strata 2 and 3.

Strata 2 and 3 contained the principal occupation of the cave. Nearly all the 13 hearths and 10 pits were radiocarbon dated and suggest an early occupation that ranged from about 1500 B.C. to 1000 B.C. Only one feature was large enough for storage (1 m by 1 m and 45 cm deep). Stratum 3 exists on the east side of the cave and relates to the initial occupation. Stratum 2 is separated into two major use areas, one in the eastern half of the cave and one in the western. I have divided the eastern half of the cave into East Clusters A, B, and C for convenience (see Fig. 3.4). In some areas, Stratum 2 has been further divided into three layers. Some layers are extremely compact, as is in Excavation Unit 27, detailed in the preface to flotation samples in Appendix B.1.

As full excavation proceeded, maize cobs were encountered in the separate cultural strata, raising hope that the period of use of maize in each stratum could be established. Accordingly, every effort was made to correlate the results of excavation with radiocarbon-dated maize samples. When dates on maize were returned, excavators realized 10 of 12 maize cobs belonging to Stratum 1 were recovered in Stratum 2. In fact, no intact maize cobs recovered from the lower stratigraphic units could be used to date the earliest introduction of maize. Instead, by necessity, flotation and maize pollen had to be evaluated in relation to the stratigraphic record and the problems inherent within each sample.

The assessment of the time maize was introduced had repercussions for the identification and interpretation of pre- and post-maize diet. Dating and stratigraphy became an important issue, but my text is limited to the relevant excavation units concerning early maize.

Radiocarbon Dating the Earliest Maize by Indirect Association and Direct Dating
A variety of answers can be posited to the question of the age of the oldest maize at High Rolls Cave, for it is easier for some individuals to accept one level of evidence over another. To answer the question concerning the earliest maize dated by association, I present three alternatives based upon (1) a maize cupule from the south half of Excavation Unit 27, (2) pollen from the north half of Excavation Unit 27, and (3) a carbonized maize embryo from Feature 11b to supplement the one direct date on early maize (Stratum 2).

1. South Half of Excavation Unit 27:
Flotation sample FS 795 from the south half of Excavation Unit 27, which contained an uncarbonized maize cupule, comes from 25 cmbs, the same depth as paired radiocarbon sample FS 797 dating 3120 ± 40 B.P. (Table B.3.2). Two wood rat fecal pellets were recovered from the sample as well as a large number of extremely young, immature fruits of three-leaved sumac, items of no known human use.

Two unburned maize cobs intruded into the south half of Excavation Unit 27: one (FS 688) 17 cmbs in historic Stratum 52 dating A.D. 1510 ± 90 B.P., and the second (FS 745) within Stratum 2, Layer 1 dating 1600 ± 70 B.P. (Table

B.3.3) The latter location lies 4 cm above FS 795. Potentially other intrusive material, like the uncarbonized maize cupule, might have reached FS 795.

If we can accept the indirectly dated maize cupule from the south half of Excavation Unit 27 as 3120 ± 40 B.C. from FS 797, the 2-sigma calibration is 1500 to 1360 B.C. and 1360 to 1320 B.C.

2. North Half of Excavation Unit 27:
Pollen in FS 96 comes from the north half of Excavation Unit 27 at 26 cmbs beneath sandal 2 (FS 93), positioned flat on the surface of the ground. The radiocarbon sample (FS 98) is from 29 cmbs, and dates to 3070 ± 70 B.P. (Table B.3.2). Potential disturbance is represented in the north half by a morning glory (*Ipomoea*) seed (FS 105) at 20 cmbs to 30 cmbs, or 11.20 to 11.30 mbd, but this Level lacks maize. Another pollen sample, FS 794, was taken at 28 cmbs, beneath sandal 5 (FS 801), but was apparently not analyzed.

If we can accept the indirectly dated maize pollen from Excavation Unit 27 north half with FS 98 as 3070 ± 70 B.P., the 2-sigma calibration for FS 98 is 1520 to 1210 B.C.

3. Feature 11b:
A carbonized maize embryo and a few cupules in flotation from Feature 11b (FS 782) come from Stratum 2, Layer 3 at 13 cmbs. No intrusive material has been recognized, not even rodent fecal pellets. The radiocarbon sample, FS 779, dates 2940 ± 60 B.P. and has a 2-sigma calibration of 1400 to 1030 B.C. (Table B.3.1; see Figure 3.5).

Direct Radiocarbon Dates on Maize
If the reader finds none of the above three indirect dates satisfactory, the oldest directly dated maize, a shank and husk (FS 1300), dates to 2840 ± 40 B.P. and has a 2-sigma calibration of 1210 to 970 B.C. (Table B.3.3)

I am inclined to accept the dated flotation from Feature 11b to approximate the introduction of maize as the sample seems more reliable than either one from Excavation Unit 27.

From the final occupation, the oldest maize, also a shank and husk (FS 139A), radiocarbon dated to 2060 ± 50 B.P. while the youngest cob (FS 146B) dates 1320 ± 80 B.P., while the remaining cobs span 310 years (Table B.3.3).

PART II. ETHNOBOTANICAL PROCEDURES IN THE TWO ROCK SHELTERS

Fresnal Shelter Ethnobotanical Analysis

Objectives and Sampling Strategy for Plant Remains
The objectives of excavation that applied to the retrieval of plant remains included determination of (1) the specific nature of the resource base, (2) the seasonal pattern of subsistence resources and possible movements of the inhabitants, and (3) the evolutionary history of plant domesticates recovered. By more deeply understanding the economic stage setting of the Late Archaic at Fresnal Shelter, it was hoped to better grasp the general principles in dietary change accompanying the adoption of agriculture. By use of the biological principles borrowed from optimal foraging theory, the author expected to better fathom traditional dietary components that were later de-emphasized or lost as well as the nature of those that were retained as life became more sedentary. Probably some items were more important than others. Optimal preservation was essential if stratigraphic variability was to be explained by variation in human behavior.

As a result, only those grid squares best protected by the rock overhang were considered for ethnobotanical study, and hearth areas were excluded (Fig. 3.1). Screened

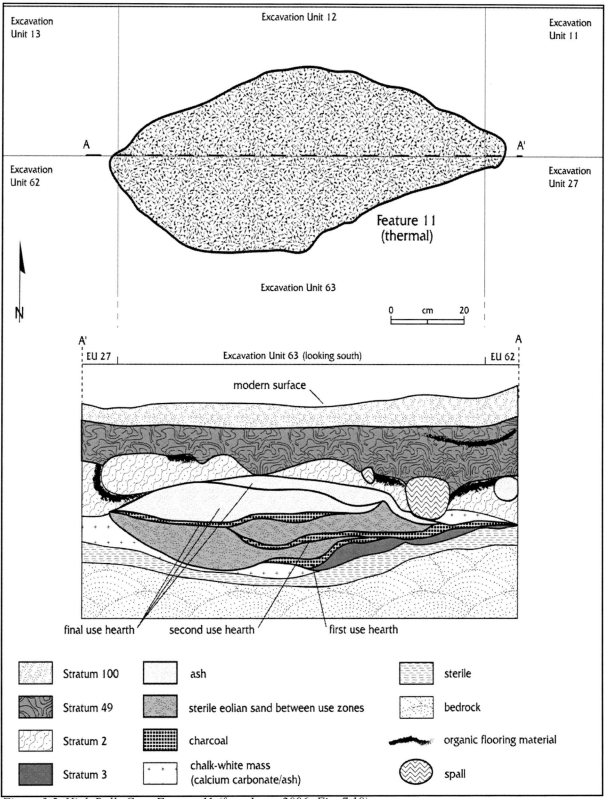

Excavation Unit 13

Excavation Unit 12

Excavation Unit 11

A

A'

Excavation Unit 62

Excavation Unit 27

Feature 11
(thermal)

Excavation Unit 63

N

0   cm   20

A'

A

EU 27

Excavation Unit 63 (looking south)

EU 62

modern surface

final use hearth   second use hearth   first use hearth

	Stratum 100		ash		sterile
	Stratum 49		sterile eolian sand between use zones		bedrock
	Stratum 2		charcoal		organic flooring material
	Stratum 3		chalk-white mass (calcium carbonate/ash)		spall

Figure 3.5. High Rolls Cave Feature 11 (from Lentz 2006: Fig. 7.18)

samples constituted the bulk of plant material analyzed. They were obtained by removal of deposits from eight 1 m squares by arbitrary depths approximating 5 cm and 10 cm in the C and D grid lines for a total of 43 levels. For a comparison of levels see Figure 3.2. Squares were named from grid lines that intersected in the northeastern corner. Outstanding floral (for example, maize and beans), faunal, and other artifactual material were cataloged by position in the square. Screens with a ¼ inch (3.2 mm) mesh suspended from tripods near the shelter opening received the level, which was sorted into typical categories such as seeds, vegetal material, bones, and flakes that were only broadly provenienced by square and level.

All the natural stratigraphic units in the B grid line were originally designated for flotation analysis, but only the 10 samples fully analyzed by 1972 are used in comparisons. Flotation samples were processed with water hauled to the shelter from Fresnal Creek and dried on screens in the shelter before being sacked. Flotation samples from seven pits in Square D 27 were studied, as the content represented the earliest secured plant material from features. Additional taxa encountered during the incomplete analysis of natural strata or ones brought to my attention by excavators were identified and included in the taxonomic catalog in Chapter 4. Of 95 squares excavated by 1971, the botanical remains from approximately 10 squares were examined.

The question of whether or not the plant material excavators sampled was representative of that originally deposited needed to be investigated for both the screened samples and those taken for flotation. In the hopes that the nature of the loss through screens might be similar from one contiguous grid square to the next, flotations from B grid line adjacent and parallel to screened ones (Fig. 3.1) were designated for "screen loss" studies. The large flotation samples obtained by excavators needed to be sub-sampled in a representative manner. For example, enough volume should be analyzed to demonstrate one sample did not differ statistically from another of equal volume from the same source. If the nature of botanical variability in strata could be established as being due to patterns of human deposition, changes in plant resource utilization might be recognized. Since the quantity of a given plant part or the presence of a genus could be altered by the amount of sample examined, the necessity to keep the volume constant seemed apparent. I hoped to analyze the smallest flotation volume possible that was typical of the depositional unit in order to minimize laboratory time.

Plant Identification from 1969 through 1972
During the time plants were identified, the state flora represented an outdated pioneering effort (Wooton and Standley 1915), and the new flora was in an early stage of preparation. To offset the lack of floral documentation, plant collecting began concurrent with the excavation efforts. Identified herbarium voucher specimens were deposited at the University of Arizona, Tucson (Table A.2). Duplicate reproductive material was retained to compare to the plant fragments recovered from Fresnal Shelter and floras of adjacent states were consulted (Correll and Johnston 1970; Kearney and Peebles 1960).

Botanical identification of fragmentary archaeological plant remains deviates from the orderly procedure presented in conventional taxonomic keys (Bohrer and Adams 1977: 41-46). In special cases, I submitted problem plant specimens to specialists such as Charles B. Heiser for *Helianthus* and Lyman Benson for some of the cacti. Jonathan Sauer identified many of the archaeological *Amarathus* to species and Lawrence Kaplan classified the cultivated beans.

Scientific names were made current using Roalson and Allred (1995).

Reference to the context of recovery was maintained through the cataloging system, which used a 01 prefix to designate the last two digits of the Santa Fe Laboratory of Anthropology site number, LA 10101. The prefix was followed by the square designation (for example C 26) and then a serial number pertaining to the square. The full catalog number (for example, 01.C26.12) was related to the field notes and a scale drawing of the level. At my insistence a duplicate field record was maintained and submitted along with the botanical material. Field sampling guidelines for pollen, soil, and radiocarbon samples were followed (HSR 1972, Section III) throughout the excavation period.

Determination of Loss Through Screening
To determine which taxa passed through the ¼ inch mesh screen and which were retained, six flotation samples from natural stratigraphic units were separated into two fractions with the screen. In each sample, 100 ml was analyzed from the retained fraction and 20 ml from the lost fraction (see Table 3.5). The error introduced by the ¼ inch mesh screens can range from changes in numerical counts of a genus and types of parts recovered within a genus, to full loss of a genus. Counts of four-wing saltbush (*Atriplex canescens)* fruits and juniper (*Juniperus)* seeds differ only slightly while those of New Mexican feather grass (*Stipa neomexicana*) florets change radically. For sotol (*Dasylirion*), the papery fruit fragments are retained by the screen, but all the burned seed is lost. The greatest error is apparent in families that typically bear disseminules smaller than the ¼ inch mesh screen. The grasses (Poaceae), members of the sunflower family (Asteraceae), amaranths (Amaranthaceae), chenopods (Chenopodiaceae), and portulaca (Portulacaceae) are strikingly underrepresented by the contents of the ¼ inch mesh screen. All evidence of grama grass (*Bouteloua* sp.), Indian

rice grass (*Oryzopsis hymenoides*), wolftail grass (*Lycurus phleoides*), Paniceae spikelets, dropseed (*Sporobulus*) florets, *Amaranthus* and *Chenopodium* seeds, and the achenes of *Iva* and *Parthenium* are consistently lost. Three of the grasses (Paniceae, dropseed, and New Mexican feather grass [*Stpia neomexicana*]) were eventually judged to be part of a list of plants frequently used in subsistence but were not retained by the screen.

Reducing the Flotation Sample Volume
High volumes of plant material were generated by flotation. For example, Square B 28, while a full meter long, extended only 15 cm toward the rear wall of the shelter. Nevertheless floating strata to a depth of only a half meter resulted in 15 liters of vegetal material. Sampling was necessary to continue analysis. A prerequisite part of the plan was to create a flotation fraction comparable to the fragments retained by a ¼ inch mesh screen. In order to accomplish the latter, the following procedures were employed:

1. The plastic sack of flotation was rotated and mixed to ensure equal distribution of all size classes.
2. Samples were scooped out, placed on ¼ inch screen mounted on a 20 cm x 20 cm frame and agitated.
3. The portion retained by the screen was divided into two lots: (a) the straw and loose fibers easily picked up with the fingers, and (b) the more solid pieces.
4. The more solid pieces were accumulated in a graduated cylinder 5 cm in diameter until 100 ml could be shaken tightly into the container.
5. Those particles lost through the screen were accumulated in a manner similar to step 4 until the 20 ml mark was reached.

After sorting and identification, each different taxon within a given catalog number

Table 3.5. Summary of Plant Material Separated by 1/4-inch Screen in Six Strata

Classification	Smaller than ¼ inch	Larger than ¼ inch
Gymnosperm		
Cupressaceae		
Juniperus seeds	5	62
Pinaceae		
Pinus edulis (nut shell)	0	**
Angiosperms, Monocotyledons		
Agavaceaae		
Dasylirion carpels	0	0.23g
Dasylirion seed	4	0
Yucca seed	0	9
Poaceae (florets or spikelets)		
Andropogoneae	0	3
Bouteloua	90	3
Chloris	1	0
Chloris crinita	7	4
Elymus/Agropyron	2	0
Lycurus phleoides	1	0
Oryzopsis hymenoides	2	0
Paniceae	79	0
Pappophorum complex	1	1
Sporobolus	0.43g	0
Stipa neomexicana	48	17
Zea mays spikelet	2	7
Angiosperm, Dicotyledon		
Aizoaceae		
Trianthema portulacastrum	1	0
Amaranthaceae		
Amaranthus utricles	47	0
Amaranthus seed	6	0
Asteraceae		
Iva achenes	26	0
Parthenium incanum achenes	27	0
Cactaceae		
Echinocereus pectinatus type areole	1	25
Platyopuntia seed	2	24
Chenopodiaceae		
Atriplex canescens fruit core	8	36
Chenopodium seed	38	0
Cheno-am seed	135	0
Cucurbitaceae		
Cucurbita seeds	f**	7

Table 3.5. Summary of Plant Material Separated by 1/4-inch Screen in Six Strata, cont'd

Classification	Smaller than ¼ inch	Larger than ¼ inch
Fagaceae		
Prosopis glandulosa endocarps	1	92
Fouquieriacae		
Fouquieria splendens calyx	0	1
Nyctaginaceae		
Mirabilis multiflora root fragments	0.059g	1.027g
Portulacaceae		
Portulaca seed	1	0
Zygophylllaceae		
Kallstroemia mericarp	1	0
Larrea tridentata carpel	9	8

*from 01.B28E.22 and 01.B28 W.1 of Unit A, 01.B28.22 and 01.B28 E.23 of Unit D, 01.B28 W.36 and 01.B28 W.37 of Unit F, and 01.B28 E.6 and 02.B29 E.7 of Unit D
**f = fragment

was entered on a marginally punched card accompanied by a notation of the quantity of the material and a description of its condition (such as parched, cracked, eroded, or cut). Where feasible, counts were formulated upon the minimum number of parts present. For example, split halves of mesquite endocarps were tallied and divided by two to obtain the total endocarps in a sample. Fragments such as pinyon nutshells, acorns, and roots were weighed in grams on a Mettler P-20 scale. Plant material from different screen levels was classified similarly except for unidentified leaves, twigs, sticks, and quids.

Testing the Adequacy of the Volume of the Flotation Sample
A Chi-square test for independence was used to investigate whether or not the volume of flotation was representative. Two random samples of equal volume from the same bag of flotation were analyzed. Two 20 ml samples of material smaller than a ¼ inch screen came from 01.B29E6 and two 100 ml samples came from Square D 27, Pit 7. The null hypothesis that there was no significant difference in the numbers of items in each taxonomic unit from a pair of samples from the same bag was tested. A 0.05 level of significance with 12 degrees of freedom for the 20 ml samples and 7 degrees of freedom for the 100 ml samples was employed. Lumping of some taxonomic categories was necessary to keep 80 percent of the hypothetical frequencies equal to or greater than five (see Tables 3.6 and 3.7). The null hypothesis was accepted in both cases and the volume of sample analyzed was considered adequate.

Exploring the Homogeneity of Natural Strata
Two methods were used to explore the question of whether or not natural stratigraphic units were homogeneous in content. Samples were taken from the eastern and western halves of two natural stratigraphic units in Square B 28 and compared for significant differences in the quantity of various taxa present (Table 3.8). Then two units (C and D) extending

Table 3.6. Number of Plant Parts in Two 20 ml Samples from 01.B29.E6*

Classification	Sample A	Sample B	Total
Monocotyledons			
Dasylirion seed	3	3	6
Poaceae florets			
Bouteloua	17	14	31
Oryzopsis or *Pappophorum* complex	1	4	5
Paniceae	12	10	22
Sporobolus	340	310	650
Stipa	17	10	27
Other	14	8	22
Dicotyledons			
Amaranthus utricles	5	3	8
Iva achenes	10	12	22
Other achenes	8	10	18
Atriplex or *Kallstroemia* (fruit or nutlet)	2	2	4
Chenopodium seed	33	14	47
Larrea carpels, *Opuntia*, *Portulaca* and *Juniperus* seed	7	4	11
Total	469	404	873

*All fragments are smaller than ¼ inch

Table 3.7. Number of Plant Parts from Two 100 ml Samples from Pit 7, Square D 27*

Classification	Sample A	Sample B	Total
Gymnosperms			
Juniperus seed	3	6	9
Angiosperms, Monocotyledons			
Bouteloua spikelet	7	8	15
Cyperaceae achene, Andropogon Paniceae and *Stipa* florets or spikelets	10	4	14
Angiosperm Dicotyledons			
Atriplex fruits	5	8	13
Cucurbita seed	7	3	10
Echinocactus areoles, Platyopuntia seed	6	10	16
Prosopis endocarps	23	29	52
Larrea carpel, *Quercus* acorn *Rhus* fruit or stone, *Yucca* seed	7	5	12
Total	68	73	141

*All fragments are larger than ¼ inch

Table 3.8. A Comparison of Quantity of Taxa Between Halves of Units A and D in Square B28*

Classification	Unit A East	West	Unit D East	West
Gymnosperm				
Juniperus seed	2	6	3	2
Angiosperm, Monocotyledon				
Cyperaceae seed, Andropogoneae,				
Lycurus, Oryzopsis, Pappophorum,				
or *Zea* spikelets or florets, Poaceae	8	8	0	0
Paniceae florets or spikelets	4	20	10	11
Bouteloua spikelets	16	19	20	33
Stipa florets	7	17	3	12
Angiosperms, Dicotyledons				
Asteraceae achenes	16	6	5	12
Cheno-am seeds	7	4	60	6
Angiosperms, Dicotyledons**				
Atriplex fruit cores	14	4		
Cactaceae areoles, seeds, *Yucca*				
seeds, other Poaceae, *Dasylirion* fruit			10	5
Cactaceae *Echinocactus* areole	3	6		
Opuntia seed				
Cucurbita seeds, *Prosopis*				
endocarps, *Larrea* carpels	7	8		
Cucurbita seeds, *Prosopis*				
endocarps, *Portulaca* seeds			6	8
Dasylirion seeds	4	3		

*Derived from samples in Unit A: 01.B28 E.22, 01.B28 W.1; and Unit D: 01.B28.E23, and 01.B28.W22.
**non-comparable groups

across Squares B 28 and B 29 were compared internally (such as Unit C in B 28 with Unit C in B 29) to see if the number of taxa were significantly different (Table 3.9).

The first test to explore quantitative differences between the eastern and western halves of the same unit utilized two Chi-square tests at the 0.05 level of significance with 10 degrees and 7 degrees of freedom, respectively. The second test to determine if numbers of taxa in the same unit in adjacent grids were significantly different utilized a Chi-square Test at the 0.95 Level of significance with 1 degree of freedom. The results of both types of tests applied to two sets of samples indicate that (1) significant differences exist in the quantity of a taxon in different halves of the same grid square and that (2) significant differences occur in the numbers of taxa in the same unit in different grid squares.

Natural stratigraphic units were not homogeneous in content, at least in the statistical manner in which the question was investigated. The results do not verify perceived stratigraphic continuity in horizontal space in the shelter or predict stratigraphic continuity when none is visible. Variability in quantity of a given taxon used in subsistence can be

Table 3.9. Differences in the Number of Taxa in the Same Strata between Squares B 28 and B 29

Stratum	Total Taxa Square B 28	Total Taxa Square B 29
C	22	33
D	20	37

explained in terms of relative availability of a plant resource at any one time, the size of the group encamped, or the location of the social unit within the shelter. In as much as all three factors might reasonably influence variability in the amount of a taxon discarded, little more definitive can be said about the meaning of quantitative vertical variability. Accordingly, the emphasis on the tables in Appendix A is on presence or absence of an item rather than quantity present.

Similarities in stratigraphic units are best perceived from tabulations of taxa present or absent. Patterns probably exist at numerous scales in the deposit, depending on the volume of sample analyzed. For example, yucca seeds and pinyon (*Pinus edulis*) shells regularly appear in the larger volumes sorted from the screens (Table A.3). However, the same items appear less frequently in the small volume of flotation samples. I regard the recovery of more species as sampled volume increases as one pattern similarly encountered in sampling modern plant communities, which are never fully homogeneous. When a sampling plot is small the number of species is also small, but as the size of the plot increases so does the number of species.

Despite the drawbacks in the analysis of taxa present in variable volumes, an unusual amount of homogeneity in the screened grid square C 29 seems apparent. The following seven taxa are common to nine levels (Table A.3): *Juniperus* seed, pinyon (*Pinus edulis*) shells, sotol (*Dasylirion*) dry fruit wings, yucca seed, mesquite (*Prosopis glandulosa*) endocarps, buffalo gourd (*Cucurbita foetidissima*) seed, and maize (Zea *mays*). The history of use of the grid square surrounding C 29 has doubtless influenced the pattern of continuous deposition. When Square C 29 was first used as a storage cist, the nearest hearth was at least a meter distant (Square C 27). Afterwards, hearths were located in adjacent grid squares. The C 29 grid square doubtless received discards from food preparation since abandonment of the cists. Regardless of how time relationships are eventually refined, it appears that certain plant resources enjoyed a long popularity.

High Rolls Cave Ethnobotanical Analysis

Objectives of Flotation Analysis
High Rolls Cave archaeologists hoped to determine the specific nature of subsistence, including patterns of processing and the seasonality of occupation and movement. Although the assessment of preservation was of interest, flotation sampling was not limited to one part of the cave. Because excavators wished to know if hearths represented specific activity areas, thermal areas were sampled for flotation. An important objective of excavation was the comparison and contrast of subsistence patterns with Fresnal Shelter and to understand

the broader implications for the prehistoric economy of the Tularosa Basin during a time when maize agriculture had been recently introduced. The documentation of a portion of the prehistory of plant domesticates was not a verbalized objective of excavators, though it became an important outcome.

Flotation Sample Distribution and Methods of Preparation

Flotation samples were obtained from both excavation units and features. Excavation units were a meter on a side and varied in depth with natural stratigraphy. Excavators designated flotation samples by a Field Sample (FS) number associated with a botanical form which gave the details of the excavation context, the cm below surface (cmbs) or cm below datum (cmbd), and cross references to additional relevant samples. Archaeologists divided the cave into eastern and western halves. I have additionally designated locations into Clusters A, B, and C in the eastern half of the cave (see Figure 3.5 and Table 3.10).

From a large array of flotation samples, 33 were selected for analysis by Teresa M. Fresquez of the Office of Archeological Studies, New Mexico. Seventeen features were investigated through 21 flotation samples. Ten of the 17 features were thermal in nature. All but two analyzed flotation samples come from Strata 2 and 3. Nine excavation units known to

contain unburned plant material were studied by means of 12 different flotation samples.

All flotation samples but one were processed by the Office of Archaeological Studies and segregated as to size with screens of mesh sizes 4 mm, 2 mm, 1 mm, and 0.5 mm. The contents were placed in labeled envelopes for my inspection. The material retained from each screen was examined from the largest to the smallest mesh with the help of a binocular microscope.

I screened an unprocessed flotation sample (FS 557) to assess potential problems in plant recovery. The sample showed erratic preservation: leathery oak type leaves accompanied a delicate tubular flower and a cheno-am seed coat. A variety of seeds had crystals formed within and upon their surface. It is highly probable that these would become part of the heavy fraction. Since the other processed flotation samples show almost no evidence of crystal formation, the fraction was not initially present or was incorporated into the heavy fraction.

The plants and the parts identified are described in the next chapter. Appendix B.1 describes each flotation sample context and the condition of the identified contents. Appendix B.2 provides taxonomic notes on identification. Appendix B.3 details dating and finally, Appendix B.4 summarizes pollen analytical research.

Table 3.10. Index to Geographic Grouping of Flotation Samples within High Rolls Cave

Location*	Stratum/Layer	Field Sample Number
East Cluster A		
F 2	2/1	80
F 7		273
F 11a**	3	263
F 11b**	2	782
EU 10	2	557
EU 12	1	187
EU 13	2	208
EU 27	2/1	742
EU 27	2/2	795
EU 27	2/3	805
EU 63	2	773
East Cluster B		
F 1	3	60
F 3	3	175
F 5	2/2	293
F 6**	2/1	267
F 22**		1063
F 23**	2/3	1075
EU 4	1	70
EU 4	2	139
EU 5	3	67
EU 33	3	1256
East Cluster C		
F 18**	2	934,935
EU 134	2/2	935
F 19**	2	964
Between A and C		
EU 88	2	853
West Cluster		
F 8**	2/1	307
F 9	2/3	310
F 13**	3	586
F 13**	3	597
F 14	2	568
F 15	3	630
F 24**		1093

*Locations include: F (Feature; EU (Excavation Unit); and F** (Thermal Feature)

Chapter 4

Distribution of Plant Taxa in the Rock Shelters with Notes Pertaining to their Nature and Potential Significance to Humans and Rodents

The mere identification of a native plant species within Fresnal Shelter and High Rolls Cave provides no assurance that it played a role in human subsistence, for it might have been gathered for other purposes or carried by wind or rodents. When I was first faced with recognizing plant species humanly consumed at Fresnal Shelter in the l970s, I was unfamiliar with the behavior and dietary habits of mice and wood rats. Since I could not readily identify rodent foraging, I felt emphasis should be on developing a scoring system for recognizing human subsistence items. Some plants within Fresnal Shelter that people might have consumed were new to me. I needed to develop a scoring system by whose rules I could reaffirm dietary components and by which I might evaluate unfamiliar ones.

THE SUBSISTENCE SCORING SYSTEM AT FRESNAL SHELTER

What follows is nothing more than an orderly plan for recognizing the role of plants in human subsistence. By adding scores based on criteria for (a) marks of processing, (b) precedent for edibility, and (c) the compatibility of ethnographic preparation technique with archaeological processing marks, the results approximate human utilization (Table 4.1). Two taxa introduced in postcontact times (*Sorghum* and *Avena*) were omitted.

The recognition of prehistoric parts or conditions that potentially represent winnowing, parching, cutting, crushing, splitting, or roasting (documented in Tables A.4 and A.5) are regarded as a source of subsistence evidence. Marks on plant material from the 4 m by 15 cm strip at the rear of the shelter (B grid) carry particular significance. Because the deposit lies so close to the rear wall, it minimizes the inclusion of plant parts inadvertently charred by virtue of being in super-heated soil near the perimeter of a hearth.

An ethnographic precedent of edibility, or at least a chemical composition known to be non-toxic, enhances the probable interpretation of the use of a genus for food. Items with no history of edibility may be raw material in finished artifacts, such as cordage or basketry, or possess woody parts used as fuel. Some may be tracked in from disturbed habitats or be components of rodent diet. A few may have lost their reputation as food.

The final additive criterion is the location of an ethnographic method of food preparation congruent with the archaeological marks of processing (or absence of marks). Gaps in the ethnographic record created imperfections in the scoring system. Such gaps may be real in the sense that people no longer use what was once regarded as a food item or they may prepare it in a different way. Other gaps may be accidental in nature as, for example, when an ethnographer incompletely records

	Score
Table 4.1 Scoring System Used To Recognize Prehistoric Subsistence Items in Fresnal Shelter	

Part I. Add scores from groups A, B and C
- A. Marks of preparation
  - Item bears no sign of processing. — 0
  - Part potentially represents a parching accident, winnowed chaff, or another single sign of preparation. — 1
  - Parts bears multiple signs of preparation: splitting, cutting, crushing, parching, roasting, etc. — 2
- B. Precedent for edibility
  - No reference to edibility of taxon part known. It may be poisonous — 0
  - The genus is only used as food outside the Southwest — 1
  - Only one group in the Southwest uses the genus for food — 2
  - More than one tribe in the Southwest eats the item or it is recovered in numerous sites in the Southwest — 3
- C. Compatibility of ethnographic preparation technique with archaeological marks of preparation
  - The two records fail to agree — -1
  - Some ethnographic records agree or no information is available — 1

Part II. Choose the appropriate number from below to multiply the score from Part I in order to further weight the probability of subsistence use.
- A. If a single example was recovered multiply by — 0
- B. If taxon part had a frequency of less than 80 percent, multiply by — 1
- C. If taxon part had a frequency of 80 percent or greater multiply by — 2

Part III. Score interpretation
- A. If the score is five or greater it is a subsistence item
- B. If the score is three or four it is a borderline subsistence item that requires more careful consideration.
- C. If the score is less than three it is unlikely to have been used in subsistence.

his observations. To minimize such error I have consulted accounts of food preparation by a large number of Southwestern ethnographers and ethnobotanists. I have subsequently selected for reporting in this chapter only the most thorough accounts congruent with the archaeological marks of preparation. In order to further keep the text as concise as possible, either the breadth of the ethnographic use or archaeological distributions are documented from published summaries.

After the above three criteria were considered, I recognized that because foods would be of the most common occurrence, they would register in high frequency. I defined high-frequency as 80 percent or better based on the sampling of 10 natural stratigraphic units along the B grid line. If this admittedly elevated standard is met, the probability of being a common food is increased by a factor of two, an arbitrary figure. This is not to say that low-frequency items are not subsistence-related. To the contrary, some low frequency genera may derive from distant or restricted habitats, or may mature in a short interval, which makes detection and gathering a crop difficult. However, the extensive nature of the sampling precluded consideration that single items played a significant role in subsistence.

Scores ranged from 3 to 12. A plant score of 5 or better ranked as a subsistence item. A score of 3 or 4 is borderline. Low-ranking items need more careful consideration. This scoring plan was tailored for the plant remains of Fresnal Shelter and was not intended as any universal solution. For example, the recognition of potential foods when in 80 percent of the 10 natural strata of equal volume relates to the high number of species recovered in flotation samples. This point is discussed in Chapter 5.

For readers unfamiliar with typical steps in the preparation of seeds, two Southwestern ethnographic sources are particularly helpful. Powell (in Fowler and Fowler 1971) describes how similarly the Southern Paiute prepared a variety of weed and grass seed. They were beaten into a basket with the aid of a fan shaped object, freed of chaff through winnowing, and roasted in a tray basket by dexterously rotating the basket to keep the hot coals and seed in motion. The roasting was said to cause many seeds to swell and burst like miniature pieces of popcorn. The seeds were then ground and the resultant meal might be eaten without further preparation. At other times the meal was made into a boiled mush by adding heated stones to the basketry container (Fowler and Fowler 1971: 39-42). Castetter and Underhill (1935: 24-25) describe how the Tohono O'odham (Papago) prepared all seed for storage through winnowing, parching, and sun drying. Parching was either done in a flat basket, as described by Powell, or by keeping the seeds in motion with the help of a stick on a piece of broken pottery laid directly over the coals. Afterwards the seeds were further dehydrated prior to storage. Seeds were never stored without being so treated for fear of mildew.

INTERPRETING PLANT REMAINS AT HIGH ROLLS CAVE FROM A LATER TIME PERSPECTIVE

When I was confronted with the analysis of flotation in 2001 at High Rolls Cave, the problem of identifying human subsistence items in Fresnal Shelter had already been largely resolved. In the process I had gathered considerable ethnographic information that might serve equally well in clarifying human plant use at High Rolls Cave. My interest in human subsistence became a subset of a larger question, "Why is the plant part present in the cave at all?" Fortunately, Stephen C. Lentz, who directed excavation, was able to secure the well-preserved contents of what I came to regard as *the mouse pantry*, FS 67. Some twenty-odd years after Fresnal Shelter, I wanted to know what signs of rodent activity were present, such as immature plant parts not characteristically used by humans, shredded plant material, or narrow strips of achenes or acorns. I was curious about where the plant once grew. Was it close enough to be introduced by the wind? Did it grow too distant to be introduced by animal vectors? Does the plant thrive with disturbance, human or otherwise? Answers to these same questions furnished a retrospective evaluation of Fresnal Shelter plant remains and provided an additional reason to group identifications in a single chapter.

Accordingly, I have organized the plant identifications from both rock shelters alphabetically by genus within a plant family so that each rock shelter identification may be dealt with accompanied by the same block of background information on distribution and ethnographic use. Plant families are also in alphabetical order by the scientific name within a conventional taxonomic framework. Cone-bearing evergreens or Gymnosperms precede the flowering plants or Angiosperms. Flowering plants are divided into monocotyledons, to which families bearing parallel veined leaves and flower parts of three (or multiples) are traditionally allocated, and dicotyledons, or plants bearing net-veined leaves and flower parts in five (or multiples) follow. The broad taxonomic outlines used in identification are repeated in Tables A.3, A.5, and A.6 as well as in Appendixes B.1 and B.2. The method of organization allows conifers to be considered as a unit, the grasses (Poaceae) to be grouped under monocotyledons, and the cacti (Cactaceae) under dicotyledons. Plant taxonomy conforms to Roalson and Allred (1995) unless otherwise indicated. Since problems in identification, recovery, and usage are often intertwined at the family level, the presentation allows for coherent discussion of these problems. The abbreviation "FS" refers to field sample number at High Rolls Cave.

CONE BEARING EVERGREENS OR GYMNOSPERMS

Cupressaceae (Cypress Family)

Juniper (Juniperus)
Only two species of juniper have been observed close to Fresnal Shelter and High Rolls Cave: one-seeded juniper (*J. monosperma*) and alligator bark juniper (*J. pachyphloea*). One-seeded juniper is found on north exposed slopes of the canyon and alligator bark juniper establishes at 1,982 m (Hutchins 1974: 32) and grows near the rolling ridge tops above the canyon proper around 2,059 m elevation. A third juniper, Rocky Mountain juniper (*J. scopulorum*) has been reported in rocky canyons above 2,135 m (Hutchins 1974: 32).

At Fresnal Shelter, the fully rounded morphology of some seeds indicates the presence of *J. monosperma*. The flat or angular faces of other seeds produced by crowding several seeds in the same fleshy cone or "berry" could represent either *J. pachyphloea* or *J. scopulorum*. The former species seems more probable because of its modern proximity to the shelter and its reputation for palatability. Several authors remark upon the sweet, mild taste of the alligator bark juniper (Castetter and Opler 1936: 45; Palmer 1878: 593; Vestal 1952: 12) relative to the berries of other junipers.

At Fresnal Shelter juniper seed has been recovered in all 10 natural stratigraphic units in the B coordinate (Table A.5). Of 94 seeds, 10 are carbonized and two appear rodent-gnawed. The seeds are also present in each of the seven pits in Square D 27, with some of the seeds in each pit being carbonized (Table A.6). Seeds and a lesser number of berries were regularly recovered in the material screened by artificial levels (Appendix A.3). Among them was one seed with a burned fruit coat attached (01. D28.152). The flotation from the B coordinates contains one partly burned fruit that has been smashed, exposing its fibrous interior.

At High Rolls Cave, two species of juniper seed were recovered in the excavation units in an uncarbonized condition: one-seeded juniper (FS 208 and FS 67, from East Clusters A and B, Strata 2 and 3, respectively) and alligator bark juniper (FS 208). Juniper seed nipped open at one end and fragmented seeds apparently resulted from mouse activity in FS 67 and FS 557. Since juniper grows on the north-facing slopes nearby, it is difficult to tell how much rodent introduction there is in other samples. FS 208 has few indications of rodent activity, yet it has juniper seed. Carbonized seed is in Feature 7 and thermal Features 9 and 11. High Rolls Cave lacks examples of burned or mashed fruits that could relate to human activity. Juniper scale leaves are found in over half the samples from both features and excavation units.

Almost every tribe in the Southwest that had access to juniper berries collected and ate them at one time or another (Lentz 1984). At one time, the pueblos of Acoma and Laguna ate the ripe berries in considerable quantities in the fall of the year or when food was scarce (Swank 1932: 50). The Zuni believed juniper berries were an ancient food that was once harvested in large quantities, boiled, roasted or dried, and ground to form meal that was made into several types of cakes (Cushing 1920: 243). The description of northeastern Yavapai processing of alligator bark juniper berries is more complete.

> ...berries pounded and ground on metate with backward-forward motion of muller. Hard seeds winnowed out by rotating motion, discarded. Meal added to water and drunk. Some meal kept in tight burden basket, later made into cake by dampening and gradually building up. Cake about 1 ft. thick, heavy; kept for several months. Temporarily cached in burden basket under rock. (E. Gifford 1936: 255)

Several methods were used to minimize the resinous flavor of the berries or cones. Cooking drives off many of the unpleasant tasting compounds. The Apache would eat the berries fresh or roast them upon heated stones and then consume them whole or ground. Sometimes the fruit was boiled in water to the consistency of mush or jelly (Castetter and Opler 1936: 45; Palmer 1878: 594; Vestal 1952: 12). The Walapai and Southern Paiute achieved a similar result by sampling the trees to find ones that bore milder flavored berries (I. Kelly 1964; Kroeber 1935: 54). The Southern Paiute crushed the berries on a metate, removed the seeds, and ate the meal.

The use and storage of juniper berries for winter is frequently mentioned. When collecting one-seeded juniper, the Western Apache sun-dried the cones before storing them for winter (Gallagher 1977: 28). The Kaibab band of the Southern Paiute regarded the juniper berries as winter products available when other foods failed (Kelly 1964: 36). The Chiricahua and Mescalero Apache ate the berries of the alligator bark juniper in July when they ripened, but one informant indicated winter

collection as well (Castetter and Opler 1936: 45). Some Ramah Navajo collected cones of alligator bark juniper for winter storage (Vestal 1952: 12). Informants indicated fruit production was erratic, much like pinyon crops (Vestal 1952: 12).

In a preceramic agricultural settlement in the Cienega Valley of southern Arizona, the seeds of juniper berries were thought to come from several kilometers away (Huckell 1995: 86). In southwestern New Mexico at Bat Cave, alligator bark juniper seeds were recovered in two of four preceramic levels as well as the two pottery levels (Smith 1950: 178). At Cordova Cave, seeds and occasionally fruits of one-seeded juniper were found in all levels from before the advent of pottery (300 B.C. to A.D.1) through A.D.1100. Lesser numbers of seeds of alligator bark juniper and Utah juniper were found in all levels as well (Kaplan 1963: 352). At Gatecliff Shelter, Monitor Valley, Nevada, some of the earliest evidence of human plant use in the shelter is recorded from Horizon 9 (1450 to1350 B.C.), which had numerous grinding stones. Hearth B contained juniper and *Chenopodium* seeds (Thomas 1983b: 155, 473-474). Juniper seeds were commonly recovered in trash and burned store rooms as well as within burials at Salmon Ruin Pueblo, in northwestern New Mexico (Lentz 1984).

Both the archaeological and ethnographic evidence suggests the berries were used in subsistence at Fresnal Shelter and at least in part at High Rolls Cave. This evidence also indicates storability and suggests that when other foods were available, juniper berries were not the top choice to eat in bulk.

At Fresnal Shelter juniper bark was seldom encountered. Some stringy bark shreds came from 01.D28.45 Level 3 along with a piece of bark with a fire-darkened exterior that had been cut cleanly at one end. A mud-encrusted bark segment came from the lower cist (Level 10) in Square C 29. One end looks pounded and the other end is frayed evenly by fire or use. Beneath the same lower cist excavators mapped the existence of still another cist that was poorly preserved. They note that cedar bark, charcoal, and ashes interrupt the sterile yellow sediment. This observation is of some interest, because later cists utilized ponderosa pine bark as a lining. This is the only place in the shelter where a distinct shift in cist lining material has been noted. One large cist was lined with a mixture of ponderosa pine bark, juniper, and grass (Table 3.2).

A pit bottom in Orme Ranch Cave in northern Arizona was lined with Utah juniper bark strips backed with Indian rice grass. All the strips of juniper bark were burned on the outside (bottom) before being placed in the storage bin, which measured 58 cm long by 48 cm wide and 28 cm deep. Within the storage bin were 12 acorns and a handful of fragments of rabbit fur blanket (Breternitz 1960: 26). Possibly much of the cave deposit is Yavapai, but there is little historic material for comparison. Breternitz also calls attention to Cist 6 in Sunflower Cave, for it is Basketmaker in age and is lined with cedar bark and grass. In Nevada at Etna Cave, juniper bark- and grass-lined storage pits range in age from Basketmaker II to Pueblo II.

Pinaceae (Pine Family)

Fir (Abies)

Two species of fir grow in the Sacramento Mountains (Hutchins 1974: 29): the white fir (*A. concolor*) and the corkbark fir (*A. lasiocarpa*). The white fir grows as low as 2,135 m and might be expected at an even lower elevation on a north-facing slope. Hutchins (1974: 29) gives the lower elevation limits of cork bark as 2,592 m.

At High Rolls Cave the sheaths that once covered terminal buds on the lateral branches of a fir tree are present in flotation samples from East Cluster A (FS 742 and FS 773) as well as between East Clusters A and C (FS 853). They were first described as pupal (?) cases in Appendix B.1. The bud sheaths may represent discards from a mouse that consumed the buds; see also the text under *Pinus*. In 1998, Mollie Toll identified charcoal from Test Pit 2, Level 1 as white fir. The tree might have grown quite close to the cave.

Pine (Pinus spp).

At High Rolls Cave a variety of pine parts probably resulted from rodent activity. Ten male (pollen-bearing) cone scales, young pine twigs with needle fascicles removed, and pinyon twigs with young needle fascicles less than 2 cm long were recovered in FS 67. Evidently mice harvested young emerging needles and the small male cones of pine heavy with pollen in spring. An entire male cone was recovered in FS 557. East Cluster A (FS 795) had two shredded pine cone scales and one identifiable as a pinyon cone scale. A cone scale tip came from the layer above it (FS 742). Pinyon pine needles or needle pairs derive from East Cluster A Stratum 2 (FS 208 and FS 557), East Cluster B Strata 1, 2, and 3 (FS 70, FS 139, FS 67), and between East Clusters A and C in Stratum 2 (FS 853).

Pinyon pine (Pinus edulis type)

Two species of pinyon are found in the Sacramento Mountains (Hutchins 1974: 30): the Mexican pinyon (*P. cembroides*) and the Colorado pinyon (*P. edulis*). The pinyon growing on the more shaded north-exposed canyon slopes nearest High Rolls Cave is *P. edulis*. It joins with alligator bark juniper near rolling ridge tops above the canyon proper around 2,059 m. It does not grow on the same side of the canyon as Fresnal Shelter.

Fresnal Shelter had pinyon-type broken seed coats recovered from every screened level with the exception of a few uppermost levels in two grid squares (Table A.3). One whole seed is carbonized (01.D28.152). Frequently both cone scales and seed coat fragments are recovered in the same screened level. In the 10 natural stratigraphic units along the B coordinate, 26 cone scales but no seed coats were recovered in 6 of the 10 stratigraphic units. In fifteen cases only the distal end of the scale was present (Table A.5). In Square D 27 cone scales were recovered in all seven pits, although only one is carbonized; nutshell fragments were in five; and pinyon needle fascicles were in one (Table A.6).

At High Rolls Cave the needles of *P. edulis* are most commonly recovered in excavation units. Only the sole of a child's fishtail style sandal (FS 1177 in Stratum 2) and *the mouse pantry* (FS 67, Stratum 3) had needles of the Mexican pinyon.

Pinyon type nutshell fragments derive from excavation units in East Cluster A Stratum 2 (FS 208, FS 557, FS 795, and FS 805), East Cluster B Strata 1, 2 and 3 (FS 70, FS 5, FS 6, FS 139, and FS 67) and between East Clusters A and C Stratum 2 (FS 853), the same locations as the pinyon needles. Only the nutshell fragments in FS 139 are burned.

Pinyon-type carbonized cone scales are preserved in thermal Features 1, 3, and 11. Carbonized nutshell fragments come from Features 3 and 9. Features 11b and 22 have uncarbonized nutshell. The recovery of uncarbonized seed coat fragments may reflect the harvest of pinyon seeds when they are naturally released from the cone and collected by rodents or humans.

The widespread utilization of pinyon nuts in the Southwest has been summarized by Gallagher (1977: 39). Simms (1987: 124) has reviewed Shoshonean pinyon procurement and processing. Gathering includes several different methods that might introduce incidental needles and cone scales to the shelter. A technique of particular interest, and a common

one, entailed the collection of immature cones that were then roasted to aid in the release of the seed. Provided processing took place in the shelter, such a treatment would result in recovering discarded burned cone scale fragments and partially roasted seeds. Carbonized cone scales symbolize an early harvest, followed presumably by others. After frost the cones release their seeds. Harvests might include picking nuts directly from the ground, shaking them from the tree onto the ground directly, or upon matting. Looting a wood rat nest, as did the Navajo, was said to circumvent a full day of labor (Vestal 1952: 13). In addition, some Paiute would store cones that had not yet opened in shallow, grass-lined pits and cover them with more grass, brush, and stones. When the stores were opened in late spring, the cones would have released the seeds (Wheat 1967: 14). In the Owens Valley of California, the Paiute chose sunny hillsides to store cones in rock-lined bins that were covered with pine boughs and finally rocks, while nuts free from cones were kept in pits lined and covered with grass (Steward 1933: 242).

The distance separating Fresnal Shelter from the stands of pinyon on the opposite canyon slope suggest people brought pinyon parts to the shelter. Since High Rolls Cave is located on the side of the canyon where pinyons grow, they may have been brought to the cave by rodents as well as humans. The cone scale fragments in Features 1, 3, and 11 may reflect the harvest of unopened cones that were stirred into a fire until the seeds or nuts were released. Carbonized nutshell in Features 3 and 9 may also be the result of this practice, or the fire was used as a wastebasket for the discarded seed coat. The vectors of uncarbonized seed or fragments are equivocal.

While examining the plant material from Tularosa Cave (2,062 m elevation) in southwestern New Mexico, Hugh Cutler commented that most of the screenings had broken pieces of corncob, grass, food fragments, and pinyon nutshells (Cutler 1952: 478). Plant remains associated with early occupation surface hearths at Bat Cave dating around 2570 ± 80 B.P. included pinyon shells (Wills 1988: 105, 109).

Ponderosa pine (Pinus ponderosa)

Ponderosa pine trees grow in various habitats between 2,135 m and 2,897 m elevation (Hutchins 1974: 31). Ponderosa pine, with its characteristics of fast growth, drought tolerance, and effective seed dispersal, acts as an early successional or invader species (Lambert 1980: 20). Such attributes may have helped ponderosa pine become one of the most widely distributed pines in North America.

At Fresnal Shelter, the distribution of ponderosa pine bark in the C and D grids (Table 4.2) appears clustered. Concentrations of bark extend laterally and vertically in adjacent artificial levels suggesting a former role in lining storage pits. Some bark remains associated with grass-lined pits (Table 4.2). When new pits were dug, older ones were disrupted and the bark dispersed. The recovery of three pieces of bark with a burned exterior in Square C 28, Level 4 and another piece from a level below may represent accidental burning rather than a form of utilization. Ponderosa pine bark evidently was the most frequently used bark for lining storage pits, but sometimes ocotillo bark (*Fouquieria splendens*) or juniper bark was also used.

Among the squares under investigation, the lower cist in C 29 represents one of the best-preserved pit linings. The effectiveness in lining the pit is demonstrated by its ability to

Table 4.2. Distribution of Ponderosa Pine and Ocotillo Bark in Grid Squares by Weight (g)

Letter	Level	Grid Number			
		28	29	30	31
C	1			ob	1.58
C	2			0.33 + ob	
C	3			22.22 + ob*	
C	4	18.07		0.75	
C	5		4.07	0.14	
C	6	34.60	7.13		
C	7			0.32	
C	8				
C	9		12.40 + ob		
C	10		117.51*		
D	1			17.10	1.02
D	2	0.44	168.64*	27.38	
D	3	65.70	12.51		
D	4	26.40			
D	5	6.63			
D	6				
D	7				

ob = ocotillo bark; also in C 29 level 9, 21.2 g; C 30 level 2, 0.99 g; C 30 level 3, 0.98 g.
* Associated with grass matting in pits

preserve the interior contents over a thousand years, despite resting in loose, moist brown soil at the time of recovery. Ponderosa pine bark, both within and below the grass-liner, evidently blocked the rise of moisture (Table 3.2).

At High Rolls Cave ponderosa pine bark scales were recovered in FS 557 (East Cluster A) and bark with signs of burning from between East Clusters A and C in Stratum 2 (FS 853).

Ponderosa pine bark can represent a by-product of the food quest. The Mescalero Apache utilized the inner bark of ponderosa pine as a source of food, either baking or boiling it. Large squares of bark were cut from the tree with a long pointed stick and the inner bark or cambium scraped off (Castetter and Opler 1936: 43 as *P. scopulorum*). The Southern Paiute cut a ring into the pine bark a little higher than the collector's head and another near the ground. The intervening bark was stripped off to obtain the mucilaginous cambial tissue in spring. Sometimes slabs were carried back to camp (Fowler and Fowler 1971: 47). While it would be hard to deny the use of bark cambium for food, the most tangible evidence for the use of bark is pit lining. For lack of contrary evidence, pit lining seems to have been its prime function at Fresnal Shelter.

The Kaiparowits Paiute liked to store seeds in bark-lined pits covered with stones in caves (I. Kelly 1964: 152). At Pine Flat Cave in southeastern Arizona, one intact ponderosa pine storage bin made by the Apache was noted. It was made by scooping out fill to insert large slabs of unmodified ponderosa pine bark. Pieces were laid flat to form a bottom and were built up to form sides about 15 cm high for a pit approximately 40 cm square (J. Gifford 1980: 183).

White pine or limber pine (Pinus strobiformis and P. flexilis)
The trees grow between 2,135 m and 2,745 m

along ridges and streams (Hutchins 1974: 30). The author collected a specimen of *P. strobiformis* at 2,288 m along the road that parallels Fresnal Canyon. On the east side of the Sacramento Mountains below Cloudcroft at 2,364 m, *P. strobiformis* is co-dominant with ponderosa pine (Lamb 1980). The balance between ponderosa pine and white pine appears dynamic enough to suggest that stands of white pine of sufficient density to collect cones might have existed anywhere around 2,348 m and that the distribution of those stands would be apt to vary between centuries.

At Fresnal Shelter, a broken seed coat (01.C30.28g) and a complete seed (01.D30.24) were recovered from Level 2 in adjacent grid squares. The relatively large seed-bearing flange seems to be characteristic of the two closely related species (Field No.1374 and USDA 1974: 30).

The Mescalero Apache whose reservation boundary begins 9.6 km to the northeast of Fresnal Shelter, gathered the seeds of *P. flexilis* while in the cone prior to their natural release (Castetter and Opler 1936: 43). Nuts might be roasted and hulled or ground shell and all and eaten.

How much the seeds were utilized in Fresnal Shelter is unknown. The large seeds could be easily picked from the shelter floor when dropped. Small seed fragments would be mistaken for pinyon. The seeds were apparently released from their cone elsewhere as cone scale fragments are missing.

MONOCOTYLEDONOUS FLOWERING PLANTS

Agavaceae (Agave Family)

Century plant (Agave)
Agave parryi grows on the south-exposed slope near Fresnal Shelter. *Agave neomexicana* was

identified from a mid-Holocene wood rat midden in Marble Canyon, 8 km to the south (Van Devender and others 1984, Table 2).

Although remains of agave were not recovered in any of the flotation samples from the 10 natural stratigraphic units in Fresnal Shelter or from the pits in Square D 27, the leaves appeared in 7 of the 43 arbitrary levels examined by screening (Table A.3). Three examples of a leaf encasing another leaf from the growing tip were recovered (Square C 29, Levels 6, 7 and 8). Four leaves were severed at both the proximal and distal ends (Square C 30, Levels 4 and 6, Square C 29 Levels 6 and 10). One lot in which the apical leaves were recovered (01.C29.131 Level 6) also had five leaves cleanly severed from a caudex, one leaf removed by ripping, and still another leaf partly cut from the caudex and then torn the remainder of the way. It is possible the juice or sap was valued for an unknown purpose. Despite the presence of an agave leaf in the C 29 Level 10 storage pit, it is of uncertain age because of disturbance. Occasional fibrous quids in 30 of 43 levels (Table A.3.) remain unidentified except for five of sotol. The concentration of 120 quids in 01.C29.13 (disturbed Level 1) is unique.

Castetter and others (1938) have reviewed the ethnographic utilization of agave by many tribes in the American Southwest. After the plants were pried from the ground with a long stick whose chisel end had been fire-hardened, the larger leaves were trimmed from the crown by a variety of tools made from flaked obsidian, quartz, or flint to a mescal hatchet made of a semi-circular blade of granite or diorite (Castetter and others 1938: 52). The Pee-Posh (Maricopa) consumed the crown after roasting with no prior mashing, but the short leaves of the baked heads were stripped off to be chopped and pounded in a mortar (Castetter and others 1938: 50).

The archaeological evidence of agave in roasting pits helped establish their former cultivation in southern Arizona (Fish and others 1980). Small samples of agave tissue from two preceramic agricultural sites in Matty Canyon represent the first and earliest documented usage of agave in southeastern Arizona (Huckell 1995: 84).

In the Guadalupe Mountains of New Mexico, southeast of the Sacramento Mountains, archaeological survey of ring middens revealed that pottery and arrow points diagnostic of the ceramic period were more likely to be associated with ring middens than were Archaic dart points. Pottery occurred almost exclusively on ring middens (Roney 1985). Below El Paso, Texas in the Eagle Mountains (near Van Horn), organic scraps in the ring middens were identified as agave (Bohrer 1994) that were exploited between 800 B.C. and ca. A.D. 1480 based on dated wood charcoal at the lowest levels (Hines and others 1994). Eighteen of the 23 assays are concentrated in the last 500 years of this span—A.D. 1000 to 1480—thus affirming the time-expansive pattern of use observed in the Guadalupe Mountains.

Sotol (Dasylirion wheeleri)

Sotol grows on the south-facing side of Fresnal Canyon where the shelter is located, which is near its upper elevation limit of 1,982 m (Hutchins 1974: 111). Plants can be found as low as 1,372 m. Flowering is from May to August.

At Fresnal Shelter, all seven pits, 9 of 10 natural stratigraphic units, and 33 of 43 screened levels contained carpel fragments. Three of the natural strata and each of the seven pits contained burned seeds (Tables A.5 and A.6). The carpels are normally recovered fragmented and devoid of seed. In both the natural stratigraphic units and the screened levels a few carpels sometimes have a deep brown or parched appearance, but none were ever carbonized. A concentration of carpel husks was found in Square C 29, Level 4 (01. C29.98).

Toothed leaf margins and leaf scraps were not as ubiquitous as the carpels in Fresnal Shelter. Spines from the margins of leaves were found in flotation and segments of sotol leaves were recovered in 13 of 43 screened levels (Table A.3). Some represent very young leaves, for the teeth are only 2 mm to 3 mm apart and the segments only 11 mm wide (Square D 28 level 5). Eight fibrous quids from 5 of 43 screened levels retained sufficient amounts of epidermal tissue to identify them as either sotol or bear-grass (*Nolina*). Since we have ethnographic accounts for roasting crowns or "hearts" of sotol (Basehart 1973: 164; Bell and Castetter 1941) and not for bear-grass (Bell and Castetter 1941: 60), it seems likely the quids represent the residue of sotol extraction. Rock shelters in the Big Bend region of western Texas have ample evidence of roasted sotol hearts (Coffin 1932: 15; Holden 1937: 69; Pearce and Jackson 1933: 130).

At High Rolls Cave, a record of sotol comes from FS 557 in East Cluster A where a single fruit and an opened carpel were recovered. A good source of sotol would be the sunny south-facing slopes across Fresnal Canyon, but it might have come from Dry Canyon as well. The plant material could have been brought to the cave as part of a stalk used for a fire drill or for some other purpose. No carbonized seed provides a suggestion of food use. It apparently is not a subsistence item.

Although the consumption of unopened sotol buds has been documented for southwestern Texas (Bryant 1974: 413), the utilization of sotol seeds is familiar only to the Tonto Apache (E. Gifford 1940: 30). The nearest analogy comes from the use of the small, round stony seeds of bear-grass (*Nolina microcarpa*) by the Isleta to make flour (V. Jones 1931: 35). The seeds are quite similar, although they belong to another genus in the same family.

The marks of utilization on the archaeological material tell the most about its use. The seeds were threshed from their enclosing papery carpels, winnowed, and parched. The presence of only a few parched carpels might be explained by the harvest of slightly immature carpels that were heated to facilitate crumbling the carpel to remove the seed.

A careful study of all the finished basketry at Fresnal Shelter may reveal a relationship to the toothed leaf margins and other scraps of sotol. The spiny leaf margins evidently do not relate to the sotol matting, for all 17 matting fragments recovered are woven from untrimmed leaves (Allan 1973: 404). However, the young leaves may have had their margins removed and used in coiled basketry. Sotol has been used as a sewing element in close-coiled basketry in the Hueco Mountains of Texas (Allan 1973: 403). The failure to recover a concentration of quids (over 50) from anywhere but Square C 29, Level 1 makes one wonder if perhaps the sotol crowns were eaten only rarely, if at all, otherwise more quids would be expected. Perhaps young leaf bases were chewed incidentally while leaves were prepared for basketry material.

Bear grass (Nolina)
Bear grass (Nolina. microcarpa) grew across the canyon from Fresnal Shelter. It can be found over a wide range of elevation from 1,372 m to 2,440 m (Hutchins 1974: 113).

At Fresnal Shelter, a leaf base (01. C29.308) and several leaf segments (01. D28.39) document the presence of the genus in the shelter. The leaves probably entered the shelter for a purpose other than subsistence, for one would expect to find the reproductive parts instead of leaves if the plant was used as food (Bell and Castetter 1941: 60; V. Jones 1931: 35). However, please see the preceding discussion of quids.

Yucca (Yucca)

Yuccas grow over a broad range in elevation but bloom early enough in the season to complete flowering by July (Hutchins 1974: 114). According to Hutchins (1974), only one species of yucca in the Sacramento Mountains has leaves broader than 1.5 cm, *Y. baccata*. Other authors would contend that *Y. Torreyi*, another fleshy-fruited species with broad leaves, also grows in the Sacramento Mountains (Benson and Darrow 1954: 69). Plants conforming to the description for *Y. Torreyi* have been observed by the author near Fresnal Shelter and a specimen of *Y. carnerosana* has been collected. However, all species are fleshy-fruited and produce thick (1 mm to 2 mm) black seeds (Correll and Johnston 1970). I refer to them as *Yucca baccata* type.

At Fresnal Shelter, 11 seeds were recovered in 4 of 10 natural stratigraphic units along the B coordinate, but no seeds were carbonized. *Yucca baccata* type seeds were also recovered in four of the seven pits in Square D 27. Of the 29 seeds, only one was carbonized. *Yucca baccata* type seeds were recovered from 36 of 43 screened levels (Table A.3). A small piece (2.5 cm by 2.5 cm by 0.7 cm) of dried flattened yucca fruit came from Level 1 (01.C30.10). The exterior was burned in several places.

Portions of yucca leaves were found in floated and screened samples. Some strips were used as thongs or ties and still bear knots. One leaf 4 cm wide appears dark and roasted and is doubled upon itself (01.C30.77). Leaf strips belong to both a broad-leaved and a narrow-leaved yucca (01.C29.131); leaf clusters and leaf bases belong to a narrow-leaved yucca (01.C29.65 and 01.C29.99) and leaf apices to a broad-leaved yucca (01.C29.15).

At High Rolls Cave, only seeds or fragments of seeds are present in deposits. Many features containing burned seeds also have bits of shiny, bubbly organic residues that might have been produced by the over-roasted fruit pulp. The seeds themselves were sometimes discarded in the fire (East Cluster A, East Cluster B, and the West Cluster), directly on the floor of the cave (East Cluster A and intermediate between Clusters A and C), or redeposited in pits or scattered elsewhere with the removal of cold ashes from firepits (East Cluster A) and provide no direct evidence of the manner of preparation. The recovery of burned seed discarded in a pit (Feature 1) records its early use in the cave (3080 ± 50 B.P., Table B.3.1) as it does in Feature 13 Stratum 3. Burned seed fragments also appear in FS 67, which is primarily a mouse pantry.

Both fully ripe and partially ripe fruit could be eaten. The fleshy fruits could be consumed raw when fully ripe, although if eaten in quantity they may cause diarrhea (Robbins and others 1916: 50; Cushing 1920: 234). The ripe fruit might be dried as well. While methods of preparation have been described using pottery (Bell and Castetter 1941), less elaborate methods were used at Picuris Pueblo, where partially ripened fruits were roasted in the coals overnight. Afterwards they might be eaten immediately or the pulp might be dried and stored (Bell and Castetter 1941: 10). Although the Kaibab Paiute did not eat the fruit raw, the fully ripe fruits were made into cakes. Green fruits were tossed into the fire and turned constantly until browned all over. Then they were removed from the fire and when cool, broken open, seeded, and dried. The pieces were later boiled to a mush. They were regarded as an important staple (I. Kelly 1964: 44).

Within historic times the Mescalero Apache cooked the tender central leaves of *Yucca baccata* in soups or stews (Castetter and Opler 1936: 39) and the Cochiti used the "hearts" for food (Lange 1968: 148). When Tewa travelers found themselves short of food, leaves of *Yucca baccata* were sometimes baked and eaten (Robbins and others 1916: 50).

Cyperaceae (Sedge Family)

Modern sedges grow in the riverbed overflow in Fresnal Canyon at 1,678 m elevation (Field Notes 1398). Members of the sedge family generally grow under moist conditions, but there are exceptions. Identification of sedges to species depends on familiarity with the floral parts and their arrangement (Kearney and Peebles 1960) that seldom accompanies archaeological achenes. To complicate matters, lenticular or trigonous achenes may be found in *Carex, Cyperus, Eleocharis,* and *Scirpus*. Fortunately, in the Sacramento Mountains species of *Carex* and *Cyperus* that have trigonous achenes grow in moist environments from 1,372 m elevation upward. In addition, the only genera with non-trigonous achenes are *Scirpus* and *Eleocharis* (Hutchins 1974: 102).

At Fresnal Shelter, no sedge achenes were recovered from the screened samples. A single trigonous achene was found in 1 of the 10 natural stratigraphic units, 01.B28.E22, Unit A. (Table A.5). An additional natural stratigraphic unit (01.B29.E25, Unit D) contained three trigonous achenes about 3.5 mm long as well as two other achenes. In Square D 27, four sedge achenes (2 mm to 3 mm long) in Pit 1 resemble the 27 in Pit 7. Since the two pits overlap (Fig. 3.3), the contents may be intermixed. In addition, Pit 7 has two larger sedge achenes that were retained by the ¼ inch screen. None of the achenes showed signs of preparation. Pit 5 in Square D 27 had a sedge achene that was smaller than the ¼ inch screen.

The presence of rodent feces together with poison ivy-type stones in Square D 27, Pits 5 and 7 suggest that rodents may have introduced the otherwise rare sedges. The evidence of Cyperaceae in Fresnal Shelter is more suggestive of environmental conditions and rodent transport than human utilization.

At High Rolls Cave a single, robust bullrush seed (*Scirpus* type) was recovered

in East Cluster A (FS 773) but from no other sample. There is too little evidence to indicate food usage.

Bullrush (*Scirpus*) achenes have been recovered from early archaeological sites in the Southwest. In northwestern Utah, *Scirpus* achenes have been recovered from 3 of 46 human feces samples of Archaic age at Danger Cave, and from 1 of 51 samples at Hogup Cave (Fry 1977: 35). At the Late Archaic Donaldson Site in Matty Canyon, southern Arizona, Cyperaceae achenes were in all but one flotation sample. Two of the achenes were trigonous in cross section. Other types or sedge achenes were no longer than 2.2 mm (L. Huckell 1995: 83). The strong Cyperaceae component in the pollen profile from the basal portion of the Matty Canyon sequence suggests marshy conditions prevailed during the Early Agricultural period.

Liliaceae (Lily Family)

Onion (Allium)

The two species of onion with exterior fibrous bulb scales (*A. macropetalum* and *A. geyeri*) flower between April and September in the Sacramento Mountains (Hutchins 1974: 110). Wild onions grew in Fresnal Canyon at 2,059 m at the top of the south-facing slope in a pinyon and juniper plant community.

At Fresnal Shelter, although the outer reticula of fibers of bulb scales were recovered in 8 of 43 screened levels, none were found in the flotation samples along the B coordinate nor in the pits in Square D 27 (see Table A.3). Some were recovered in the rodent-disturbed cist (01.C29.308) that had the grass and ponderosa pinebark-lining. The largest collection (O1. C30.77 Level 4) represents about 15 individual plants. One intact group of three to five plants is encrusted with mud, charcoal, and spalls.

The Navajo dig the bulbs in early spring and eat the entire plant raw or cooked with meat

(Steggerda and Eckardt 1941: 221). They may singe the bulbs in hot ashes to remove some of the strong taste from them; they are then eaten or stored for winter. Onions are eaten by the Mescalero Apache, Tohono O'odham, Navajo, Hopi, and various others of the Pueblos (Castetter 1935: 15).

Wild onions were recovered from Murrah Cave in western Texas in Val Verde County near Del Rio. The cave contains evidence of preceramic, preagricultural life ways (Holden 1937: 70). Small wild onions were also recovered from a rock shelter from a similar cultural context in Seminole Canyon in the same area (Pearce and Jackson 1933: 130). Coprolite analysis from a Late Archaic (800 B.C. to A.D. 500) rock shelter near the confluence of the Pecos and Rio Grande in Texas had onion bulbs and scales in 24 of 41 coprolites studied (Bryant 1974, Figure 3).

Poaceae (Grass Family)

Historically-introduced grasses are present in the uppermost disturbed levels of Fresnal Shelter. Eleven grains of *Sorghum* and a single grain of oats *(Avena fatua* type) were recovered in the two upper levels (Table A.3) Both genera have their origin in the Old World and could have been incorporated into the historic dung of domesticated animals.

The following section documents the occurrence of grass taxa at Fresnal Shelter, except for a small, unidentified residue of spikelets, florets, and vegetative portions. Unidentified grass taxa occur quite sporadically, therefore they would seem to lack significance over any extended period of time.

Conventional taxonomic keys allow identification to species with whole specimens of plants. Identifications based only upon florets and spikelets permit one to sometimes classify to tribe (e.g., Andropogoneae or Paniceae), to

genus (e.g., *Sporobolus*), and at other times to species. Occasionally a species can be recognized on the basis of florets or spikelets alone, such as side-oats grama (*B. curtipendula*), New Mexico feather grass, and Indian rice grass. In other cases the specific identification is a consequence of a genus being monotypic—that is represented by a single species. When I identified grasses from Fresnal Shelter in the 1970s, a number of species were monotypic (Gould 1951) including wolftail, California cottontop (as *Trichachne californica*, but *now Digitaria californica), Trichloris crinita* (but now *Chloris crinita)*, and maize (*Zea mays*).

Beardgrass (Andropogoneae class)
At Fresnal Shelter, fragments of the grass heads were recovered in 12 of 43 screened levels, and as unmodified spikelets in 5 of 10 natural stratigraphic units. In Square D 27, unmodified spiklets are present in Pits 1 and 6.

Grama grass (Bouteloua)
Of the three listed below, two modern species of grama grass collected on the slopes of Fresnal Shelter grow within a broad range of elevation. Black grama *(B. eriopoda)* grows on dry sandy plateaus and rocky slopes mostly between 1,068 m and 1,830 m but occasionally higher (Gould 1951: 149). Blue grama (*B. gracilis*) can be found mostly from 1,220 m to 2,440 m (Gould 1951: 149). Side-oats grama (*B. curtipendula*) ranges between 762 m and 2,135 m (Gould 1951: 143).

Most species of grama retain portions of the reproductive structure that looks like a small curled feather, consisting of the rachis and glumes, while the florets fall free on maturity. Identifications to species from Fresnal Shelter are problematical because of the separation of reproductive parts from each other. Side-oats grama (*B. curtipendula*) is an exception. While trampling could be a factor for the disassociation of florets and spikelets from the rachis, it is also possible that mature grasses, or even ones that had shed their florets were initially brought to Fresnal Shelter.

At Fresnal Shelter, *Bouteloua* reproductive parts occur in 13 of 43 screened levels, in all 10 natural stratigraphic units (201 spikelets in total), and in six of the seven pits in Square D 27 (160 spikelets in total). The remnants of the flowering heads appear slightly abraded when recovered, which may be only the product of foot traffic rather than threshing. Side-oats grama was identified in 5 of 10 natural stratigraphic units as 10 spicate branches but not elsewhere within the shelter.

The lack of grains at Fresnal Shelter, despite abundant floral parts, is a matter for speculation. Perhaps most grass was harvested after maturity, possibly for bedding. If all nearby grass species were arbitrarily harvested for bedding, then the abundance of grama grass would support an interpretation of desert grassland with scattered shrubs on the slopes of Fresnal Shelter, as it is today. Other explanations for the lack of grain may include the consumption of grain by mice or other rodents or loss through processing the flotation sample.

At High Rolls Cave, grama grass spikelets are recovered from five excavation units and from Feature 5. Although black grama was the only identifiable species from High Rolls Cave, at least one other grama species was present. Four lots are from excavation units in East Cluster A (Stratum 2) and one from East Cluster B (FS 67) in Stratum 3. One of the spikelets in FS 67 was of the black grama type (*B. eriopoda*).

Only the Western Apache have harvested the grain of grama grass (Reagan 1929: 155).

Chloris crinita (Trichloris crinita, Trichloris mendocina, Trichloris fasciculata)
This grass is native to northern Mexico and

adjoining portions of the United States (Gould 1951: 33). *Chloris crinita* can grow at elevations lower than 1,220 m (Gould 1951: 34, as *T. mendocina*) and as high as 1,525 m (Hutchins 1974: 93). The grass was most commonly seen in the 1970s growing on the outskirts of Alamogordo (elevation 1,327 m) in disturbed ground. The natural disruptions that can foster heavy populations can be deduced from the literature. It can grow in "deep alluvial silty soil... near intermittent creeks and along ditches" (Correll and Johnston 1970: 243) or on rocky hills and mesas (Hutchins 1964: 92).

At Fresnal Shelter the grass heads have been recovered in 5 of 10 natural stratigraphic units. In stratigraphic unit 10, the 37 spikelets are deep golden brown rather than normal cream (Table A.5). Otherwise the remaining spikelets appear unmodified. Five of seven pits in Square D 27 have a total of 40 unmodified spikelets, and there are more in 13 of 43 screened levels (Table A.3. and A.5). A rodent nest interior was lined with the soft heads of this grass in the cist in Square C 29 Level 10 (Table 3.2).

I can find no ethnographic reference to *Chloris*, yet it is in Fresnal Shelter at 1,922 m, well beyond its natural elevation limits. A dead specimen of this grass was observed on the lip of the shelter when I visited the site in 1970. The seed was doubtless carried by excavators who commuted daily in 1969 from Alamogordo, where *C. crinita* grew in abundance. I believe prehistoric foot traffic from lower elevations could have effectively introduced it to the shelter slopes long ago too. Heads could have been accidentally collected when other grasses were harvested at lower elevations as well.

Feather finger grass (Chloris virgata type)
Feather finger grass grows in disturbed habitats such as roadsides, swales, and desert washes at

1,678 m elevation or below (Gould 1951: 131), although Hutchins (1974: 58) allows an upper range of 1,830 m.

At Fresnal Shelter, no remnants of this grass were recovered in the screened levels, but the genus was present in 2 of the 10 natural stratigraphic units. Thirteen spikelets of *C. virgata* type were recovered in Pit 6 of Square D 27. Due to its rarity in the shelter, it probably did not grow on the slopes, but was introduced from lower elevations in an accidental manner. The grain is apparently not harvested.

Arizona cottontop (Digitaria californica, formerly Trichachne californica)

Arizona cottontop grows in open, well-drained soil often in steep, rocky slopes from 305 m to 1,830 m (Gould 1951: 296). The grass flowers primarily from August to November (Gould 1951: 296). This grass might have once shared dominance with side-oats grama and black grama as happens in desert grasslands in southern Arizona after long periods of protection from grazing (Cable 1979: 10, 18).

At Fresnal Shelter the grass is found in 8 of 43 screened levels, and in 3 of 10 natural stratigraphic units. In Square D 27, a single spikelet came from Pit 2 and six spikelets were recovered from Pit 6 (Tables A.3, A.5, and A.6).

Wild rye, wheat grass (Elymus/Agropyron complex)

Wild rye grass (*Elymus canadensis*) grows along the margins of Fresnal Creek today, but not abundantly. It can range from 1,372 m to 2,592 m in elevation (Hutchins 1974: 62). Under agrading conditions and higher water tables this grass may have been more widespread. Another species (*E. glaucus*) grows in open woods and meadows from 1,525 m to 2,135 m (Hutchins 1974: 62).

At Fresnal Shelter no evidence of the rye grass complex was apparent in the screened levels. However, 6 of 10 natural stratigraphic units had a total of 13 unmodified florets, and a floret was recovered in Square D 27, Pit 5.

At High Rolls Cave rye grass was encountered in five samples. Six florets with the grain removed and one flattened rachis were in *the mouse pantry* in East Cluster B (FS 67). In East Cluster A Stratum 2, a spikelet was in FS 557 and another in FS 773. Two carbonized grains of the rye grass complex were recovered in Feature 11a (Stratum 3) and another carbonized grain was in Stratum 2 (FS 187) in East Cluster A. Despite the sparse record, it appears the rye grass complex grain was used as food by both mice and people, though perhaps not with regularity.

Elymus was important to the Paiute (Chamberlin 1964: 368, I. Kelly 1932: 99, Steward 1933: 244). At Gatecliff Shelter in Monitor Valley of central Nevada, *Elymus* grass grains were the most common type of grain recovered and possibly date as far back as 1300 B.C., in Horizon 7 (Thomas 1983b: 155, 484).

Lovegrass (Eragrostis)

The perennial Chihuahua lovegrass (*Eragrostis erosa*) grows on rocky hills from 1,372 m to 2,288 m (Hutchins 1974: 65).

At Fresnal Shelter, no lovegrass was recovered from the screened levels, but unmodified spikelet segments were found in 5 of 10 natural stratigraphic units. Square D 27, Pit 1 contained 17 spikelets and Pit 5 had only one spikelet. No evidence of direct utilization of *Eragrostis* shows on any of the recovered parts from Fresnal Shelter.

At High Rolls Cave, complete inflorescences of *E. erosa* were recovered from FS 955 and FS 956 as macrobotanical material and are likely represented in the more fragmented parts recovered by flotation. A few singed spikelets or segments of the inflorescence were recovered from East Cluster B, Stratum 1 with five of eight grains carbonized. Infloresence segments were recovered in Stratum 2 in East Cluster A and East Cluster B. East Cluster B Feature 5 has a mixture of 49 carbonized and uncarbonized grains. Intermediate between East Clusters A and C, two grains of lovegrass were recovered. Each flotation sample also contains wood rat fecal pellets and the one from Feature 5 has those of a mouse. Lovegrass introduction could be due at least in part to rodent activity and in part to human food preparation.

The Ethiopian domestic grain known as teff is an *Eragrostis* (*E.teff*). *Eragrostis* is documented as a food grain for the Paiute (Palmer 1878: 602, Steward 1933: 243) and for the lower Colorado River tribes (Castetter and Bell 1951: 187). *Eragrostis diffusa* type grains were apparently used by the Hohokam in La Ciudad, Phoenix (Bohrer 1987: 84).

Wolftail (Lycurus phleoides)
Wolftail grows on disturbed ground and rocky slopes from 1,525 m to 2,440 m (Hutchins 1974: 71). Fresnal Shelter had no evidence of this grass recovered from screened levels, but unmodified florets were recovered in 6 of 10 natural stratigraphic units and in five of seven pits. I have found no ethnographic precedent for its use.

Indian rice grass (Oryzopsis hymenoides)
Indian rice grass, though seldom noted in the Tularosa Basin today, was once a conspicuous part of sandy grassland plant communities. Chapter 2 discusses its former distribution. Present evidence suggests that Indian rice grass was atypical of alluvial soils in and near the Sacramento Mountains. A reconnaissance on May 13, 1981 of loamy soils in La Luz Canyon (Township 15 S, Range 11 E, Section 27) failed to reveal Indian rice grass, despite observing New Mexican feather grass, which was just starting to head. The area was explored on the premise that if the rangeland was in good

enough condition for New Mexican feather grass to grow, Indian rice grass might be found there as well.

At Fresnal Shelter, despite the occurrence of Indian rice grass in only 3 of the 10 natural stratigraphic units in the B coordinate (Table A.5), the grass was probably used for food. Other stratigraphic units in the B coordinate also contained evidence of the grain. A carbonized floret was found in 01.B28E.24, Unit F, and another carbonized floret was recovered in another sample from 01.B29E.25, Unit D. The presence of hairless florets (01.D30.24, 01.B29E.25, Unit D) and a floret with a cracked lemma (01.B28W.17, Unit C) serve as indicators of parching. All specimens fit the known range of variation in *Oryzopsis hymenoides*. The distinctive kinked capillary pedicels were not recognized nor were any lenses of processed chaff observed.

At High Rolls Cave, a carbonized floret of Indian rice grass was recovered from Feature 6, a thermal pit radiocarbon dated 28500 ± 70 B.P. (Table B.3.1). The record is unique at High Rolls Cave.

The widespread ethnographic utilization of Indian rice grass in the Southwest has been summarized by various authors (Bohrer 1975a; Doebley 1984; V. Jones 1938). The actual process of removing chaff by burning, and the possible parching of the seed is described by Fowler (1976) and V. Jones (1938).

Indian rice grass forms a conspicuous part of the prehistoric plant record in northern Arizona and New Mexico. Flotation analysis of Archaic sites from the Navajo Mines Archaeological Project in the San Juan Basin of New Mexico revealed large numbers of charred Indian rice grass grain in sample after sample, indicating a consistent emphasis on this particular grass (Toll and Cully 1994: 107). It was recovered at White Dog Cave, a Basketmaker II site in northeastern Arizona, as well as at a broad scatter of prehistoric pueblos arching from the Hopi Reservation into the Four Corners area and over to Santa Fe (Bohrer 1975a; V. Jones 1938).

Panic Grasses (Paniceae)
Because of a cluster of shared botanical characteristics, a number of genera belong to the botanical tribe Paniceae (Gould 1951: 38). When fragmentary heads are present, persistent bristles found at the base of the spikelet allow recognition of the genus *Setaria*. When only spikelets are present, a few genera like *Cenchru*s (burgrass) and *Chloris crinita* (Arizona cottontop) can be recognized. When only spikelets are present, the botanical key prohibits the separation of *Setaria* from *Panicum*; additional characteristics are needed. It is the spikelets of these two genera that are grouped under the tribe Paniceae in Fresnal Shelter.

Setaria macrostachya grows on the south-facing slopes of Fresnal Shelter today. Besides the genus *Setaria*, eight species of *Panicum* potentially might be subsumed under the tribe Paniceae, as they grow in the area (Hutchins 1974: 80).

At Fresnal Shelter, spikelets or florets of Paniceae have been recovered from each of the 10 natural stratigraphic units. Of the 12 spikelets, nine are dark brown and three are carbonized (Table A.5). Since the floret bracts naturally range from cream to brown in different species, and even vary within a species (*Panicum halli*), the dark coloration may not be created by parching. Paniceae florets or spikelets were recovered in all seven of the pits investigated by flotation in Square D 27 (Table A.6). In Pit 3 two florets have unevenly darkened lemmas that are cracked. Their condition is suggestive of parching. Within unit BB of Square B 30, five spikelets have glumes and sterile lemmas that are deep brown, allowing no conclusions in regard to human usage.

Four of the five species of *Panicum* that

have been collected in the southwestern United States for food—*P. bulbosum, P.capillare, P. hirticaule, and P. obtusum* (Doebley 1984)—can be found in northern Otero County where Fresnal Shelter is located (Hutchins 1974: 79-80). Because of the ethnographic use of Paniceae, the ubiquity of Paniceae in flotation samples, and the carbonized nature of some florets, it seems reasonable to conclude the grains of Paniceae were gathered for food at Fresnal Shelter.

At High Rolls Cave the best evidence for Paniceae consumption by humans comes from Stratum 3 Feature 3 with a *Setaria macrostachya* type floret that looks cracked by parching, but not carbonized. It may have been a component of early human diet in High Rolls Cave.

A case can be made for Paniceae being part of rodent diet. In FS 67 (*the mouse pantry*), 11 of 18 Paniceae florets are of *Setaria macrostachya* type. Florets whole but with the grain absent come from Stratum 1 (FS 70) and Stratum 2 (FS 139 and Feature 5). In addition, FS 773 has 22 florets of *Setaria macrostachya* where mice have been active.

Members of Paniceae have been collected for grain in many parts of the world (Harlan 1975: 17), though their prehistory is not well understood. *Setaria italica* may have first come into cultivation in northern China (Harlan 1975: 72). Plains bristlegrass (*Setaria* cf. *macrostachya*) has been recovered in the fill of Coxcatlan Cave, Tehuacan, Mexico (Smith 1967: 236) while the genus has been identified from the same locale in prehistoric human feces (Callen 1967: 266). Coprolite analysis from a Late Archaic (800 B.C. to A.D. 500) rock shelter near the confluence of the Pecos and Rio Grande rivers in Texas had *Setaria* grains in 2 of 41 coprolites studied (Bryant 1974: Figure 3).

Pappophorum complex

The *Pappophorum* complex includes three genera, *Pappophorum*, *Enneapogon*, and *Cottea*. All have been delineated by Gould (1951: 29) as belonging to a botanical class bearing nine or more nerves or awns on the lemma. No attempt has been made to segregate the genera involved.

Pappus grass (*Enneapogon desvauxii*) grows on dry hills and mesas, usually in scattered clumps from 1,372 m to 1,982 m in elevation (Hutchins 1974: 63). *Cottea* is only occasional on rocky slopes at 1,525 m or lower (Gould 1951: 100) and has a range that extends through southern New Mexico (Hitchcock 1950: 225). *Pappophorum mucronulatum* grew at 1,525 m elevation (Table A.2).

At Fresnal Shelter *Pappophorum* complex florets were recovered in 5 of 43 screened levels, 7 of 10 natural stratigraphic units, and in three of seven pits in Square D 27 (Pits 1, 2, and 5). No record of ethnographic use has been discovered.

Tobosa grass (Pleuraphis cf mutica = Hilaria cf mutica)

Tobosa grass grows on dry, sandy rocky slopes and plains mostly between 610 m and 1,830 m (Gould 1951: 161).

At Fresnal Shelter two florets were recovered in one natural stratigraphic unit (Table A.5). I have found no human food use for this grass.

Dropseed grass (Sporobolus)

Various species inhabit a wide elevation range from the Tularosa Basin up to 1,982 m.

Many species of dropseed in the Southwest are early successional ones and can abound locally. Gatherable quantities of dropseed (*S. contractus* and *S. giganteus*) were probably once obtained in sandy or sandy loam soil in the Tularosa Basin (Table 2.1). I have observed that *S. airoides*, S. *contractus*, and S. *cryptan-*

drus are very responsive to moisture and may mature harvestable grain in either early summer or at various points through the subsequent growing season depending on rainfall. As the common name for the grass indicates, the grain is easily freed from its membranous bracts. Such qualities help explain its present and past popularity.

Alkali sacaton (*S. airoides*) grows on the south-facing slope of Fresnal Shelter as isolated plants. Concentrations suitable for harvesting would be downstream towards the Tularosa Basin where a variety of plant communities contain stands of the grass (Table 2.1). Alkali sacaton can become established with disturbance (Aldon and Garcia 1972) and competes well against grama and galleta grass under heavy sedimentation (Hickey and Springfield 1966). Further, it makes little difference if the sediment is rich in sand, clay (Hubbell and Gardner 1944: 42), or alkali (Wooton and Standley 1912: 80). Because of these characteristics, monocultures might be anticipated on alluvial fans, and agrading stream or arroyo margins or canyon forks with gentle slopes that spread floodwater.

Giant sacaton *(S. wrightii)* grows in dense clumps on deep alluvial soils relatively free of harmful amounts of alkali (Aldous and Shantz 1924: 106). Such locations periodically acquire moisture through flooding or groundwater seepage (Meinzer 1927: 25). Favorable conditions might be postulated in La Luz Canyon or further west near the perimeter of the Tularosa Basin in pre-contact times, but a specimen actually grew much closer at the confluence of Fresnal and Salado canyons at 1,678 m elevation (Table A.2).

At Fresnal Shelter every one of the 10 stratigraphic units along the B coordinate possessed the chaff (empty florets) of *Sporobolus*. Chaff was also present in six of the seven pits in Square D 27 (Table A.6). Because chaff was so abundant, counting was impractical. For example, 1,003 florets weighed 0.06g. A total of 0.789 g of florets derived from the 10 stratigraphic units. In only one natural stratum (01. B28W.24, Unit F) was a grain of *Sporobolus* present, and it was fully carbonized. Four screened lots (C28.85, C28.126, C29.133, and C30.82) retained barren panicle fragments. The last lot had a typical *Sporobolus* type rachis with closely appressed rachillas, traits that appear in several species. In disturbed Level 1 of Square C 31 were two caryopsis (grains) with the swollen, starchy interior protruding along the fractured surface (01.C31.18). Level 2 of the same square contained two parched seeds and a burned one (01.C31.25). One of the natural stratigraphic units (01.B28.W24, Level F) had four expanded cracked caryopses, one carbonized caryopsis, and appressed rachis fragments.

The almost total lack of parched or carbonized seed until the upper disturbed levels of Fresnal Shelter would seem to indicate that parching was far from usual. If Fresnal Shelter were an open site and only carbonized grain preserved, one would receive the erroneous impression the grass was infrequently gathered. The recovery of chaff and small portions of the infloresence may mean that whatever the source of the gathered grain, it did not receive its final winnowing until people returned to Fresnal Shelter.

At High Rolls Cave the dropseed grain is under-represented in flotation samples. In FS 67 (*the mouse pantry*), only 48 grains were recovered from the flotation fraction in contrast with 497 grains from the heavy fraction. The near total lack of chaff typifies the manner of mouse grain transport in the cheek pouches. In contrast, humans beat the seed and loose chaff into a container that then requires winnowing.

Carbonized dropseed grass was recovered in Feature 1, Stratum 3, which dates 3080 ± 50 B.P. as well as in Feature 11b. Dropseed grass

is widespread in Stratum 2. Of seven flotation samples in East Cluster A, four contain burned grain. Two (FS 208 and FS 773) have unburned grain and chaff as well. East Cluster B, thermal Feature 23 contained carbonized grain while the West Cluster, thermal Feature 13 had an uncarbonized grain.

The yellow grains with dark embryos in FS 67 segregate into two size classes in length, 0.75 mm and 1.5 mm. The larger size appears to be unique to giant dropseed grass (*S. giganteus*). In the stratum above FS 67, Teresa M. Fresquez also identified giant dropseed grass among bulk plant remains. However, giant dropseed has not been collected in the White Mountains, which is part of the Sacramento Mountains (Hutchins 1974: 89). It is found on the White Sands Missile Range in gently undulating to level, deep sand (Table 2.1). It also grows on sandy hills, washes, and river flats mostly from 1,220 m to 1,830 m (Gould 1951: 224).

Among the dropseed grains in FS 67 were two brown grains of the alkali sacaton type (*S. airoides*). An alkali sacaton type grain still in the husk was in FS 773 as well. Concentrations of alkali sacaton suitable for harvesting would grow downstream towards the Tularosa Basin where a variety of plant communities contain stands of the grass (Table 2.1). The remaining small dropseed grains could be more local, such as sand dropseed (*S. cryptandrus*). The latter is abundant and weedy in sandy soil, but less frequent in tighter, finer disturbed soils (Correll and Johnston 1970). Mice evidently pilfered edible grains like alkali sacaton and giant dropseed that humans harvested at a distance and brought to High Rolls Cave.

Sporobolus has been recovered at the Donaldson Site in the Cienega Valley, a Late Archaic site with maize agriculture (Huckell 1995: 83). Flotation analysis of Archaic sites from the Navajo Mines Archaeological Project in the San Juan Basin of New Mexico revealed grain of *Sporobolus* (Toll and Cully 1994: 106). The remains of alkali sacaton (*Sporobolus airoides*) were recovered from preceramic and ceramic levels of Bat Cave in Catron County in west-central New Mexico. Of 11 coprolites analyzed from the ceramic period (A.D. 200 to 1000), six contained seeds of *Sporobolus* while only one had evidence of maize in the form of pollen (Trigg and others 1994).

New Mexico feather grass (Stipa neomexicana)

Today, relict stands of this cool season grass can be found on steep slopes and hill crowns or ridges between Fresnal and La Luz Canyons and due west of the shelter on Horse Ridge (1,830 m to 1,982 m). Chapter 2 discusses its former distribution.

Compared to most grasses, New Mexico feather grass bears a large grain. The main bracts that enclose it (lemma and palea) are less than 2 mm in diameter, but extend for some 10 mm, terminating basally in a sharp drill point (callus tip) useful for self-planting. The opposite end is topped by what appears as a thin wire, twisted apparently from two strands (an awn) that finally extends into a miniature feather-like structure. In burned material, the callus and the awn are typically recovered.

At Fresnal Shelter, all 10 natural stratigraphic units along the B coordinates contained the reproductive parts of *Stipa neomexicana* (Table A.5). Segments of burned awns, remains of callus tips, and splintered lemmas devoid of seed probably represent efforts to release the grain from the indurate lemma encasing it. Five of the seven pits in Square D 27 contained similar evidence (Table A.6).

In 1971, two grid squares excavated by following natural stratigraphy (E 22 and F 18) showed extensive burned lenses of *Stipa*. In Square E 22, level 3m, a lens of *Stipa* spread diagonally from southeast to northwest. The excavator estimated that when the level was

screened, 80 percent or more of the *Stipa* was lost. In the next level below it, a hearth area surrounded by burned soil, had a smaller lens of *Stipa* on its eastern side. When the lens was floated it produced about 3/4 liter of chaff. The chaff consisted of the pubescent distal awns, the stout base of the awns (frequently burned), the roasted and splintered lemmas, and the fire-singed hairy callus tips of *Stipa neomexicana* (01.E22.50). In Square F 18, two successive levels, 13c and 14c, each 4 cm thick, carried a predominance of *Stipa* in the gray soil, but only token evidence survived the screening process (01.F18.72 and 01.F18.81). Judging from the residues present, more grass was collected at one time than could ever have been collected from the slopes fronting the shelter. It probably grew on gentler slopes that were more easily harvested.

At High Rolls Cave the early use of New Mexico feather grass is evident in the two carbonized awn bases and the carbonized awn segment in two pits in East Cluster B, which were dated 3080 ± 50 B.P. and 2970 ± 40 B.P. (Table B.3.1). Further evidence of its use is preserved in thermal Features 11a and 11b in East Cluster A and in two other thermal features in the West Cluster representing Strata 3 and 2. In East Cluster A Stratum 2, only awn segments were recovered in two flotation samples (FS 557 and FS 805) while in two additional samples a variety of parts including awn segments, carbonized callus tips, and splintered lemmas were recovered (FS 187 and FS 773).

Other than the remains from Fresnal Shelter and High Rolls Cave, the human utilization of this particular species is unknown in the literature, although the Owens Valley Paiute (Steward 1933: 243) and Kawaiisu Paiute of Kern County California utilized the similar *Stipa speciosa* in late spring and considered the harvest very important as a food source. Zigmond (1981: 66) described how the Kawaiisu collected the grass in bunches, spread it to dry, and then "threshed" it by burning. The seeds were gathered and winnowed by dropping them from one basket into another. A second Kawaiisu informant told of the grass being dried for a day or two and the seeds beaten out.

Although the grass could have been spread to dry and then burned at High Rolls Cave and Fresnal Shelter, it appears that the grains were beaten free from the hard coats after firing. What remains is the chaff from burning and winnowing. The lemma that ensheaths the grain is normally pubescent and the very tip or callus is quite hairy. At High Rolls Cave in FS 208, the lemmas are smooth and many are singed to a deep brown. Where the removal of callus hairs is incomplete, the lack of pubescence on the lemma suggests exposure to fire. On one, a portion of the hairs still clings to the lemma. Such variability is to be expected, because full control of the firing process is impossible. The lemmas are all splintered longitudinally to remove the grain by an unknown technique. The three to five splintered lemmas of New Mexico feather grass in *the mouse pantry* sample (FS 67) at High Rolls Cave all appear fire-singed. These may have been pilfered from the original processing area.

Maize (Zea mays)

Because maize is a non-native cultigen from Mexico, we can be assured that humans were the introductory vector. At Fresnal Shelter, TAMS radiocarbon dates on maize range from 2945 ± 55 B.P. to 1665 ± 55 B.P. (Tagg 1996: 319), potentially representing 1300 years of maize cultivation. Once maize was brought into the shelter, however, rodents evidenced a keen interest in the grain and its storage in small caches, a subject covered in greater detail in Chapter 2 under biotic forces in site formation.

At Fresnal Shelter, corn kernels were screened from 26 of 43 levels They are pres-ent in greatest abundance in 9 of 10 levels in Square C 29, similar to the cultivated beans in 8 levels. Cobs were recovered in 20 levels in the screened grid squares (Table A.3).

Five of the seven pits in Square D 27 have either kernels or cob cupules (Table A.6). The oldest maize date derives from a cob from Pit 3, radiocarbon dated 2945 ± 55 B.P., while the charcoal scatter in Pit 3 dates 3150 ± 70 B.P. Cupule or cob segments came from two natural strata (Table A.5).

Signs of processing were infrequent. Only three grains observed by the author were carbonized: catalog number 01.C30.53 from Level 3, .01.C29.162 in Level 6, and 01.C29.188 from Level 7. Four were swollen and cracked from parching (catalog numbers 01.C28.85, Level 6; 01.C29.162, Level 6; and 01.C29.245, Level 9). Perhaps more might have been recovered if thermal areas were investigated. No evidence of fire-singed husks that might indicate roasting was seen.

Male spikelets (tassel fragments) that appear worn and abraded were recovered from 4 of the 10 natural stratigraphic units along the B coordinate (Table A.5). Tassel fragments were reclaimed in Square C29, level 5 (01.C29.103) and Level 6 (01.C29.131 and 01.C29.154).

Only a few salient features of maize morphology can be given, primarily from cobs encountered in the C 27 to C 29 and D 26 to D 29 grid squares. Of 34 cobs, row number ranges from 8 to 18. Half the cobs (17) have 12 rows, four have 8 rows, seven have 10 rows, five have 14 rows, and one has 18 rows. The latter cob comes from disturbed Level 2 (01. C27.5). All five cobs with 14 rows are from outside the C and D grid squares (01.F.26.13a and 01.F26.20).

Walton Galinat observed some cobs with deep narrow cupules resembling the very primitive pre-Chapalote (for example, 01.E26.25) as well as some cobs approaching

Maize de Ocho (e.g., 01.F29.9) and many cobs of the PIma-Papago type. Only one example of a carbonized cob was noted (01.B27.85). The kernels ranged from tan to brown to reddish brown. Kernels were of flour starch in composition or had a thin flinty outer coat and a flour starch interior.

Volney H. Jones described maize from the El Paso phase (A.D. 1100 to 1350) sites near Alamogordo and the Bradley site east of the Organ Mountains as having slender cobs and small kernels with row numbers usually ranging from eight to twelve with a few having as many as fourteen. He thought the maize would classify as Pima-Papago (Lehmer 1948: 95), a type described in the literature only a few years earlier. Thus there appears to be a considerable continuity in the type of maize grown in the area according to the sketchy information we now have available.

At High Rolls Cave, carbonized embryos of maize kernels preserve in some samples. The embryo is rich in oil compared to the starchy endosperm and may separate from it. Carbonized embryos have been recovered in East Cluster A Stratum 2 in FS 187, in Feature 11b, and in FS 557 (Appendix B.1). In FS 557 the top half of one embryo is 2.7 mm long. I would expect it to be from a fully mature kernel because my own measurements on length of five mature embryos averaged 4.5 mm. Small embryos may either be immature or come from small kernels. In FS 187 two embryos measure only 1 mm and 1.5 mm long. In Feature 11b two embryos resemble the size of the two in FS 187, while the top half of another embryo fragment is 1.5 mm long (Appendix B.1).

Other parts of maize were encountered in flotation. Feature 11b had a few carbonized cupules and kernels. East Cluster B, Stratum 2 FS 139 had two cob shanks with the base of husk attached and one singed by fire, pieces of husk both burned and unburned, and a carbonized cupule. FS 795 Stratum 2 had a cupule

with tough glumes while FS 805 had cross section fragments from the cob. Feature 5 had a carbonized maize husk. FS 67, *the mouse pantry*, had two kernel fragments in the heavy fraction of flotation.

Our knowledge of cob row number at High Rolls Cave is still incomplete, although a variety of cobs have been dated to Stratum 1 times (Table B.3.3). Both a 12 and an 18 row cob (FS 110) derive from Stratum 1, Level 1. In FS 146 six cobs had 12 rows and one cob possibly had 10 rows.

Many of the techniques used for preparing wild grains for consumption could be transferred to the preparation of maize. The grain could simply be parched. Or after parching and grinding, the meal could be mixed with water and drunk. Pinches of meal might be taken with sips of water. Making gruel of the ground grain and heating it with hot stones could have been practiced. Ears might be roasted in the husk. Dough wrapped in cornhusk could be baked in a pit; flattened dough could be cooked on a stone griddle or in the ashes. The flavor could be altered by mixing different kinds of seed flour with the corn meal.

Of all these methods of maize preparation, we only have direct evidence of parching at Fresnal Shelter. The partly expanded condition of some grains could easily result from heating a flinty outer-coat until the steam inside caused partial swelling before it escaped the grain. The fully mature carbonized embryo fragment from High Rolls Cave probably survived a parching accident. I believe the ultra-small carbonized embryos came from either immature or small kerneled maize that was roasted at High Rolls Cave. The fire-singed husks are suggestive of roasted maize in the ear. The one carbonized cupule may indicate cobs were infrequently used as fuel at High Rolls Cave.

Perhaps most intriguing is the worn, abraded nature of the male spikelets in Fresnal Shelter. It is hard to attribute their condition to wear from trampling when other plant parts from different species are well preserved. Crushing or pounding to release any remaining pollen might provide an explanation that veers toward medicinal or ceremonial interpretation. For example, in San Ildefonso Pueblo, corn pollen is recommended for heart palpitations (Curtin 1947: 119) and in many of the Rio Grande Pueblos it is an ingredient in sacred cornmeal (Curtin 1968).

In the Hueco area of Texas, in Cave 1, a small (9.6 cm long) pear-shaped buckskin pouch filled with a powdery substance resembling cornmeal lay above the right hand of a male between the age of 56 and 75 years. Several coiled baskets, a checker-weave basket of sotol leaves, and a 89 cm long, unpeeled shaft with two 23 cm feathers fastened with sinew and split yucca leaves were enclosed with the body by a fur blanket (Cosgrove 1947: 161-162). Maize was in evidence in nearly every site in the Hueco area, and the author assigned a Basketmaker age to this particular find (Cosgrove 1947).

Typhaceae (Cattail Family)

Cattail (Typha)
Cattail (*T. domingensis*) grows today in Fresnal Canyon at 1,678 m near its upper elevation limit, but the broad leaved cattail (*T. latifolia*) ranges from 1,220 m to 4,440 m in elevation. All species flower between May and July (Hutchins 1974: 32-33).

At Fresnal Shelter about 45 pistillate portions of spikes of *Typha* were recovered in Square E 17 level 8 (01.E17.200). All the heads measure no more than 5 mm in diameter and have the distally located staminate (pollen bearing) spike missing. The immature and unmodified appearance of the pistillate spikes suggests that the absent terminal pollen-bearing spike was valued. A wide variety of vegetal and cultural material is present in the stratigraphic unit, and no special context for the find was noted. If the pollen was indeed collected as food only one instance at Fresnal Shelter has been noted.

At High Rolls Cave a total of two cattail seeds came from FS 187 and FS 853 in Stratum 2. The pollen record is far more extensive (Appendix B.4) and pertains exclusively to the broad-leaved cattail (*Typha latifolia*) because only pollen tetrads were recovered. Richard Holloway (2002) believes the plants were intentionally brought to the cave because of the high pollen concentration values. For example, one pollen sample (FS 1006) had 2,592 grains per gram, a very high number.

A cattail marsh served as a prehistoric food bank. When other plant resources were exhausted, the marsh was a resource. Toll and Cully (1994) point out that riparian food plants tend to grow in dense patches and produce sizeable edible parts, allowing for efficiency in food gathering. Cattail alone is a rich source of food. The young shoots of cattail can be eaten fresh in the spring when they are abundant, but also to some extent during the summer. The young flower stalks, especially the pollen-producing apex, can be scraped and used alone or as an additive to other flours. Later when the flower stalk is mature, the down can be set afire and the tiny seeds eaten. Towards the end of the growing season the rootstalks are rich in starch, and can be eaten raw, boiled, or baked (Harrington 1967: 223). Experimental harvests of cattail pollen have yielded up to 9,360 kcal per hour of labor compared to the rootstalks that only yield 128 kcal to 267 kcal per hour (R. Kelly 1995, Table 3-3).

Cattail pollen has formed part of religious rites of Pueblo (White 1942: 175), Apache (Linskens and Jorde 1997), and Navajo and has also been used as a source of food elsewhere in the Southwest. The literature concerning its employment is widely dispersed and varied in content. Cocopa utilization seems especially pertinent because the pollen was brought back to camp to dry before it was extracted (E. Gifford 1933: 268; W. Kelley 1977: 39). Both men and women would wade waist deep in water to collect bundles of the stems, which were taken home and sun-dried four to five hours. A shallow depression 45.7 cm (18 inches) in diameter was dug and lined with a cloth. Four sticks were placed upright to support another cloth and enclosed a third cloth. The operator disengaged the pollen from the stalk with the set of cloth covers so that it would not blow away (E. Gifford 1933: 268). The Paiute in northwestern Nevada had no trouble collecting baskets of pollen in a short time. Green cattail leaves were laid on a bed of hot coals. Pollen made into cakes by mixing it with a little water were laid on the leaves and covered by more leaves. Coals were placed on top of the leaves as well to promote baking (Wheat 1967: 11).

Dual sources of evidence from Bat Cave suggest the consumption of cattail pollen. The remains of numerous pistillate heads and a small staminate head of *T. latifolia* were recovered from ceramic levels (Smith 1950: 166). In another study from Bat Cave (Trigg and others 1994: 215), 1 of 11 coprolites from the ceramic period (A.D. 200-1000) had cattail pollen in considerable quantity and in clumps.

DICOTYLEDONOUS FLOWERING PLANTS

Aizoaceae (Carpetweed Family)

Horse purslane (Trianthema portulacastrum)
Horse purslane, an annual, grows between 305 m and 1,525 m elevation (Hutchins 1974: 167; Kearney and Peebles 1960: 281) in cultivated or otherwise disturbed ground.

At Fresnal Shelter one seed coat of horse purslane was recovered in a natural stratigraphic unit (Table A.5). Although the seed has been found in prehistoric contexts suggestive of economic utilization among the Hohokam of southern Arizona (Gasser 1982a: 223), the single recovery at Fresnal Shelter may represent an accidental introduction or a rare instance of utilization. At the Late Archaic Donaldson Site, in the Cienega Valley of southeastern Arizona, seven flotation samples contained a total of 31 horse purslane seeds (Huckell 1995: 89).

Amaranthaceae (Amaranth Family)

Pigweed (Amaranthus)
Amaranthus cruentus is an introduced domesticated species from Guatemala and Mexico (Sauer 1950b, 1967). Like the Pueblo dye plants and the specimen collected by Wislizenius in 1846 in Cusihuiriachic, Chihuahua (Sauer 1950a: 415), the *A. cruentus* from High Rolls Cave bears dark seed.

A. powellii is an annual herb growing near water and disturbed ground from 1,372 m to 2,440 m elevation (Hutchins 1974: 154). It ranges from western Texas, Colorado, New Mexico, and Arizona into northern Mexico (Wooton and Standley 1915: 212).

A. torreyi grows from 1,068 m to 1,678 m in southern Arizona (Kearney and Peebles 1942: 280). It extends from western Texas to Nevada southward into Mexico in the Upper Sonoran Zone (Wooton and Standley 1915: 211).

A. wrightii is found from western Texas to southern Colorado, New Mexico, and Arizona. The species is found in waste ground in central and southern New Mexico from 1,068 m to 1,525 m elevation. It flowers from August to October (Martin and Hutchins 1980: 633).

At Fresnal Shelter amaranth utricles or capsules were recovered in 8 of 10 natural stratigraphic units and from each of the seven pits in Square D 27. A total of 17 black seeds came from the natural stratigraphic units and pits, but none were obviously carbonized (Tables A.5 and A.6). Since carbonization may warp the seed until the generic identity disappears, others may be subsumed under the artificial category cheno-ams discussed in the goosefoot family, Chenopodiaceae.

The utricles and associated parts hold the best potential to identify the species. However, natural variation in the morphology of utricles within any one species precludes positive identification unless the utricles are highly typical.

Enough typical utricles exist from Fresnal Shelter to indicate the following species are present: *A. cruentus*, *A. powellii*, *A. torrey,* and *A. wrightii* (Table 4.3). The latter two species grow below 1,678 m. The reader should understand that *A. Powellii* in particular varies so much in utricle cap and sepal characters that, in some instances, parts identified as *A. cruentus* may represent poorly developed *A. powellii*.

It is more likely, however, that the cultivated species *A. cruentus* is present, according to Jonathan D. Sauer, who kindly provided the identifications.

Because *A. cruentus* identification in natural stratigraphic unit four is based upon a large number of utricle caps and bases (Table 4.3), it is particularly reliable. Both *A. cruentus* and maize were recovered from Square D 27, Pit 3. The scattering of charcoal in the pit produced a corrected radiocarbon date of 3150 ± 70 B.P., but the amaranth may have entered the pit at a later date, as was the case with maize.

At High Rolls Cave, *A. cruentus* type chaff has been documented in East Cluster A in Stratum 2 (FS 208 and FS 773). In FS 208 the papery capsules or utricle caps were recovered in association with seeds and chaff of dropseed, goosefoot, and New Mexico feather

Table 4.3. *Amaranthus* Identifications from Fresnal Shelter

Location	Identification			Sample		
	A. cruentus	*A. powellii*	*A. torreyi*	cap	base	seed
Natural Strata						
3		x		7		1
4	x	x		44	22	2
5	?x	?x		3	2	6
6		x		5		
7		?x	x	8	8	
8		x	x	13	15	
9		x	x	12	11	
10		x	x	1	1	
Pits in D 27						
1		x	x		5	
2		x		10	4	4
3	x			3		1
4		x		9	5	2
5		x			19	
6		x	x	1	10	
7		x		3	2	
Other Strata						
01.B28W22. D			x	1	5	
01.B28W24. F	x	x	x	**u	u	u
01.B29E23. CC		x	x	10	10	
01.B29W8. CC'			x		1	
01.B30.15 BB (*A. wrightii*)				1	1	

* Idenitified by Jonathan D. Sauer in 1971
** Specimen unavailable for tabulation

grass. When seeds are winnowed to remove the chaff, the separation is imperfect; some seeds are usually lost with the chaff. FS 208 is from an ash deposit above matted organic material 15 cm to 36 cm below surface. Evidently cold ash became the recipient of residues from parching and winnowing. The context in which it was found suggests it was raised for its seed or grain.

The other *A. cruentus* from Stratum 2 (FS 773) has abundant diagnostic chaff that was radiocarbon dated 2640 ± 40 B.P. (Table B.3.3). All but one of the 38 oval dark brown or black amaranth seeds have seed coat parted enough to see how thin they are compared to the single exception (Appendix B.1). Because thin coats tend to inhibit germination, we could be looking at a cultivated form of amaranth seed, readily identifiable in the same sample from chaff as *A. cruentus* type.

At High Rolls Cave, *A. powellii* type utricle bases (0.5 ml) were recovered from FS 773 and could have been harvested from cultivated fields or other locations. The eight utricle bases of *A. torreyi* in the same sample reveal some exploitation of lower elevation habitats. I found no evidence of *A. palmeri*, a modern agricultural weed near Alamogordo.

In the Cienega Valley of southeastern Arizona, the Late Archaic Donaldson and Los Ojitos sites contained seeds of *Amaranthus* obtained through flotation (Huckell 1995). At Gatecliff Shelter, Monitor Valley, Nevada in Horizon 8 (1350 B.C.), *Amarathus* seeds came from a hearth (Thomas 1983b: 155). Carbonized amaranth seeds were recovered from a San Jose hearth near Grants, New Mexico radiocarbon dated 6880 to 400 B.P. (Agogino and Feinhandler 1957; Agogino and Hester 1958). One of the most common remains in two preceramic levels of Bat Cave is *Amaranthus powelli* (Smith 1950: 172, 179). In the Basin of Mexico at the Zohapilco Site, the Playa I phase (6000 to 5300 B.C.) sediments contain carbonized seeds of *Amaranthus* (Niederberger 1979). In Chihuahua, Mexico at Cerro Juanaquena, amaranth seeds from a site dated by maize at about 3070 B.P. have been reported (Hard and Roney 1998). Near Durango, Colorado, one lot of uncarbonized *Amaranthus* seeds came from a small, narrow-necked twined bag included with a burial of a young woman wrapped in a fur cloth robe (Jones and Fonner 1954: 95; Morris and Burgh 1954: 41;) placed in a dry crevice at a Basketmaker II site. The Durango amaranths are intriguing, for if the amaranth seed were native, why would it be saved in a small bag as if it were a precious item? Other reports span upward in time.

The archeological record of cultivated amaranths is extremely sparse. Cultivated species date from about 3500 to 2300 B.C. in Pueblo, Mexico with the recovery of *A. cruentus* in the Abejas phase of Coxcatlan Cave and in later levels. *A. hypochondriacus* is represented in Zones IV and V in the cave (200 B.C. to A.D.700) and possibly earlier (Sauer 1969). The latter species was also identified by Jonathan D. Sauer under the synonym of *A. leucocarpus* at Tonto National Monument in southern Arizona, a site which existed around A.D. 1300 (Bohrer 1962: 107-108). The Bureau of Plant Industry identified *Amaranthus* seed from Bee Cave Canyon Shelter in the Trans-Pecos of Texas as *A. paniculatus* (Coffin 1932: 33). The scientific name was one applied to a cultivated amaranth by W.E. Safford, also of the Bureau of Plant Industry some 15 years earlier, and is a synonym of *A. cruentus*. The archaeological seeds were contained in three reed tubes stoppered with grass, which were cached beneath the edge of a large stone. Although undated, the other artifacts and assemblage of subsistence items from the shelter show strong similarities to those of Fresnal Shelter.

Religious reasons for perpetuating cultivated *A. cruentus* need consideration as the Fresnal Shelter recovery context lacks clues on usage. Both the Zuni in the southwestern United States and the Huichol of Jalisco, Mexico have similar traditions regarding amaranth seeds. The Zuni say that their rain priest carried amaranth seeds in reed tubes (*et'towe*) from the undermost world (Stevenson 1915: 65). Two sets of reed tubes, one filled with water and the other with edible seed symbolized life, including rain and vegetation (Stevenson 1904: 24, 163). The Huichol leave diminutive forms of reed canes as generalized prayers for rain, health, and good crops or prayers for longevity (Dutton 1962: 42; Lumholtz 1900: 80-81; Lumholtz 1973: 162). In Aztec Mexico in preconquest times, the ground grain was kneaded into a dough and formed into mountains in honor of the rain gods (Tlaloques) or into images such as the war god or the god of fire at other ceremonies (Sauer 1950b: 569, Table 1). Household ceremonies were held for the mountain or rain gods with individual offerings also (Sauer 1950b: 570).

At Hopi, Zuni, and the Rio Grande Pueblos, *A. cruentus* was used to impart a pinkish hue to piki or paper bread (Sauer 1950a: 414). The Zuni did this by grinding the inflorescence to a fine meal (Stevenson 1915: 87) and soaking it in water. Additionally, the Zuni rubbed the crushed, moistened inflorescence on their cheeks as a rouge (Stevenson 1915: 83). An unidentified amaranth was used to color maize dough bright red in Guerrero, Mexico (Sauer 1950a: 412).

The Southern Paiute used a cultivated amaranth for grain. The tops were broken off in a burden basket and the heads spread to dry. After drying the heads were rubbed between the palms to release the seeds into a tray and then winnowed. The dried seeds were made into a gruel, but when eaten fresh in mush the heads were ground on the metate, pods and all (I. Kelly 1964: 41). Grain amaranths in Mexico were commonly toasted, ground, and stirred into water to make a beverage.

We have little historic information how grain amaranths were cultivated in the southwestern United States. In the 1870s, Edward Palmer and John Wesley Powell indicate the Southern Paiute usually cultivated grain amaranths near the river bottoms and harvested them in conjunction with wild species (Bye 1972). The Kaibab Paiute apparently planted their grain amaranth (I. Kelly 1964: 39) separate from their maize crop in a plot about 7.7 m on a side where water was accessible for irrigation.

A. cruentus is thought to originate as a domestic grain crop in southern Mexico or Guatemala, the only region where the cultigen is grown within the range of its probable progenitor, *A. hybridus* (Sauer 1967). *A. cruentus* is a minor component of the grain amaranths of Mexico, but the prevailing Mexican race lacks the heavy red plant color and dark seed pigmentation seen among dye amaranths of the Rio Grande Pueblos. It is grown in a few villages in Puebla and Sinaloa and on the southern and western fringes of the "great preconquest Mexican grain amaranths" (Sauer 1950a: 415). The Mexican race of *A. cruentus* was grown by the Tarahumara of Chihuahua and collected by Wislizenius in 1846 without comment (Sauer 1950a: 415). Dark seeded forms of *A. cruentus* are now commonly grown in the wet tropics and some temperate regions along with the dark seeded form of *A. hypochondriacus*. Although they are usually planted as ornamentals and pot-herbs, they sometimes have magical, reputedly medicinal or other esoteric uses (Sauer 1967: 125).

Anacardiaceae (Sumac Family)

Poison ivy (Rhus radicans type)
Poison ivy grows in damp woods, edges of meadows, and along stream banks from 1,525 m to 2,440 m elevation (Hutchins 1974: 302).

At Fresnal Shelter oblong poison ivy type

stones with a slight constriction at the equator were found in Pits 5 and 7 in Square D 27. A flattened glabrous fruit coat was found in a natural stratigraphic unit and fruit stones were found in D 28, D 29, and D 30 (Tables A.3 and A.5). Since I have found no reference to Southwestern Indian utilization of the fruit, I assume the species was introduced by rodents from somewhere near. While poison ivy no longer grows in the vicinity, a spring or seep near the shelter might have provided a suitable habitat.

Three-leaved sumac (Rhus trilobata)
Threeleaf sumac can grow on dry rocky slopes from 1,372 m to 1,982 m elevation (Hutchins 1974: 302).

At Fresnal Shelter fruits and stones of *R. trilobata* type came from 3 of 10 natural stratigraphic units along the B coordinate. One of the four fruits was dark and had a charred peduncle while another had its coat spread out as if pounded. Stones and fruits have also been recovered from 7 of 43 screened levels and in five of the seven pits in Square D 27. One stone from a pit has been carbonized (see Tables A.3, A.5, and A.6).

At High Rolls Cave, threeleaf sumac (*Rhus trilobtata* type) floral and fruiting parts are fairly well represented in half of the excavation units. The fruit stones, broken or whole, are most widespread, followed by the fruits. They are found in East Cluster A Stratum 2 in FS 557, FS 208, and throughout the three levels in Excavation Unit 27 (FS 742, FS 795, and FS 805) and in East Cluster B Stratum 2 (FS 139), as well as in Stratum 3 (FS 67). FS 853 contains a half of a stone and another fragment.

The condition of floral and fruiting parts (Appendix B.1) in the deposits at High Rolls Cave strongly implicates rodents in the introduction of threeleaf sumac. A large number of just-blossomed and immature fruits were in FS 557 and FS 795. Flotation FS 67 carried the most complete range of parts in the residue. Besides fruit stones, the sample had a whole array of young to mature fruits as well as the infloresence axis. About 2 ml of stone fragments were in the heavy fraction. Because of numerous fecal pellets of mice, I suspect they were the collectors. However, wood rats are known to store new growth of plants within foraging distance, including threeleaf sumac (VanderWall 1990: 261).

The pattern of threeleaf sumac recovery in thermal features suggests they were unused when mice and wood rats introduced parts of threeleaf sumac, and were reclaimed later for human purposes. In the features the recovery of fruiting parts is less frequent and less diverse. Feature 3 has a carbonized fruit coat and Feature 11 has carbonized stones, stone fragments, and a carbonized inflorescence axis. Features 22 and 23 have the carbonized remains of immature fruits (see Appendix B.1).

The fruits of threeleaf sumac can be eaten raw. Sometimes the berries are washed, dried, and stored in ollas. Preparation usually involved grinding the fruit and soaking the mash in water prior to drinking the liquid (E. Gifford 1932: 211; Kroeber 1935: 55; Nequatewa 1943: 20; Palmer 1878: 597; Vestal 1952: 35). Variations in preparation involve the addition of dried or cooked agave to the soaking meal (Castetter and Opler 1936: 37; E. Gifford 1932: 212; Kroeber 1935: 55). The author is aware of only one reference to a method of preparation that might darken the fruit with heat. The Kaiparowits Paiute would "clean" the fruit with hot ashes to improve the flavor, but otherwise prepared them similarly (I. Kelly 1964: 153).

In the Late Archaic sites of Los Ojitos and Dondaldson in the Cienega Valley of southeastern Arizona, the carbonized stones were recovered in flotation samples (Huckell 1995: 90).

Apiaceae (Parsley Family)

At High Rolls Cave two excavation units from East Cluster A, Stratum 2, each had a single mericarp. One (FS 773) was uncarbonized and the other (FS 795) was carbonized. Pollen in a human coprolite indicates consumption (Appendix B.4). The family level of identification makes ethnographic comparisons of little value.

Apocynaceae (Dogbane Family)

Dogbane (Apocynum)
Dogbane or Indian hemp grows in open or disturbed ground between 1,372 m and 2,745 m (Hutchins 1974: 367-368). *Apocynum suksdorfii*, a perennial that ascends to 1.8 m in height, was collected at 2,047 m elevation in a marshy area in Fresnal Canyon.

At Fresnal Shelter when screening Square C 29 level 6, five splints 3 cm to 7 cm long from the same type of stem were recovered (01. C29.131). The details of cellular structure of the stem cross section compare favorably with *Apocynum*. The one segment with the shredding exterior fibers matches the appearance of stems of *Apocynum* collected after frost. The presence of fibers on only one splint suggests the pieces were discarded following removal of the fibers. The manufacture of cordage from *Apocynum* is to be anticipated. McBrinn (2005: 53) speculates that cordage from Fresnal Shelter that appears processed differently is dogbane.

The Southern Paiute use *Apocynum* for tump lines on burden baskets (I. Kelly 1964: 81) and for the twined weft of rabbit skin blankets (I. Kelly 1964: 68). Dogbane or Indian hemp was in common use in the Southwest in the 19th century.

The Indians of Southern Utah, California, and Arizona use the fiber prepared from the stems of this plant to make rope, twine and nets; and before the advent of Europeans it was used in the manufacture of various articles of clothing. In order to remove the fibre the wood stems are first soaked in water, the bast with the bark is then easily removed. The latter being washed off, leaves a soft, silky fiber of a yellowish brown color which is very strong and durable. I have seen ropes made of it that have been in constant use for years. (Palmer 1878: 649)

In northwestern Nevada, Paiute men collected bundles of *Apocynum* plants after the plants had shed their leaves from the first frost (Wheat 1967: 15), just as the Fresnal specimens evidently were. As such, the *Apocynum* represents a late fall or winter visit or stay at Fresnal Shelter. The Paiute considered stalks that stood in the field for more than a year too weak to use. Men selected the tall stalks, scraped off the thin reddish stem epidermis, and split the stem lengthwise. The pith was cracked in short sections and loosened from the fiber. If any moisture were left in the pith, it would not break easily (Wheat 1967: 55-57).

Apocynum fiber for cord making was recovered in Seminole Canyon, Site 1, in Val Verde County, near Del Rio, Texas from a pre-corn, preceramic context (Pearce and Jackson 1933: 135). Archaeological *Apocynum* cordage was found in the vicinity of El Paso, Texas (Roberts 1930: 11). Cordage for snares was made of both *Apocynum* and *Yucca* in the Hueco area (Cosgrove 1947: 137). Cordage of *Apocynum* is reported in a Basketmaker cave in Kane County, Utah (Nusbaum 1922: 103). At Gatecliff Shelter in Monitor Valley, Nevada in a post A.D.1300 level, *Apocynum* cordage was recovered as well as wrapped bundles of heavily macerated *Apocynum* fibers cached within a grass bundle (Thomas 1983b: 498). What is possibly a netting fragment represents a high level of craftsmanship with extreme maceration of fiber and 3.5 to 8 twists per cm (Thomas 1983b: 280, 288). Not even the recent archaeological references provide criteria used in what may be difficult identifications. Bast fibers of a tall, herbaceous plant found in a Basketmaker II site in Durango, Colorado could not be satisfactorily compared to *Apocynum* or milkweed (*Asclepias*) and remain unidentified (Jones and Fonner 1954: 104).

Asteraceae (Sunflower Family)

A small residue of unidentified taxa is sparsely represented in the shelter.

Desert holly (Acourtia nana = Perezia nana)
Desert holly is a low, perennial herb that grows on dry plains, mesas, and slopes from 1,372 m to 1,982 m elevation (Hutchins 1974: 556). At Fresnal Shelter a round, spiny edged leaf of desert holly came from flotation sample 01.B28W.8 Unit B and from a screen, 01.C29.234. I found no reference for use as food for this plant.

Ragweed (Ambrosia confertiflora)
Ragweed occupies disturbed ground between 1,372 m and 1,982 m (Hutchins 1974: 460) and has tiny fruits bearing as many as 10 hooked spines that aid in their transport. At High Rolls Cave ragweed occurs as a single fruit in East Cluster B in FS 67, Stratum 3 and in FS 139, Stratum 2. No indications of economic use are present.

False tarragon (Artemisia dracunculus type)
False tarragon, a perennial herb, ranges from 1,068 m to 2,745 m in open coniferous forests (Kearney and Peebles 1942: 1002). It has been more recently described growing in moist, open slopes and meadows and near streams in the Sacramento Mountains (Hutchins 1974: 465). The latest habitat description may be due to the historically increased density of conifer-ous forests affected by both fire control and overgrazing. I am familiar with false tarragon as a plant of disturbed ground, typically viewing patches of it along the railroad right of way between Roswell and Portales, but also along roadsides in pinyon-juniper country. The plant bears its tiny (1 mm long) seeds in minute clusters on abundant heads that are only 3 mm to 4 mm in diameter. Plant identification manuals indicate it flowers between July and October. I know it as a late maturing plant (self-seeded in my flower beds for a number of years) whose seeds are ripe in Portales around mid-October or even afterward.

At Fresnal Shelter 12 heads of *Artemisia dracunculus* type were obtained from Pit 1 in Square D 27 and eight brownish heads were from a single natural stratigraphic unit.

At High Rolls Cave in East Cluster A the Stratum 3 portion of Feature 11a and an early pit (Feature 7) preserve carbonized achenes of false tarragon. Nearby within Stratum 2, additional achenes were recovered (FS 187, FS 208, FS 557, FS 773, and FS 782). In East Cluster B burned achenes discarded in pits in Stratum 3 (Features 1 and 3) represent early human use. Use extends to Stratum 2 in a thermal area in East Cluster C (Feature 19) and nearby (FS 853) as well as in the West Cluster (Feature 8).

Burned false tarragon achenes tend to shorten to 0.5 mm and broaden while shedding their longitudinal stripes, making recognition difficult. Uncarbonized achenes in FS 208 and unusually well preserved carbonized achenes in Feature 8 permitted initial identification. Mice apparently ignored them, for they are absent from FS 67. If so, the seed might be stored more safely.

False tarragon (*A. dracunculus*) and another species (*A. wrightii*) were among the seeds gathered by the Southern Paiute (Bye 1972: 92, I. Kelly 1964: 42). The ground seeds were used to make a strong-flavored mush

(Bye 1972: 92).

Rabbitbrush (Chrysothamnus spp.)

Various species of rabbitbrush grow on dry hills and plains up to about 2,135 m, but sometimes even at higher elevations (Hutchins 1974: 476-478). Rabbitbrush (*C. nauseosus*) growing along roadsides, trailsides, and arroyo margins indicate a degree of disturbance is needed for its establishment. The species has been suspected as an indicator of prehistoric fields (Dunmire and Tierney 1995: 149).

At High Rolls Cave rabbitbrush floral parts are evident in two of the upper stratigraphic units: one in East Cluster A towards the close of intensive use of the cave in Stratum 2, Layer 1 (FS 742) and in East Cluster B Stratum 1 (FS 70).

Cudweed or everlasting (Gnaphalium type)

Two species of cudweed are anticipated up to 2,135 m in the Sacramento Mountains or the nearby Capitan Mountains (Hutchins 1974: 555).

At High Rolls Cave cudweed type leaves were noted in East Cluster A in FS 773, Stratum 2, and in East Cluster B Stratum 3 (FS 67 and FS 1256) and Stratum 2 (FS 139). The leaves, especially the lower side, are covered with a short, densely matted soft white wool, described by the botanical term *tomentose*. Because the leaves have little apparent use to humans and they are in *the mouse pantry* (FS 67), their presence serves as a potential indicator of rodent activity.

Sunflower (Helianthus annuus type)

Sunflower grows in disturbed ground from 1,372 m to 2,745 m elevation (Hutchins 1974: 544). A specimen was obtained from Fresnal Canyon at 2,028 m. The botanical structure (pappus) needed to distinguish sunflower from goldeneye (*Viguiera*) drops readily from the achene and is rarely recovered in archaeological material.

Archaeological achenes from Fresnal Shelter that were at least 4 mm long and glabrous were classifieds as sunflower (*Helianthus annuus* type) and those 2 mm to 3 mm long with appressed pubescence and high, symetrical shoulders were classed as goldeneye (*Viguiera dentata* type). The use of the word *type* acknowledges that other species may have achenes that mimic these. The apparent distinction was based on four modern field collections in Fresnal Canyon identified by Charles B. Heiser and deposited with the Indiana University Herbarium (Appendix A.2).

At Fresnal Shelter sunflower type achenes were recovered in 7 of 10 natural stratigraphic units and in five of seven pits (Tables A.5 and A.6). Most of the achenes were whole, but in Square D 27, Pit 6, longitudinal halves and longitudinal strips were present. There were no carbonized achenes. Human use of the achenes is uncertain.

Although the Paiute parched and ground the achenes (Jones and Fonner 1954: 96; Palmer 1878: 602) it is possible the archaeological seed was neither hulled nor parched. Cowboy Cave, an Archaic site in southeastern Utah, has unroasted seed with the hulls present but split away (Jennings 1980: 208). Sunflower seeds have been used in the Great Basin and the northern periphery of the southwestern United States (Jones and Fonner 1954: 96).

Marsh elder (Iva ambrosiaefolia type)

Modern specimens of the plant have been collected by the author between 1,678 m and 1,962 m elevation in Fresnal Canyon. The species has been described as infrequent in the Trans-Pecos deserts in late summer and fall, having a distribution that extends south to the states of Durango and Zacatecas, Mexico (Correll and Johnston 1970: 1629).

At Fresnal Shelter the tiny achenes (about 1.2 mm long) of *I. ambrosiaefolia* type were found in all 10 natural stratigraphic units along the B coordinate and in each of the seven pits in Square D 27 (Tables A.5 and A.6). A handful of *Iva* achenes and related chaff of bracts and flowers (01.C29.126) was recovered prior to screening, but retention by the screens was rare. Despite the dark brown or black exteriors observed in some achenes, none bears evidence of parching or burning on the interior of the thin coat. Other achenes have tan, corky coats that probably indicate immaturity (Correll and Johnston 1970: 1629).

At High Rolls Cave, the achenes, while not numerous, occur uncarbonized in a variety of samples. In East Cluster A, they are in Stratum 2 (FS 208, FS 557, FS 773, and FS 805) and in East Cluster B in Stratum 2 (FS 139) and in Stratum 3 (FS 67 and 1256). One achene appears carbonized in a thermal deposit (Feature 19) but is uncarbonized in another (Feature 11b). It also occurs in a pit (Feature 5).

Given the ubiquity of this tiny achene it is not surprising one might accidentally be part of a thermal feature. With this possible single exception, the lack of seed processing evidence negates its use as a dietary item. The plant might have been valued for its leaves for some other purpose and the achenes are simply discards.

Almost all the reported uses of *Iva* in the southwestern United Sates are medicinal. The Shoshone use *I. axillaris* for stomach ache and cramps and the Paiute make a plaster of the mashed leaves for sores and itches (Train and others 1941: 91). Chamberlin (1964 [1911]: 372) indicates *I. xanthifolia* being used but indicates linguistic confusion with *Chenopodium*. *I. xanthifolia* is used by the Navajo to relieve itchy skin (Wyman and Harris 1941: 64) and as a poultice for boils (Wyman and Harris 1951: 48). The same species is used by the Ramah Navajo for coughs, the flu, and witch protection (Vestal 1952: 52).

Carbonized *Iva xanthifolia* achenes derive from Basketmaker III contexts near Cimarron, New Mexico (Kirkpatrick and Ford 1977). In the eastern United States, *I. annua* was apparently cultivated in prehistoric times for its edible achene (Asch and Asch 1978). The achenes could have been roasted or boiled.

Mariola (Parthenium incanum)

The rather bitter, aromatic low shrub grows on the lower south-facing slopes near the bottom of Fresnal Canyon, along the path to Fresnal Shelter. It can be found elsewhere growing in dry plains and hills from 1,372 m to 1,830 m elevation (Hutchins 1974: 547).

At Fresnal Shelter the achenes were found in 10 of the natural stratigraphic units along the B coordinate and in five of the seven pits in Square D 27 (Tables A.5 and A.6). The achenes are so small it is a wonder they were retained by the screens in four levels (Table A.3). No modification of the achene by parching was observed and no ethnographic references commenting on edibility were located. Mariola evidently was not a subsistence item. Mariola was recovered in wood rat nests in Marble Canyon (Van Devender and others 1984, Table 2). Its distribution in Fresnal Shelter may be related to wood rat activity.

Crown beard (Verbesina enceloides type)

This flower of disturbed habitats grows from 1,372 m to 2,135 m elevation (Hutchins 1974: 550).

At Fresnal Shelter an achene of *Verbesina* originated in a natural stratigraphic unit. The isolated recovery in Fresnal Shelter bears no strong implication for human consumption.

At High Rolls Cave in East Cluster A, 15 achenes were recovered in Stratum 2 (FS 773), and one in Stratum 2, Layer 2 (FS 795). In East Cluster B four achenes were recovered in *the mouse pantry* (FS 67, Stratum 3). The apparent interest of mice in the achene may explain its distribution in the cave. No ethnographic references to the use of *Verbesina* for food were found.

Goldeneye (Viguiera dentata)

Goldeneye, a perennial, grows on dry slopes and in canyons 1,372 m to 2,135 m elevation (Hutchins 1974: 551). Two species of *Viguiera* were collected in Fresnal Canyon, *V. dentata* at 1,678 m elevation, and *V. stenoloba* at 1,830 m. Modern *V. dentata* could be the descendant of prehistoric populations in the canyon.

At Fresnal Shelter three heads of the *V. dentata* type with achenes still adherent were recovered from screens (01.C29.234, 01.C31.18, 01.D28.72). An achene from Square D 27 Pit 5 had the distinctive pappus (fimbriate squamellae) adhering to it. *Viguiera dentata* type achenes were recovered in 5 of 10 natural stratigraphic units and in all seven pits (Tables A.5 and A.6). All the achenes are whole, although some may show signs of insect damage or mechanical abrasion by the loss of some pubescence on the achene.

Archaeological achenes at Fresnal Shelter, which were 2 mm to 3 mm long with appressed pubescence and high symmetrical shoulders, were classed as goldeneye (*V. dentata* type). Achenes of *V. stenoloba* are glabrous and 3.5 mm long (Correll and Johnston 1970: 1647). When examining the material from High Rolls Cave, I thought the loose achenes of both sunflower (*Helianthus*) and goldeneye (*Viguiera* spp) overlapped each other in size, mottling, and hairiness and were easily confused even when uncarbonized. Pending better criteria to tell the species apart, I combined the two genera into a single identification at High Rolls Cave.

At High Rolls Cave two excavation units in East Cluster A Stratum 2 have two achenes each (FS 557 and FS 773), and there are six in an intermediate position between Cluster A and Cluster C in FS 853. A single achene comes from Feature 5. Single carbonized achenes come from two thermal contexts: in East Cluster B (Feature 23) and in East Cluster C (Feature 19).

The mouse pantry sample (FS 67) contains an array of 85 sunflower or goldeneye achenes. In addition, many disc flowers, identifiable only to the sunflower tribe, have the floral tubes partially eaten, leaving only the base and a bulge for the ovary. Floral heads with chaffy bracts that would hold the achenes are absent. However, the presence of both flowers and fruit suggests the plants grew within the home range of mice and were harvested by them. Presumably the mouse climbed the stalk in order to acquire both flowers and achenes. Longitudinal split strips of achene coats attest to the method of preparation by mice.

Because one achene in FS 67 appears partly burned on the shoulder, it may have come from a human harvest. The accumulation of achenes suggests this category was an accessible part of mouse diet. Consequently, both exterior sources and human stores of the achenes might be subject to considerable mouse predation. Nevertheless, people may have harvested some and parched them as revealed in thermal Features 19 and 23.

Achenes of *Viguiera multiflora* were formerly eaten in Utah and Nevada (Chamberlin 1964[1911]: 373; Yanovsky 1936: 63). Another hint of palatability comes from the utilization of the leaves of *V. helianthoides* as a green by the Tarahumara (Pennington 1963: 128). In contrast, the pungent roots of *V. decurrens* are used as a fish poison (Pennington 1963: 110). The resemblance of *V. dentata* to the sunflower is striking, although the heads and flowers are smaller. The visual analogy suggests a use similar to the annual sunflower. Actual evidence for using sunflower (*Helianthus*) seeds in Fresnal Shelter is not all that clear.

Berbericaceae (Barberry Family)

Algerita (Berberis fremontii)

Algerita with its small, holly-like evergreen leaves grows on dry pinyon-juniper hillsides and mesas 1,678 m to 2,440 m elevation (Hutchins 1974: 190). Algerita grows on the same slope as Fresnal Shelter and probably is the source for scattered leaves. Vigorous shrubs bear red berries in the fall. A yellow dye can be made from the wood and roots (Kearney and Peebles 1942: 332).

At Fresnal Shelter spiny leaf fragments came from flotation 01.B29E.2, Unit B; 01.B29E.23, Unit CC; and 01.B30E.14, Unit CC'. A fruit stone was recovered in Square D 27 Pit 5 (Table A.6) and another from a screened level (01.C26.85).

At High Rolls Cave, algerita leaves were recovered from East Cluster A (Stratum 2, FS 557) and East Cluster B (Stratum 1, FS 70).

Boraginaceae (Borage Family)

Stickseed (Lappula redowskii type)

Stickseed grows on disturbed ground from 1,372 m to 2,745 m elevation (Hutchins 1974: 394). Each nutlet bears a crown of barbed prickles that aid in its transport. One armed nutlet of this borage was recovered in East Cluster A (FS 742). Another stickseed comes from *the mouse pantry* (FS 67) in East Cluster B.

Brassicaceae (Mustard Family)

Peppergrass (Lepidium spp.)

Many species of peppergrass in the Sacramento Mountains thrive on disturbed ground over a wide range in elevation and have a relatively long period of flowering (Hutchins 1974: 205-206). Mustards, however, are spring bloomers.

A seed resembling peppergrass (*Lepidium* type) appears carbonized in thermal Feature 13 in the West Cluster and another carbonized seed is in FS 853, intermediate between East Clusters A and C. What may be a variant seed is uncarbonized in East Cluster A (FS 742). Three coprolites from children contain pollen from the mustard family (Appendix B.4).

Seeds of peppergrass (*Lepidium*) were used as food and flavoring by Arizona Indians (Kearney and Peebles 1960: 332). The seeds were recovered in archaeological sites from Pueblo I to Pueblo III times in northeastern Arizona in the St. Johns area in 10 of 17 sites (Gasser 1982b: 34).

Cactaceae (Cactus Family)

Pincushion cactus (Coryphantha strobiliformis)

When Lyman Benson examined representative cacti from Fresnal Shelter in 1971, he noted *Coryphantha strobiliformis* (01.C29.95, level 4). The species grows in grassy limestone areas around 1,220 m (Martin and Hutchins 1980: 1352). At Fresnal Shelter the classification of a few tubercles of *Mammillaria* type cactus (Tables A.5 and A.6) should include the similar appearing *Coryphantha*.

Barrel (Echinocactus) and hedgehog (Echinocereus spp.) cacti

Turk's head barrel cactus (*Echinocactus horizonthalonius*) grows on dry alkaline hills from 1,372 m to 1,678 m elevation (Hutchins 1974: 326). My identification of spine clusters and stems of Turk's head barrel cactus were verified by Lyman Benson. Hedgehog cacti grow in dry, rocky places in the Sacramento Mountains up to 2,440 m elevation (Hutchins 1974: 327). The spines easily detach from the succulent, tasty fruits at maturity, greatly aiding dispersal.

In Fresnal Shelter, 9 of the 10 natural stratigraphic units contain the spine bearing areoles of *Echinocactus horizonthalonius*.

All but 1 of 45 areoles have spines reduced to stubs by burning. Six of the seven pits in Square D 27 also have areoles with burned spines. *E. horizonthalonius* is present in 19 of 43 screened levels (see Tables A.3, A.5, and A.6). The spines range so much in size that it appears that plants of very small diameter were exploited as well as larger ones.

Lyman Benson thought several cacti to be a variety of *Echinocereus pectinatus* but the missing upper areoles would be needed for critical identification (01.B26.36, 01.B27.43 level 3, and 01.C29.154 level 6). The reference to other specimens of *E. pectinatus* in the tables in Appendix A can only be considered provisional. Five of the 10 natural strata along the B Grid line also contain areoles resembling *Echinocereus pectinatus* with 15 of 20 examples showing a similar charring of the spines (see Table A.5).

The screens retained cacti showing the manner of their procurement and preparation. Two cacti have the taproot sharply severed from the stem (01.C29.193 and 01.C29.154). Several *E. horizonthalonius* specimens have their tops (stems) cleanly severed, leaving only the woody stem base and roots (01.D28.18 and 01.C29.154). Cacti like *Echinocereus pectinatus* have ashes clinging to roasted epidermal tissue that has missing spines (01.C29.38). Other examples (01.C29.205) show strips of roasted epidermis and roots severed and burned. Only one stem of *Echinocactus horizonthalonius* is longitudinally split. Its flesh is intact but the spines are burned to the base (01.C29.154).

Several methods of preparation recorded in the literature would produce the modification in the cacti deposited in Fresnal Shelter. The Southern Paiute of the Kaibab Plateau of Arizona would toss the body of the hedgehog cactus (*Echinocereus engelmannii*) into the fire to remove the spines and skin (I. Kelly 1964: 45). Palmer noted the use of the stem of *Echinocactus johnsoni* as a source of food among

the Southern Paiute (Bye 1972: 97). The single archaeological example of a longitudinally split stem of *Echinocactus* may represent the application of the flesh as a poultice, as do the Kaibab Paiute (I. Kelly 1939: 153).

In northern and western New Mexico hedgehog cacti have been found in similar condition in other archaeological sites. The plant remains from Pindi Pueblo included the outer charred rinds of *Echinocereus* (Stubbs and Stallings 1953: 141). Fragments of the shoot and root crowns come from Cordova Cave (Kaplan 1963: 354), and the genus is reported in Tularosa Cave (Cutler 1952: 479) and Jemez Cave (Alexander and Reiter 1935: 64).

At High Rolls Cave hedgehog cactus seed was recovered in Stratum 2 from East Cluster A (FS 742 and Feature 11b) and intermediate between East Clusters A and C (FS 853) as well as in the Stratum 3 *mouse pantry* (FS 67). The latter location suggests it was an item in rodent diet when available. The fruits have been collected by the Navajo (Vestal 1952: 37) and the Apache (Castetter and Opler 1936: 41), as well as by the Acoma and Laguna (Swank 1932: 42).

Prickly pear and cholla (Opuntia)

Species of prickly pear generally range between 1,372 m and 2,288 m in the Sacramento and White mountains as does the cane or tree cholla, *Opuntia imbricata* (Hutchins 1974: 331-332). The eastern prickly pear *(O. humifusa)* no longer inhabits New Mexico. It grows on prairies, open woodlands, and rock ledges on various soils in moister parts of the Great Plains. It is found in the eastern third of Kansas and Oklahoma, western Missouri and from Minnesota to Florida, with widely scattered stations beyond the Rocky Mountains (Barkley 1986: 157). The seed margin is characterized as much less than 1 mm broad and firm and even (Barkley 1986: 157).

In 1971, Lyman Benson identified a cholla

fruit, probably *Opuntia imbricata*, and the fruit of the eastern prickly pear (*Opuntia humifusa*, as *O. compressa*) from Square C 29 level 3 of Fresnal Shelter (cat. no. 60 and 65). Level 3 has radiocarbon dated charcoal and one maize kernel from a cache of 239 (Table 3.3). The whole fruits could have been rodent transported as might the one dated kernel in a cache.

At Fresnal Shelter the recovery of prickly pear cactus seed (*Platyopuntia*) in 23 of 43 screened levels and in 8 of 10 natural stratigraphic units and in all seven pits (Tables A.3, A.5, and A.6) suggests the utilization of the succulent fruits. Of the 28 seeds from natural strata, three are carbonized.

In High Rolls Cave what at first seems like an extensive record of prickly pear seeds (8 of 11 excavation units) is comprised half the time of either single whole seeds (FS 557, FS 742, and FS 1256) or single seeds that have had the embryo removed (FS 187 and FS 805). In FS 67, one seed is unmodified but six others have had the embryo removed from one flat face of the seed. In FS 139 (Stratum 2), the seed is burned on one face but the embryo is also excavated from it. The seeds in FS 795 have dark brown exteriors, but other aspects of their condition may indicate decay. Features 5 and 22 have uncarbonized seed that appears eroded until they almost have a furry appearance. Since some wood rats are known to swallow the seed whole, it may go through the digestive tract relatively intact (Spencer and Spencer 1941). Perhaps this is true of humans too!

Three Stratum 3 features in East Clusters A and B provide possible evidence of humanly parched seed: Features 7 and 11a retained a carbonized embryo and a seed while Feature 3 had two carbonized seeds as well as a burned fragment of prickly pear tissue; the only really good indication we have that joints were roasted. In Stratum 2 (FS 208) the lone carbonized prickly pear seed may have been removed from a parching tray and deposited in the cold ashes.

High Rolls Cave has inconclusive examples of human consumption of prickly pear pads. In East Cluster A, a small stem fragment and two pieces of epidermis with glochids could be from either prickly pear or cholla in FS 208 (Excavation Unit 13), as is a single areole with glochids in FS 773 (excavation unit 63). The remnants could be the by-products of rodent consumption. Wood rats will sometimes use prickly pear joints to fortify their homes as well.

The burned seeds from Fresnal Shelter and High Rolls Cave imply people had some role in fruit consumption. Carbonized seeds of prickly pear may result from accidental burning when the seeds were parched prior to cracking them on the metate. Missing embryos indicates rodents utilized the seed for their own purposes. Presumably people discarded the seeds after eating the fruit pulp most of the time and made use of the seed only when thrift was a necessity. High Rolls Cave evidenced such behavior in Stratum 3 and sporadically later.

At Fresnal Shelter a number of epidermal fragments of stem pads recovered from the screens have spine bases and glochids that appear singed (01.C28.106, Level 7; 01.C29.127, Level 5; 01.C30.77, Level 4; 01.C31.2, Level 1; and 01.C28.114, Level 6). Other *Opuntia* stem pad fragments unmarked by fire (Table A.3) may have been gathered by either rodents or humans. We see evidence of more frequent consumption of roasted prickly pear pads at Fresnal Shelter than High Rolls Cave.

It is worth noting that cooking evidently increases the palatability of prickly pear stems or pads. At Acoma and Laguna the joints of *O. polycantha* (prickly pear) are singed in hot coals and boiled with dried sweet corn in the winter (Swank 1932: 57). The Gosiute roasted the pads of the same species in hot coals after removing the spines (Chamberlin 1964 [1911]:

375). Since no pottery was recovered at Fresnal Shelter and High Rolls Cave, the Gosiute custom would account for joint fragments with singed glochids best.

The Walapai separated the prickly pear seeds from the pulp, and dried the pulp for storage. After parching and pounding, the seeds were eaten or stored (Kroeber 1935: 50). The Southeastern Yavapai followed a similar practice but did not often save the seed (E. Gifford 1932: 210). The dried fruit pulp was packed in a basket or kept in a dry place like a pit in a cave. The bottom and sides of the pit were lined with straw and the cached fruit covered with straw and stones or earth.

Coprolites from Tamaulipas, Mexico show that some epidermal tissue was roasted and some was not prior to consumption (Callen 1965: 342). In southwestern Texas between 800 B.C. and A.D. 500, eight coprolites contained evidence of eating prickly pear cactus fruits, cactus stems, and cactus flowers in conjunction with agave flowers (Bryant 1974: 413). In the lower Pecos river of Texas, coprolites regularly contain fiber from the flattened stems or pads. Most seeds when recovered are fragmented, as if they had been pounded prior to consumption (Sobolik 1988). A Late Archaic coprolite from Culbertson County, Texas has fragmented seeds of prickly pear frequently charred compared to whole seeds (Holloway 1983).

Capparidaceae (Caper Family)

Rocky Mountain beeweed (Cleome serrulata)
Rocky Mountain beeweed grows on plains, mesas, and hills from 1,372 m to 2,440 m elevation (Hutchins 1974: 214). A single seed of Rocky Mountain beeweed (*Cleome serrulata*) was recovered from Square D 27, Pit 6 (Table A.6).

The uses of *Cleome serrulata* as a boiled green have been summarized by Adams and others (2002) and Castetter (1935: 24). The

consumption of the dried seeds in winter mush by Acoma and Laguna (Swank 1932: 37) is less well known. Charred *Cleome* seeds have been recovered in Ancestral Pueblo archaeological sites in the Four Corners Area, including the lower Chaco river of New Mexico (Toll 1983, Table 17.5).

Chenopodiaceae (Goosefoot Family)

Four-wing saltbush (Atriplex canescens)
Four-wing saltbush can tolerate strongly saline soils in and near the Tularosa Basin as well as soils rich in clay, sand, or gravel. It grows on dry hills and mesas in the Sacramento Mountains up to 1,982 m in elevation (Hutchins 1974: 144).

At Fresnal Shelter every one of the 10 natural stratigraphic units along the B grid line contains the remains of the winged fruits or expanded calyx of *A. canescens*. Typically only the stubs of veins protrude from the central portion of the dry fruit. All but 5 of 156 fruits have their bracts or wings eroded from them in just such a manner. Two fruits are carbonized and five appear parched. Since the delicate utricle caps of *Amaranthus* and the perianth of *Chenopodium* are preserved in the same strata, no depositional conditions should be anticipated that preclude the preservation of the fruiting bracts of four-wing saltbush. The erosion would have had to take place prior to deposition. Seventeen of 43 screened grid squares and each of the seven pits contain eroded fruits (see Tables A.3 and A.6).

At High Rolls Cave four-wing saltbush fruits were found singly in Stratum 2 East Cluster A (FS 208), East Cluster B, (FS 742 and Feature 5), and in an intermediate position between Clusters A and C (FS 853). All but the last specimen were ragged in appearance, but were essentially whole. The fruit wings in FS 853 were missing but the remaining veins on the core did not appear chewed. The fruits apparently were lost from branches brought for another purpose.

Most ethnographic references document the use of the seed of various species of *Atriplex* for food (Stevenson 1915: 66; Yanovsky 1936: 21). However, at Acoma and Laguna both the seeds and the expanded calyx of *A. argentea* are eaten as food and for the salty taste (Swank 1932: 31). I found the papery fruit bracts of *A. canescens* to have an agreeable flavor. The chewing of the dry fruits to obtain the taste and nutrients left them as eroded as the ones found in the Fresnal Shelter deposits. I do not know if other animals would eat saltbush fruits in just such a manner. Fourteen fruits of *A. canescens* have been recovered from a shelter (CS561) occupied solely by animals in Chevelon Canyon, Arizona (Briuer 1977: 270). The reported erosion of some fruits may have been created by moisture now in the lower levels of the shelter, but insufficient details are provided to determine this.

Goosefoot (Chenopodium type)

Goosefoots are annual herbs that are frequently found in disturbed ground from 1,372 m to 2,440 m elevation (Hutchins 1974: 146-7).

At Fresnal Shelter *Chenopodium* seed or perianth derives from 6 of 10 natural stratigraphic units along the B coordinate and from six of seven pits in Square D 27 (Tables A.5 and A.6). Only one seed from a pit appears carbonized. A few seeds were recovered in screens by chance, for the seeds are smaller than the mesh (Table A.3).

At High Rolls Cave *Chenopodium* seed has been recovered in 10 of 12 excavation units and in 13 of 17 features. Seeds identifiable as *Chenopodium* were so well represented in flotation from High Rolls Cave that counting their numbers proved impractical. The harvest of wild seed persisted throughout the occupation of the cave.

The seeds of species of *Chenopodium*

were used as a source of food by a variety of tribes in the western and southwestern United States (Castetter 1935: 21, 23; Yanovsky 1936: 22). The northeastern Yavapai plucked the mature tops and spread them on a flat surface for threshing. The winnowed seeds were parched with coals in a basket, ground on a metate, boiled, and eaten (Gifford 1936: 256). The Akimel O'odham (Pima) prepared the seed by parching and grinding, after which the flour might be eaten as pinole or combined with other meal (F. Russell 1908: 73). The Navajo threshed the seeds from dried plants on a blanket, winnowed them, ground them to loosen the perianth, winnowed them once again, washed, dried, and finally ground them into a flour to be used in combination with maize flour (Vestal 1952: 25). Vestal's account is so detailed that it opens the possibility that the seeds were not necessarily parched. Castetter (1935: 23), in describing the former use of the seeds by the Rio Grande Pueblos, indicates the seeds were ground *or* parched and then used in making cakes or mush. Both references invite speculation that parching might constitute an optional step in preparation, as is apparently the case with *Amaranthus*.

In the Cienega Valley of southeastern Arizona, the Late Archaic Donaldson and Los Ojitos sites contained numerous seeds of *Chenopodium* obtained through flotation (Huckell 1995). At Gatecliff Shelter, Monitor Valley, Nevada some of the earliest evidence of human plant use in the shelter is recorded from Horizon 9 (1450 B.C. to 1350 B.C.) in conjunction with numerous grinding stones. Hearth B contained juniper and *Chenopodiium* seeds (Thomas 1983b: 155, 473-474).

Cheno-ams

The artificial category cheno-ams comprises seeds lacking the criteria that distinguish the genera *Chenopodium* and *Amaranthus*. The term is applied to poorly preserved archaeological specimens.

At Fresnal Shelter some cheno-am seeds are typical of those processed by people. Of 180 seeds, one is popped, one is carbonized, one is cracked, and 37 are deflated (Table A.5). The deflated seeds probably represent immature ones that drifted free from the heavier seed during winnowing. The popped and carbonized seed could result from parching. The cracked seed probably came from pounding or grinding, for only a direct hit on the small seed coat would be expected to crack it contrary to the natural suture line.

At High Rolls Cave cheno-ams seeds derive from all samples from excavation units and features except Feature 5 and Feature 7. Mixtures of carbonized and uncarbonized seed come from the excavation units. The seeds that are clearly carbonized come from an ash pit (Feature 9) and two thermal areas (Features 8 and 11). A record as extensive as this, from all stratigraphic units and nearly all contexts, underlines its importance as a food source.

Tiny goosefoot and pigweed seeds (less than 2 mm in diameter) have a similar morphology. To visualize the seed coat imagine two pie pans with their orifices joined. The seed coats tend to split apart along the perimeter of the pie pan orifices when they degrade. Inside the pie pan covers, next to the rim, is a curved Italian sausage, which is the embryo. The center of the pie pan is filled with a white, starchy nutritious cake, the endosperm. Often, when the fresh seed is burned, the endosperm in the middle swells and splits the seed coat apart. Sometimes the seed coat remains joined as if by a hinge.

In FS 853, some burned and unburned cheno-am seeds lack endosperm. In addition, one roasted larva was recovered. It appears the seed was stored long enough to become infested with insects. Most of the time we infer that seeds were stored and do not recover direct evidence. Historic seed collectors parched seed prior to storage. If this custom were followed at High Rolls Cave, the process was either not consistent or not efficient. When larvae were not killed by parching, the depredations into stored seed diminished its food value.

In the same sample (FS 853) some cheno-ams have the uncarbonized seed coat separated from the interior. Given that the seeds measure about 1 mm in diameter, the technology of seed coat removal appears beyond the control of the human occupants of the cave. I postulate that the seed swelled on imbibing water, and the seed coat cracked and peeled back. The condition of cheno-ams lacking seed coats even in samples containing more delicate papery utricle caps and bases or perianth may serve as a reminder that these now dry samples were at one time subject to considerable moisture, even if transitory in nature.

Among the exfoliating seed coats of cheno-ams in FS 853 were six that looked thin and fragile compared to the others. They may be a product of degradation, but also may represent cultivated amaranth seed bearing thin coats that were not recognizable.

Convolvulaceae (Morning Glory Family)

Morning glory (Ipomoea)

Morning glory species such as *I. purpurea* or *I. hirsutula* will grow on disturbed ground over a broad range in elevation while other species may be restricted to moist ground or even dry slopes (Hutchins 1974: 380-381). Five modern species of *Ipomoea* grow in the Sacramento Mountains (Hutchins 1974: 380).

Ipomoea seed was recovered from a screened grid (01.C29.58) and from two flotation samples (01.B29E.23, Unit CC and 01.B29E.25, Unit D). There can be no doubt that the dark seed from Unit D is carbonized, as the coat chipped by a dissecting needle revealed a carbonized layer beneath.

A single carbonized seed of *Ipomoea*

came from Los Ojitos, a Late Archaic site along a tributary of Cienega Creek in southeastern Arizona (Huckell 1995: 90). Three carbonized seeds of *Ipomoea costellata* were recovered from the Escalante Ruin group in southern Arizona, an apparently new record in Hohokam sites (Hall 1974: 204).

Although the author has discovered no reference to the edibility or other recognized property of the seed in the American Southwest, deeper in Mexico the seeds of morning glory (*Ipomoea violacea*) and the Aztec ololiuqui (*Rivea corymbosa*) have been utilized for their psychoactive attributes (Hofman 1972: 255, Schultes and Hofman 1980: 244). The Zapotec Indians grind the seeds of *Ipomoea*, soak them in water and drink the strained liquid (Schultes and Hofman 1979: 163). Elsewhere in Mexico, *I. pedicillaris* seeds were used as a purgative (Altschul 1973: 235). Various species of *Convolvulus* and *Ipomoea* contain derivatives of ergoline, from which the active principle of lysergic acid (LSD) is derived (Hofman 1972: 257). The data suggest that any usage probably took place in a medicinal or ceremonial context rather than as a component of normal diet. Other psychotropic genera have been reported in early shelter deposits in northeastern Mexico and the Trans-Pecos of Texas, and at least one cache suggests ritual use (Adovasio and Fry 1976).

Cucurbitaceae (Squash Family)

Squash and buffalo gourd (Cucurbita spp.)
The buffalo gourd (*C. foetidissima*) grows in disturbed ground and plains 1,372 m to 1,982 m (Hutchins 1974: 453). The light, dry fruits, which are the size of a tennis ball, are well adapted to spread by floodwaters to a new location in canyons and on alluvial fans. I have observed buffalo gourd fruits in late fall and winter collapse from decay instead of being opened by rodents. The edible seeds in buffalo gourd fruits are surrounded by a fibrous pulpy matrix rich in bitter cucurbitacin compounds that would repel rodents. They would find it difficult to transport whole gourds any distance.

At Fresnal Shelter the seed coats of *Cucurbita* were recovered in 8 of 10 natural stratigraphic units along the B coordinate. Of the 26 seed coats recovered, 19 were split in half along natural suture lines. One of the split seed coats shows evidence of parching. Remains of 14 seeds were also recovered in five of seven pits in Square D 27, primarily as seed coats split along natural suture lines. *Cucurbita* seed coats were retrieved in 33 of 43 screened levels. The bulk of the seed coats belong to the buffalo gourd (*C. foetidissima*). Several were exceptionally narrow with a sharp, pointed apex (01.C30.28g.) but were within the broad range of variation of *C. foetidissima*. More importantly, the seed coat anatomy matched the wild species rather than the introduced cultivated melon, *Cucumis melo*. The screens also contained many pieces of exocarp or shell that had thin, cleanly broken edges and peduncle scars that matched the small size of *Cucurbita foetidissima*. The broken edges of the exocarp appear to come from fully dried (unwarped) fruit, which becomes available a month or two after frost. Since Fresnal Shelter is near the elevation limit for the species, the bulk of the fruits would have been obtained down canyon.

The cucurbit material that might possibly belong to cultivated squash or pumpkin comes primarily from the uppermost levels of the shelter. A few pieces of exocarp are unevenly thickened and corky in texture (01.D30.4, Level 1). The edge of one piece appears rounded and sanded and is almost a full mm thick (01.D29.30, Level 2). Another piece of thick exocarp has warped inward on drying and has a seed buried in the fibrous matrix (01.D29.30, Level 2) One exocarp has a broader curvature than can be found in buffalo gourds, but it may simply be flattened (01.D29.14, Level 1). The base of one peduncle has such a large diameter (1.5 cm) that it could be from a cultivated type (01.D30.34).

Only one exocarp fragment comes from a deep enough level to broach the question of early cultivation. The fragment (01.C29.103) bears a prominent floral scar 1.7 cm diameter. In order to investigate the relationship of the size of the floral scar to the size of the fruit, a collection of 75 modern *Cucurbita foetidissima* fruits was made. Of these, only nine bear floral scars 1 cm to 1.5 cm in diameter. The development of the floral scar evidently relates to the persistence of dried flower, which apparently stimulates the development of the scar tissue. In some instances the dried flower was retained after the gourd was fully mature. When this happened the flower had to be removed to measure the abnormally large scar. Since the size of the floral scar bears no relationship to the size of the fruit, no credence should be given the presence of a large floral scar as an indicator of a cultivated species.

At High Rolls Cave four seeds of the buffalo gourd (*Cucurbita foetidissima* type) were recovered from *the mouse pantry* (FS 67). I believe that they were pilfered from the human pantry rather than represent an independent acquisition. Cucurbitacins are extremely bitter. A lethal dose for a small mammal is in the neighborhood of a millionth of the animal's body weight (Nabhan 1985: 168). Before the mouse absconded with the seeds they would have been well washed in preparation for human consumption.

The utilization of *Cucurbita foetidissima* seeds for food survived in the Southwest into historic times (Corbusier 1886: 327; Palmer 1878: 651; and Rothrock 1878: 44 as *C. perennis* Gray; F. Russell 1908: 70; Sparkman 1908: 229). The Akimel O'odham roasted the seeds prior to eating them (F. Russell 1908: 70) and the Southern Paiute ground the seeds to prepare

them for mush (Bye 1972: 93).

The ethnographic literature omits vital steps needed to prepare palatable seed. In order to release the dried seed from the bitter pulp, mechanical abrasion or threshing is required followed by winnowing to concentrate the seed. Unless the seeds are well washed the bitter cucurbitacin in the surrounding pulp imparts a similar taste to the seed. Parching releases an appetizing aroma and dries the coat so it is easily pulverized. The dried seed contains 31.6 percent protein, 26 percent oil, and 31 percent fiber (Lancaster and others 1983). The coats do not readily darken or burn when parched.

The remains of buffalo gourd *(C. foetidissima)* have been recovered in southwestern New Mexico in three caves whose elevations exceed 2,000 m, which would probably indicate exploitation of a lower-elevation resource. Cordova Cave preserved the remains of buffalo gourds from preceramic levels (300 B.C. to A.D.1) to A.D. 1100 (Kaplan 1963, Table 1). Kaplan determined that the fruits had not undergone human selection for size during the occupation of the cave. At Tularosa Cave one of the most obvious wild plants used was the buffalo gourd. Many masses of fruit pulp (with the seeds absent) were recovered in some levels (Cutler 1952: 479). At Bat Cave the remains of the buffalo gourd were recovered in a preceramic level and a post-ceramic level (Smith 1950: 179).

Ericaceae (Heather Family)

Bearberry or kinnikennick (*Arctostaphylos uva-ursi*)

Bearberry is a low, prostrate shrub that grows from 2,135 m to 3,050 m on shaded or partially shaded slopes. It flowers from May to July (Martin and Hutchins 1981: 1460). I have seen it growing on the north side of the Capitan Mountains beneath an overstory of widely spaced ponderosa pines. While it has not been reported from the Sacramento Mountains, the species is expected (Hutchins 1974: 356).

Both the bearberry seed and heather family pollen were recovered from different excavation units in East Cluster A (Appendix B.1 and B.4). No other genera are expected in the Sacramento Mountains. Its modern distribution indicates the species evidently grew at a higher elevation than High Rolls Cave. The darkening by fire of 3 of 19 seeds and carbonization of one (FS 773) implies humans discarded the fruits.

Birds, bears, and other animals eat the fruits (Kearney and Peelbles 1960: 633). The species could have been eaten fresh or dried, ground and made into mush as we learn from broad ethnographic information (Yanovsky 1936: 50). The leaves have been smoked by the Navajo with mountain tobacco, *Nicotiana attenuata* (Vestal 1952: 38). How the plant was used remains equivocal, but its presence indicates journeying to higher elevations to obtain it.

Fabaceae (Pea or Legume Family)

Mesquite (Prosopis)

Only one species, *Prosopis glandulosa*, grows in the area (Hutchins 1974: 273), although *P. glandulosa* var. *torreyana* has been called through error *P. juliflora* or *P. chilensis* in many publications (Correll and Johnston 1970: 784). Low mesquite trees or shrubs grow on the slopes where Fresnal Shelter is located, near its elevation limits at 1,982 m (Hutchins 1974: 273). Steep slopes and high elevation create harsh conditions for pod production. High Rolls Cave is less suitable for mesquite. Sandy grasslands or the lower elevation canyon junctions with more favorable temperatures and ground water regimes (Table 2.1) would foster productivity (see Felger 1977: 155 and Simpson 1977: 79). Historically, a band of mesquite about 4 km wide and 48 km long fronted the Sacramento Mountains near Alamogordo (Meinzer 1927: Fig. 6).

The indehiscent pods of mesquite have a mealy, edible outer portion and a hard inner portion (endocarp) surrounding each seed. A sample of 100 pods from the junction of Fresnal Canyon and Salado Canyon contained a mean of 17 endocarps (s.d. = 2.56). Mesquite pods mature in the fall and are amenable to drying and storage.

Endocarps were recovered in abundance in Fresnal Shelter. In material excavated in Squares C and D, endocarps are present in the lowest level and in nearly every level upward (Table A.3). Endocarps were also recovered in 9 of the 10 stratigraphic units along the B coordinate and in all seven of the pits excavated in Square D 27 (Tables A.5 and A.6).

Split endocarps were far more common than burned ones. In the screened material, only one endocarp in 7,000 was carbonized and in the flotation samples another endocarp was noted as carbonized. Burned pods are believed accidental and bear no relation to food preparation. However, the state of the remaining endocarps may be relevant. In the natural stratigraphic units half the endocarps were split along natural suture lines and devoid of seed. The empty endocarps should not imply that the seed was necessarily used to that extent. Kangaroo rats (*Dipodomys*) and pocket mice (*Perognathus*) can be prolific users of mesquite seeds and wood rats collect the pods (Simpson 1977: 45). A single carbonized seed was recovered from a natural stratum (Table A.5) and more carbonized seed was recovered from four of the seven pits investigated in Square D 27. Six carbonized seeds were in the screened material (01.D30.50).

A storage cist (Table 3.2) lined with grass had numerous "seeds" (endocarps?) of mesquite imbedded in the grass lining that seems to indicate the pit once held mesquite pods. Apparently any storage was short term as I failed to note any holes in the endocarp where bruchid beetles had emerged. Apparently, the pods and sometimes the seeds were utilized in subsistence at Fresnal Shelter.

The flotation samples at High Rolls Cave may not indicate the actual importance of mesquite. While nine flotation samples have endocarps, 10 sediment samples contain mesquite pollen (Appendix B.4). Pods may have decayed in portions of the cave leaving only adherent pollen. The endocarps from Stratum 2 come primarily from six flotation samples in East Cluster A (Appendix B.1). The greatest quantity came from FS 208 and FS 773, which had 31 and 37 endocarps, respectively. East Cluster B had one flotation sample with endocarps as did another sample nearby.

Several surveys document the various ways the edible pods of mesquite can be prepared into nutritious food (Bell and Castetter 1937; Felger 1977). The pods were typically ground and then the meal formed into a cake or made into a drink. The seeds might be either ground with the pods or separated and parched by tossing in a basket with live coals (Bell and Castetter 1937: 22, 24). The low incidence of burned endocarps at Fresnal Shelter and High Rolls Cave probably is explained by the characteristic processing of mesquite pods.

The dry pods can be stored up to a year, or possibly longer. The Cahuilla, for example, made coarse-coiled outdoor granaries. They were perched on platforms or poles and the interiors were plastered to protect them from field mice and kangaroo rats. Emergency supplies were stored in dry caves as well (Bean and Saubel 1972: 111). The Southern Paiute in Death Valley stored mesquite pods more simply. Clusters of pits were dug in the gravel alluvial fan of Furnace Creek a short distance uphill from the sand dunes that were covered by mesquite. The location presumably minimized damage from rodents that had extensive burrows in the mesquite covered sand dunes. The pits average 0.6 m to 0.9 m below the surface,

with a broad mouth of about 1.5 m that narrows to around 0.6 m in diameter at the base. Coarse gravel and cobbles thrown up during the excavation of the pit create rock circles on the surface. One excavated pit had an initial lining of sand followed by a lining of alkali sacaton (*Sporobolus airoides*) grass 8 cm to 10 cm thick. Another had a lining of desert holly (*Atriplex hymenelytra*). Each retained some mesquite pods. While the pods were gathered in late May or early June, they were stored for the following early spring lean period (Hunt 1960).

Common bean (Phaseolus vulgaris)
Common beans were domesticated in the New World and introduced to New Mexico before the use of pottery was known. A bean from Bat Cave was radiocarbon dated 2140 ± 110 B.P. and one from Tularosa Cave 2470 ± 250 B.P. in 1984 (Wills 1988: Table 18).

At Fresnal Shelter common beans are distributed in the uppermost levels in Squares C 30 and D 31 and deeper in a storage cist and one pit (Table 4.4). They were recovered in 11 of 43 screened grid square levels (Table A.3). Three dated beans indicate storage pits were used relatively late in the Fresnal Shelter occupation. In Square C 29 the beans seem to be dribbled throughout the depth of the cist. The C 11 bean type from Level 7 (C29.202A) does not agree in date with the maize kernel or charcoal in the same level (Table 3.3). In Square D 27 169 beans have accumulated in Pit 1. One of the C 11 type beans (01.D27.103A) radiocarbon dated at 2015 ± 65 B.P. in 1991 and a C 29 or C 30 bean type dated 2085 ± 60 B.P. The dates suggest new use or reuse of Pit 1, and the latter bean is the oldest bean dated by TAMS (Tagg 1996: 317). Four or possibly five bean types from Fresnal Shelter have been identified by Lawrence Kaplan that follow his earlier descriptions (Kaplan 1956): the violet striped bean (type C11), the pinto bean (type

Table 4.4. Distribution of Types of Common Beans in Grid Squares

Letter	Level	Grid Number 27	29	30	31
C	1			1 C 11, 1C*	
C	2			3 C 11	
C	3		1 C 11		
C	4		1 C 11		
C	5		1 C 13		
C	6		1 C 11		
C	7		4 C 11		
C	8		3 C*		
C	9		3 C 11 1 C*		
C	10		17 C 29 or 30 5 C 11		
D	1		1 C 11	1 C 11	
D	2				
D	3-9				
D	10a	1 C*			
D	11a	10 C 29 or 30 159 C 11 11 C*			

* Unclassified as to type

C13), a mottled tan bean known as Jacob's cattle (type C14), and a bean type resembling the blue dye bean (type C29) or another dark variety (type C30). Two bean types, the pinto and Jacob's cattle, have a single representative in the material examined (01.C29.129, 01.B27.70). The pinto bean derives from level 5 of Square C 29 (Table 3.3).

The majority of beans are in excellent condition, with coats intact and still glossy, although their color is consistently darker than their modern counterparts. A few bean coats have been corroded, apparently by ashes (01. C29.268, 01.C29.290). A pair of carbonized cotyledons was recovered from disturbed Level 1 (01.C30.12).

Mature beans may have been treated like other native seeds in perceramic times. We know that the Cocopa and Havasupai parched and ground beans to meal, which was then added to hot water to make a soup or mush (E. Gifford 1933: 264; Weber and Seaman 1985: 227). The Tarahumara follow a similar practice to make a refreshing drink after a long journey or a spate of work (Pennington 1963: 156). One author (Kennedy 1966: 55) likened one Tarahumara method of bean preparation to that of corn, for the dried beans are roasted in a small olla with sand, ground twice on the metate, and then boiled. The product is drunk as a hot soup or eaten cold when it congeals.

The violet striped bean (Type C11) predominates in numbers and in distribution throughout the stratigraphic record (Table 4.4). The violet striped bean (type C11) has been used in modern times as a string bean when immature and as a shelled bean for boiling when mature (Kaplan 1965: 153). The deep burgundy pods of this bean give it a striking appearance. The mature bean takes no more than an hour to boil at 1,220 m elevation; it cooks quickly. The violet striped bean was the most abundant and widespread bean type in the prehistoric Southwest (Kaplan 1965: 153). It was also the most widely distributed bean in Fresnal Shelter. The same variety, recovered in a cave along the Rio Zape in Durango, Mexico, dated to 1300 B.P. (Brooks and others 1962).

Fagaceae (Beech Family)

Oak (Quercus)

Different oak species range in elevation beginning at 1,372 m with *Q. turbinella* to 2,592 m elevation (Hutchins 1974: 126-127), but are nowhere evident on the south-facing slopes of Fresnal Shelter today, although present on the opposite side of the canyon near High Rolls Cave. The variety of shapes, sizes, and textures of oak leaves (including leathery evergreen types) from the shelter exceeds what is found in the immediate canyon vicinity now. Historic depredations of oak thickets and woodlands by goats has been chronicled in the Near East (Guest 1933: 81). In this country livestock consumption of shrub live oak (*Q. turbinella*) and other species is also well documented (USDA 1937: B125; Dayton 1931: 20-25).

At Fresnal Shelter of 43 screened levels, 28 contain narrow, longitudinal strips from acorn shell. Four of the 10 natural stratigraphic units and two of seven pits in Square D 27 had evidence of acorns (see Tables A.3, A.5, and A.6). The narrow strips of acorn shell look like rodent discard. No acorn caps were recovered anywhere. The best evidence of human utilization is one crushed acorn devoid of its content (01.B29E.30, Unit E).

At High Rolls Cave acorns derive from two samples in each of East Clusters A and B. In the former cluster, one sample (FS 557) had a proximally decapitated acorn along with leaves, while another contained an immature acorn (FS 795). An acorn strip came from the heavy flotation fraction in *the mouse pantry* and other acorn strips, an acorn shell fragment, and leaves were in Stratum 2 (FS139) from East Cluster B. The collective evidence indicates exclusive rodent utilization, though there is historic precedent for human use.

Both sedentary and migratory peoples in the Southwest utilized acorns (Gallagher 1977: 45). Acorns shared top rank with *Agave* as part of the nine staples of the Western Apache (Goodwin 1935: 62). The Mescalero Apache would eat the acorns of *Q. grisea* and *Q. Gambellii* either raw or slightly roasted, pounded, and mixed with dry fruit or fat. The practice of gathering ripe acorns from the ground (Gallagher 1977: 43) might explain why no acorn cups form part of the archaeological record. The Kaibab Paiute ate acorns roasted in ashes from *Q. gambelii* and *Q. turbinella*, but the acorns were not a staple (I. Kelly 1964: 44).

Fouquieriaceae (Ocotillo Family)

Ocotillo (Fouquieria splendens)

Spiny wands of ocotillo grow from root crowns on the south-facing slope near Fresnal Shelter, close to its limits of 1,982 m elevation (Hutchins 1974: 320). The leaves appear following rain.

The carbonized base of a calyx comes from a single natural stratigraphic unit along the B coordinate (Table A.5). Although bark was recovered from 17 of 43 screened levels (Table A.3), it is found in greatest concentration in Squares C 29 and C 30. In three instances the bark seems to relate to pit function (Table 4.2). When no ponderosa pine bark was at hand to line a pit, the locally available ocotillo bark evidently substituted. The Cahuilla Indians of southern California are said to eat the flowers and capsules of ocotillo (Kearney and Peebles 1942: 584).

Garryaceae (Silk Tassel Family)

Silk tassel (Garrya)

Two species of the evergreen shrubs grow in dry hills and canyons at elevations of 1,372 m to 2,288 m (Hutchins 1974: 354). *Garrya wrightii,* which can be a small tree, occupies the sunny slopes near Fresnal Shelter and must have been growing fairly close to High Rolls Cave at one time. It is one of the shrubs associated with the pinyon-juniper woodland and ranges from western Texas to Arizona, and into northern Mexico (Kearney and Peebles 1942: 658; Lamb 1971: 56).

At Fresnal Shelter the leaves of *Garrya* were recovered in 22 of 43 screened grid levels and in 3 of 10 natural stratigraphic units (Tables A.3 and A.5). At High Rolls Cave silk tassel leaves were recovered from Stratum 2 in East Cluster A and in Stratum 2 in East Cluster B.

The Las Vegas Paiute boiled sprays of the shrub for heart trouble (I. Kelly 1939: 162) and Palmer (1878: 654) reports the leaves were used for an internal tea for ague and colds. Some species have the bitter alkaloid garryin, which is used medicinally (Kearney and Peebles 1942: 658). A bundle of leaves and twigs wrapped with a strip of bark was recovered at Tonto National Monument in Arizona (Bohrer 1962: 89) and may have been collected for medicine.

For lack of more convincing evidence, the loose leaves in Fresnal Shelter and High Rolls Cave probably represent nothing more than wind scatter. Silk-tassel ranks moderately high in palatability as goat browse (Chapline 1919: 13) especially in summer (USDA 1937: B81) and may have been heavily grazed historically.

Lamiaceae (Mint Family)

At High Rolls Cave a shiny brown nutlet belonging to the mint family was in East Cluster A (FS 795) and another nutlet was half way between East Clusters A and C (FS 853).

True sage (Salvia type)

The two species of *Salvia* known in the Sacramento Mountains, *S. reflexa and S. subincisa,* range from 1,372 m to 2,288 m in elevation. Flowering begins in either July or August (Hutchins 1974: 413). *Salvia reflexa,* an annual herb with tiny sky blue flowers, can be found in woods and rocky slopes.

At Fresnal Shelter two calyxes and a nutlet of *Salvia* were recovered from 2 of 10 stratigraphic units sampled along the B coordinate (Table A.5). The nutlet has its apex removed and the embryo missing. The calyxes resemble those of *Salvia reflexa,* which are pubescent along the ribs. Two other flotation samples contain evidence of *Salvia.* One sample has a nutlet with the tan crescent marks typical of *S. reflexa* (01.B28W.24, Unit F) and the other (01. B30E.14, Unit CC') contains the basal ribbed portion of the calyx.

At High Rolls Cave the recovery of seven *Salvia* type nutlets in *the mouse pantry* (FS 67) may explain the presence of one other *Salvia* type nutlet in FS 773, where a great deal of finely shredded material typical of mouse activity was recovered. In the two rock shelters mice are implicated in the introduction and use of *Salvia* despite an ethnographic record as a human resource.

Salvia seeds have a history of human use as a beverage; they have the property of becoming mucilaginous when wet. The Huichol, Tarahumara (Beals 1932: 62), and other people in central and northern Mexico cultivated a species of *Salvia* for the seed used in a beverage (Havard 1896: 44; Bukasov 1930: 532) while the Akimel O'odham of southern

Arizona employed the wild *S. columbariae* similarly (Russell 1908: 77). The nutlets of the latter species might also be made into a mush rather than steeping them in water for a drink (Palmer 1878: 604). In southern California the seed was roasted and ground before dissolving in water for a beverage or mush (Rothrock 1878: 48). In contrast, at Cochiti Pueblo the leaves are chewed as a treatment for diarrhea (Lange 1968: 151).

Malvaceae (Mallow Family)

Globemallow (Sphaeralcea spp.)
Hutchins (1974: 314–317) describes the perennial globemallow (*S. angustifolia*) with a preference for dry roadsides and disturbed ground from 1,372 m to 2,135 m. Other species may not respond to disturbance so readily.

At High Rolls Cave globemallow only appears as carbonized seed in thermal features in East Cluster A (Feature 7) and East Cluster B Stratum 3, Features 1 and 3. All the available data suggest their use was early, that is 3080 ± 50 B.P. in Feature 1 (Table B.3.1).

The Kaiparowits Paiute used globemallow seeds within an environment that was relatively impoverished of food plants compared to other Paiute. Kelly (1964: 151) remarks that the subsistence problems in the Kaiparowits area must have been acute. Near Chaco Canyon National Monument a Navajo informant indicated that the seeds of a globemallow (*S. lobata*) were eaten (Elmore 1943: 63). Carbonized globemallow seeds have been reported from LA 19374, an Archaic site along the lower Chaco River in northwestern New Mexico (Toll 1983: Table 17.4). Globemallow seeds in later archaeological sites in northeastern Arizona in the St. Johns area were recovered in 7 of 17 sites (Gasser 1982b: Table 5).

Nyctaginaceae (Four O'clock Family)

Umbrella wort (Allionia incarnata)
This sprawling, perennial with viscid herbage grows on dry slopes and plains from 1,372 m to 1,982 m in elevation (Hutchins 1974: 159).

At Fresnal Shelter, one fruit of *Allionia incarnata* was recovered from Square D 27, Pit 6. The herb has no known use. Its fruits can be rather viscid while still green. Its inclusion in the pit is probably accidental or the work of rodents. Narrow strips of sunflower achenes suggest rodent activity in this pit (Table 3.4).

Spiderling (Boerhavia wrightii type)
Spiderling grows from 1,372 m to 1,982 m on dry hills and mesas (Hutchins 1974: 160). It flowers from August to September.

At High Rolls Cave the carbonized fruit comes from an East Cluster B thermal area (Feature 23). The singular recovery implies no subsistence use.

Desert four o'clock (Mirabilis multiflora)
Desert four o'clock is a perennial that can be found from Colorado to southern Utah and from western Texas to Arizona and Mexico (Correll and Johnston 1970: 580). It thrives on well-drained soil and partial shade in elevations from 1,372 m to 2,287 m (Hutchins 1974: 162). In northern New Mexico and Arizona it can be found beside pinyon and juniper trees or where sandstone escarpments join the valley floor. In Fresnal Canyon the plants grow on dry, rocky, south-facing slopes of limestone origin. The leaves, stems, and ultimately flowers may appear as early as June or just prior to frost, depending on environmental conditions. In winter the bleached, dichotomously branched stems mark its location until spring winds sweep the brittle superstructure away. The plant has thick storage roots. One specimen was collected on the slopes of Fresnal Shelter with roots as thick as a person's wrist. The

plant yielded seven pounds of root excluding the smaller segments (Field No. 1410).

Archaeological specimens of roots were identified by comparison of the raphide filled root fragments with large rooted perennials including the following Nyctaginaceae with macroscopically similar tissue: *Abronia elliptica, A. fragrans, Mirabilis multiflora, M. linearis,* and *M. longiflora.* Only *M. multiflora* possessed the properly colored and textured root surface to match the prehistoric material (Bohrer 1975b).

At Fresnal Shelter fragments of the thick root of *Mirabilis multiflora* were recovered from all 10 natural stratigraphic units along the B coordinate (Table A.5). Some fragments are carbonized and three pieces in one stratigraphic unit appear masticated. Root fragments have been recovered in 20 of the 43 screened levels and in all seven of the pits in Square D 27 (Tables A.3 and A.6). Some larger pieces of the root have the bark darkened with ashy spots and some show disorganized tissue characteristic of mastication. One is split longitudinally. Seeds were occasionally recovered in the screening of the C and D grids (Table A.3).

The Pueblo Indians of Arizona and New Mexico and the Navajo and Spanish who have close contact with the Pueblo Indians know of desert four o'clock. The root was characteristically ground for food, pulverized for medicine, and chewed as a hallucinogen (Bohrer 1975b). Because of its ubiquity in Fresnal Shelter it is thought to have been a food rather than a lesser-used medicine. The fresh root has a flavor akin to earthy potatoes. Chewing results in a mouthful of fibrous residue that ejects as finely dispersed fragments (Bohrer 1975b).

Oleaceae (Olive Family)

Ash or fresnal (Fraxinus)
Velvet ash *(F. pennsylvanica ssp. velutina)* grows along streams, canyons, and slopes from 1,525 m to 2,440 m in elevation (Hutchins 1974: 362). Trees were growing at streamside below Fresnal Shelter at the time of excavation..

An incomplete samara or winged-fruit of *Fraxinus* was recovered from 1 of 10 natural stratigraphic units (Table A.5). Another samara with wings burned and broken was recovered in an additional flotation sample (01B29E2, Unit B). The association with humans is apparent but the reason is obscure, unless a tree grew on the slope nearby.

Portulacaeae (Purslane Family)

Purslane (Portulaca)
Different species of purslane, annual succulent herbs, occupy disturbed habitats in a broad range of elevations in the Sacramento Mountains. Blooming may start as early as July (Hutchins 1974: 168).

At Fresnal Shelter two seeds of purslane, or verdolaga, were recovered in 2 of 10 natural stratigraphic units (Table A.5). An additional seed was recovered from another stratigraphic unit that was floated (01.B30.E14, Unit CC') and another from a screened level. Although the seed is naturally dark, no evidence of parching could be discerned.

At High Rolls Cave the two pits in East Cluster B with the earliest dates (Feature 1, 2970 ± 40 B.P. and Feature 3, 3080 ± 50 B.P.) have one and two seeds, respectively, that appear carbonized. Since seeds have been recovered from no other feature, it could be that the seed was more extensively used in the early years of the cave's occupation, similar to the use of globemallow (*Sphaeralcea*) seed. In East Cluster A Stratum 2, five purslane seeds were recovered from FS 208 and FS 34 seeds along with capsule lids and bases from FS 773. Other *Portulaca* seeds were recovered from Feature 6, from FS 853, and the heavy fraction of FS 67.

Although mice could be vectors for purslane seed, I would not expect them to transport intact capsules. The recovery of the capsule lids as well as the capsule base in FS 773 represents processing clues for concentrating purslane seed. The Zuni custom (Cushing 1920: 244) of collecting piles of the succulent plants and allowing the seeds to mature within the pile comes to mind. When the dead plants were shaken, all the tiny seed would concentrate at the bottom of the pile, along with loosened portions of the capsule that would need to be winnowed from the seed.

The seeds of *Portulaca* were eaten by both the Navajo and Zuni (Standley 1912: 458), although the details of preparation are rarely reported. The Southern Paiute ground the seeds into flour and consumed the product as mush (Bye 1972: 95). No specific mention of parching *Portulaca* seeds has been encountered.

Examples of archaeological seed recovery include the Late Archaic Donaldson Site in Matty Canyon (Huckell 1995: 88); the Hay Hollow Site in Arizona, 300 B.C. to A.D. 300 (Bohrer 1978, Table 3); various Hohokam sites (cited in Huckell 1995); the Arroyo Hondo Site near Santa Fe, A.D. 1270-1425 (Wetterstrom 1986: 12); and a cache of seed in a Chupadero Black-on-white pitcher, of El Paso Phase, A.D. 1200 to 1425 near the southern border of the Tularosa Basin in Doña Ana County (Phelps 1968). Purslane seeds were recovered from sites west of the Jarilla Mountains (Doleman and others 1992: 207).

Ranunculaceae (Crowfoot Family)

At Fresnal Shelter an achene was recovered whose beak and general shape suggest it has affinity with this family (01.F26.24). Genera of the crowfoot or buttercup family typically grow in moist habitats in the Southwest. Presumably the achene was introduced by humans, but the reason is unknown.

Rosaceae (Rose Family)

Mountain mahogany (Cercocarpus)
Mountain mahogany can be found from 1,830 m to 2,440 m in elevation (Hutchins 1974: 226) in the Sacramento Mountains. However, no shrubs were observed growing on the south face of Fresnal Canyon near the shelter. Mountain mahogany is reported as good goat and sheep browse (Chapline 1919, McDaniel and Tideman 1981: 104) and may have been heavily grazed in the canyon historically.

At Fresnal Shelter nine leaves of *Cercocarpus* (mountain mahogany) were recovered in 4 of 10 natural stratigraphic units along the B coordinate. Six of the leaves were fragmentary. Several other strata in the B coordinate not used in the above tabulation contain *Cercocarpus* leaves. Some of the minced leaves in 01.B29.E2, Unit B appear parched, and a fragment from 01.B30.W3, Unit AA has been burned. The association of *Cercocarpus* with humans is apparent but no ethnographic food use of the leaves has been located.

Apache plume (Fallugia paradoxa)
Apache plume grows on dry slopes, canyons, and hills between 1,525 m and 2,288 m in elevation. (Hutchins 1974: 227). Dense stands often grow where soil moisture runs deep, such as along arroyo margins, sandy flats, or disturbed sites (Dunmire and Tierney 1995: 134). Goats browse this shrub (Chapline 1919).

At Fresnal Shelter, 1 of 10 natural stratigraphic units contained a half-burned leaf of Apache plume *(Fallugia paradoxa)* (Table A.5). At High Rolls Cave fragmentary leaves of Apache plume were recovered in Stratum 2 (FS 853, FS 795, and carbonized in FS 773). Since the leaves were discarded, perhaps the wood was valued instead.

Plum or cherry (Prunus)
Chokecherry (*Prunus serotina, P. virginiana*)

and wild plum (*P. americana*) are found along streams 1,372 m to 2,288 m in the Sacramento Mountains (Hutchins 1974: 234).

At Fresnal Shelter the rotund pits of chokecherry (*Prunus*) have been recovered in some of the screened material from the C and D grid coordinates (Table A.3). The pits likely belong to *Prunus serotina,* which commonly grows in the nearby Fresnal Canyon bottom today. Chokecherries have been eaten either fresh or dried by many Rio Grande Pueblos (Castetter 1935: 46).

At Fresnal Shelter one small ellipsoidal pit that derives from C 28, Level 6 (01.C28.85) likely represents *P. emarginata,* which was collected at 2,288 m (Appendix A.2) in the Sacramento Mountains. A larger ellipsoidal pit derives from the disturbed soil beneath manure (01.C28.08, Level 2). It could either be a modern commercial introduction, or the wild plum (*Prunus americana*), which is similar. The latter species grows in the Sacramento Mountains (Hutchins 1974: 234).

At High Rolls Cave pollen from the rose family was recovered from three fecal samples, suggesting an edible species like chokecherry (Appendix B.4).

Rutaceae (Rue Family)

Hop tree (Ptelea)
The hop tree can grow as a shrub up to 1.8 m high on rocky canyon slopes between 1,525 m and 2,592 m in elevation (Hutchins 1974: 288). The shrubs or small trees have a strong odor and are not eaten by livestock; some persons suffer dermatitis as a result of contact with the plant (Kearney and Peebles 1960: 495).

A single fruit with eroded wings (01. C28.88, Level 6) came from Fresnal Shelter. At High Rolls Cave one fruit came from Stratum 2 in East Cluster A (FS 742) and another from East Cluster B Stratum 1 (FS 70).

The Tarahumara make a wash of the leaves and root of a *Ptelea* to relieve rheumatic pains (Pennington 1963: 184). The fruits have been recovered from Jemez Cave (Alexander and Reiter 1935: 64) and Bat Cave (Smith 1950: 173)

Solanaceae (Potato Family)

Ground cherry (Physalis type)
Ground cherries are annual or perennial herbs that grow between 1,372 m and 2,135 m in elevation (Hutchins 1974: 419-421).

At Fresnal Shelter one ellipsoidal light brown seed 1.1 mm in diameter of the *Physalis* type was recovered in a natural stratigraphic unit (Table A.5). At High Rolls Cave *Physalis* seeds were recovered as a macrobotanical sample in Stratum 1 in excavation unit 69.

Ground cherries have been in common use by the Rio Grande Pueblos, usually being boiled but sometimes eaten fresh. The fruits were also utilized by the Hopi and Zuni (Castetter 1935: 40). Direct evidence of prehistoric consumption of fruits at Mesa Verde comes from coprolite analysis (Stiger 1979).

Because of its rarity in Fresnal Shelter and High Rolls Cave *Physalis* probably held no dietary significance for the occupants.

Wild tobacco (Nicotiana trigonophylla)
The plants do well in washes or near streams, in sandy soil, and disturbed habitats at low elevations (Adams and Toll 2000: 144). In the Sacramento Mountains it can be found as high as 1,830 m in canyons (Hutchins 1974: 419). Historic collections of *N. trigonophylla* have been made in Mexico in Chihuahua, Sinaloa, Sonora, and Durango. (Goodspeed 1954: 385) as well as in the American Southwest where the species has been cultivated (Winter 2000: 125).

N. trigonophylla seeds, through the way they are planted, may become overly large after many generations. If a species is being planted thickly, so that competition between plants is severe, the seeds with the most food reserves (endosperm) will be able to out-compete the other seedlings and live to set seed. If some seed is planted more deeply than normal, and the shallow seed dies of drought, then a similar form of selection might take place. If either happens often enough, seed selection will be for the most food reserves, which could mean a larger seed or one with more calories. Certain variants of *N. trigonophylla* may have been valued enough by shamans to be planted. So if strains of *N. trigonophylla* were being planted and cared for (cultivated) over many human generations, an increase in seed size is possible.

The leaves recovered in High Rolls Cave have the shape, size, and texture of the basal rosette of leaves of the wild or semi-wild *Nicotiana trigonophylla* (Winter 2000: 124, Figure 13). The oblanceolate, delicate appearing herbaceous leaf fragments are preserved in East Cluster A (FS 557, FS 742), East Cluster B (FS 67), and FS 853. While the leaves at High Rolls Cave appear quite small, large leaves may have been differentially degraded.

Some leaves in two of the samples (FS 557 and FS 742) have been rolled. Seven leaves in FS 742 bear signs of manipulation. Three are rolled starting from the petiole, two are rolled beginning at the tip of the leaf, and two are undetermined. One seems to be rolled from a longitudinal strip of leaf blade, as one margin is intact and another torn. FS 557 has another leaf that has been rolled from the apex so that the petiole is exposed, forming a small, flattened package 6 mm by 5 mm. One gets the impression that each little leaf roll was regarded as potent.

Additional tobacco parts accompany two leaf samples. One sample that has the rolled leaves (FS 742) also contains three tubular flowers; the best preserved seems to be *N. trigonophylla* (see Appendix B.2, Taxonomic Notes). In FS 853 a tobacco leaf was recovered in company with 254 tobacco seeds, *Nicotiana*

rustica type.

Cultivated tobacco (Nicotiana rustica type)

Nine tobacco (*Nicotiana rustica* type) seeds from FS 1256, Stratum 3, and 254 seeds from FS 853, Stratum 2 were recovered. The seeds, instead of being 0.5 mm in length as in *N. trigonophylla*, have a mean of 1 mm (s.d. .073, n=49) and best resemble *N. rustica* or possibly *N. attenuata* in size (Adams and Toll 2000: 145). The growing of tobacco in small, isolated tracts is common (Winter 2000) and would not be limited by elevation in the species.

It may be that the tobacco seeds represent a strain of *N. trigonophylla,* cultivated as described above. To accomodate both possibililties, I have identified the tobacco seeds as the *N. rustica* type. The designation *type* implies that other species may duplicate the appearance of *N. rustica*. The *N. rustica* type seeds in FS 853 have been TAMS dated at 2860 ± 40 B.P. (Table B.3.3).

If the seeds actually are *N. rustica*, they represent a very early introduction into the Southwest, and may be an early varietal or even weedy form no longer grown. Such an early date of acquisition fuels speculation that tobacco was present in the eastern United States in the Early Woodland period (before A.D. 1) or even in the preagricultural Archaic period (Winter 2000: 108).

Tobacco (Nicotiana spp.)

At High Rolls Cave eight uncarbonized and ten carbonized tobacco seeds were reported from Feature 6, a thermal pit in East Cluster B, while a single carbonized seed from FS 187 in East Cluster A was also reported. In addition, two tobacco seeds were encountered in Excavation Unit 8 in the modern surface topsoil of the cave.

At High Rolls Cave the context of recovery of all the tobacco seeds has been associated with signs of rodent activity (Appendix B.1). Considering the circumstances of deposition, it is perhaps best to assign the tobacco to the general dates for Stratum 2, in the range from

3260 ± 60 to 2890 ± 50 B.P. The variety of parts recovered seems to negate the possibility that tobacco was obtained by trade.

Prehistoric tobacco seeds have been recovered in an early agricultural village near Tucson, dating 398 to 169 B.C. (Adams and Toll 2000: 152).

The role tobacco may have played in the lives of the inhabitants of High Rolls Cave is open to conjecture. The Akimel O'odham, Tohono O'odham, and Tarahumara keep a number of tobacco species available, including the wild *N. trigonophylla* and the cultivated *N. rustica* and *N. tabaccum* (Bye 1979: Winter 2000: 4). Among the Tarahumara, *N. rustica* was valued for smoking in evening ceremonies and as a purifier of people, animals, and fields (Bye 1979: 41). In the Tarahumara community of Rejogochi, smoking *N. rustica* was used to enhance the effect of maize beer drinking (Merrill 1978: 112). The historic role it played in general among Native Americans and the Pueblo peoples may provide other parameters within which one's imagination may roam:

> Tobacco is a recreational drug, a mood altering, addictive substance, a deadly carcinogen, and a sacred, vision producing force that links the user with the spirit world. It is a metaphor for life and death; it provides a balance between the worlds of humans and spirits; it is a supernatural agent during life-crisis ceremonies; it is the food of the gods. (Winter 2000: 3)

> For the Pueblos in general, the ceremonial use of tobacco brings fog, clouds, and rain, gives luck for ceremonies and heals and nourishes people. Tobacco is used during initiation ceremonies and political meetings, and it induces the growth of flowers, crops and other forms of food. The cloud-like puffs of smoke appeal to the clouds, producing rain and fertility. (Winter 2000: 44-45)

Ulmaceae (Elm Family)

Hackberry (Celtis reticulata type)

The netleaf hackberry grows near streamside along Fresnal Canyon near Fresnal Shelter. It can range in elevation from 1,372 m to 1,830 m (Hutchins 1974: 128).

In Fresnal Shelter the stones of *Celtis* fruits occurred in 18 of 43 screened levels (Table A.3). A stone was noted in only one natural stratum (01.B29E.2, Unit B). Hackberry fruits were eaten by many of the Pueblo Indians of the Rio Grande Valley and extensively used by the Acoma and Laguna (Castetter 1935: 21). The Apache (Castetter and Opler 1936: 46) ate the fruits fresh or ground them into cakes for winter use. Since the stones are whole, the fruits may have been eaten when available. Wood rats are known to collect hackberries (VanderWall 1990: 262).

Zygophyllaceae (Caltrop Family)

Contrayerba (Kallstroemia)

Kallstroemia species are trailing annual or perennial herbs with a range of adaptation from the low deserts up to 2,135 m (Hutchins 1974: 285). *Kallstroemia* is closely related to the introduced puncture vine (*Tribulus*). *Kallstroemia* differs from puncture vine by possessing orange rather than yellow flowers and by bearing a series of nutlets with harmless tubercles instead of four or five double-pronged spikes.

At Fresnal Shelter three consecutive natural stratigraphic units contained a total of seven mericarps (Table A.5). Three mericarps have their walls broken and the seed missing. One split carbonized mericarp fragment comes from Pit 4, Square D 27 (Table A.6). One dry fruit with beak longer than the body came from the screens (01.D30.46, Level 4) and classifies as *K. parviflora*. A whole carbonized mericarp comes from a natural stratum (01.B29E.25, Unit D) and three mericarps come from .01B30E14, Unit CC'. At High Rolls Cave in East Cluster A Stratum 2, FS 795 contained two mericarps and FS 773 had a mericarp missing the seed and a fruit with the apex cut. Opened mericarps devoid of seed suggest rodent activity while the carbonized mericarp indicates some possible association with humans.

A single carbonized nutlet was recovered at Los Ojitos, a Late Archaic site in southern Arizona (Huckell 1995: 90). No human food uses are known. Spanish Americans esteem the ground root for fever, dysentery, sore eyes, and other afflictions (Curtin 1947: 68).

Creosote bush (Larrea tridentata)

Creosote bush grows on the south-facing slopes of Fresnal Canyon near Fresnal Shelter, which represents an extreme adaptation in elevation. It was reported as very common in late Holocene wood rat nests in nearby Marble Canyon at 1,690 m (Van Devender and others 1984, Table 2). Most floras list the shrubs as growing below 1,678 m elevation.

At Fresnal Shelter 9 of 10 natural stratigraphic units along the B coordinate had 25 carpels of creosote bush. A minimum of 17 leaves were recovered in 6 of the 10 stratigraphic units, with at least three leaves burned. Carpels were in three of the seven pits in Square D 27. Carpels or fruits occur in 7 of 43 screened levels (Tables A.3, A.5, and A.6). Fully carbonized leaves come from flotation sample 01.B30W.2, Unit AA. The fire-marked leaves indicate there was some utilization of the shrub, but no ethnographic references ever suggest that this resinous plant was used as food.

At High Rolls Cave, East Cluster A, Stratum 2 (FS 208), contains half of a single fruit of a creosote bush. The nearest source would be far beyond the range of rodent vectors. It is likely the branches were brought to the cave for some other purpose and the fruit discarded.

A Late Archaic coprolite from Culbertson County, Texas has an 18.5 percent concentration of creosote bush pollen (Holloway 1983, Table 3). Such a singular high percentage from an insect pollinated plant suggests a cultural use, quite possibly a medicinal one.

Unidentified quids

At Fresnal Shelter quids of unknown composition were recovered from 30 of 43 screened levels (Table A.3). Only disturbed Level 1 had a high concentration (120) of quids (01.C29.13). There were never over 50 in any other level. When quids were identified at Antelope House in Canyon de Chelly, Arizona, fibers of yucca leaves, maize husks, and bean pods predominated (Zauderer 1975).

TERMITE FECAL PELLETS AT FRESNAL SHELTER

Two families containing five genera of wood dwelling termites are known from native habitats in the southwestern United States. Over half of the nine species live below 1,130 m. Termite fecal pellets can be introduced into habitation areas through transport of locally gathered firewood containing colony chambers and passageways. The burning of the encasing wood might slowly heat and eventually carbonize the pellets (Adams 1984). Termite pellets, usually in a carbonized condition, have been reported at archaeological sites in southern and central Arizona, in northwestern New Mexico at Salmon Ruin, as well as at Fresnal Shelter (Adams 1984, Table 3). Attempts to identify the species that produced the fecal pellets that might allow inferences on environment have been frustrated by wide variations in pellet size produced by variable burning conditions (Adams 1984).

At Fresnal Shelter two uncarbonized termite fecal pellets derive from a grass-lined cist that had mesquite seeds (01.C26.85). One carbonized termite pellet comes from 01.C31.18, Level 1 and another from 01.C30.22, Level 2. Both levels are disturbed.

Chapter 5
Fresnal Shelter

The plant preservation beneath the protection of the cliff overhang was unusual. Delicate structures like grass florets and amaranth capsules (utricles) were preserved. A flotation sample consisted of 20 ml of minced plant material smaller than a ¼ inch screen and 100 ml of plant material larger than a ¼ inch screen from a variable volume of matrix that had already been floated. On average, a flotation sample took 20 hours to sort. I have never seen such a complexity of fine plant preservation. Flotation samples were limited to unburned material, except for a few burned lenses of New Mexico feather grass. No flotation samples were obtained from hearths.

An average flotation sample from one of the ten natural stratigraphic units contained 35 taxa (range 24 to 44). A total of 54 different taxonomic units are represented in the 10 flotation samples. It would have been easier to make a distinction between what was frequent and what was rare if only half the taxonomic units (27 in this case) were represented in any given flotation sample. In order to provide a conservative interpretation of what taxa were really common in the 10 natural stratigraphic units when so many taxa were present in each sample, a high cut-off percentage was used for potential food recognition. If a taxon occurred in 80 percent or more of the natural stratigraphic units it was considered a potential food. Had I used an even larger flotation sample, the same taxonomic units might appear in very nearly every sample, providing no contrast.

From the analysis of the entire Fresnal Shelter study 104 different taxonomic units were recovered, which includes identifications that vary from family and generic level to species. In addition, four varieties of the common beans were recognized.

COMPARING NATURAL STRATIGRAPHIC UNIT FLOTATION AND SCREENED SAMPLES

Technical factors used in the method of retrieval of plant remains undoubtedly affect results (Bohrer 1981a). The screen loss samples provide insight as to what vegetal items might be missing, but one is left with lingering doubts about whether the limited testing was broadly applicable. For example, did differences in spatial distribution of various taxa exist within the shelter?

Natural stratigraphic units of equal volume lacked pinyon nutshell in the flotation, yet nutshell was present in 40 of 43 screened levels. Maize kernels are in 26 of 43 screened levels, yet no kernels were recovered along the B grid line near the rear wall, at the very perimeter of human activity.

One tends to find a greater frequency of prickly pear seeds, four-wing saltbush fruits, creosote bush carpels, Turk's head barrel cactus areoles, and desert four o'clock root in the flotation along the back wall than in the screened squares. It is also true that the similar high recovery rates of the same items are found in the flotation from pits in Square D 27 rather than screened squares.

Perhaps the rear of the shelter was favored for masticated residue ejected from the human mouth. This might account for the saltbush fruits and might account for the disparity in frequency of recovery of desert four o'clock root. Small root fragments lost through the levels using the ¼ inch mesh screen would sharply decrease the number of strata showing it present compared with flotation.

Locations toward the rear of the shelter may have some peculiar attraction to rodent rummaging. Some support of this idea comes from the recovery of rattlesnake vertebrae along the B grid line. In addition, there is evidence of rodent activity in almost all of the seven pits examined (Table 3.4). It is possible rodents would find the prickly pear seeds and redeposit them. Conceivably a similar mechanism might be operative with the Turk's head barrel cactus areoles. Rodents might glean any remaining flesh from the areole and redeposit it at such a location. An unknown rodent might chew the wings off of the saltbush fruits. However, the numerous intact creosote bush carpels remain a mystery. They are distributed in 9 of 10 natural stratigraphic units at the rear of the shelter, but are only in three of seven pits and in only 17 of 43 screened levels.

Because of the foregoing skewed distributions, I postulated that the rear of the shelter would more readily accumulate chaff from winnowing dropseed grass and sotol, as diurnal up-canyon winds created by rising hot air would move chaff against the rear of the shelter. My expectation that dropseed chaff (empty florets) might be deposited in such a manner was not met. There was more chaff in six flotation samples from Square D 27 (0.948 g) than there was for 10 natural stratigraphic units (0.78 g). When I consider the results in

the light of my own winnowing experience, I realize strong winds are detrimental to the winnowing process, as too much seed is carried away with the chaff. Because of this, the chaff might be more evenly distributed.

COMPARING FLOTATION FROM NATURAL STRATIGRAPHIC UNITS AND SEVEN PITS FROM SQUARE D 27 WITH SCREENED LEVELS

The strong similarity between recovery of plants of ethnobotanical interest in natural stratigraphic units and flotation from seven pits in Square D 27 is apparent. Items smaller than the ¼-inch screen are as common in the small pits (or nearly so) as they are in the natural stratigraphic units, as is true for the larger fraction (Table 5.1).

What is of interest about the seven pits is that the location is away from the extreme rear of the shelter. We would like to know if the residue from edible plants larger than the ¼-inch screen from the pits resembles the screened levels (Table A.3). In most respects the comparison is good, but fewer screened levels have saltbush fruit cores, prickly pear seeds, Turk's head barrel cactus areoles, and four o'clock root fragments. Apparently explanations offered in regards to the position of flotation samples in natural stratigraphic units at the extreme rear of the shelter are not adequate to explain the contrast with the selected taxa from the screened levels.

If one examines the occurrence of saltbush fruit cores, prickly pear seeds, Turk's head barrel cactus areoles and four o'clock root fragments in screened levels along the C grid line in comparison to the D grid lines (Table A.3), they are better distributed along the C grid line than the D grid line, but still depleted compared to flotation in D 27 and along the B grid line. Apparently as one moves toward the front of Fresnal Shelter in this particular sector

Table 5.1. Comparison of Plant Parts in Flotation by Screen Size		
Part larger than ¼ inch screen	D 27 Pits	Natural Strata
Mesquite endocarps	7/7	9/10*
Burned seed of mesquite	4/7	0/10
Pine cone scales	7/7	6/10
Nut shells	5/7	0/10*
Juniper seeds	7/7	10/10*
Four o'clock root fragments	7/7	10/10*
Saltbush fruit cores	7/7	10/10*
Prickly pear seeds	7/7	8/10*
Buffalo gourd	5/7	8/10*
Sotol carpels	7/7	9/10*
Turk's head cactus	6/7	9/10*
Maize kernels	5/7	0/10*
Part smaller than ¼ inch screen	D 27 Pits	Natural Strata
Paniceae	7/7	10/10*
Dropseed chaff	6/7	10/10*
New Mexico feather grass	5/7	10/10*
Amaranth utricles	7/7	8/10*
Cheno-ams seeds	6/7	7/10
Goosefoot seeds	5/7	3/10
Sotol seeds	5/7	3/10
Purslane seeds	1/7	2/10

* Common in diet; see discussion in text.

(Squares 28, 29, 30, and 31) there are fewer of the items in question.

IDENTIFICATION OF COMMON DIETARY COMPONENTS

The application of the scoring system (Table 4.1) to the plant remains from Fresnal Shelter resulted in the ranking of the subsistence scores. Twenty-three taxa with scores of five or higher were likely used for food, fifteen taxa with scores of three or four are more equivocal in the role they played, and 39 taxa are least likely to have been used for food (Table 5.2).

Of the 23 taxa, some must have been more important than others.

Because natural stratigraphic unit samples of equal volume offer the most complete sample in size range and presumably time, those same taxa found in 80 percent or more of the natural stratigraphic units were isolated from the 23 as potentially common or basic foods (Table 5.1). As a result, the 23 taxa reduce to only 12. While pinyon nuts and maize have a high subsistence score in Table 5.2, they do not qualify for an 80 percent frequency in natural stratigraphic units (Table 5.1).

The 12 segregated taxa occur in the flotation from the seven pits in Square D 27

Table 5.2. Ranked Subsistence Scores of Plant Material from Fresnal Shelter

Scientific Name	Common Name	Components	Score*
Juniperus	juniper	2 (2 3 1)	12
Sporobolus	dropseed	2 (2 3 1)	12
Paniceae	panic tribe	2 (1 3 1)	10
Setaria	bristlegrass		
Amaranthus seeds	pigweed	2 (1 3 1)	10
Echinocactus			
horizonthalonius	Turk's head	2 (2 2 1)	10
Cucurbita foetidissima	buffalo gourd	2 (1 3 1)	10
Prosopis glandulosa	mesquite	2 (1 3 1)	10
Dasylirion wheeleri	sotol seeds	2 (2 2 1)	10
Mirabilis multiflora	four o'clock	2 (2 2 1)	10
Stipa neomexicana	New Mexico feathergrass	2 (2 1 1)	8
Agave	century plant	1 (2 3 1)	6
Dasylirion wheeleri	sotol quids	1 (2 3 1)	6
Yucca	yucca seed, leaves	1(2 3 1)	6
Rhus trilobata type	threeleaf sumac	1 (2 3 1)	6
Echinocereus cf pectinatus	rainbow cactus	1 (2 3 1)	6
Atriplex canescens	four-wing saltbush	2 (1 1 1)	6
Pinus edulis type	pinyon	1 (1 3 1)	5
Oryzopsis hymenoides	Indian rice grass	1 (1 3 1)	5
Zea mays	maize, corn	1 (1 3 1)	5
Mammillaria type		1 (1 3 1)	5
Opuntia sp.	prickly pear	1 (1 3 1)	5
Chenopodium	goosefoot	1 (1 3 1)	5
cheno-ams		1 (1 3 1)	5
Cyperaceae (Sedge family)	sedge	1 (0 3 1)	4
Elymus/Agropyron	wild rye	1 (0 3 1)	4
Allium	onion	1 (0 3 1)	4
Helianthus annuus	sunflower	1 (1 2 1)	4
Iva amrosiaefolia		2 (0 1 1)	4
Viguiera dentata		1 (1 2 1)	4
Phaseolus vulgaris	common bean	1 (0 3 1)	4
Quercus	oak	1 (0 3 1)	4
Salvia reflexa type		1 (0 3 1)	4
Portulaca	purslane	1 (0 3 1)	4
Prunus cf. serotina	chokecherry	1 (0 3 1)	4
Celtis	hackberry	1 (0 3 1)	4
Pinus strobiformis type	white pine	1 (0 2 1)	3
Pinus ponderosa	ponderosa pine	1 (0 2 1)	3
Eragrostis	lovegrass	1 (0 2 1)	3
Nolina microcarpa	beargrass	1 (1 0 1)	2
Amaranthus cruentus	dye amaranth	1 (0 1 1)	2
Parthenium incanum	mariola	2 (0 0 1)	2
Cercocarpus	mountain mahogany	1 (1 0 1)	2

Table 5.2. Ranked Subsistence Scores of Plant Material from Fresnal Shelter, cont'd

Scientific Name	Common Name	Components	Score*
Kallstroemia		1 (1 0 1)	2
Larrea tridentata	creosote bush	2 (0 0 1)	2
Andropogoneae	beardgrass	1 (0 0 1)	1
Aristida	three-awn	1 (0 0 1)	1
Bouteloua curtipendula	side-oats grama	1 (0 0 1)	1
Chloris crinita		1 (0 0 1)	1
Chloris virgata	feather finger grass	1 (0 0 1)	1
Digitaria californica	California cottontop	1 (0 0 1)	1
Pappophorum complex (*Pappophorum, Enneapogon, Cottea*)		1 (0 0 1)	1
Pleuraphis cf mutica	tobosa grass	1 (0 0 1)	1
Lycurus phleoides	wolftail	1 (0 0 1)	1
Rhus radicans type	poison ivy	1 (0 0 1)	1
Garrya wrightii	Wright silk-tassel	1 (0 0 1)	1
Typha	cattail	single occurrence	
Trianthema portulacastrum		single occurrence	
Apocynum	dogbane	single occurrence	
Acourtia nana	desert holly	single occurrence	
Artemesia dracunculus	sage	single occurrence	
Verbesina		single occurrence	
Berberis	holly-grape	single occurrence	
Coryphantha strobiformis		single occurrence	
Opuntia imbricata	cane cholla	single occurrence	
Cleome serrulata	beeweed	single occurrence	
Ipomoea	morning glory	single occurrence	
Fouquieria splendens	ocotillo calyx	single occurrence	
Allionia incarnata		single occurrence	
Fraxinus sp.	ash	single occurrence	
Ranunculaceae cf.	crowfoot family	single occurrence	
Fallugia paradoxa	Apache plume	single occurrence	
Prunus emarginata		single occurrence	
Ptelea	hop tree	single occurrence	
Physalis	groundcherry	single occurrence	
Kallstroemia parviflora		single occurrence	
Avena	oats	historic	
Sorghum	sorghum	historic	

*A score of 5 or more is a subsistence item; a score of 3 or 4 is a borderline subsistence item.

either meet or closely approach the percentage recovered in natural stratigraphic units (80 percent), thus providing supporting evidence (Table 5.1). In the screened levels the expectations of comparable high frequencies were realized for (1) juniper, 95 percent; (2) sotol (*Dasyliron wheeleri*) carpels, 72 percent; (3) mesquite (*Prosopis glandulosa*), 98 percent; and (4) buffalo gourd (*Cucurbita foetidissima*), 72 percent. Thus, 8 of the 10 taxa in the natural stratigraphic units are also very common in screened levels. Four taxa were under-represented in screens: four-wing saltbush were in 40 percent of the levels, Turk's head barrel cactus in 44 percent, prickly pear seeds in 53 percent, and desert four o'clock in 65 percent.

In the above delineation of common foods, I have omitted reference to pinyon *(Pinus edulis* type) and maize. Pinyon cone scales were in only 60 percent of the 10 stratigraphic units, but well represented in screens as nut fragments (91 percent, 40 of 43 levels). Locations for the disposal of pinyon cone scales (processing residue) evidently differed from where the pinyon nuts themselves were cracked in this part of the shelter.

The opportunities to incorporate maize kernels in the deposits in the 15 cm wide strip at the rear of the shelter seem relatively limited. Strata along the B grid line contain primarily tassel fragments. The floated natural strata lack maize kernels entirely and contain only two cob segments. In contrast, many maize kernels once lost on the forward shelter floor apparently remained in the area, though transported by rodents or moved by trampling or digging. Consequently, the number of screened levels retaining maize evidence need consideration. With 32 of 43 of screened levels retaining maize cobs or kernels (74 percent), corn exceeds buffalo gourd (72 percent) and sotol carpels (72 percent) in rank, already recognized as basic foods. As a result, maize was included as one of the common or important foods. On the nega-

tive side, some of the corn present in Square C 29 levels may be over-represented by late intrusions, effectively raising their frequency, at least in terms of the earliest occupants. It is one of the hazards of cave deposition.

In summary, of the original 23 items likely used for food, 8 to 14 seem to have been used often, the final number depending on how one evaluates the last six taxa from screened levels. For the purposes of discussion on the pages that follow, I will emphasize all 14 taxa.

1. juniper
2. sotol
3. Paniceae grass(es)
4. dropseed grass
5. New Mexico feather grass
6. amaranth
7. four-wing saltbush
8. mesquite
9. Turk's head barrel cactus
10. buffalo gourd
11. desert four o'clock root
12. prickly pear fruits
13. pinyon nuts
14. maize

Equivocal subsistence items with scores of three and four (Table 5.2) can be evaluated further. Cogent arguments for human consumption can be made for common beans (*Phaseolus vulgaris*), white pine seeds (*Pinus strobiformis* type), and wild onion (*Allium*) bulbs. The habitat of white pine in ponderosa pine forests lies beyond the home range of rodents as does the native home of the common bean south of the United States border. The large bunch of onions precludes rodent transport. People are believed to be the vector in each case.

A series of genera all grow on the slopes of the shelter, in the riparian canyon bottom some 61 m below the shelter, or might have grown there in the past like members of the sedge family (Cyperaceae), sunflower (*Heli-*

anthus), and sage (*Salvia*). The 100 m home range radius of wood rats (Wells 1976: 228) could extend from the canyon bottom to the shelter. For many genera there is as much good reason to interpret their presence as due to rodent foraging as to human foraging. In fact, the two records may overlap. *Yucca* seeds are in Pit 3 of Square D 27 with no sign of rodent disturbance and many other seeds have been discarded near thermal areas, suggesting human use. However, humans can eat the seeds and mice are quite omniverous. Acorns shell strips typify rodent foraging. Hackberry (*Celtis*) and chokecherry (*Prunus serotina* type) pits are in screened levels but not in Square D 27 pits or natural stratigraphic units, a distribution I find difficult to evaluate as well, and prefer to suspend judgment.

Pending more convincing evidence, I have demoted sedge (Cyperaceae), sunflower *(Helianthus), Iva,* purslane (*Portulaca*), sage *(Salvia),* and goldeneye *(Viguiera)* from the list of questionable human dietary items. I believe ponderosa pinebark, grama (*Bouteloua*) grass, *Elymus/Agropyron,* and lovegrass (*Eragrostis*) were not used in human diet. The most tangible reason for the presence of the bark derives from its probable role in lining pits. The three grasses now grow on the slopes of the shelter and could have grown there in the past. They could have been collected for non-subsistence purposes by either man or rodents (for example, bedding or nest lining). The case for consuming pine bark and the three grasses is relatively weak.

MEDICINAL CEREMONIAL PLANTS

While the shelter is replete with the by-products of subsistence activities, whether by humans or rodents, relatively few items deviate readily from such an interpretive framework into the realm of medicinal or ceremonial usage. Among those suspect items are a longitudinally split stem of Turk's head barrel cactus (*Echinocactus horizonthalonius*), the burned seed of wild morning glory (*Ipomoea*), fragments from the heads of a cultivated amaranth *(A. cruentus*), and pollen bearing tassel segments of maize. All but the barrel cactus might have been secured from a cultivated plot. The interested reader is referred to the more detailed discussions of each within Chapter 4.

SEASONALITY

In the warm deserts of the American Southwest, the addition of soil moisture at particular points in time typically affects the seasonal capacity to produce flowers and fruits. The phenological pattern is best understood in the Mohave Desert. There a critical amount of rain of at least 25 mm winter or early spring rains (from 50 to 125 mm) that stimulates vegetative growth of shrubs followed by flowering and fruiting through the month of May (Beatley 1974: 858). While the pattern in the Tularosa Basin and the Chihuahuan Desert is not as well understood, it is fairly safe to assume that rainfall plays a large role in predicting the flowering and fruiting of higher plants. However, moisture is not strongly correlated with calendar dates except when the average precipitation for a period increases as in July and early August.

One might categorize the fruit forming response of various plants to desert conditions into having a pattern of (1) true, (2) qualified, or (3) shifting seasonality (Bohrer 1975c; Adams and Bohrer 1998: 130). True seasonality means the timing of seed maturation is little altered by the vagaries of weather. Trees, shrubs, or other components of riparian habitats are apt to belong to this category, such as mesquite and chokecherry. Many cacti that have the ability to store water also express true seasonality. Some cool season perennial grasses might also be regarded as having true seasonality, such as Indian rice grass and New Mexico feather grass, as fall and winter moisture allow them to mature grain in late spring quite regularly. The cooler temperatures in which these grasses grow and store carbohydrates together with lessened root competition doubtless provides some advantage when rainfall is limited.

Most trees and shrubs exhibit a strategy of qualified seasonality such as is expressed in the production of pinyon nuts, banana yucca fruits, and acorns. Proper environmental conditions must extend over several years for banana yucca fruit production (Wallen and Ludwig 1978) and for pinyon nuts (Lanner 1981). If the fruit or nuts mature, they regularly mature in the fall and at no other time of year.

Other plant species have developed a pattern of shifting seasonality in response to erratic rains. So long as temperatures are conducive to growth, moisture triggers their eventual maturation. Among species of former economic importance to humanity are the dropseed grasses such as alkali sacaton (*Sporobolus airoides*), spike dropseed (*S. contractus*), and sand dropseed (*S. cryptandrus*). Harvestable grain may be available as early as June or at later dates until October, depending on rainfall. For human consumers, the chances of obtaining a grain crop during the year remain extremely good so long as the patches are well monitored.

When one uses food plants to evaluate the times of year Fresnal Shelter was occupied it is important to recognize that all the evidence is not equally valuable (Adams and Bohrer 1998: 130). Relatively few plants found in the shelter have a well-defined season of collection (Table 5.3). This may be due in part to the shifting strategy of maturation previously described. For other plants the regular season in which the reproductive parts first mature differs substantially from the length of time these same parts are available for procurement. For example, mature alligator juniper berries cling to the tree

through early winter before they finally fall. Although four-wing saltbush fruits mature in the fall they persist into December and sometimes as long as April (U.S.D.A. 1974: 241). Sotol stalks retain their seed long after maturity. Finally, certain perennial available parts of plants carry little seasonal information, such as fleshy roots or the stems of hedgehog cacti and prickly pear. One therefore must reject many species that might otherwise furnish evidence of seasonal shelter occupation.

From Table 5.3 one can see that the shelter was occupied in late spring, again in mid-summer, in fall, and as late as mid winter. The mid-winter habitation deduced from buffalo gourds relates to their cleanly broken fruit edges indicative of full maturity. The gourd shell pieces are cleanly broken with sharp edges indicating they were fully dried. With the first killing frost in the Tularosa Basin margins in October or as late as November, it would take one to two months for the fruit shells to dry sufficiently to form a clean, unwarped break under pressure.

The evidence for possible sequential patterning of behavior comes from two sources, the cool season grasses and the lining of the storage pits. One of the cool season grasses, Indian rice grass, typically matures prior to New Mexico feather grass, even at the same elevation (Rio Puerco notes). The postulated habitat of Indian rice grass in sandy portions of the Tularosa Basin and New Mexico feather grass in the foothills would imply a movement in spring from a lower elevation to a higher one. The irregular record of Indian rice grass tells us, however, that this scheme was not typical. The second possibility rests on the assumption that if storage caches were usually formed in the fall, the practice of lining some caches with ponderosa pinebark suggests trips to higher elevations may have preceded their formation.

A pattern of occupation throughout the

Table 5.3. Plants Whose Reproductive Parts Best Document Seasonal Procurement

Taxon	Part harvested	Remarks
California cottontop grass	mature plant	August to November
Indian rice grass	grain	late spring
New Mexican feather grass	grain	late spring following Indian rice grass
Maize	tassel	mid to late summer
Cattail	pollen	late spring (May to July)
Dogbane	stem fibers	after frost and into late fall
Four-wing saltbush	fruit	fall to early winter depending on how long fruits cling to shrub
Buffalo gourd	fruit	late fall (well after frost) and early winter
Piñon	nut	late fall
Prickly pear cactus	fruit	fall
Mesquite	pod	early fall
Oak	acorns	fall
Banana yucca	fruit	fall

entire year seems possible. If one considers the fourteen subsistence items isolated as of special dietary importance, four bear a pattern of fall maturity (prickly pear fruit, pinyon, mesquite, and buffalo gourd, Table 5.3). Nine of the remaining subsistence items have no well-defined season of collection. In contrast, the taxa found in all nine levels of Square C 29 (juniper, pinyon, yucca, sotol, maize, mesquite, and wild gourd) are known to mature in the fall and are available for various lengths of time thereafter, except possibly sotol.

Some seasonal information from deer comes from determining the approximate age of six deer at death, using tooth eruption patterns. Three were killed in late summer or fall when the animals were 12 to 18 months. Two other individuals, no older than six months, were killed in the first fall of their lives. The one maxilla amenable to aging indicates the animal was no older than a month and was killed in late summer. No evidence suggested any mid-winter hunting of deer (Wimberly and Eidenbach 1981: 25-26).

The large number of plants that seem to have no marked season of maturation should serve as a warning that the almost year around availability of many foods allowed use of the shelter at highly variable times. Archaic populations reaped the added harvest produced by precipitation in the form of either plant or animal life whenever favorable conditions or good fortune permitted. Further, the caching of even small amounts of food gave even more elasticity to a potentially flexible pattern of shelter occupation.

Plant species that appreciate more water than is available today and were recovered in Fresnal Shelter came from a variety of locations and had no documentation as to their age include Cyperaceae or sedge, cattail, ash fruits, poison ivy-type stones, and a member of the buttercup family. Trigonous sedge achenes in natural stratigraphic Unit A and numerous sedge seeds in Square D 27, Pit 7 suggest higher levels of moisture. The eastern prickly pear *(Opuntia humifusa)* now grows in the eastern third of Oklahoma and Kansas where rainfall is higher.

SIZE, NUMBER, AND NATURE OF LARGER PITS IN RELATION TO WINTER OCCUPANCY

Assuming for the moment that Fresnal Shelter was occupied in the winter months, an examination of the number, size, and superposition of the storage pits (Table 3.4) makes storage seem inadequate. Any expansion of storage space within the shelter appears impractical in retrospect, as so little of the shelter is fully protected from the elements. The storage pits have no structural aspects like rock slab-lined interiors to discourage rodent predation. Their ability to retain stored food must rely on the presence of people in the shelter during the period of stored food utilization. The success of rodents in pilfering maize kernels is evident from the caches archaeologists uncovered. Except for mesquite in the grass-lined wall of one pit, the humanly lost food and discards blend with residue of rodent consumption and we lack direct evidence of what people stored in the pits. Maize, mesquite pods, pinyon nuts, and buffalo gourd all mature in the fall and can be stored when dry.

As long as people used the shelter in the winter months, the maximum of three relatively shallow pits that were available at any one time would have been insufficient to supply even a small family over the winter dormancy period. Supplies were likely cached elsewhere and then brought to the shelter for consumption. One might postulate that caches of pinyon nuts were kept nearby and that large caches of mesquite pods were kept close to where they were collected. I would also think that this could be true of maize itself. Mesquite pods, maize on the cob, and to a lesser extent, pinyon nuts are bulky items for their weight. All would need to be stored at least initially near where the crops were harvested (Thomas 1983a: 85). Storage outside the shelter bears its own risks because of the reduced monitoring of rodent activity day and night. Since alligator bark juniper berries cling to the trees for an extended period during the winter, I am not sure how much caching might be necessary to preserve the resource from competing animals.

A considerable amount of trekking down canyon to secure stores of mesquite and maize would be needed to replenish supplies periodically. I believe while either mesquite pods or maize were being transported, the dried fruits of the buffalo gourd could be located easily and added to the load on the return trip to the shelter, as would the fruits of the four-wing saltbush.

Since all five storage pits were used for trash disposal before the abandonment of Fresnal Shelter, it is quite possible that use as a winter base camp ceased, while occupation continued for other purposes.

Estimated Size and Nature of Collecting Territory

The rhythmical dispersal of people from and their return to a central place fosters its own cultural geography. The *extended range* is the area commonly monitored relative to resource abundance and distribution. Not only does this include the radius of the core area or campground, but the *foraging radius*, which is the area systematically searched and exploited by task specific work parties leaving camp to forage but returning home each night. Further out is the *logistical radius* defined by special task groups staying away overnight or longer (Thomas 1983a: 88,89). Field camps often were occupied for two or three weeks, but sometimes for months (Thomas 1983a: 89). Keep in mind that each resource has its own variables, such as transport and labor costs, that may modify an average or ideal zone configuration for any given group.

The dominant pattern of mule deer bone deposits suggests whole deer carcasses were brought to Fresnal Shelter. High frequencies of skull fragments, lower legs, hoofs, and unscraped hides imply the hunting area must have been near (Wimberly and Eidenbach 1981: 26). The few bones from a pronghorn, big horn sheep, and bison (N= 8) exemplify possible long distance hunting (HSR 1972; Wimberly and Eidenbach 1981: 23).

The astute reader of Chapter 4 may have noticed that the upper elevation limits of certain plant species indicate that they grew lower than Fresnal Shelter. This information helps trace the foraging and logistical movements of the former inhabitants of Fresnal Shelter from their home base.

One would need to travel at least 2.7 km down canyon to the junction of Fresnal Canyon and Salado Canyon (1,678 m) to obtain many plant resources (Table 5.4). This is at the upper elevation limits of growth for a semi-weedy pigweed (*Amaranthus torreyi*), feather finger grass (*Chloris virgata*), and Turk's head barrel cactus recovered at Fresnal Shelter. Although the location represents a rather limited area of relatively flat bottom land, its resources would be in substantial agreement with the archaeological plant remains, except for *Amaranthus wrightii* and the weed grass *Chloris crinita*, which normally do not exceed 1,525 m.

Regular forays may have extended even further into the margin of Tularosa Basin to a location likely to incorporate potentially good agricultural land in lower Fresnal Canyon at 1,586 m or as far as the Randy Berger farm (elevation 1,470 m) north of La Luz. At 1,586 m one might encounter stands of alkali sacaton or other dropseed grasses (*S. contractus, S. cryptandrus,* and *S. flexuosus*), grasses of the Paniceae tribe, hackberry, narrow leaved yucca, buffalo gourd, mesquite thickets, and four-wing saltbush (HSR 1973: 438). Given the possibility of fallow fields in either location, increases in annual weeds such as amaranth (*A. torreyi*), goosefoot, feather finger grass, horse purslane, and perennials of disturbed ground, such as *Chloris crinita* grass and four-wing saltbush, might be predicted. When maize was maturing a portion of the inhabitants might have stayed in temporary field camps to protect the crop.

When all Fresnal Canyon junctions are compared, the junction with La Luz Canyon at 1,525 m taps the largest drainage basin and would be apt to carry floodwaters most often. More frequent floods would foster a greater abundance of many plant resources. The more reliable ground water level at this particular location might also foster better crops of mesquite pods than the immediate Fresnal Shelter area. Although the La Luz Canyon junction has higher relative costs in terms of energy spent in travel, a larger caloric return might be expected due to the increased efficiency in gathering from denser, more extensive and diverse stands of food resources (Table 5.4).

Table 5.4. Location, Composition amd Distance of Food Patches from Fresnal Shelter

Patch Type and Location	Patch Content	Distance one-way from Fresnal Shelter
Stands of white pine, up canyon 2288 m	white pine nuts	4 km
Piñon-juniper woodland above Fresnal Shelter 2059 m	Piñon nuts, juniper berries	0.8 km
Semi-desert hills, rockland on slopes of Fresnal Shelter or in canyon bottom 1922 m	wild onion, sotol, agave, yucca, hedgehog and prickly pear cactus desert four o'clock, three-leaf sumac, chokecherry acorns, mesquite, hackberry	0 to 92 m
Junction with La Luz Canyon 1525 to 1586 m	Yucca, panic grass, dropseed grass, Turk's head barrel cactus, prickly pear, four-wing saltbush, hackberry, goosefoot, pigweed (*A. torreyi*, *A. wrightii*) buffalo gourd, mesquite, weed grass, *Chloris crinita*	6.4 km
Junction with Salado Canyon, nearly level alluvial soil, 1676 m	same as La Luz Canyon, except *A. wrightii,* and weed grass, and *Chloris crinita,* are absent	2.4 km
Footslope grasslands, 1,312 to 1,982 m	New Mexico feathergrass; Turk's head barrel cactus to 1676 m.	variable
Tularosa Basin margin, 1312 to 1525 m	mesquite, four-wing saltbush, alkali sacaton grass, weed grass, *Chloris crinita*	variable
Low sand dunes southeast of Alamogordo; also within White Sands National Monument, and north of it.	Indian rice grass, dropseed grasses	24 km

All canyon junctions provide opportunities for flood waters to spread and deposit sediment. Each junction might have more dropseed grass, buffalo gourd, and other wild resources relative to Fresnal Shelter.

For a transported weed, *Chloris crinita* grass was in some abundance in Fresnal Shelter. *Chloris crinita* is recovered in 15 of 43 screened levels, all of which also have maize (Table A.3). The eleven levels that lack maize also lack *Chloris crinita*. *Chloris crinita* occurs with dropseed grass in nine levels. The grains of the latter are so small they may have been lost from some screened levels entirely. *Chloris crinita* accompanies either dropseed or maize (or both) in eleven levels. Although the association of maize and dropseed with the low elevation weed grass *Chloris crinita* may be coincidental, a down canyon orientation for procurement of many wild resources and agricultural activity seems plausible.

Maximum Distance Traveled to Higher Elevations

Evidence concerning the maximum distance people traveled for plant food at higher elevations seems more direct, although such trips, resulting in bringing back nuts of the white or limber pine, appear to have been quite rare. The pine now grows intermixed with ponderosa pine beginning about 2,135 m in elevation. Procurement would necessitate a hike of about 4 km up canyon from Fresnal Shelter.

Maximum Distance Traveled to Lower Elevations

Arguments concerning the maximum distance people traveled for food at lower elevations depend on how three observations of Indian rice grass should be interpreted: (1) its low incidence in stratigraphic units (3 of 10), (2) the lack of burned lenses that result from process-ing, and (3) the failure to recover the distinctive kinked capillary pedicels. The evidence could mean that people infrequently visited the shelter when grain was available in late June or early July and therefore left little residue. Alternatively, the evidence could imply habitats where monocultures grew were so restricted that it was infrequently gathered. In other words it could have been a minor component of a grassland, but not a dominant. The same evidence could be used to argue that the grass grain was gathered and threshed at a distant location and then carried to the shelter.

I find it difficult to accept either of the first two interpretations that would seem to carry the connotation of local procurement. Local procurement implies local processing, and I would expect to recover the evidence. There is no obvious reason why New Mexico feather grass and dropseed grass were processed in the shelter and not Indian rice grass, as long as they all grew in the vicinity.

The contention of long distance transport of Indian rice grass can be supported by the location of Archaic sites in gypsum and quartz sand dunes where the grass could grow. Archaic sites have been noted in the quartz sand adjacent to the lava flow near Three Rivers (Wimberly and Rogers 1977: 435) and in the gypsum dunes of White Sands National Monument, which have artifacts comparable to the Archaic tools found within Fresnal Shelter (Eidenbach and Wimberly 1980: 89). In the southern Tularosa Basin, evidence of Archaic plant collecting activities in sandy areas takes the form of fire hearths, grinding stones, and monzonite rocks cracked by rapid cooling, as would happen in stone boiling (Doleman and others 1992).

Processed grain could have been carried to Fresnal Shelter from the Tularosa Basin. One must traverse about 24 km to reach White Sands National Monument where Indian rice grass grows today. It apparently survived at the monument as a result of its relative inaccessibility to grazing. The quartz sand west of Three Rivers and the low sand dunes 24 km south of Alamogordo (Maker and others 1972) also represent potential habitats. Any intervening sandy areas that were being recently colonized by Indian rice grass (where it would grow in dense stands) would become prime collecting areas. Areas like these may have been part of the logistical radius of the extended range, an area commonly monitored for resource distribution and abundance (Thomas 1983a: 89).

The single specimen of cactus, *Coryphantha strobiliformis,* probably came from an alkaline grassy area in the Tularosa Basin proper around 1,220 m. Its unique presence may be the result of an expedition rather than typical travel to field camps.

Summary of Travel

We are probably viewing two superimposed travel patterns that have now become intermingled in the shelter deposits. The first is one of logistical long distance transport. It probably results from infrequent collecting trips in late June and early July from the Tularosa Basin when a reserve of Indian rice grass was brought along, and from late fall travel to about 2,134 m in elevation to transport surpluses of white pine nuts to the shelter. These rarely recorded events imply potential travel some 24 km or less out into the Tularosa Basin and about 4 km up canyon.

Second, another travel pattern probably results from relatively short distances (a minimum of 6.4 km) due to rhythmic dispersal and return to the shelter for various periods of time (refuging of Hamilton and Watt 1970: 263; foraging radius of David Hurst Thomas 1983a: 89) or by frequent alteration in activities between elevations between 1,470 m and 1,586 m and Fresnal Shelter. All 14 items of dietary importance might have been secured approximately

6.4 km down canyon and 0.8 km up canyon from Fresnal Shelter. Only pinyon and juniper would grow up canyon (Table 5.4).

RISK MINIMIZATION OR MAXIMIZING THE RELIABILITY OF FOOD PROCUREMENT

Of the 14 different plant foods recognized as important, those seen in the same location year after year were favored. Trees (mesquite, pinyon, and juniper); shrubs (four-wing saltbush); succulents (hedgehog and prickly pear cactii, and sotol); and perennials such as buffalo gourd, New Mexico feather grass, and dropseed grasses predominated. Stationary wild resources could be monitored easily by trips up and down the canyon. Their appearance either near the shelter or in multiple patch types (Table 5.4) reduced search time to a minimum. Annuals are represented by maize, amaranth, and a few species of Paniceae grasses. In general people stayed close to water, to their fields, and to the margins of the canyon in which they lived.

A RANKED COMPARISON OF SCREENED LEVELS WITH AND WITHOUT MAIZE

Any comparisons between different types of deposits or within the same deposit suffer from the uncertainty that the taxa in question have either moved horizontally or vertically since their original deposition. In Square C 29, thanks to radiocarbon dating, we know maize has undergone vertical movement and that some levels have been enriched with corn by the activities of the later occupants. The percentage of screened levels with maize is apt to be inflated, and can only be regarded as an approximation.

Regardless of the presence of maize, the three taxa commonest to all screened levels are the plant resources that could be stored and used over the winter months: mesquite pods, juniper berries, and pinyon nuts (Table 5.5). Any deviation from being in 100 percent of the levels is when maize is present. The steady collection of mesquite, juniper, and pinyon, even when maize is lacking, suggests continual use of Fresnal Shelter as a winter base camp. It appears that when maize was absent from the winter diet, more pinyon, mesquite, and juniper compensated for the loss. Otherwise, I would expect aseasonal items like hedgehog cactus, prickly pear stem pads, and four o'clock root to occupy a higher percentage of the levels without maize.

The fondness of many living groups for pinyon nuts and the reliance of others on mesquite are well documented in Chapter 4 concerning the ethnographic literature. Because juniper berry consumption has been less prominent in the records of customary use, I think some scholars have unwittingly downgraded the potential juniper berries have as a food. From the review of historic juniper berry consumption in Chapter 4 in conjunction with the prehistoric record, it is apparent that the berries also helped people survive the winter months.

No undisturbed areas could be identified as preagricultural in composition in this study. The disruption caused by rodent burrows or pits intruding into older deposits in areas of good preservation has been extensive. The use of mesquite, juniper, pinyon, and perhaps buffalo gourd seed approximates the reconstruction of the cold season segment of preagricultural diet in Fresnal Shelter.

A trend exists toward higher rates of recovery of hedgehog cactus, desert four o'clock root, and prickly pear stem joints from

Table 5.5. Ranked Comparison of Content of Screened Levels With and Without Maize

Taxon	With maize % (fraction)	Without maize % (fraction)
Mesquite endocarps	97 (31/32)	100 (11/11)
Juniper seed	94 (30/32)	100 (11/11)
Piñon shell	91 (29/32)	100 (11/11)
Yucca seeds	84 (27/32)	73 (8/11)
Buffalo gourd seed or shell	81 (26/32)	64 (7/11)
Sotol carpels	78 (25/32)	54 (6/11)
Acorn fragments	66 (21/32)	64 (7/11)
Prickly pear seeds	56 (18/32)	45 (5/11)
Hedgehog cactus parts	50 (16/32)	18 (2/11)
Desert four o'clock root fragments	50 (16/32)	36 (4/11)
Prickly pear stem joints	50 (16/32)	18 (2/11)
Turk's head barrel cactus areoles	44 (14/32)	45 (5/11)
Four-wing saltbush fruit cores	38 (12/32)	45 (5/11)
Quids, unidentified	72 (23/32)	64 (7/11)

levels with maize (Table 5.5). The heavier use of sotol seeds seems to be part of the same propensity. Evidently while task groups monitored fields of maize to protect them, they consumed plant resources readily accessible within the canyon and available during the growing season. I believe the trend can be interpreted in terms of collecting activities being tethered to the requirements of successfully raising maize and later, beans. In order to stay close to the fields (or work parties to stay close to the fields), Fresnal Shelter was used more intensively for collecting plant products that grew nearby and down canyon. The wild plants they may have utilized until maize was mature, is an acknowledgement of the importance of the domesticated plant and the role it probably played as a storable winter resource. Julian H. Steward (1938: 19) remarks that digging roots (four o'clock in this case) often was a leisure activity that did not require residential movement. Desert four o'clock roots certainly take time and patience to obtain, given the size and extent of the roots. And it would make sense to use the seeds of sotol as a renewable resource rather than destroy the entire plant by roasting the crowns, as at Hinds Cave in the lower Pecos of western Texas (Dering 1999). Fresnal customary plant use seems well adapted to intensified living in a restricted area.

In years when no maize was grown, the priorities of wild harvests changed in obscure ways. The weed grass *Chloris crinita* is absent. A lower diversity of plants was used. If drought were involved, the decrease in use of four o'clock root may be caused by the increased effort to dig the roots in hard soil, reducing the net caloric return for labor considerably. The average number of taxa in levels without maize is less, but the range of variation is quite high.

THE ROLE OF FRESNAL SHELTER FROM EARLIEST DATED MAIZE TO THE START OF A

VERY MOIST PERIOD (2945 ± 55 B.P. TO 2770 ± 70 B.P.)

David Hurst Thomas (1983a: 73) provides a Binfordian definition of a base camp as one that functions in processing, manufacturing, and maintenance. Field camps differ from base camps because of their short-term occupation (Thomas 1983a: 80), with subsistence heavily weighted towards either plant or animal consumption, with locations close to the point of procurement, and with low artifact diversity (Thomas 1983a: 79-80). Base camps, particularly of collectors, should exhibit the storage of food and implements. Thomas also adds evidence of children, since they would be reared primarily in a base camp.

Thomas (1983a: 78) develops other criteria for base camps that only are defined relative to field camps. Higher levels of food consumption would be expected to produce high levels of discard as compared to a field camp. Lithic production is better-planned and executed of higher quality materials for more permanent tools. Recreational items or ceremonial items are more abundant. As valid as the differences may be, they are difficult to recognize when produced as part of a gradient in behaviors.

The recognition of field camps as distinct from base camps in the archaeological record is complicated by a variety of behaviors that may have taken place in a single location and their subsequent obscurement by post-depositional conditions (Thomas 1983a: 80). Seasonal base camps, temporarily abandoned, can become short-term field camps a few months later. Areas that had once been a residential base are often reoccupied by task groups to harvest plants, to collect basketry material, and so forth. Some field camps may be re-occupied year after year, some logistically oriented for several weeks or as long as three months (Thomas 1983a).

A multifunctional archaeological site, as

seems to be the case with Fresnal Shelter, can be created from distinct behavioral entities. I have adopted Thomas's various operational definitions (mid-range theory) to help identify some ways Fresnal Shelter functioned.

Dietary Arguments for a Short-Term Winter Base Camp

A number of arguments can be marshaled for the use of mesquite, pinyon, and juniper in the winter. Their presence in all eleven levels lacking maize (Table 5.5) underlines the probable role these items once played in winter subsistence. The three foods are available close to the time needed, offer easy storage, and the highest return in kilocalories per hour for effort expended (Chapter 7). Of the five relatively large storage pits still found in place, one still retained mesquite seeds (endocarps?) intermixed in the grass lining. The observation that in the Great Basin most caches for winter consumption tend to be near the projected winter residence (Thomas 1983a: 85) provides ethnographic support for the use of Fresnal Shelter as a short-term winter base camp.

If one accepts the above arguments in support of a short term winter base camp in non-maize bearing screened levels, one can extend the same arguments to include maize, as it ripens in the fall, is amenable to storage, and provides a high caloric return for effort. In most levels where maize is present, it accompanies mesquite, pinyon, and juniper (Table 5.5).

Mesquite pods and ears of maize are high bulk items that were probably harvested at lower elevations and temporarily stored nearby. They would be transported later to the area of winter residence as Thomas (1983a: 81) suggests. The presence of field camps to harvest mesquite and maize is assumed. I failed to note any mesquite endocarps with bruchid beetle holes from beans reinfected from long-term storage. Complete and rapid consumption

seems indicated. Buffalo gourd seed is found in a greater number of screened levels that also have maize (81 percent) as compared to levels that lack maize (64 percent) in Table 5.5. Dried buffalo gourds are conspicuous on the margins of washes as one travels to lower elevations where maize was likely grown. As people returned to Fresnal Shelter with stored maize or mesquite it would be convenient to gather dried gourd fruits as well. The oily seed is energy rich and preparation can be deferred as needed as is true for maize.

Geographic Arguments for a Short-Term Winter Base Camp

The geographic position of Fresnal Shelter makes it suitable for winter occupancy as it is close to water and extensive stands of fuel. Late fall food resources, such as pinyon and juniper, are near. In addition, sunshine penetrates Fresnal Shelter in winter. Finally, the location of Fresnal Shelter high on the canyon margin minimizes cold air drainage from the Sacramento Mountains.

Cultural Arguments for a Short-Term Winter Base Camp

Base camps of collectors should show evidence of food storage, relevant tools, and evidence of children. The digging sticks, metates, manos, at least some fire-cracked rock, as well as the hearth for a fire drill in Fresnal Shelter typify the domestic equipment for food processing in a preceramic culture. Of 152 sandals that were classified into 13 styles, half were two-warp sandals finished in a fishtail heel (Styles l, 9, and 11). Of these, 25 belonged to children (Merchant 2002, Table 36). An infant was also buried in the shelter (HSR 1973).

The evidence of manufacture versus maintenance becomes confounded archaeologically. I interpret the discard of worn, perishable items as a sign of maintenance behavior in as much as something of a less fragile nature presumably replaced it. But in a sense, the unseen item that replaced it was likely manufactured. Thus fragments of a pitched basket (that might have been a water jug), sandals, and cordage bits appear as random discards, while checker weave mats survive as recycled fragments in storage pits. The presence of rabbit fur cordage (Moots 1990), presumably part of a woven fur wrap or blanket is one frequent artifact that suggests winter occupancy. Among the lithic debris we are told there is considerable evidence of biface resharpening (R. Jones 1990). Bone dice were also recovered (Irwin-Williams 1979). In summary, the dietary, geographic, and cultural arguments suggest a base camp. The strongest evidence is for a winter base camp, but additional possibilities present themselves.

Role Either as a Residential Base Camp or Temporary Field Camp or Both

After a period of low availability of food resources over the winter, the maturation of New Mexico feather grass in late May or early June was an important event that had little variance from year to year, as it belongs to a class of cool season grasses (Bohrer 1975a) known to thrive on sparse winter moisture. New Mexico feather grass probably was as high a ranked food item as might be found locally at this time of year (Chapter 7). Logistical parties came back to Fresnal Shelter and processed the grain. However, we do not know how long they encamped.

Dropseed grasses typically respond to moisture during the growing season by flowering and setting seed. Seed maturation characteristically depends on available moisture, and given the erratic nature of thunderstorms that sweep the landscape in summer and fall, dropseed fails as a good seasonal indicator. And yet we know that logistical parties returned

from gathering the crop to winnow the chaff within the shelter. But we do not know when, nor how long people remained.

From the maize tassels recovered, we know people were in the shelter long before crop maturity. We also know that prickly pear stems, hedgehog cactii, and desert four o'clock root fragments are more consistently represented in levels with maize. While the vegetative portions indicate no season, they may have sustained people as maize was maturing. During growing seasons when maize was not planted, travel away from Fresnal Shelter could have been more extensive. Fresnal Shelter could have served as one field camp in a variety of residential moves, some of which took people out into the Tularosa Basin to gather Indian rice grass.

Role as a Temporary Camp for Butchering Deer

Because there is no sign of mid-winter kill of deer at Fresnal Shelter, the use of the shelter as a temporary logistical camp for butchering deer remains compatible with the use of Frenal Shelter as a winter base camp. The estimated season of deer kill in late summer to early fall (Wimberly and Eidenbach 1981: 25-26) places at least some collecting parties outside of Fresnal Shelter either in field camps or short-term base camps. This would be the season that maize fields might need protection from animal predation.

The use of Fresnal Shelter as a butchering station was quite limited compared to other activities in the shelter. The large mammal bone analysis from Fresnal Shelter produced a count of 26 deer-spanning at least 1,500 years. The presence of a high percent of low muscle mass bone elements indicates the shelter was near enough to the kill area that the deer were taken to the shelter for butchering. At some point most bones that carried the larger muscle mass were carried elsewhere. An appropriate time might have been when others were encamped near maize fields to protect the crop.

THE ROLE OF FRESNAL SHELTER FROM THE EARLIEST INTRODUCTION OF BEANS UNTIL ABANDONMENT (2085 ± 60 B.P. TO 1550 B.P.)

The latest date for growing maize in Fresnal Shelter is 1665 ± 55 B.P., calibrated at one-sigma, A.D. 264 to 428 (Tagg 1996: 317). Toward the end of occupation of Fresnal Shelter we have indications that the pattern of living may have changed.

> 1. Large storage pits are used for discard.
>
> 2. The earliest common beans date to 2085 ± 60 B.P.
>
> 3. Cultivated squash may have been grown.
>
> 4. A cob with 18 rows was recovered from disturbed level 2.
>
> 5. Turkey feathers in Square C 31 and C 32 are limited to levels 1 and 2 except for a cache of feathers in a small pit in Square C 32 (Appendix A.1), suggesting minimal disruption and a late introduction.
>
> 6. Feather artifacts may be relatively late and relatively rare.

The array of cultigens may have changed with the arrival of domesticated beans. Changes in squash morphology in the upper levels suggest another domesticated crop. We lack evidence of domesticated amaranth toward the end of occupation. The 18-row cob from the upper disturbed level may be intrusive or may signify either indigenous selection or outside introduction of new genetic material.

Artifacts of feathers are uncommon. Feather cordage was not reported by Moots (1990) or McBrinn (2005), who examined 491 specimens of cordage from varied locations. Cordage with split feather shafts inserted into it and wrapped tightly around it derive from Square 01.D18.26, Level 2. Feather-wrapped twine was also recovered in a pit made into B29E, Unit F. A string-and-feather ornament from Fresnal Shelter (unprovenienced) was illustrated by Irwin-Williams (1979: 42).

If Fresnal no longer served as a winter base camp, what may have once been a field camp near the maize growing area could have become a residential base. People may have become proficient with raising maize. Fresnal Shelter could have become a logistical camp for the harvest of pinyon and juniper. Additionally, people were seeking dry spots in the shelter to leave beans around 2015 ± 65 B.P. All these remarks are approximations of what really might have happened, as there is even less stratigraphic control within the upper levels of the shelter itself than elsewhere.

WHO WERE THESE PEOPLE?

They were a Late Archaic agricultural people who had cultural ties to Mexico, if we can judge by the perishable artifacts. They were by no means an isolated pioneering outpost. Adults wearing various sandal styles lingered long enough to replace their worn footwear at Fresnal Shelter. Such travelers may also have left their own stylized bifaces, some of which show influences seen in the Trans-Pecos and among the Cochise-Mogollon. Doubtless a variety of people were attracted to the nearby Tularosa Basin, particularly as the vegetation was enriched by more predictable rains during the early part of the Late Archaic. We know other people were living in Fresnal Canyon during the era when the earliest maize came into use. High Rolls Cave was less desirable for year around living because of its shady north-exposure. When all prime living spaces were apparently occupied so early, the canyon was, in a sense, overcrowded.

The people were plant collectors: people who relied on food storage to help survive the winter. But the occupants of Fresnal Shelter were cultivators of maize and later, beans: a people who sent work groups or portions of their household to tend the fields while others maintained residence at Fresnal Shelter. They left a record of vigorous plant collecting and processing. When crops were nearing maturity and needed guarding from predators, much of the population might have been down canyon, engaged in work parties—including some on collecting expeditions for dropseed grass, leaving a small segment of hunters at Fresnal Shelter on the look out for deer. Since no plant record was recovered from Fresnal Shelter that was preagricultural in nature, we can only surmise the nature of earlier subsistence from occupational levels that lack maize, but in which winter resources of pinyon, juniper, and mesquite are prominent. At times people may have traveled or lived away from Fresnal Shelter. On moonlit nights Fresnal Shelter would resonate with the sound of scurrying mice, wood rats, and later with the cries of an owl who left his meal pellets behind on the littered shelter floor.

Chapter 6
High Rolls Cave

Unlike most Late Archaic sites in the Southwest, High Rolls Cave preserved uncarbonized plant material, though unevenly. The extensive stratigraphy coupled with generous radiocarbon dating fostered the hope of segregating different episodes of Archaic occupation. Since Fresnal Shelter lacked flotation from thermal features, the carbonized plant remains from High Rolls hearths were of special interest.

Additional information on High Rolls Cave is presented in earlier chapters. Chapter 3 discusses the problem of recognizing signs of rodent activity, the stratigraphic context in which plant remains were recovered, and chronology and dating maize. Chapter 4 reviews the condition of plant parts of each taxon and whether the wind or animal vectors might have introduced the taxon. The tendency of a species to thrive with disturbance, human or otherwise, is also addressed, as well as any ethnographic data that might assist with interpretation. Discussions of cultivated maize, amaranth, and tobacco from High Rolls can be found there. Concerns regarding taxa from High Rolls Cave in Chapter 4 were in many ways similar to those for Fresnal Shelter. They helped identify the species people consumed or were otherwise of ethnobotanical importance. The context of recovery of each sample appears in Appendix B.1. and the analysis of pollen in Appendix B.4. The analysis of vertebrate bone contains important evidence concerning subsistence and seasonality.

IDENTIFICATION OF DIETARY COMPONENTS

Vertebrate Bone Remains

The largest number of bones impacted by human activity can be attributed to the hunting of mule deer (*Odocoileus hemionus*), bighorn sheep (*Ovis canadensis*), and pronghorn (*Antilocarpa americana*). When the minimum number of individuals per stratum is estimated (Akins 2002:, Tables 13, 14, 15), the bulk of the bone can be attributed to deer and bighorn sheep and the lesser amount to pronghorn. When Strata 1, 2, and 3 are considered, of the 37 or 38 individuals estimated, 20 are deer, 7 bighorn sheep and 10 to 11 pronghorn. Some of the deer, bighorn sheep, and pronghorn bones show signs of carnivore scavenging.

The most common small mammal was the cottontail rabbit (*Sylvilagus* sp.) with the largest in size approximating the Eastern cottontail. When the distribution of the cottontail rabbits is viewed on a stratum-by-stratum basis, probably no more than 16 mature and 18 immature individuals are represented in the whole site (Akins 2002: 15). In Stratum 2 the rabbit bones show signs of carnivore alteration. It is only in Stratum 3 that the cottontail bones bear evidence of heavy burning (Akins 2002: Table 5). Wood rats (*Neotoma* sp) were believed to be the primary rodent inhabiting the shelter based on bone part distributions. Wood rat bones are recovered in almost every stratum (Akins 2000: 12); some show possible thermal alteration.

Bones of turkey (*Meleagris gallapavo*) were in Stratum 1 (FS 197), Stratum 2 (FS 206 and FS 217), Stratum 2, Layer 1 (FS 740), Stratum 2, Layer 2 (FS 1100), and in disturbed strata (FS 492). The distal end of the tibiotarsus in Stratum 2 (FS 217) showed oblique cut marks. The two bones from FS 206 came from Excavation Unit 13, from which a flotation sample (FS 208) was obtained as well. No eggshells or immature skeletal elements that might indicate domesticated turkeys were recovered. The recovered pieces of eggshell more likely belong to the prairie chicken, for they resemble that bird's eggs in size and coloration.

Plant Remains

Interpretation and Flotation Samples

Flotation samples from features and excavation units at High Rolls are placed chronologically from oldest to youngest in Table 6.1 and Table 6.2. While Table 6.1 uses actual radiocarbon dates of all features, only six radiocarbon dates are available for the 12 excavation units. The radiocarbon dates of the samples can be found in Tables B.3.1, B.3.2, and B.3.3. The linear ordering of samples can be deceptive. Sometimes two samples may have the same radiocarbon date, but may have been in actual use at different points in time. Or two features may have overlapping radiocarbon dates but may have been in use at the same time. Certain thermal features, either because of archaeological or botanical evidence (see threeleaf sumac), were believed reused after a period of abandonment. In addition, rodents may introduce items at random. It is unrealistic to imagine a single sequence of feature use from Table 6.1. Archaeologists who further analyze the context of radiocarbon dates in all locations may modify my limited perspective on dating.

The flotation record from features may under-represent some dietary items. Note that mesquite, prickly pear, and perhaps juniper berries, foods typically prepared without the use of fire, have a weaker record of use in features than in excavation units (Tables 6.1 and 6.2). The use of the flotation process itself evidently impairs the recovery of dropseed grass grain, for much more was recovered from the heavy fraction of FS 67 than the light fraction (Chapter 4 and Appendix B.1). Table 6.3 combines the frequency of use in *all* flotation samples from features and excavation units and ranks them from most common to most rare. Note that globemallow seed is restricted to features and only buffalo gourd is absent from features. All in all, the lists of taxa are essentially similar, but differ in rank. Table 6.3 probably underestimates the role of maize in the diet, a subject discussed in the following chapter.

Pre-maize Diet: Chronological Analysis of Flotation from Features

The number of times a given taxon appears in dated features, totaled on the right hand side of Table 6.1, provides a rough measure of the most common items recovered through time. Note that taxa of high frequency use fire in their preparation: pinyon nuts, fruits of yucca, New Mexico feather grass, dropseed grass, false tarragon, and chenopodium. Such remains might be preserved in a less protected site.

The nature of pre-maize diet can be evaluated from Table 6.1. For example, if we assume the sample from Feature 11b represents the adoption of maize (2940 ± 60 B.P. with a 2-sigma calibration of 1400 to 1030 B.C.), then at least some samples to the left of it represent a pre-maize diet.

The plant content of Features 1 and 3 from Stratum 3 could represent either pre-maize diet or derive from early years of its adoption. Apparently globemallow and purslane seeds were collected and parched during Stratum 3 times, which spans from 3460 ± 60 B.P. to 3250

Table 6.1. High Rolls Plant Foods Arranged Chronologically from Oldest to Youngest by Carbon-14 Dated Features

Feature	11a	15	24	1	3	9	23	5	11b	18	13a	13b	8	22	6	2	Total
Botanical Sample																	
Trees																	
Pinon cone scales or nut fragments				c	c	c		x	c			x		x	c		8
Juniper seeds						c		x	x								3
Mesquite									c								1
Desert Succulent Seed																	
Yucca baccata type	c			c	c		xc		c	c		c			c	c	9
Prickly pear				c	c		x	x	xc								5
Hedgehog cactus														x			1
Grass Grains																	
Rye grass	c																1
Love grass								x									1
Rice grass								x									1
Panic grass					c										c		2
Dropseed grass				c	c		c	x	xc		x				c		7
New Mexico feathergrass	c							x	c			c	c	x			6
Maize								c	c								2
Other Annual or Perennials																	
Amaranth																	
False tarragon															xc		1
Sunflower/goldeneye						c	c		c	c	x	c	c				7
Chenopodium		c	c														2
Cheno-am	c			c	xc	c	c		c	c	c	xc	c	x	xc	x	13
Globe mallow	c			c	c		c		c	c	c	xc	c		c	c	11
Purslane	c			c													2
Peppergrass				c											x	x	3
Tobacco															xc		1
Number of Taxa	6	1	1	9	10	4	6	7	12	3	6	6	3	3	8	3	

c = carbonized; x = present

* Omitted are undated Feature 19 and Features 7 and 14 of uncertain date

Table 6.2. High Rolls Excavation Unit Plant Foods Arranged Chronologically from Oldest to Youngest Stratigraphic Unit by Field Sample Number

Excavation Unit	33	27	27	4	5	13	10	63	27	88	12	4	
Stratum/layer	3	2/3	2/2	2/2	2	2	2/3	2/3	2/1	2	?2	1	
Field Sample Number	1256	805	795	139	67	208	557	773	742	853	187	70	SUM
Trees													
Pinon cone scales			c		x		c	x					4
Pinon nut fragments		x	x	x	x	x	x	x		x	x	x	10
Juniper seeds		x	x		x	xc	x		x	x	x	x	9
Mesquite endocarps			x	x	x	x	x	x		x	xc		8
Desert Succulent Seed													
Yucca baccata type		c	x		xc	x		xc		x	c		7
Prickly pear	x	x	x	c	x	c	x	x	x	xc	x		11
Hedgehog cactus					x				x	x			3
Grass Grains													
Rye grass					x		x		x		c		4
Love grass				x			x			x		xc	4
Panic grass		x	x	x	x			x		x		x	7
Dropseed grass	x	x	x		x	x		x		x	xc	x	9
New Mexico feathergrass		c			x	xc	c	xc			c		6
Maize		x	x	xc	x		c				x		6
Other Annual or Perennials													
Amaranth			x		x	xc		x		x	c		6
False tarragon	x					c		xc		x	c		5
Sunflower/goldeneye					x	x	c	x		x			5
Chenopodium	x	x	xc		x	x	xc	x	x	c	xc		10
Cheno-am	x	x	xc	x	xc	xc	xc	x	x	xc	xc	x	12
Globe mallow													0
Purslane					x			x		x			3
Peppergrass									x	c			2
Buffalo Gourd					x								1
Tobacco	x								c	x	c		4
Number of Food Taxa including Tobacco	6	10	12	7	18	12	12	14	8	17	14	6	

c = carbonized; x = present

± 60 B.P. Feature 7 was omitted from Table 6.1, as the date appears too old. Yet by its content of globemallow and purslane seeds (Appendix B.1), it approximates the age of Features 1 and 3. Well after the introduction of maize, the collection of purslane seeds continues but globemallow seed apparently terminates in Stratum 3. Like the globemallow seed, the evidence for the consumption of plains bristle grass (*Setaria macrostachya*) is restricted to Feature 3. The two carbonized wild rye grass complex grains in Feature 11a in Stratum 3 only reappear once more in flotation (FS 187). A botanical record of food stress may be reflected in the carbonized seeds of prickly pear from Features 3 and 11a, which could represent seed parching

Table 6.3. Frequency and Ranking of Dietary Components in all Excavation Units and Features

Excavation Units	Frequency#	Rank	Features	Frequency#	Rank
Cheno-am seed	12	1	*Chenopodium* seed	13	1
Prickly pear seed	11	2	Cheno-am	10	2
Chenopodium seed*	10	3	*Yucca baccata*	9	3
Piñon*	10	3	Piñon*	8	4
Juniper seed*	9	4	False tarragon achenes	7	5
Dropseed grass*	9	4	Prickly pear seed*	7	5
Mesquite*	8	5	Dropseed grass*	7	5
Panic grass*	7	6	New Mexico feathergrass*	6	6
Yucca baccata	7	6	Juniper seed*	4	7
New Mexico feathergrass*	6	7	Globemallow	3	8
Maize*	6	7	Purslane	3	8
Amaranth*	6	7	Sunflower/ goldeneye achenes	3	8
False tarragon achenes	5	8	Panic grass*	2	9
Sunflower/ goldeneye achenes	5	8	Maize*	2	9
Hedgehog cactus	4	9	Ryegrass complex	1	10
Rye grass complex	4	9	Mesquite*	1	10
Lovegrass	4	9	Lovegrass	1	10
Purslane seed	3	10	Peppergrass	1	10
Tobacco	3	11	Hedgehog cactus	1	10
Peppergrass	2	12	Tobacco	1	10
Buffalo gourd*	1	13			
Globemallow Sotol seed*		0			

based upon presence or absence
* Item important at Fresnal Shelter

accidents. Feature 3 also contains a fragment of roasted prickly pear epidermal tissue, the only really good indication in the entire site that joints were roasted.

Additional signs of possible dietary stress come from the utilized bone. In Stratum 3 the heavily burned cottontail rabbit bones provide the strongest evidence of human rabbit consumption in the entire sequence of strata. Possible thermally altered wood rat bones were recovered in Stratum 3 and Stratum 2. Cottontail rabbit consumption could imply low availability of both larger animals and the inability to capture a sufficient number of wood rats inhabiting the cave.

Flotation from Stratum 2 Excavation Units
When flotation samples from excavation units are arranged chronologically (Table 6.2), a strong record of wild plant use throughout Stratum 2 times is evident. The lack of dietary compositional contrast in excavation unit samples with maize and without maize provides little evidence of food stress compared to Table 6.1 and the zoological record.

By examining the six highest ranked food items shared in both excavation units and features (Table 6.3), one obtains a more balanced perspective. New Mexico feather grass and false tarragon seed rank in the top six only in features, while mesquite, panic grass, and juniper rank in the top six only in the excavation units. The top six ranks shared by both excavation units and features include cheno-ams, *Chenopodium*, pinyon nuts, prickly pear, and dropseed grass. There are many ways one might simplify Table 6.3, but this method highlights eleven foodstuffs of highest frequency as follows:

1. cheno-ams
2. Chenopodium
3. Paniceae grass(es)
4. dropseed grass
5. New Mexico feather grass
6. false tarragon seed
7. juniper berries
8. mesquite pods
9. pinyon nuts
10. prickly pear fruit
11. Yucca baccata type fruit

Synthesis of Flotation from Stratum 2 and 3
The attention at High Rolls Cave to small seed gathering apparently preceded the adoption of maize agriculture and also followed it. Not all of the species are annuals like chenopodium and purslane are, but they are plants that bear small but numerous seeds such as dropseed

grass and false tarragon. The use of globe-mallow seed and plains bristle grass (*Setaria macrostachya*) may have been restricted to pre-maize diet or its early introduction.

The occupants of High Rolls Cave tend to either create or follow disturbance of the pinyon-juniper plant community to assure themselves of collecting highly productive annuals and perennials. Diverse plant entities such as ryegrass, love grass, false tarragon, globemallow, peppergrass, purslane, a member of the parsley family, sunflower, and golden-eye apparently were unique resources in High Rolls Cave. People were able to continuously harvest early successional species over a period of 500 years.

Pollen Analysis and the Nature of Diet
Pollen studies from High Rolls Cave (Holloway 2002 and Appendix B.4) provide additional evidence of plant usage. Five more excavation units have maize pollen than noted through flotation, bringing the total to 11. Features 5 and 6 contain a unique record of maize pollen as well. Mesquite pollen occurs in eight excavation units beyond those previously noted for having mesquite. Pollen from the rose family recovered in Strata 2 and 3 may be of ethno-botanical importance. Concentrations of rose family pollen were in eight excavation units in East Clusters A and B and three excavation units in the West Cluster. Significantly, pollen from the family was recovered in three fecal samples indicating the plant part was edible. Members of the carrot or parsley family and the mustard family were also consumed, judging by residual pollen in fecal samples and distribution of pollen of each type in four other excavation units. The use of peppergrass in the mustard family was proposed from flotation evidence, and the pollen record reinforces the supposition. While a few cattail seeds were recovered in flotation, apparently the pollen was of more significance as a foodstuff. Cattail pollen

appears in a particularly high concentration in one excavation unit in the West Cluster (EU 59) and is documented in four other excavation units.

SEASONALITY IN STRATUM 2 AND 3

The best plant species useful in establishing the seasons when High Rolls Cave was occupied are relatively few in number and are heavily biased toward spring and fall (Table 6.4). Pollen from willow in the cave is indicative of early spring occupation (Appendix B.4). Its relatively heavy pollen is poorly transported by the wind, but is readily transported by insects. Its presence in the cave suggests it may have been carried in on willow shoots, which could have been a raw material for basketry or perhaps the catkins were valued as food (Rea 1997: 195). The high concentration of mustard pollen in human coprolites carries seasonal information, for the mustard family is also insect-pollinated and restricts its blossoming to the cool season, generally spring. Similarly, the harvest of a cool season grain like New Mexico feather grass also indicates spring occupation, though it could be as late as June. Cattail (*Typha latifolia*) flowers between May and July depending on elevation. Its pollen was recovered in concentrations high enough to suggest human consumption.

Plant species recovered in High Rolls Cave that typically mature in the fall include maize, cultivated amaranth, prickly pear fruits, yucca fruits, and pods of mesquite. Pinyon nuts are normally released from their cones relatively late in the fall, but burned cone scales suggest people roasted the cones to release the nuts prior to frost. Due to nut introduction by rodents from nearby pinyon trees, we have ambiguous evidence that pinyon nuts were harvested after the frost.

Documenting the presence of people in High Rolls Cave using the summer harvest of wild plants proved impractical. Many of the utilized plants (Table 6.3) demonstrate shifting seasonality, when reproduction is confined to a time when temperature and moisture are conducive to growth. Thus dropseed grass might be available in mid-June some years or not until July or far into the fall depending on the nature of the rainfall. Cheno-ams, goosefoot, globemallow and false tarragon typically have or could have a similar flexibility in maturation. Although maize pollen was recovered, it might have arrived clinging to ears of maize brought to the cave. No maize tassel fragments preserved in High Rolls Cave that might have otherwise indicated mid-summer presence.

Immature artiodactyl bones commonly and consistently document a July to August occupation throughout Stratum 2 and Stratum 3. The evidence contrasts with the absence of fall and the scarcity of artiodactyls killed in late fall (November and December) (Atkins 2002: 42). Similarly, there is a lack of evidence that young pronghorn were killed from October to March and to only infrequent butchering of deer and bighorn sheep ewes in winter (Atkins 2002: Table 23). The author suggests 1) only mature animals were hunted, 2) other resources may be more important, and 3) High Rolls Cave was not used as a hunting camp.

Inasmuch as the mildness, severity, or duration of any one season in New Mexico is far from predictable, the human response to the more limited calendar-defined seasons should also vary. Part of the season, High Rolls Cave may not have been used either for plant collecting or as a base camp for hunting. Sometimes the harvest of maize or pinyon may have had priority over hunting. Similarly, the recovery of the seed of buffalo gourd may represent a singular post-frost incident. Following the final pinyon harvest, the occupants typically might have departed for a cold season encampment in or near the Tularosa Basin. In winter the slopes

Table 6.4. Plants from High Rolls Cave Whose Reproductive Parts Best Document Seasonal Procurement

Taxon	Part harvested	Timing
Willow	pollen	early spring
Mustard family	seed?	spring
Rye grass	grain	late spring
Indian rice grass	grain	late spring
New Mexican feather grass	grain*	late spring, following Indian rice grass
Cattail	pollen	late spring (May-July)
Piñon	nut*	fall
Prickly pear cactus	fruit*	fall
Mesquite	pod*	early fall
Banana yucca	fruit	fall

*of special dietary importance

to High Rolls Cave were covered with snow at times, and the north-facing cave opening could not shield people from severe storms. A cave abandoned in the cold season might have served as a lair for carnivores that gnawed bones from cultural levels, for grey fox, ringtail, and coyote occupied High Rolls Cave in historic times. It is also possible that dogs were partly responsible for bone damage.

ROLE OF HIGH ROLLS CAVE STRATUM 2 AND 3

During Stratum 2 and 3 High Rolls Cave served as a logistical base camp for families from spring when the first bees visited the willows in Fresnal Canyon until the last pinyon nut was gathered in fall; in short, during the growing season. The recovery of children's sandals suggests the presence of families while the record of processing of both plant and animal remains both within and outside of thermal features strongly supports the assertion. Most occupants apparently were absent during winter plant dormancy. I have assumed that a portion of the maize that was raised was cached near their winter residence. The diverse evidence suggests human occupation of High Rolls Cave typically encompassed the growing season only. The term *semi-sedentary* might describe their mode of living. Conceivably, we may be observing a pattern of transhumance that alternates between the Tularosa Basin in winter and High Rolls Cave during the remainder of the year.

Stratum 1 Notes on Subsistence

Assessment of dietary usage from Stratum 1 is limited to one or possibly two flotation samples, FS 70 and FS 187. The latter sample was recovered at 46 cmbs, which seems unusually deep for a sample of a late date. The material used for the radiocarbon date (FS 188) may have been intrusive and not reflect the age of FS 187. Among the potential food items in FS 70 are cheno-ams, dropseed grass, juniper, and pinyon nuts, which are all frequently recovered in Stratum 2.

Radiocarbon-dated maize from the last occupation have cobs, shanks, and husk intact. All but 3 of 17 unburned cobs from the final occupation have been displaced from Stratum 1 into Stratum 2 and preserved in East Clusters A and B. The oldest maize plant parts from the final occupation, a shank and husk, radiocarbon date to 2060 ± 40 B.P. and the youngest cobs date to 1320 ± 80 B.P. (Table B.3.3).

During Stratum 1 High Rolls Cave no longer served as a logistical base camp in the same way, for there are no thermal features. So little has been preserved that its manner of use is puzzling. The one lot of seven maize cobs from Excavation Unit 4, Stratum 2 at 50 cmbs (FS 146) displays a uniformity of row number that suggests that ears saved for their seed were either cached or shelled at High Rolls Cave. Each of six cobs had 12 rows and one cob may have had ten rows.

Stratum 1 has a pronghorn and a bighorn bone fragment with the remainder identified as deer or medium artiodactyl bones (Akins 2002: 46). Most of the artiodactyl bones belong to mature animals, but immature deer bones suggest some deposition in both summer and winter (Akins 2002: 43). Long bones and rib bones are most common and in this respect are similar to the high processing seen in Stratum 3 (Akins 2002: 56). Rabbit bones show signs of carnivore alteration. Bones of turkey (*Melea-*

gris gallapavo) were in Stratum 1 (FS 197).

Travel Between the Tularosa Basin and High Rolls Cave

I initially assumed High Rolls people traversed Fresnal Canyon via La Luz Canyon to the Tularosa Basin. Considering the amount of residue of mesquite pods and mesquite pollen, many trips must have been necessary to transport bulky pods from the Tularosa Basin margins to High Rolls Cave. However, they left no evidence of use of Turk's head barrel cactus or the fruit wings of saltbush, and only minimal evidence of low elevation disturbed ground plants was recovered. The record is minimal when compared with Fresnal Shelter. The few *Amaranthus torreyi* capsules could have come in with other wild amaranth heads from a lower elevation. It makes me wonder why High Rolls Cave deposits did not also preserve some of the low elevation *Chloris crinita* weed grass, at least by nesting mice. Instead, the furry leaves of local *Gnaphalium* probably provided nest lining.

To reconcile my observations of the plant record with the travel route, I believe High Rolls people must have entered the Tularosa Basin via Dry Canyon, to the immediate south of Fresnal Canyon. Very few riparian disturbed ground plants would be encountered. The route would have been shorter by about half (4.8 kilometers) and much steeper. The modern highway that goes past High Rolls also ascends the Tularosa Basin via Dry Canyon.

Medicinal or Ceremonial

While my research objective was to identify human food use, cultivated amaranth, maize, and tobacco also have potential religious importance (Chapter 4). Excavation Unit 27 contained what may be a fortuitous mix of items partly introduced by rodents, or some might have been used to supplicate the supernatural. Feather fragments were recovered in two contiguous levels of flotation in FS 742 and a split feather in FS 795. An unburned morning glory seed comes from the north half of Excavation Unit 27, and both a flower of native tobacco (*Nicotiana trigonophylla* type) and rolled leaves were recovered from FS 742.

Additional macrobotanical items may be of potential importance. Mollie S.Toll (1998) identified charcoal (FS 20) from test pit 2, level 1 as white fir and either spruce or Douglas fir. Wood of these species has the potential to symbolize evergreen trees that grow at high elevations near rain bearing clouds. The single unburned seed of morning glory (*Ipomoea,* FS 6) and *Datura* (FS 955) may simply be rodent-introduced into Stratum 1 or may have been obtained for some hallucinatory function. Charred morning glory seed was recovered from Fresnal Shelter.

Chapter 7
Behavioral Ecology, Optimal Foraging, and the Diet Breadth Model

The criteria that animals used to select their diets have been the focus of considerable interest and research. Many believe the selection of food is not a random affair on the part of a given animal but one produced by a process that has evolved by Darwinian natural selection to maximize fitness.

Few will deny the apparent behavioral adaptations different species of animals display in acquiring their food. But within any one species there is a range of variation. Those portions of a population that are more successful in acquiring food (better adapted) are more apt to survive the natural selection pressure in their environment; they are more fit. They live to raise healthy progeny and their descendants contribute more progeny. The application of natural selection theory in anthropology to the study of the shaping of human society has become known as behavioral ecology. Behavioral ecology analyzes choices with respect to their impact on reproduction, health, and survival (R. Kelly 1995: 51). For example, a model was developed for the Ache of Paraguay that assumes foragers will spend time in those activities that lower the mortality rates of their children and increase their own reproductive rates (Hill and Hurtado 1989: 441). Optimal foraging theory comprises one aspect of behavioral ecology. Some key features are listed below.

1. Foraging behavior shows bio- logically or socially heritable variation and this affects the degree of contribution of a given behavior to the next generation (Smith 1983).

2. A range of possible foraging behavior exists, implying the existence of constraints (Smith 1983).

3. Natural selection will favor those individuals in a population that contribute most to subsequent generations (Pyke and others 1977: 138).

4. Over a period of time, the average foraging behavior in a population will change toward one that gives maximum fitness (Pyke and others 1977: 138).

5. Increased growth or speed of development relate to increased intake of food in many studies (Schoener 1971: 372). If increased growth implies earlier reproduction or reproduction at a larger size, fitness may be increased (Schoener 1972: 372). The increased energy that is needed for reproduction also suggests a relationship between food intake and reproductive output (Schoener 1972: 372). In other words, to maximize rates of food acquisition is equivalent to maximizing fitness. While fitness itself is difficult to measure (Smith 1983: 626), the net intake of calories per unit of time can be measured.

Optimal diet models were developed to predict which of an array of resources will be exploited if an organism attempts to maximize, for example, rates of food acquisition (net energy intake per unit of time). In order to achieve maximum foraging efficiency the forager is assumed to rank potential food sources by the amount of energy in any given food gathered per unit of time (that is kcal per hour less the energy expended in harvesting and processing, known as handling time).

Optimizing behavior for rates of food acquisition might result from a number of factors. One might be the condition of low food availability, which has been documented for fish, mollusks, and many birds (Schoener 1971: 381). Another factor might be the desire to minimize exposure to climatic extremes or to attack by enemies. Still another factor might result from an organism trying to secure more time for non-foraging activities essential for fitness, such as reproductive behavior. Finally behavior that optimizes rates of food acquisition might relate to an attempt to acquire excess food for sharing with others to enhance reproductive fitness by anticipating reciprocity (R. Kelly 1995: 54). Conceivably, optimal diet models might encompass an objective to maximize specific nutrients if they are in short supply.

The diet breadth model predicts only whether a resource will be taken by a forager when encountered at random in a fine-grained or homogenous environment (Keegan 1986; R. Kelly 1995: 90). The fine-grained diet breadth model generates a number of predictions (Smith 1983: 628) about what a forager will do upon encountering a prey source at random.

1. A widely diverse diet results from low availability of high-ranked resources (R. Kelly 1995: 100).

2. As availability (that is, search cost) of high-ranked resources or prey fluctuates, optimal diet breadth shrinks or expands. Evidence of decreased selectivity under conditions of low food availability has been established for both invertebrates and vertebrates (Schoener 1971: 381), which creates an expansion in diet breadth. If a higher ranked resource becomes available, a lower ranked resource will be dropped from the diet (R. Kelly 1995: 87), shrinking the diet breadth.

3. The inclusion of a resource or prey type should depend on the availability of higher ranked prey types, not on its own availability. After a prey type is encountered, the decision to invest handling time is a function of the degree of probability that a higher ranked prey type will be encountered in the time to handle the observed prey (Keegan 1986: 94).

4. Prey or resource types should be added or dropped from the diet in rank order of handling efficiency as kcal per unit of time (equivalent to post-search cost or post-encounter return rate of R. Kelly 1995). Lower ranked items move in and out, but higher ranked items are pursued whenever encountered. High-ranked prey types should be harvested even if rarely encountered. If rarely encountered, they will make only a small portion of the diet (R. Kelly 1995: 88).

5. If travel to obtain food at a distance is a factor, only selected items will be obtained (Jones and Madsen 1989). There will be a distance at which the energy used in gathering and transporting equals the amount of energy obtained, known as the maximum transport distance.

In the diet breadth model, each resource

is ranked in terms of the net amount of kilo-calories per hour. Energy used for resource acquisition needs to be allocated into *search costs* and *handling costs*. The latter includes harvesting, preparation, and cooking. The division helps to account for the influence of changes in patch density on harvesting deci-sion as well as the potential for technological changes that may occur through more efficient harvest methods or food preparation. In reality it costs energy to *search* (travel). In practice, only post-encounter rates (handling) have been subtracted from the final kilocalories per hour. This is because the necessary *search* costs ulti-mately relate to the density of an item in the environment; its encounter rate (or its *general* abundance or rarity) has little effect on choices made in foraging.

Consequently, sheer resource abundance is not a predictor of utilization. Acquisition decisions depend on what other high-ranked resources are available that would provide an average higher return in terms of kilocalories per hour. This is fortunate for those who work with the prehistoric plant record, for former density, or even relative density is difficult to estimate. Plant density is accommodated in optimal foraging theory in the harvest time. The number of kilocalories per hour harvested from a dense patch will exceed the number of kilocalories per hour harvested from a widely dispersed patch.

Patches are difficult to define because the scale used to define them can vary so much. Patterns can vary from a small area of grass in a forest to a more extensive prairie, to an area the size of the Great Plains. A patch might mean a clone of hedgehog cacti. However defined, patches have discontinuities in environmental character states from their surroundings. These discontinuities have biological significance and matter to an organism. The patch structure of an environment is that which is recognized by or relevant to the organism under consideration.

Patchiness is organism-defined and must be thought of in terms of the perceptions of the organism (Wiens 1976: 83). The patch choice model makes the following assumptions:

1. Resources are dispersed in patches rather than homogeneously across a landscape (R. Kelly 1995: 90)

2.The forager does not return to the patch until the resources are renewed.

3. Patches are responded to in a fine-grained manner if they are en-countered sequentially and ran-domly in direct proportion to their frequency in the environment (R. Kelly 1995: 90; Wiens 1976: 84).

To the extent that people walked vegeta-tion transects up and down Fresnal Canyon, the last assumption seems apt. But Kelly believes foragers do not encounter patches randomly, but choose their destination before they leave camp (R. Kelly 1995: 92). This is equivalent to responding to patches in a coarse-grained manner. Preference for certain patches is shown (Wiens 1976: 84). On the other hand, Keegan (1986) considers each patch as fine-grained (homogeneous), but the distribution of each plant community as coarse-grained or hetero-geneous. This perspective is important in the diet breadth model, which predicts the outcome of random searching in a fine-grained environ-ment. Despite the differing evaluations of grain size response, the patch choice model suggests that foragers should choose the highest return rate patches, given their environmental knowl-edge (R. Kelly 1995: 92). Additionally, Wiens (1976: 84) points out that ambiguity exists in the grain concept that is resource or function specific, since an environmental mosaic can be utilized in a fine-grained fashion for some functions (feeding) and a coarse-grained man-ner for another (nesting).

Gardens can be conceptualized as *managed patches* and foraging within them is random (Keegan 1986: 95). The time to prepare the patch is considered *search time* that is shared by all the cultigens that are raised in the patch. Search time is shared equally with all the *prey* or crops that are raised in the patch. Foraging within a patch for what is mature is random. However, handling time is unique to each crop. The diet breadth model proposes that handling time includes planting, harvesting, and processing of each crop or prey type.

Group movements are related to the environment through foraging efforts (R. Kelly 1998: 9) and ethnographic data suggest that 10 km to 15 km is the maximum distance a forager can gather food and still return to camp the same day. Foragers rarely travel this far and rarely deplete a foraging area for food (R. Kelly 1998: 9). Where resources are patchily distributed, maximum foraging efficiency is obtained by aggregating in a central place and sending out foraging parties (R. Kelly 1995: 120). R. Kelly (1998: 10) further indicates the distance from a residential camp at which a forager can procure resources at an energetic gain is limited by the return rates of those resources.

Whether or not to remain in one location is based not only on what is available at that location, but also on what is available elsewhere (R. Kelly 1998: 11). A group or individual may remain in one place by absorbing an increase in real costs if people search farther and father away. Alternatively, the group, if it chooses to stay, may experience a decline in real returns if they decide to live on shorter supplies or inferior foods within easy reach. Kelly (1995: 152) remarks that sedentism can be a product of local abundance in a context of regional scarcity.

"The frequency of residential movements decreases as resource patches become more spread out, while the length of logistical forays increases" (R. Kelly 1995: 152). In deserts where water sources are localized, water may be more a determinant of residential moves than foraging considerations (R. Kelly 1995: 126). In addition to water, modern hunter-gatherers are frequently tethered to agricultural plots (their own or those of sedentary neighbors) and to sources of welfare and wage labor (R. Kelly 1995: 127).

Optimization models of central place foraging theory predict that the further a forager travels from camp, the more selective his or her choice of resources (R. Kelly 1995: 135). Once a forager has traveled far from his home base, any extra time to select a better prey may be small compared to travel time to and from the central place (Pulliam 1981: 66). The transportability of a resource also becomes a factor for foragers who can carry an item only in their hands or in a burden basket. In the Great Basin, the largest burden basket at the Utah Museum of Natural History was 64.3 liters (Jones and Madsen 1989: 529). The caloric value of a basket load becomes important in determining the maximum transport distance.

The decision to reside at the location where food is stored or to transport the resources to another location, however, depends on the return from moving one set of resources versus the return rate expected from each area's local resources (Jones and Madsen 1989). A high return rate (kcal per hour) should be the best indicator of whether collection in excess of consumption is likely (Jones and Madsen 1989). A bulky resource, even with a high caloric return rate, cannot be transported easily. A relatively small weight transports as a large volume (Jones and Madsen 1989, R. Kelly 1995: 135). Whole cobs with kernels and mesquite bean pods serve as examples. But neither the return rate, nor the caloric value per unit of volume, nor the cost of transportation are sufficient to predict whether a resource is a good candidate to exploit.

FAVORABLE ASPECTS OF OPTIMAL FORAGING STRATEGY AT THE ROCK SHELTERS

When comparing the dietary choices in the two rock shelters with predictions or hypothesis based on optimal foraging models, the results may serve as a tentative evaluation of the theory (Winterholder 1981: 19). Because uncertainties in kilocalories per kilogram are only magnified when net caloric value is determined, it may be too soon to apply such figures in anything more than a preliminary assessment. Nevertheless, many observed effects seem to match the causes proposed by optimal foraging theory.

I. A Widely Diverse Diet Results from Low Availability of High Ranked Resources

At Fresnal Shelter the most frequent high-ranked resource was deer (Table 7.1). During the occupation of the shelter 26 deer were harvested. Even if one narrows the time frame of occupation of Fresnal Shelter to 1500 years, not many deer in any one year were harvested. The low kill rate and the widely diverse plant diet are intermixed in the deposits.

At High Rolls Cave, in Stratum 2, the most frequent of the high-ranked resources were deer (14), bighorn sheep (6), and antelope (7-8), for a total of 27 or 28 animals. The largest number of animals killed corresponds in rank to the kilocalorie per hour return rate of each (Table 7.1). In Stratum 2 (the major occupation of High Rolls Cave), the harvest of a single animal in any one year was unusual. The widely diverse plant diet in Stratum 2 has been documented in the preceding chapter.

II. As Availability of High Ranked Resource or Prey Fluctuates, Optimal Diet Breadth Shrinks or Expands

Shrinkage
At High Rolls Cave the small, difficult to col-

lect seed of globe mallow likely would rank far below maize in terms of kilocalories per unit of labor. It is only in Stratum 3 that globe mallow seed is part of diet and cottontail bones bear evidence of heavy burning (Akins 2002: Table 5). Globe mallow seed is no longer recovered in Stratum 2 when records of maize begin. If a higher ranked resource becomes available, a lower ranked resource will be dropped from the diet (R. Kelly 1995: 87).

Pollen typical of the mustard family was recovered in four human coprolites (Holloway 2002, and Appendix B.4). The only identifiable mustard seed from flotation is peppergrass. It blooms in spring and is recovered infrequently (Tables 6.1 and 6.2). Pollen may have mixed with the seeds when they were collected. The relatively low ranking of peppergrass in terms of kcal per hour (Table 7.1) suggests there were relatively few times when little else was available to collect. A similar case might be made for sunflower or goldeneye.

Expansion with Maize Agriculture
At Fresnal Shelter mesquite, pinyon, and juniper rank as the highest wild plant resources in caloric return per unit of labor (Table 7.1) and would be taken as encountered. They are also storable. The ubiquity of mesquite pods, pinyon nuts, and juniper berries in screened levels led to the inference that they served as winter base camp dietary staples. But if supplies were insufficient to sustain the occupants through the winter, according to the diet breadth model, the choice of the relatively high-ranked maize as an addition (Table 7.1) is reasonable, as is its occasional absence as a lower ranked resource. Diet breadth increased with the addition of maize. In as much as maize ranks higher than the stems of cacti (presumably), it would be more readily adopted into the winter subsistence economy.

High Rolls Cave maize adoption came in a period of wide fluctuations in climate, caus-

Table 7.1. Comparison of Kilocalories per Kilogram of Selected Animal and Plant Food Sources Ranked by (Net) Kilocalories per Hour

Resource: kcal per kg	kcal per hour	Literature Source
Deer, bighorn sheep: 1258	17,971 to 31,450	Simms 1987, Table 5*
Pronghorn: 1258	15,725 to 31,450	Simms 1987, Table 5*
Jackrabbit: 1078	13,475 to 15,400	Simms 1987, Table 5
Cottontail rabbit: 1078	8983 to 9800	Simms 1987, Table 5
Cattail pollen: 1040	2750 to 9360	Simms 1987, Table 11, Table 5*
Mesquite pods: 3480 to 4280	1733 to 2522	Doelle 1976: 68 (*P. juliflora*)
Piñon nuts: 4880 to 6336	841 to 1408	Simms 1987
Juniper berries: 5200 to 5500	?	Lentz 1979: 112 (*J. osteosperma*)
Panic grass grain: 4212	?	Kelrick and Macmahon 1985, Table 2 (*Panicum milaceum*)
Needle and thread grass grain: 4181	?	Kelrick and Macmahon 1985, Table 2 (*Stipa commata*)
Maize flour: 4100		Carpenter and Steggerda 1939, Table 2
Maize:	711 to 1133	Hudspeth 2000: 369**
Grain amaranth: 3910	?	Rodale 1977: 37 (*A. hypochondriacus*)
Yucca fruit, dry: 3900	?	Wetterstrom 1986: 172
Buffalo gourd seed: 3604	?	Lancaster and others 1982
Peppergrass seed: 3160	537	Simms 1987 (*Lepidium fremontii*) Tables 5 and 11
Sunflower achenes: 3650	467 to 504	Simms 1987, Tables 5 and 11
Indian rice grass: 4100	?	Wetterstrom 1986, Table 32
Indian rice grass: 4058	?	Kelrick and Macmahon 1985, Table 2
Indian rice grass: 3900	?	Carpenter and Steggerda 1939, Table 2
Indian rice grass: 2850	?	Thomas 1983: 65
Indian rice grass: 2740	301 to 392	Simms 1987, Tables 5 and 11
Great Basin wild rye: 2800	263 to 473	Simms 1987, Tables 5 and 11
Alkali muhly or dropseed: 2420	162 to 294	Simms 1987, Tables 5 and 11 (*Muhlenbergia asperifolia* or *Sporobolus asperifolius*)
Sotol seeds: 3049	?	Earle and Jones 1962, Table 1
Prickly pear fruit: 2175	?	Wetterstrom 1986, Table 2

*Processing time equals time taken to put resource in storable form. Final cooking and preparation time omitted (Simms 1987:15).

**Maximum possible return rates for field type with soil/water control from new fields with high labor costs to old fields with high labor costs for lower Rio Chama, New Mexico A.D. 1100-1600. Figures chosen to illustrate Hudspeth's estimate of lowest return rate. Hudspeth merges field preparation, planting and harvesting costs to the ear-free-from-the-husk stage.

ing high-ranking prey to vary in availability. Dietary stress in Stratum 3 times may have motivated people to include maize in their diet. The introduction of a high-ranking plant resource like maize may have resulted from the lack of availability of a higher ranked prey like artiodactyls. Simms (1987: 46) indicates that a hunter will abandon pursuit of prey if he can do better by searching and processing an alternative resource. The consumption of a presumably low-ranking seed food (globe mallow) can not be detected in Stratum 2. The adoption of maize at High Rolls Cave during a period of wide climatic fluctuations reinforces arguments at Fresnal Shelter for adopting maize as a supplement to winter diet.

Even though maize approaches mesquite and pinyon in kilocalories return per hour of labor, High Rolls Cave maize ranks only in eighth or ninth place in ubiquity (Table 6.3). This low ranking may be due to destruction of cobs through decay or burning or to the transport of the crop to a winter residence. The net kcal per hour suggests it should be recovered more frequently. The broader record of maize pollen in Stratum 2 would more nearly meet the expectations of optimal foraging theory.

Fluctuations in Diet Breadth
A decision to remain in Fresnal Shelter not only depends on what is available at that location, but also on what is available elsewhere. The comment that sedentism can be a product of local abundance in a context of regional scarcity (R. Kelly 1995: 152) comes to mind. There is a cost to remaining in place and using food with a lower return rate. A decision to remain in residence while maize matured was done at the cost of expanding the diet to include more (presumably) lower ranked items such as flattened stems of prickly pear, stems of hedgehog cacti, and the roots of desert four o'clock. The decision to transport maize and mesquite to Fresnal Shelter for winter use could have been made in consideration of additional winter resources available up canyon, such as fuel, pinyon nuts, and juniper berries. Its occupants were tethered to water and agricultural plots in years in which a crop could be raised, as are some modern hunter-gatherers. Fresnal Shelter inhabitants lived in conjunction with neighbors. The group that lived across canyon in High Rolls Cave may have created some social factors that influenced subsistence choices.

When native vegetation became lush and promoted the development of large animal herds, we might predict the increasingly available high-ranked game may have fostered a decision to drop the lower ranked maize from the diet. Both rock shelters may have been abandoned during a prolonged wet period, perhaps accounting for the gap in dated maize. If Fresnal Canyon sedentism originated as the product of local abundance amidst regional scarcity, the circumstance faded with the onset of moist climatic conditions.

III. The Inclusion of a Prey Type Should Depend on the Availability of Higher Ranked Prey Types, Not on its Own Availability

At Fresnal Shelter no evidence suggested any mid-winter hunting of deer (Wimberly and Eidenbach 1981: 25-26) and at High Rolls Cave late fall hunting of artiodactyl could be documented only once. Granting that High Rolls Cave occupants might have a winter residence at another location, low availability of artiodactyls in winter may have necessitated storage and use of high-ranking plant food.

IV. Prey or Resource Types Should be Added or Dropped from the Diet in Rank Order of Handling Efficiency, Kilocalories per Unit of Time

At Fresnal Shelter mesquite, pinyon, and juniper rank as the highest wild plant resources in caloric return per unit of labor (Table 7.1) and would be taken as encountered. They are the most frequent plant resources in the 43 screened levels. Only two levels are anomalous. Level 5 in Square C 28 contained a hearth in the northeast corner, one small maize cob and kernel, and an acorn. Level 3 in Square C 31 had just maize, mesquite, buffalo gourds, and quids.

At High Rolls Cave the most commonly recovered plant resources include some that may have been partly rodent-introduced (juniper, pinyon, and prickly pear), many whose kilocalories per hour of labor is unknonwn, and a confusing differential distribution between features and excavation units. The high rate of recovery of mesquite in excavation units (Table 6.2) does suggest a parallel pursuit of a food item that ranks high in kilocalories per unit hour of labor.

The observation that high-ranked prey types should be harvested even if rarely encountered and thus comprising only a small portion of the diet (Kelly 1995: 88) is illustrated by the use of cattail pollen at High Rolls Cave. The high rank of cattail in terms of kcal per hour, which is competitive with rabbits (Table 7.1), suggests that it was regularly collected during the short season it was available.

V. If Travel to Obtain Food at a Distance is a Factor, Only Selected Items will be Obtained

Fresnal Shelter people traveled away from their residential base camp at times to obtain Indian rice grass in the Tularosa Basin.

At High Rolls Cave occupants left their base camp for the Tularosa Basin to procure giant dropseed grass and Indian rice grass. Since Indian rice grass is a cool season grass available in late spring and giant dropseed grass is available sometime in the summer or fall, two separate trips of approximately 24 kilometers were needed to obtain unique items.

VI. Collectors Relied on Logistical Mobility

The nature of the plant remains at both rock shelters indicates movement of individuals or task specific groups was out from and back to a residential camp. Harvested plants that thrive in patchy habitats like arroyo banks, fire-induced mosaics of vegetation, grassy slopes, rock outcrops, and flood plains were brought to the shelter for processing and consumption. A strategy of logistical mobility achieves maximum efficiency in the harvest of the patchy plant resources (R. Kelly 1995: 120).

At Fresnal Shelter logistical movements

best represent preparations for winter, but might have persisted over the entire year. Low quality summer-seasonal plant information prevents judgment.

At High Rolls Cave logistical movements took place during the growing season. Collectors went out, procured resources, and returned for hundreds of years. The seasonal analysis of animal remains suggest only sporadic visitation in the dormant season. The winter residence could have been elsewhere.

TROUBLESOME ASPECTS OF OPTIMAL FORAGING STRATEGY AT THE ROCK SHELTERS

A variety of observations on the archaeology of Fresnal Shelter and High Rolls Cave benefit from optimal foraging theory as it is now understood. But as the literature is reviewed, it is apparent that there is room for refinements that would lead to better understanding.

The kilocalories per kilogram of given plant resources may vary for a number of reasons, including differing laboratory methods used in calculating kilocalories (Table 7.1). The figures offered for Indian rice grass by K. Jones (1983) and Simms (1987) are the results of experimental efforts. Carpenter and Steggarda (1939) depended on grain already processed by skilled Navajo families. Maize varieties may also differ in caloric values. The figure for mesquite pods represents the caloric value for the pods alone without the seeds. If the seeds were parched, ground, and consumed, as is probable at Fresnal Shelter, the caloric value would undoubtedly increase. The nearest caloric value for New Mexico feather grass comes from the related but smaller-grained needle and thread grass. Only two sets of authors (Carpenter and Steggarda 1939; Kelrick and Macmahon 1985) explain the method used in obtaining the caloric value, and they differ. Thus, even in determining kilocalories per kilogram, a variety of factors affect results.

Many food items formerly procured at Fresnal Shelter and High Rolls Cave lack basic data needed to rank foods according to net kilocalories per hour of labor. For example, no information is available on caloric content or collecting efficiency of New Mexico feather grass. From what we know about the related needle and thread grass, it could be relatively high in kcal per kg. If the labor in processing were not excessive, it might have been a relatively high-ranking food resource in late spring. Its ranking of use at High Rolls Cave (Table 6.3) suggests this might be the case. I know of no kilocalories per kilogram for the vegetative parts of cacti. Caloric values for alligator bark juniper berries would be comparable to the large, dry Utah juniper berries (Table 7.1). When we do have figures available (for example Simms 1987), they are based on a relatively short period of developing skill, compared to a woman's lifetime of perfecting customary techniques in harvesting. If all information were available, the dietary items could be ranked in terms of kcal per hour and compared to the frequency of recovery within a given season.

As optimal foraging develops within the biological sciences, additional understandings may be of value when applied to human behavior. The rarity of higher-ranking plant species is frequently cited as a reason for collecting others of lower value. Yet the labor in harvesting some plant resources can leave few kilocalories to benefit the harvester. Expanded understanding of the way herbivores forage (Provenza 2003) may elucidate additional reasons for diverse human dietary choices during the Archaic. All herbivores, not just human vegetarians, eat a wide array of plant species. The bulk of a meal normally contains less than 10 species, typically three to five species. Researchers are finding that both high rates of intake and high rates of nutrient intake influence food selection in herbivores, although neither herbivores nor fish, birds, or mammals) invariably select nutritious food.

All plants have compounds that create toxic effects in animals that eat them. Humans most commonly encounter enzyme inhibitors that interfere with digestion like protease inhibitors in barley, wheat, rice, many legumes, and other plants. Physiological irritants might be the second most commonly encountered toxic effects; they include raphide crystals (found in beets and rhubarb) as well as irritant oils (Leopold and Ardrey 1972). To obtain nutrients, herbivores must eat plants that contain different kinds of toxins. Different plant toxins produce different effects on the body. Both nutrient imbalances and toxins cause animals to satiate and limit food intake. Most secondary compounds in plants limit how much of a given species an herbivore can eat. In order to obtain sufficient nutrients, a variety of plant species that contain different toxins need to be eaten.

Yet unrecognized deviations from adding or dropping plant dietary items in rank order of handling efficiency by humans may result from efforts to balance nutrient intake against toxicity factors, as in herbivores. For example, large chunks of four o'clock root remained uneaten in Fresnal Shelter. The irritating raphide crystals in the roots may have promoted satiation. Modern collectors have parched grains that dissipate certain toxins like protease inhibitors. An array of irritating oils or resins in juniper berries may be minimized by heating them or by selecting trees that offer the most palatable berries. Differing traditional diets and different ways of food preparation by the occupants of each rock shelter may have served to counterbalance inherent toxicity factors and foster the well-being of the inhabitants.

Uniquely Human Aspects of Optimal Foraging Strategy

As optimal foraging strategy attempts to predict human behavior, conduct not characteristic of other animals becomes apparent (R. Kelly 1995: 95). Humans often will pursue game longer than other animals will track their prey. Resources often are processed at times when it would be impractical to obtain them. The parching and grinding of seeds serve as an example. The total amount of food obtained also has importance along with the rate of food acquisition.

The capacity to manage patches of vegetation for their own benefit is not unique to humans. Construction of prairie dog towns fosters a disturbed plant community while beaver dams promote vegetation adapted to their life style. But humans have the capacity to manage patches of vegetation through the use of fire. I feel hard pressed to think of other animals that use fire as a tool to promote their own diet.

The well-placed and well-timed touch of a fire brand to a pinyon and juniper plant community can create a diverse mosaic of vegetation that fosters a whole series of useful, small seed producing plants. The people from High Rolls Cave kept the plant community in an early successional stage to harvest many more species spread throughout the growing season and were able to continuously do so over a period of 500 years. But their neighbors in Fresnal Shelter made different choices. Why the difference?

Patch management allows people to prosper longer in one location or to live at greater density. In arid locations patch management sustains people who are tethered to limited sources of water. Under conditions of growing regional population, patch management could compensate for more limited territory or access to territory. An opposite condition described in the foraging radius model predicts a decline in return rates resulting from increased search time (R. Kelly 1995: 143). Both agricultural pursuits and deliberate disturbance of the nearby native plant community must have worked against what might otherwise be a normal successional trend. *But under what conditions does deliberate disturbance of natural habitats take place?*

A variety of observations on the archaeology of Fresnal Shelter and High Rolls Cave benefit from optimal foraging theory as it is now understood. But are the factors invoked from optimal foraging theory necessarily the causative ones? Alternative hypothesis have not been rejected or even considered. As we understand more about the ranking of dietary items in south central New Mexico we may find it less satisfactory. Optimal foraging theory is still being refined. As additional early sites are unearthed and published, there will be more pieces of the puzzle to fit proposed models. Doubtless Fresnal Shelter and High Rolls Cave will be reexamined.

Chapter 8
Fresnal Shelter and High Rolls Cave

Archaeology examines cultural behavior across long time periods, but it is too coarse-grained to record individual events. Robert Kelly (1995: 334) has remarked that archaeology is a difficult route for knowledge of the past—especially hunter-gatherers who leave few remains behind. At Fresnal Shelter and High Rolls Cave, we are looking at a shared period of initial adoption of maize, which lasted some two hundred years, followed by a second and probably more erratic maize growing occupation. Stratigraphically, the two periods are merged in Fresnal Shelter, but remain separate at High Rolls Cave. Ecological, biological, and cultural variables all had a role in decisions made by each occupation that affected subsistence.

Reconstructing elements of diet, seasonality, and mobility have been research objectives of both Fresnal Shelter and High Rolls Cave. Determination of the evolutionary history of cultigens was an objective at Fresnal Shelter, but, given the nature of the evidence, could not be achieved. Instead, at High Rolls Cave we could date the early appearance of a cultivated form of tobacco (*Nicotiana rustica* type) and of an amaranth (*A. cruentus* type) in the southwestern United States (Table 8.1). The tobacco was recovered with a wild species of the same genus; *N. trigonophylla*, and the amaranth in conjuction with a series of native species. This suggests the rock shelter occupants thought the cultivated species had attributes that were valued beyond the local species, though in just

what way is unknown. Both the amaranth and tobacco are believed to originate to the south, along with maize.

COMPARISONS AND CONTRASTS

Plant Dietary Use

The inhabitants of High Rolls Cave and Fresnal Shelter both exploited the margins of the Tularosa Basin selectively by collecting New Mexico feather grass from the foothills, and mesquite pods and dropseed grass from lower elevations. When plant-collecting trips were undertaken deeper into the Tularosa Basin, both groups had limited objectives. Fresnal Shelter people left an erratic record of bringing back Indian rice grass. High Rolls Cave people left a single record of Indian rice grass in late spring and of giant dropseed grass later in the growing season.

Both groups of people from High Rolls Cave and Fresnal Shelter made limited use of elevations much higher than they were located for plant foods. At Fresnal Shelter the people probably journeyed as high as 2,288 m for white or limber pine nuts while High Rolls Cave people collected bearberry around 2,135 m or higher. Each represents an isolated recovery of an item obtained at a higher elevation, although bearberry is also documented by pollen in another sample from High Rolls Cave.

Of the 11 dietary items than rank sixth or better at High Rolls Cave, 7 shared importance at Fresnal Shelter (Table 6.3). The frequent use of yucca fruit at High Rolls Cave is a superficial difference only. At Fresnal Shelter no thermal areas were investigated with the use of flotation samples, but 81 pecent of the screened squares have yucca seed (Table A.3). Due to the close proximity of pinyon and juniper trees to at High Rolls Cave, the high frequency of their seeds may result from combined human and rodent consumption. Still, the burned pinyon cone scales affirm human use, as does the context of recovery of some juniper seeds.

The many food items common to both rock shelters suggest that within the dietary ranking framework of net kilocalories per hour of labor, choice and availability coincide. Both pinyon and mesquite provide very high net kilocalories return per hour of labor. Many items with only high kilocalories return per kilogram (Table 7.1) may prove to be high in net kilocalories return per hour of labor, simply because one is initially dealing with a calorie-dense resource. High-ranking plant resources will always be used when encountered, even if they are rare and comprise a small portion of the diet. For example, in late spring when New Mexico feather grass matured, it presumably yielded the highest net kilocalorie per hour available at that season and its abundance was regularly harvested at both rock shelters.

Additional dietary items common at Fresnal Shelter (Table 5.2) were absent from High Rolls Cave. The people living at Fresnal Shelter made abundant use of plants that grew in the drier portion of the canyon and lower elevations: sotol seeds, desert four o'clock root, prickly pear pads or stems, buffalo gourd seed, the starchy wings of the fruit of the four-wing saltbush, and roasted stems of Turk's head barrel and hedgehog cacti. Despite the wide distribution of desert four o'clock root and the stems of hedgehog and Turk's head barrel cacti,

use was restricted to Fresnal Shelter. One gains an impression the inhabitants were thoroughly familiar with the potential of lower elevation plants and made extensive use of them. It also appears that their maize fields were down canyon from Fresnal Shelter.

High Rolls Cave (Table 6.3) illustrates notable variances from Fresnal Shelter diet. Hedgehog cactus was limited to fruit collecting in comparison with Fresnal's roasting of stems. The emphasis on the collection of small seeds at High Rolls Cave contrasts to the known subsistence orientation at Fresnal Shelter. For example, rye grass, love grass, false tarragon, globemallow, peppergrass, purslane, a member of parsley family, sunflower, and goldeneye apparently were limited to use in High Rolls Cave. The focus at High Rolls Cave on small seed gathering apparently preceded the adoption of maize agriculture and followed it, for the use of cheno-ams, *Chenopodium*, purslane, and false tarragon is continuous. Globemallow seed collection accompanied by rye grass, plains bristle grass, and prickly pear seed mark the pre-maize small seed complex.

There were distinct differences in some aspects of diet that were characteristic and repetitive for each group. As far as can be determined from the deposited plant remains in both rock shelter, each has retained its own dietary traditions.

Resolution of Dietary Differences

Several variables may influence presumed use or non-use. At High Rolls Cave globemallow and false tarragon seeds were restricted to firepit locations that were not sampled in Fresnal Shelter. The near absence of buffalo gourd and failure to use saltbush fruits may be due to a combination of factors such as vacating High Rolls Cave in the wintertime, use of Dry Canyon as a route of entry, and use of fields at higher elevations. The drying of flotation on screens in the shelter may have resulted in the loss of small grains like dropseed or the seeds of tobacco. If beans were left in High Rolls Cave in Stratum 1, they may have decayed.

If the initial occupation of Fresnal Shelter began as a winter base camp, it seems likely they utilized many plant resources in the Tularosa Basin at other times of the year. The recovery of a single cactus (*Coryphantha strobiliformis*) at Fresnal Shelter typical of elevations around 1,220 m is perhaps symbolic of that potential. The people at Fresnal Shelter evidently took advantage of some natural disturbance in their quest for food from lower elevations. Indian rice grass and many species of dropseed grass thrive under natural disturbance, as they are early successional grasses. Buffalo gourd from the arroyo margins and saltbush similarly can spread by disturbance. Fresnal Shelter people went beyond natural disturbance by cultivating the soil for domesticated crops, which promoted native amaranth and *Chenopodium*.

Yet, at Fresnal Shelter, minimal disturbance of habitat and preservation of harmony with nature seemed to be an important part of their cultural approach to subsistence choices. Apparently the harvest of pinyon nuts and juniper berries from the adjacent highlands was conducted without habitat disruption, which would have left a trail of useful small seed bearing plants. The collecting of other wild plant products are frequently ones from native, undisturbed perennial vegetation such as New Mexico feather grass, sotol seeds, mesquite, four o clock root, roasted bodies of hedgehog cacti, Turk's head barrel cacti, and prickly pear.

From the very first evidence of occupation at High Rolls Cave, the people were familiar with highland resources from pinyon and juniper to cheno-ams, purslane, and globemallow, and false-tarragon seed as well as the securing of deer or bighorn sheep. They initially

may have fully used a series of fire-disturbed mosaics within the pinyon-juniper plant community in the Sacramento Mountains for plant collecting and hunting while dipping into the margin of the Tularosa Basin for seasonally high-ranking resources. Later, in the vicinity of High Rolls Cave, it is probable that extra measures were taken to perpetuate the disturbed ground small-seeded annuals and perennials that they collected in conjunction with agricultural products. It would have kept their foraging radius short and allowed tethering to a permanent water source in Fresnal Canyon over an extended period of time. High Rolls Cave was apparently used as a higher elevation base camp during the growing season for logistical collecting and for agriculture.

Partitioning of Plant Resources

If one envisions a continuum of plant harvests from undisturbed habitats to extremely disturbed habitats and a second continuum of exploitation of low elevation resources to the exploitation of high elevation resources, I would place Fresnal Shelter at the low end of harvesting plants from disturbed habitats and with a bias toward harvesting low elevation plant resources. High Rolls Cave would come at the upper end of the continuum of harvesting plants from disturbed habitats and to typically do so at higher elevations.

We know Fresnal Shelter was occupied, though perhaps intermittently, for a long time preceding the introduction of maize (Tagg 1996). The nature of the herbs and grasses of disturbed ground trekked in by the inhabitants that were raising maize suggests many were limited to elevations around 1,525 m. Some of their food resources, including Turk's head barrel cactus, buffalo gourd, saltbush fruits, and dropseed grass would grow only in abundance at lower elevations. Both lines of evidence suggest that their fields were located at a lower elevation than Fresnal Shelter.

If lower elevation agricultural plots were already in use, it seems likely that High Rolls occupants would seek agricultural land at higher elevations. At High Rolls Cave the herbs and grasses of disturbed ground seem to be local in nature. Their fields could have been rich in the useful globemallow, cheno-ams, purslane, and sunflowers. Rye grass and false tarragon were nearby. The two different lines of evidence seem compatible.

Fresnal Shelter must have been in obvious use when a group came to occupy High Rolls Cave. Wills (1988: 45) raises the possibility of the development of obligatory or formal relationships between groups as a potential response to increasing population density. The author posits that such a development is favored with at least two conditions: 1) an increased potential for conflict and/or (2) an increase in social control of access to resource areas. The trend would be from informal, frequent sharing to infrequent and more formal exchange relationships. Lack of knowledge of particular resource patches used by each group creates uncertainty. Wills (1988: 46) predicts that hunter-gatherer groups might begin to focus on locally available but less frequently used resources to avoid procuring resources in areas controlled by other groups and avoiding associated obligations. While Wills developed the theoretical background as a means of explaining the adoption of agriculture, it appears as a useful theoretical framework to explain the dietary differences that accommodate two peoples based in the same canyon at similar elevations.

Cultigen Radiocarbon Dates and the Climatic Record

High Rolls Cave and Fresnal Shelter mirror similar agricultural events in other contemporary archaeological sites straddling the U.S. border with Mexico. Virtually all the earliest maize sites in the American Southwest as well as the Cerro Juanaquena in northwestern Chihuahua appear contemporaneous (Hard and Roney 1998: 1661). The inhabitants of both rock shelters lived in the same canyon near the margin of the Tularosa Basin at a propitious time.

Stalagmite records of former climate support an interpretation of a drier middle Holocene ending about 2050 B.C. A period follows with intervals of slightly greater effective moisture than at present and that terminates around 1050 B.C. (Polyak and Asmerom 2001: 150). The early dates on cultigens in both rock shelters suggest similar times of introduction (Table 8.1).

The stalagmite bands indicate the onset of significantly greater annual moisture begins in 1050 B.C. and ends in A.D.250 (Polyak and Asmerom 2001: 150). The dates approximate the dated temporary abandonment of High Rolls Cave and a lack of dated maize in Fresnal Shelter. It is not obvious from the disturbed upper levels in Fresnal Shelter that there is a hiatus in occupation. However, the last date on wood charcoal (ISGS 969) falls at the beginning of the very wet period (2770 ± 70 B.P.) and the next date, upon a radiocarbon-dated bean (2015 ± 65 B.P.), has a 1-sigma calibrated date of 87 B.C. to A.D. 65, toward the end of the wet period. The hiatus in dating (Tagg 1996) may reflect a gap in occupation similar to High Rolls Cave.

In the late Holocene the region experienced the wettest interval between 850 and 650 B.C. (Polyak and Asmerom 2001: 150) when High Rolls Cave was vacated. At least southern New Mexico and the Tularosa Basin vegetation should have benefited greatly. Where were the former occupants of High Rolls Cave and what were they doing? According to optimal foraging theory, efforts should have been focused on hunting animals and collecting plants with the

Table 8.1. Earliest Cultigen Dates from High Rolls Cave and Fresnal Shelter*

Origin	Item	Source of Date	Date BP	Cal 2 Sigma BC
High Rolls Cave	maize embryo	context	2940 +/- 60	1400 to 1030 BC
High Rolls Cave	maize husk	TAMS**	2880 +/- 40	1210 to 970 BC
High Rolls Cave	*Nicotiana rustica* type	TAMS	2860 +/- 40	1200 to 940 BC
High Rolls Cave	*Amaranthus cruentus* type	TAMS	2640 +/- 40	1110 to 900 BC
Fresnal Shelter	maize	TAMS	2945 +/- 55	1369 to 941 BC

*Tables B.3.1 and B.3.3
**Tandem Accelerator Mass Spectrometer

highest rates of return. People from High Rolls Cave and even Fresnal Shelter may have left the canyon for a time to exploit higher ranked resources in the Tularosa Basin. Perhaps the raising of maize was suspended.

Possibly significantly greater annual moisture did not continue as heavily as the start of the dry period approached (A.D. 250, Polyak and Asmerom 2001: 150). High Rolls Cave was dry enough then to preserve the dated maize cobs that belonged to Stratum 1 times, mainly between 350 B.C. to A.D. 340. Fresnal Shelter exhibits late cultigen dates that closely approximate the Stratum 1 occupation at High Rolls Cave. The interval begins at Fresnal Shelter with a bean that has a 1-sigma calibrated date of 87 B.C. to A.D. 65. The interval closes with a maize kernel that has a 1-sigma calibrated date of A.D. 264 to 428 (Tagg 1996: 317).

SOME REASONS FOR THE ADDITION OF MAIZE AGRICULTURE

In a perceptive review of the explanations for the adoption of agriculture in the Southwest, William Doleman (Doleman and others 1992: 184) has noted that recent models of the adoption of agriculture share the same elements: (a) a model of pre-horticultural hunter-gatherer subsistence, (b) a "stress factor" of varying importance such as environmental change or demographic pressure, (c) an argument that available cultigens were either better than or a back-up alternative to wild resources, or a way of reducing risk and increasing predictability of food sources, and (d) an emphasis on the value of cultigens as storable resources as they increase the availability of food.

When High Rolls was earliest occupied, oscillations in precipitation might initiate sufficient food stress for inhabitants to consider maize agriculture as a potential solution. High Rolls Cave has numerous clues from both plant and animal deposits in Stratum 3 of broadening the resource base in response to food stress (Chapter 6). By Stratum 2 times when agriculture products form part of the diet, signs of food stress are no longer evident.

In this sense, maize played an important role. Table 7.1 presents kilocalorie per hour figures for pinyon, mesquite, and maize that suggest maize was a competitive alternative to wild foods in terms of optimal foraging strategy. The erratic swings toward increased effective moisture give credence to motivate people to expand dietary choices with the adoption of a relatively high-ranking crop (in terms of kilocalories return per hour of labor) like maize. All factors combined constitute the most probable interpretation of the archaeology of High Rolls Cave. Something similar may have transpired at Fresnal Shelter

The balance between population and resources is dynamic. At High Rolls Cave I could detect some stress on resources during a period of climatic oscillation, but could not pinpoint the stress on resources that may be the concomitant result of a rise in local population. Admittedly, we could also be viewing an archaeological solution to an overpopulation problem, through intensification of food production by means of agriculture without the expansion of territory (Wills 1988). Intensification usually means an increase in the range of resource use. In terms of optimal foraging theory this equates with moving down in rank order of dietary items or, in other words, increased cost in work per unit of return. Wills (1988) has laid the theoretical groundwork for such a prediction.

The postulated climatic reasons for its initial adoption at High Rolls Cave and Fresnal Shelter may not be the same ones that caused them to resume raising maize before the close of the wet period. Surveys in the southern Tularosa Basin indicate an expanding population during the late Archaic (Doleman and others 1992; Miller and Kenmatsu 2004: 212), and a parallel expansion in the adjoining highlands might reasonably be expected. Given the influx of people attracted to favorable habitats for game, the balance of population to resources may have shifted towards overpopulation. The need to increase the range of food resources may have resurfaced.

SEDENTARY AND SEMI-SEDENTARY

At Fresnal Shelter we can identify the base camp function in winter through mesquite, pinyon, juniper, and maize in relation to storage facilities and the favorable geographic location. We can identify the use of Fresnal as a hunting field camp, because the heavy muscle mass bones were carried elsewhere. But base camp and field camp distinctions in regards to a wild crop like dropseed grass remain obscure because our seasonal information for summer and fall occupancy is poor. We are fortunate to know of several particular points in time, but not what happened in between. Continuity of occupation during the warm season is suggested by the trend in use of prickly pear pads, desert four o'clock root, and Turk's head barrel cactus that accompany maize in screened levels.

At High Rolls Cave the base camp function can best be documented with plant remains in spring and fall and with immature artiodactyl bones in July and August. In contrast, indications of winter butchering are relatively scarce. Considering the cave opened onto a shaded north slope, it did not offer conditions desirable for family living following the harvest of pinyon nuts. A semi-sedentary mode of existence seems probable.

High Rolls Cave probably was not suitable for occupation during an interval of heavy rainfall. So far, no dates from Fresnal Shelter indicate it was occupied either.

Dietary Elements from Fresnal Canyon Archaic in Pueblo Food Traditions

Some of the small seeds at High Rolls Cave recall Zuni traditions about what life was like before they grew maize. *Artemisia wrightii* and *Chenopodium leptophyllum*, lumped under the Zuni name, *kiatsanna*, which literally translates as *small seeds*, were among the earliest foods (Stevenson 1915: 66) along with *Amaranthus blitoides* (Stevenson 1915: 65). *Artemisia wrightii* is an herbaceous species like false tarragon from High Rolls Cave. Sayatashas Night Chant (Bunzel 1932: 714) recites the names of the ancient seeds that the Zuni esteemed, and Cushing (1920: 244-245) translates three of the archaic Zuni terms for the seeds. *Sutoka* is the old name for *Chenopodium* seed. *Kushutsi* is the archaic name for purslane or portulaca. He also provides the archaic name for still another ancient small seed, *mitaliko*, and translates it as "father in law of corn." He says the seeds were gathered in the same manner as *Chenopodium*. He indicates the plant resembles *Chenopodium* but probably belongs to another genus; the seeds were less rich and more nearly like maize that other native foods. His description sounds remarkably like amaranth, and even one that might have been cultivated. Stevenson (1915: 65) includes the amaranth as having been brought in a sacred reed tube of the rain priests and scattered over the earth. Among the historic Pueblos, including Zuni, a black-seeded amaranth (*A. cruentus)* was grown as a minor dye plant (Sauer 1950a: 414). The Zuni also considered juniper berries an ancient food that was once harvested in quantity.

Plants that have come down through tradition often bear the connotation of being good for you, and hence become part of the medicinal memory, as for the Tewa who mix the ground root of desert four o'clock with corn meal as a medicine (Robbins et al 1916: 60). Among the Pueblos, tobacco is believed to impart benefits. Some eastern Pueblos use *N. rustica* in their rituals (Adams and Toll 2000: 150). The use of the inflorescence of dark-seeded amaranth to color paper bread is but a small shift away from mixing the ground seeds with corn flour as food.

Stories of how people faced food shortages may incorporate reference to juniper berries as at Acoma, Indian rice grass at Zuni, and alkali sacaton or dropseed grass with the Hopi. I marvel that traditional food items remembered by the Pueblos are traceable to the Archaic. Even the institutionalized periodic burning of vegetation at Acoma (Bohrer 1983) might have had a start in less formal practices during the Archaic.

This study ponders some details of life during what may be an initial pulse of agriculture in south central New Mexico and highlights how modestly we understand the principles upon which preceramic peoples made dietary decisions. Archaeology is a difficult route for knowledge of the past--especially hunter-gatherers, even when they leave abundant plant remains behind.

Appendix A

Fresnal Shelter:
Content of Excavation Units and Features

Table A.1. Fresnal Shelter Feathers Identified by Charmion McKusick, Sept. 1, 1971

Catalogue No.	Identification,* Level, Remarks
01.B26.25	Turkey feather; Level 2, 103 cmbd, 2cd 10 cm; Rats nest in NE corner
01.B27.66	Unidentified
01.C26.6	Swift; Level 2, 118 cmbd (Level 1 is 48 cmbd)
01.C26.42	Turkey feathers; Level 4, 170 cmbd
01.C26.66	Turkey feathers; Level 2? 140-150 cmbd
01.C26.74	Turkey feathers; Level 3? 150-160 cmbd
01.C26.87	White-throated Swift
01.C27.63	Unidentified split quill; Level 5, 166-177 cmbd
01.C28.91	Unknown feathers; Level 6, 146-156 cmbd
01.C28.122	Steller's jay, Turkey with evidence of heat on feather, Red-shafted Flicker; Level 7, 156-166 cmbd
01.C29.125	Feather bundle artifact "matted feathers;" Level 5, 132-136 cmbd
01.C29.135	Feather bundle artifact "matted feathers;" Level 6, 136-146 cmbd
01.C29.213	Turkey, quill of vulture; Level 8, 151-156 cmbd
01.C30.26	one Red-shafted Flicker, one Swift, one Turkey feather; Level 2, 116-126 cmbd (Level 1 is 107-116 cmbd); Found with a cache of juniper seeds at 126 cmbd; Pinecone material was beneath juniper
01.C31.8	Turkey feathers; disturbed Level 1, 126-131 cmbd
01.C31.14	Turkey, Steller's jay; Level 1, 126-131 cmbd
01.C31.30	Turkey feather; Level 2, 131-136 cmbd
01.C32.36	Turkey feathers; Level 3, 127-132 cmbd; From small circular hole 10 cm diameter and 7 cm deep filled with ashes and vegetal matter
01.C32.42	Turkey feathers; Level 4, 132-142 cmbd; From same hole as Catalogue No. 01.C32.36
01.C32.44	Turkey feathers; Level 4, 132-142 cmbd; From same hole as Catalogue No. 01.C32.36
01.D26.8	Swift feather; Level 1 with "cow dung"
01.D26.53	Turkey feather; Level 3, 150-156 cmbd; In loose vegetal material
01.D27.16	Turkey feather; Level 2, 125 cmbd
01.D28.58	Turkey feather fragment; Level 4, 126-136 cmbd; Rodent disturbed NE corner
01.D28.80	Swift feathers; Level 5, 136-146 cmbd

Table A.1. Fresnal Shelter Feathers Identified by Charmion McKusick, Sept. 1, 1971, cont'd

Catalogue No.	Identification,* Level, Remarks
01.D30.7	Turkey feather fragment; Level 1, 109-116 cmbd
01.D31.23	Red-shafted Flicker; Level 2, 126-136 cmbd
01.E26.43	Turkey feather; Level 6, 129-136 cmbd
01.E26.100	White-throated Swift; No provenience data found
01.F26.48	Turkey feathers; in NE quadrant on sloping rock, 73-93 cmbd
01.J26.3	White-throated Swift
01.J26.76	White-throated Swift
01.J26.39G	White-throated Swift
01.J27.10	White-throated swift
01.J27.18E	Unknown + White-throated Swift
01.J27.22	White-throated Swift, Turkey; vegetal fiber
01.J27.49	White-throated Swift
01.J27.68	White-throated Swift
01.J27.89	White-throated Swift
01.J27.97	White-throated Swift

*Identifications with Taxonomic Classifications

Turkey (*Meleagris gallapavo*)
White-throated Swift (*Aeronautes saxatalis*)
Red-shafted Flicker (*Colaptes auratus collaris*)
Turkey Vulture (*Cathartes aura*)
Steller's Jay (*Cyanositta stelleri*)

Table A.2. Modern Plant Voucher Specimens from the Fresnal Canyon Vicinity, Sacramento Mountains, New Mexico

Unless otherwise indicated, all plants have been deposited with the University of Arizona Herbarium. In the following table, specimens are listed by their taxonomic classification followed by the collector's field number, the accession number, and the specimen's elevation. Authors of scientific names may be found in Correll and Johnston 1970, Kearney and Peebles 1960, and Gould 1951. Taxonomy follows Roalson and Allred 1995.

FERNS AND FERN ALLIES

SELAGINELLACEAE
Selaginella mutica (Bohrer 1348; 176389; 6,300 ft.)
PTERIDACEAE
Notholaena sinuata (Bohrer 1418; 182495; 6,300 ft.)

GYMNOSPERMS

CUPRESSACEAE
Juniperus monosperma (Beggelman 34; 182460; 6,300 ft.)
Juniperus pachyphloea (*J. deppeana*) (Bohrer 2350:176391; 7,260 ft.)
PINACEAE
Picea pungens (Bohrer 1739; 189998; 8,500 ft.)
Pinus edulis (Beggelman 29; 182457; 6,300 ft.)
Pinus strobiformis (Bohrer 1374; 176412; 7,500 ft.)

MONOCOTYLEDONOUS FLOWERING PLANTS

AGAVACEAE
Agave parryi (Bohrer 1335; 176380; 6,000 ft.)
Nolina microcarpa (Bohrer1372; 176955; 6,300 ft.)
Nolina microcarpa (Bohrer 1349 176390; 7,260 ft.)
Yucca carnerosana (Bohrer 1394; 182486; 5,500 ft*)
COMMELINACEAE
Commelina dianthifolia (Bohrer 1463; 181257; 7,000 ft.)
JUNCACEAE
Juncus saximontanus (Bohrer 1486; 182524; 6,710 ft.)
Juncus mexicanus (Bohrer 1399; 182487: 5,500 ft.)
LILIACEAE
Allium cf. *Geyeri* (Bohrer 1405; 182489; 6,500 ft.)
Allium Geyeri (Bohrer 1351; 176392; 7,260 ft.)
POACEAE
Agropyron smithii (Beggelman 17; 182449; 6,000 ft.)
Agropyron smithii (Bohrer 1360; 176402; 7,260 ft.)
Agrostis gigantea (*A. alba*) (Beggelman 9; 182444; 6,000 ft.)
Agrostis scabra (Beggelman 23; 182445; 6,000 ft.)
Agrostis semiverticellata (Beggelman 24; 182454; 6,000 ft.*)
Agrostis stolonifera (*A. palustris*) (Beggelman 23; 182453; 6,000 ft.)
Aristida purpurea var. *fendleriana* (*A. fendleriana*) (Bohrer 1435; 142500; 6,450 ft.)
Aristida parishii (Bohrer 1473; 181262; 7,000 ft)
Bothtriochloa laguroides subsp. *laguroides* (*Andropogon saccharoides*) (Bohrer 2396; 182488; 5,500 ft.)
Bouteloua curtipendula (Beggelman 72; 182475; 6,000 ft.)
Bouteloua eriopoda (Bohrer 1414; 181261; 6,300 ft.)
Bouteloua eriopoda (Bohrer 1472; 181261; 7,000 ft.)
Bouteloua gracilis (Bohrer 1413; 182481; 6,300 ft.)
Bouteloua gracilis (Bohrer 1468; 181260; 7,000 ft.)
Bouteloua hirsuta (Bohrer 2467; 181259; 7,000 ft.)
Bromus arizonicus (Bohrer 1485b; 182523; 6710 ft.)
Cf *Elymus* spp.(*Sitanion hystrix*) (Bohrer 2479;182518; 7,000 ft.)

Table A.2. Modern Plant Voucher Specimens from the Fresnal Canyon Vicinity,
Sacramento Mountains, New Mexico, cont'd

Elymus canadensis (Beggelman 36; 182461; 6,000 ft.)
Elymus cinereus (Bohrer 1738; 189999; 6,650 ft.*)
Elymus glaucus (Beggelman 15; 182448; 6,000 ft.)
Elymus lanceolatus (Bohrer 2747; 1900907)
Eragrostis intermedia (Bohrer 1474; 182472; 7,000 ft.)
Eragrostis intermedia (Bohrer 1409; 181241; 6,300 ft.)
Erioneuron avenaceum (*Tridens grandiflorus*) (Bohrer 1480; 181266; 5,900 ft.)
Erioneuron pilosum (*Tridens pilosus*) (Bohrer 1433; 181253; 6450 ft.)
Koeleria macrantha (*K. cristata*) (Bohrer 1475; 181263; 7,000 ft.)
Lolium perenne (Beggelman 59; 182471; 6,000 ft.)
Lycurus phleoides (Bohrer 1466; 181258; 7,000 ft.)
Lycurus phleoides (Boher 1417 181245; 6,300 ft.)
Muhlenbergia asperfolia (Bohrer 1745; 190005; 6,800 ft.)
Muhlenbergia tenuifolia (*M. monticola*) (Bohrer 1434; 182499; 6,450 ft.)
Muhlenbergia porteri (Bohrer1408; 182491; 6,300 ft.)
Muhlenbergia rigida (Bohrer 1470; 182519; 7,000 ft.)
Panicum obtusum (Bohrer 1392; 182477; 5,000 ft.)
Pappophorum vaginatum (*P. mucronulatum*) (Beggelman 80; 182477; 5,000 ft.)
Phragmites australis (*P. communis*) (Bohrer 1485; 182522; 6,710 ft.)
Poa pratensis (Bohrer 2376a; 766414; 7,500 ft.)
Polypogon monspeliensis (Bohrer 1487; 181269; 6,700 ft.)
Setaria macrostachya (Beggelman 70; 182474; 6,300 ft.)
Sporobolus airoides (Bohrer 1372; 176410; 4,744 ft.)
Sporobolus airoides var. *wrightii* (Bohrer 1397; 181238; 5,500 ft.)
Sporobolus cryptandrus (Bohrer 1395: 182480; 5,500 ft.)
Sporobolus cryptandrus (Bohrer 2476; 181264; 7,000 ft.)
Stipa eminens (Bohrer 2415; 181244; 6,300 ft.)
Stipa eminens (Bohrer 1478; 181265; 5,900 ft.)
Stipa neomexicana (Bohrer 1479; 5,900 ft.)
Stipa robusta (Bohrer 1357; 176399; 7,260 ft.)
Stipa scribneri (Bohrer 1471; 182520; 7,000 ft.)
TYPHACEAE
Typha angustifolia (Bohrer 1401; 181239; 5,500 ft.)
Typha domingensis (Bohrer 1402: 181240; 5,500 ft.)

DICOTYLEDONOUS FLOWERING PLANTS

AMARANTHACEAE
Amaranthus graecizans (Bohrer 1750; 190010; 6,800 ft.)
Amaranthus hybridus (Bohrer 2457; 182513; 6,000 ft.)
ANACARDIACEAE
Rhus microphylla (Bohrer 1731; 190011; 5,400 ft.)
Rhus trilobata var. *pilosissima* (*R. aromatica var pilosissima*) (Beggelman 25; 182455; 6000 ft.)
APIACEAE
Conium maculatum (Beggelman 13; 182446; 6,000 ft.)
Ligusticum porteri (Bohrer 1382; 176422; 6,800 ft.)
Pastinaca sativa (Bohrer 1339l; 176383; 5,900 ft.)
APOCYNACEAE
Apocynum suksdorfii (Bohrer 1483; 181268; 6,710 ft.)
ASTERACEAE
Acourtia nana (*Perezia nana*) (Bohrer 1331; 176378; 6,000 ft.)
Ambrosia confertiflora (Bohrer 1752; 190021; 5,400 ft.*)
Ambrosia psilostachya (Bohrer 1465; 182517; 7,000 ft.)
Arctium minus (Beggelman 56; 182478; 6,000 ft.)
Artemesia dracunculus (*A. dracunculoides*) (Bohrer 1728; 190038; 6,500 ft.)
Artemesia dracunculus (*A. dracunculoides*) (Bohrer 1482 181267 6,710 ft.)

Table A.2. Modern Plant Voucher Specimens from the Fresnal Canyon Vicinity, Sacramento Mountains, New Mexico, cont'd

Artemesia ludoviciana (Bohrer1421; 181246; 6,300 ft.)
Bahia dissecta (Bohrer 1741b; 190002; 6650 ft.)
Berlandiera lyrata (Bohrer 1364; 176406; 5,500 ft.)
Berlandiera lyrata (Bohrer 1459; 182514; 6,900 ft.)
Cirsium cf. *undulatum* (Beggelman 20; 182452; 6,000 ft.)
Cirsium undulatum (Bohrer 1356; 176398; 7,260 ft.)
Chaetopappa ericoides (*Leucelene ericoides*) (Bohrer 1354; 176396; 7260 ft.)
Gaillardia pinnatifida (Bohrer 1481; 182521; 5,500 ft.)
Grindelia nuda var. *aphanactis* (*G. aphanactis*) (Bohrer 1484; 1815121; 6,710 ft.)
Gymnosperma glutinosum (Bohrer1730; 19037; 6,000 ft.)
Helianthus annuus (wild type) (Bohrer 1737; Ind.U.; 6,650 ft.)
Helianthus ciliaris (Bohrer 1373; 176411; 4744 ft.)
Iva ambrosiaefolia (Bohrer 1731; 190032; 6,400 ft.)
Iva ambrosiaefolia (Bohrer 1390; 181236; 5,500 ft.)
Parthenium incanum (Bohrer 1338; 176382; 6,000 ft.)
Pectis angustifolia (Bohrer 1462; 182515; 7,000 ft.)
Perityle staurophylla (*Laphamia staurophylla*) (Bohrer 1333; 176369; 6,000 ft.)
Tetradymia canescens (Beggelman 40; 182464)
Thelesperma longipes (Bohrer 1379; 176419; 7,500 ft.)
Thelesperma subnubum (Bohrer 2352a; 176319; 7,260 ft.)
Verbesina enceliodes (Bohrer 1479; 190009; 6,800 ft.)
Verbesina encelioides (Bohrer 1355; 176397; 7,260 ft.)
Viguiera dentata (Bohrer 1729; Ind. U.; 6,000 ft.)
Viguiera dentata (Bohrer 1736; Ind. U.; 6,650 ft.)
Viguiera stenoloba (Bohrer 1336: 176952; 6,000 ft.)
BERBERIDACEAE
Berberis fremontii (Beggelman 5; 182441; 6,000 ft.)
BRASSICACEAE
Diplotaxis cf. *tenuifolia* (Beggelman 1; 182438; 6,000 ft.)
Lesquerella purpurea (Beggelman 43; 182466; 6,350 ft.)
CACTACEAE
Echinocactus horizonthalonius (Bohrer 1368; 176424; 5,500 ft.)
Echinocereus fasciculatus? (Bohrer 1384; 176426; 7,260 ft.)
Echincereus pectinatus (Bohrer 1371; 176426; 7,260 ft.)
Coryphantha vivipara var. cf. *radiosa* (*Mamillaria cf radiosa*) (Bohrer 1370; 176427;   7,260 ft.)
CAPPARIDACEAE
Koeberlinia spinosa (Bohrer 1367; 176409; 5,900 ft.)
CHENOPODIACEAE
Ceratoides lanata (Eurotia lanata) (Bohrer 1412; 181243; 6,300 ft.)
Chenopodium graveolens (Bohrer 1456; 181256; 6,000 ft.)
Sueda torreyana (Bohrer 1393; 182483; 5,500 ft.)
CONVOLVULACEAE
Ipomoea purpurea (Bohrer 1744; 189942; 6,800 ft.)
CUCURBITACEAE
Cucurbita foetidissima (Beggelman 48; 182468; 6,000 ft.)
FABACEAE
Acacia neovernicosa (*A. vernicosa*) (Boher 1365; 176407; 5,900 ft.)
Amorpha nana (Bohrer 1378a; 176956; 7,500 ft.)
Dalea formosa (Bohrer 2429; 181250; 6,450 ft.)
Hoffmanseggia glauca (*H. densiflora*) (Bohrer 1391; 182479; 5,500 ft.)
Krameria lanceolata (Bohrer 1431; 181251; 6,450 ft.)
Melilotus albus (Beggelman 3; 182440; 6,000 ft.)
Prosopis glandulosa var. *torreyana* (Beggelman 50; 182469; 6,300 ft.)
Vicia pulchella (Bohrer 1734b; 190000; 6,650 ft.)
FAGACEAE
Quercus gambellii (Beggelman 30; 182458; 6,000 ft.)

Table A.2. Modern Plant Voucher Specimens from the Fresnal Canyon Vicinity,
Sacramento Mountains, New Mexico, cont'd

Quercus grisea (Bohrer 1748; 190008; 6,800 ft.)
Quercus pungens var. *vasseyana* (Bohrer 1742; 190003; 6,800 ft.)
Quercus undulata? (Bohrer 1380; 176420; 7,500 ft.)
GARRYACEAE
Garrya wrightii (Bohrer 1381; 176421; 6,800 ft.)
GERANIACEAE
Geranium caespitosum (Beggelman 67; 182473; 6,000 ft.)
HYDRANGEACEAE
Fendlera rupicola (Bohrer 1346; 176388; 6,300 ft.)
Fendlerella utahensis (Bohrer 1464; 182516; 7,000 ft.)
Philadelphus microphyllum (Bohrer 1376b; 176415; 7,500 ft.)
LAMIACEAE
Hedeoma drummondii (Bohrer 1746; 190006; 6,800 ft.)
Salvia reflexa (Bohrer 1743; 190004; 6,800 ft.)
Trichostema arizonicum (Bohrer 1411; 182492; 6,300 ft.)
NYCTAGINACEAE
Mirabilis multiflora (Bohrer 1410: 181242; 6,300 ft.)
OLEACEAE
Forestiera neomexicana (*F. pubescens* var. *glabrifolia*) (Bohrer 1743; 182503; 6,800 ft.)
Fraxinus cuspidata (Bohrer 1343; 176385; 6,300 ft.)
Fraxinus velutina (Beggelman 51; 182470; 6,000 ft.)
Menodora scabra (Bohrer 1359; 176401; 7260 ft.)
OXALIDACEAE
Oxalis alpina (*O. metcalfei*) (Bohrer 1441; 182502; 6,800 ft.)
POLYGONACEAE
Eriogonum alatum (Bohrer 1734; 190001; 6,650 ft.)
Eriogonum jamesii (Bohrer 1732; 190033; 6,000 ft.)
PORTULACACEAE
Talinum pulchellum (Bohrer 1442; 182024; 6,800 ft.)
RANUNCULACEAE
Clematis drummondii (Bohrer1415; 182494; 6,300 ft.)
RHAMNACEAE
Condalia spathulata (Bohrer 1366; 176408; 5,900 ft.)
Condalia viridis (Beggelman 46; 182467; 6,350 ft.*)
ROSACEAE
Cercocarupus montanus var. *paucidentatus* (Beggelman 77; 182476; 6,350 ft.)
Cercocarpus montanus (Bohrer 1358; 176400; 7260 ft.)
Fallugia paradoxa (Beggelman 6; 182442; 6,300 ft.)
Holodiscus dumosus (Bohrer 1375; 176413; 7,500 ft.)
Prunus emarginata (Bohrer 1376 c; 176416; 7,500 ft.)
Prunus serotina ssp. *virens* (Bohrer 1362; 176404; 5,500 ft.)
Prunus serotina ssp *virens* (Bohrer 1488; 182525; 7250 ft.)
Prunus virginiana (Beggelman 37; 182462; 6,000 ft.)
Rosa stellata (Bohrer 1733; 189994; 6,650 ft.)
Rosa stellata (Bohrer 1352b; 176394; 7,260 ft.)
RUBIACEAE
Galium rothrockii (Bohrer 1428; 182498; 6,450 ft.)
RUTACEAE
Ptelea trifoliata ssp. *angustifolia* (*P.angustifolia*) (Bohrer 1361; 176403; 5,500 ft.)
Ptelea trifoliata ssp. *angustifolia* (*P. angustifolia*) (Bohrer 1459; 181510; 6,900 ft.)
SALICACEAE
Populus fremontii (Bohrer 1340; 176384; 5,900 ft.)
SCROPHULARIACEAE
Castilleja sessiflora (Beggelman 18; 182450; 6,000 ft.)
Maurandya antirrhiniflora (Beggelman 31; 182459; 6,000 ft.)

Table A.2. Modern Plant Voucher Specimens from the Fresnal Canyon Vicinity,
Sacramento Mountains, New Mexico, cont'd

SOLANACEAE
      Nicotiana trigonophylla (Bohrer 1427; 182497; 6,300 ft.)
      Solanum douglasii (Bohrer 1353; 176395; 7,260 ft.)
      Solanum jamesii (Bohrer 1406; 182490; 6,300 ft.)
ULMACEAE
      Celtis reticulata (Bohrer 1363; 176405; 5,500 ft.)
VISCACEAE
      Arceuthobium vaginatum (Bohrer 1377; 7,500 ft.)
VITACEAE
      Parthenocissus inserta (*P. vitacea*) (Bohrer 1420; 182496; 6,300 ft.)
      Vitis arizonica (Beggelman 41; 182465; 6,000 ft.)

*Unlisted in Roalson and Allred 1995

Table A.3.1. Distribution of Plant Remains in Screened Squares by Level

Taxonomic ID	Part ID	C28-2	C28-3	C28-4	C28-5	C28-6	C28-7	C29-1	C29-2	C29-3	C29-4	C29-5	C29-6	C29-7	C29-8	C29-9	C29-10	C30-1	C30-2	C30-3	C30-4	C30-5	C30-6	C30-7	C31-1	C31-2	C31-3
Cupressaceae																											
Juniperus	seed	2	3	4		6	7	1	2	3	4	5	6	7	8	9	10	1	2	3	4	5	6	7	1	2	3
	berries					6	7		2			5	6	7	8	9		1	2	3	4	5	6		1	2	3
Pinaceae																											
Pinus edulis	nutshell	2	3	4		6	7	1	2	3	4	5	6	7	8	9	10	1	2	3	4	5	6	7	1	2	3
P. ponderosa	bark		3	4		6		1		3		5	6			9	10		2	3	4			7	1		
P. strobiformis	seed																		2								
Agavaceae																											
Agave	leaves												6	7	8		10			3	4		6				
Dasylirion	fruit/carpels		3			6	7	1	2	3	4	5	6	7	8	9	10	1	2	3	4	5			1	2	3
Dasylirion nolina	quid										4											5					
Dasylirion	leaf segments						7	1	2			5	6	7	8	9	10			3							
Yucca	seed		3	4		6	7		2	3	4	5	6	7	8	9	10	1	2	3	4	5	6	7	1	2	3
Liliaceae																											
Allium	bulb scales												6				10	1		3	4	5					
Poaceae	florets, spikelets																										
Andropogoneae											4	5		7	8	9			2	3					1		
Aristida																											
Avena fatua																											
Bouteloua						6	7		2		4		6	7					2								
Chloris crinita						6	7		2			5		7		9		1	2								
Digitaria californica							7											1	2						1		
Oryzopsis hymenoides																											
Paniceae						6	7		2		4		6			9			2	3			6		1		
Pappophorum	complex											5							2	3							
Setaria	inflorescence								2						8												
Sorghum	grain								2									1	2						1		
Sporobolus						6	7		2		4		6	7		9		1	2	3		5	6		1		3
Stipa neomexicana									2				6			9		1	2						1		
Zea mays	grain		3		5	6	7		2	3	4	5	6	7	8	9	10	1	2	3	4		6		1		
Zea mays	cob		3		5	6			2	3	4		6	7	8		10		2						1	2	3
Amaranthaceae																											
Amaranthus	seed/utricles	2				6													2								
Anacardiaceae																											
Rhus trilobata type	stones						7												2	3							
Rhus radicans type	stones																										
Asteraceae																											
Iva	achene					6	7												2	3							
Parthenium incanum	achene																		2	3							
Cactaceae																											
Echinocactus horizonthalonius	areoles							1	2		4	5	6		8	9			2		4	5			1		

Table A.3.1. Distribution of Plant Remains in Screened Squares by Level, cont'd

Taxonomic ID	Part ID	C 28						C 29										C 30							C 31		
		2	3	4	5	6	7	1	2	3	4	5	6	7	8	9	10	1	2	3	4	5	6	7	1	2	3
Echinocereus pectinatus type	stem			4					2		4	5	6	7	8	9		1	2	3	4	5					
Platyopuntia	seed		3			6	7		2			5	6			9	10	1	2				6		1	2	3
	stem or pad					6	7	1			4	5					10		2		4				1		
Chenopodiaceae																											
Atriplex canescens			3			6	7		2				6			9			2	3		5			1		
Chenopodium	seed													7						3					1		
Cheno-am	seed					6					4		6													2?	
Convolvulaceae																											
Ipomoea										3																	
Cucurbitaceae																											
Cucurbita	seed		3	4		6	7	1	2	3	4	5	6	7	8	9	10	1	2			5	6	7	1	2	3
Fabaceae																											
Phaseolus vulgaris	seed									3	4		6	7	8	9		1	2						1		
Prosopis glandulosa	endocarp	2	3	4		6	7	1	2	3	4	5	6	7	8	9	10	1	2	3	4	5	6	7	1	2	3
Fagaceae																											
Quercus	acorn		3	4	5	6		1			4	5	6	7	8	9	10	1	2	3			6		1		3
Fouquieriaceae																											
Fouquieria splendens	bark			4								5	6		8	9			2	3		5			1		
Garryaceae																											
Garrya	leaf	2					7			3	4		6				10	1	2	3	4	5	6		1		
Nyctaginaceae																											
Mirabilis multiflora	seed		3								4				8	9	10	1	2								
	root					6			2	3	4	5	6	7		9		1	2	3		5			1		
Portulacaceae																											
Portulaca	seed										4																
Rosaceae																											
Prunus	stone	2	3			6	7						6		8				2	3							
Rutaceae																											
Ptelea	fruit					6																					
Ulmaceae																											
Celtis	stone												6	7		9	10	1	2						1	2	3
Zygophyllaceae																											
Kallstroemia parviflora	fruit																										
Larrea tridentata	carpel/fruit		3			6										9			2	3							
Miscellaneous																											
Quids		2	3	4		6	7	1	2	3		5	6		8		10	1	2	3	4	5			1	2	

Table A.3.2. Distribution of Plant Remains in Screened Squares by Level

Taxonomic ID	Part ID	D 28						D 29				D 30				D 31			Total Number
		2	3	4	5	6	7	1	2	3	4	1	2	3	4	1	2	3	of Levels (n=43)
Cupressaceae																			
Juniperus	seed	2	3	4	5	6	7	1	2	3	4	1	2	3	4	1	2		41
	berries		3	4	5	6		1	2	3	4	1	2	3	4	1	2		31
Pinaceae																			
Pinus edulis	nutshell		3	4	5	6	7	1	2	3	4	1	2	3	4	1	2		40
P. ponderosa	bark	2	3	4	5			1	2	3		1	2			1			24
P. strobiformis	seed																		1
Agavaceae																			
Agave	leaves																		7
Dasylirion	fruit/carpels				5				2	3	4	1	2	3	4	1	2		31
Dasylirion/Nolina	quid			4		6						1							5
Dasylirion	leaf segments	2			5					3									
Yucca	seed			4	5	6	7		2	3	4	1	2	3		1	2		35
Liliaceae																			
Allium	bulb scales													3			2		8
Poaceae	florets, spikelets																		
Andropogoneae				4	5	6						1							12
Aristida															4				1
Avena fatua													2						1
Bouteloua					5				2			1	2	3	4				13
Chloris crinita								1	2		4		2	3		1		3	15
Digitaria californica									2	3	4	1							8
Oryzopsis hymenoides													2						1
Paniceae		2			5	6				3			2						15
Pappophorum complex												1		3					5
Setaria	inflorescence									3									3
Sorghum	grain												2						4
Sporobolus		2		4	5	6		1		3		1	2	3			2		24
Stipa neomexicana				4	5				2			1	2			1			11
Zea mays	grain							1	2		4		2	3		1		3	26
Zea mays	cob	2	3	4	5						4		2						20
Amaranthaceae																			
Amaranthus	seed/utricles																		3
Anacardiaceae																			
Rhus trilobata type	stones				5	6	7							3					7
Rhus radicans type	stones						7				4		2						3
Asteraceae																			
Iva	achene																2		5
Parthenium incanum	achene				5				2										4
Cactaceae																			
Echinocactus horizonthalonius	areoles	2			5	6	7	1							4	1	2		19
Echinocereus pectinatus type	stem	2						1			4		2			1			18
Platyopuntia	seed				5	6	7		2			1	2	3	4		2		23
	stem or pad	2				6		1			4		2						14

Table A.3.2. Distribution of Plant Remains in Screened Squares by Level, cont'd

Taxonomic ID	Part ID	D 28	D 29	D 30	D 31	Total Number of Levels (n=43)
		2 3 4 5 6 7	1 2 3 4	1 2 3 4	1 2 3	
Chenopodiaceae						
Atriplex canescens	fruit	4 5 6	3	3 4	2	17
Chenopodium	seed	5				4
Cheno-am	seed	5				4
Convolvulaceae						
Ipomoea						1
Cucurbitaceae						
Cucurbita	seed	4 5 6 7	2 3 4	2 3	1 3	33
Fabaceae						
Phaseolus vulgaris	seed		1		1	11
Prosopis glandulosa	endocarp	2 3 4 5 6 7	1 2 3 4	1 2 3 4	2 3	42
Fagaceae						
Quercus	acorn	3 6	2 3 4	1 2 3 4	2	28
Fouquieriaceae						
Fouquieria splendens	bark		1 4	1 2		13
Garryaceae						
Garrya	leaf	4 5 6	3 4	1 2 4	1	22
Nyctaginaceae						
Mirabilis multiflora	seed	5 7	3	4		11
	root	2 6 7	1 2	1 2		20
Portulacaceae						
Portulaca	seed					1
Rosaceae						
Prunus	stone	3 5 6	2	3		13
Rutaceae						
Ptelea	fruit					1
Ulmaceae						
Celtis	stone	4 5 6	2	1 2 3 4	2	18
Zygophyllaceae						
Kallstroemia parviflora	fruit			4		1
Larrea tridentata	carpel/fruit	5	3			17
Miscellaneous						
Quids		4 5 6	1 2 3 4	1 2 3	3	30

Table A.4. Identification of Ten Natural Strata with Original Volume of Floated Matrix Sampled

Sample No.	Source	Unit	Matrix Volume (L)	Remarks
1.	B28.E22	A	7.125	
2.	B28.E5	B	3	
3.	B28.E17	C	9.75	
4.	B28.E23	D	9.375	
5.	B28.W37 B28.W36	F F	1.50 1.50	screen loss fraction screen retained fraction
6.	B29.E3	C	1.50	
7.	B29.E6 B29.E7	D D	1.50 1.50	screen loss fraction screen retained fraction
8.	B29 E30	E	5.25	
9.	B29.E11 B29.W5	P CC	record absent 15.00	screen loss fraction screen retained fraction
10.	B30.E17	BB	record absent	

Table A.5. Condition and Distribution of Plant Parts in Ten Natural Stratigraphic Units*

Classification	Part and Condition	1	2	3	4	5	6	7	8	9	10	Percentage
Cupressaceae												
Juniperus seeds	Of 94 seeds, 10 are carbonized, two are rodent-nipped, and three are split	1	2	3	4	5	6	7	8	9	10	100
	Two fruits are unmodified; one is partly burned and smashed. Fragments appear crushed.						6	7	8	9		40
Pinaceae												
Pinus edulis	Of 26 cone scales, 15 are distal ends.					5	6	7	8	9	10	60
	Two fascicles of needles											
P. ponderosa	Bark not consistently sorted.					5	6				10	
Agavaceae												
Dasylirion	Fruit carpels weight 1.3 g. Of 33 entire fruits, one is deep brown and two are parched.	1	2	3	4	5	6	7		9	10	90
	All five seeds are burned.					5	6	7				
	Of 12 spines from the margin of young leaves, one is charred.	1	2		4							
Yucca	A split leaf is knotted					5						
	Leaf base present.						6	7				
	Of 11 seeds, only one is thin and fragile.							7	8	9	10	
Cyperaceae	One trigonous achene is present.	1										
Poaceae (florets/spikelets)												
Andropogoneae	Ten spikelets are unmodified.	1		3					8	9	10	
Aristida	One floret is unmodified.											
Bouteloua curtipendula	Ten spikate branches are unmodified.					5	6	7		9	10	
Bouteloua (other) spp.	Unmodified spikelets total 201.	1	2	3	4	5	6	7	8	9	10	100
Chloris	Of two spikelets, one is bleached and one is brown.					5	6					
Chloris crinita	Of 54 spikelets, 34 are in sample 10. The latter are a deep or golden brown.					5	6		8	9	10	60
Digitaria californica	Of five florets, one is singed.								8	9	10	
Elymus/Agropyron	13 florets are unmodified.					5	6	7	8			
Eragrostis	Eight spikelet segments are unmodified.				4		6		8	9	10	
Hilaria	Two florets are unmodified.											
Lycurus phleoides	Unmodified spikelets total 34.					5	6	7	8	9	10	
Oryzopsis hymenoides	Of three florets, one is hairless and one is golden brown.	1					6	7				
Paniceae	Of 174 florets or spikelets, nine are brown and three are carbonized.	1	2	3	4	5	6	7	8	9	10	100
Pappophorum complex	Of 13 spikelets, one is singed brown.	1	2		4		6	7		9	10	70
Sporobolus	Florets weighed 0.78g. No grain present.	1	2	3	4	5	6	7	8	9	10	100
Stipa neomexicana	Burned awn segments, splintered lemmas, and callus tips are equivalent to 147 florets.	1	2	3	4	5	6	7	8	9	10	100

Table A.5. Condition and Distribution of Plant Parts in Ten Natural Stratigraphic Units,* cont'd

Classification	Part and Condition	1	2	3	4	5	6	7	8	9	10	Percentage %
Zea mays	The 45 male spikelets have abraded or eroded tips.	1	2					6	7			
	Cupule or cob segments are unburned.		2							9		
Aizoaceae												
Trianthema portulacastrum	One seed coat present				4							
Amarathanceae												
Amaranthus	A minimum of 90 utricles are present.			3	4	5	6	7	8	9	10	80
	Of 11 seeds, two remain in their utricles.				4	5	6		8	9		
Anacardiaceae												
Rhus trilobata type	Of two stones, one is cracked.			3				7				
	Of four fruits, one is dark with a charred peduncle and one is spread as if pounded.											
Rhus radicans type	One glabrous, flattened intact fruit coat.			3				7		9		
Asteraceae												
Artemesia dracunculus	Eight brownish heads are in one lot.										10	
Helianthus annuus type	Seven achenes are present.	1		3	4		6	7	8		10	70
Iva achene	51 achenes are present.	1	2	3	4	5	6	7	8	9	10	100
Parthenium incanum	Many of the achenes have bracts and florals parts as well.	1	2	3	4	5	6	7	8	9	10	100
Verbesina	One achene is present.	1										
Viguiera dentata type	12 achenes are present.	1			4		6	7		9		50
Cactaceae												
Echinocactus horizonthalonius	Of 45 areoles, all but one have the spines burned to the base.	1	2	3		5	6	7	8	9	10	90
Echinocereus pectinatus	Of 20 areoles of this type, 15 show stumps of burned spines.		2	3	4		6	7				50
Opuntia cf. *leptocaulis*	The stem is present.								8			
Platyopuntia	Of 28 seeds, three are carbonized or parched. The embryo is absent from 18.	1	2			5	6	7	8	9	10	80
Mammillaria	Of the seven nipples capped by spiny areoles, only one has burned spines.						6			9		
Chenopodiaceae												
Atriplex canescens	The fruit bracts or wings on all but five of 156 fruits are eroded with vein stubs protruding. Of those with eroded wings, two are carbonized and five appear parched.	1	2	3	4	5	6	7	8	9	10	100
Chenopodium	Three unmodified seeds are present.			3	4			7				
	Five perianths are present.											
Cheno-ams	Of 180 seeds, 37 are deflated, one is cracked, one is carbonized, and one is popped.	1		3	4			7	8	9	10	70
Cucurbitaceae												
Cucurbita foetidissima	Of 26 seeds, 19 are split in half, one is parched and split, and nine are irregularly broken.		2	3	4	5	6	7	8	9		80

Table A.5. Condition and Distribution of Plant Parts in Ten Natural Stratigraphic Units,* cont'd

Classification	Part and Condition	Distribution** 1 2 3 4 5 6 7 8 9 10	Percentage %
Cucurbita foetidissima (cont.)	Shell fragments are present. The single peduncle is carbonized.		
Fabacae			
Prosopis glandulosa	Of the 181 endocarps, 57 are hinged open, 34 halves have been parted, and 1 endocarp is carbonized. A single seed is carbonized. 6 leaflets are present	1 2 3 4 5 6 7 8 9	90
Fagaceae			
Quercus	Acorn shell frags are present. One acorn is crushed open, one is possibly roasted.	7 8 9 10	
Fouquieriaceae			
Fouquieria splendens	One carbonized base of a calyx	2	
Garryaceae			
Garrya	Unmodified leaves are present.	5 6 9	
Lamiaceae			
Salvia reflexa type	Two calyxes were recovered.	5	
	One seed has the apex removed and the embryo is missing.	9	
Nyctaginaceae			
Mirabilis multiflora	Minced root fragments weight 4.24 g. Six of 10 strata have some carbonized pieces. Three pieces in one stratum appear masticated.	1 2 3 4 5 6 7 8 9 10	100
Oleaceae			
Fraxinus	One samara has the wings broken away.	6	
Portulacaceae			
Portulaca	Two seeds are present.	4 7	
Rosaceae			
Cercocarpus	Of nine leaves, six are fragmentary.	1 3 6 9	
Fallugia paradoxa	The partly carbonized portion of a leaf is present.	10	
Solanaceae			
Physalis	One unburned seed.	4	
Zygophyllaceae			
Kallstroemia parviflora	Of seven mericarps, three are open and have the embryo missing.	6 7 8	
Larrea tridentata	A total of 25 carpels are present.	1 2 3 5 6 7 8 9 10	90
	(5 carpels = 1 fruit). There are at least 17 leaves.	1 2 3 8 9 10	

* See Appendix A, Table A.4 for catalog numbers

** Sample volume is 120 mL.

Table A.6. Condition and Distribution of Plant Remains in Seven Pits* in Square D27

Classification	Parts and Condition	Distribution** 1 2 3 4 5 6 7
Cupressaceae		
Juniperus seeds	Of 45 seeds, 19 are carbonized. Some in each pit are carbonized.	1 2 3 4 5 6 7
Pinaceae		
Pinus edulis	Distal ends of cone scales are in each pit. Nutshells are in five pits, needles are scattered. Pit 5 had three examples of fascicles of two needles.	1 2 3 4 5 6 7
Agavaceae		
Dasylirion	Carpels weigh 1.2g. All 14 seeds are carbonized.	1 2 3 4 5 6 7
Yucca	Of 29 seeds, 16 are in Pit 3. One seed in Pit 3 is carbonized.	
Cyperaceae	Of 31 achenes, 27 were in Pit 7.	1 5 7
Poaceae (florets, spikelets)		
Andropogoneae	Unmodified spikelets are present.	1 6
Aristida	Florets are present.	1
Bouteloua	Spikelets total 160.	1 3 4 5 6 7
Chloris crinita	There are 40 unmodified spikelets.	6
Chloris virgata	Spikelets total 13.	
Digitaria californica	Of the seven spikelets, six are in Pit 6.	2 6
Elymus/Agropyron	One floret is present.	5
Eragrostis	Of 17 spikelets, 16 are in Pit 1.	1 5
Lycurus phleoides	A total of 94 spikelets are present.	1 2 4 5 6
Paniceae	Of 127 florets or spikelets, one spikelet is deep brown and two florets have unevenly darkened lemmas that are cracked (parched?).	1 2 3 4 5 6 7
Pappophorum complex	There are only 3 or 4 spikelets.	1 2 5
Sporobolus	Florets weigh .948 g.	1 2 3 5 6 7
Stipa neomexicana	A minimum of 18 florets were present. Some of the callus tips were carbonized. Lemmas were in slivers.	1 2 4 5 6
Zea mays	Of the 16 kernels, 11 were in Pit 1. One kernel was cracked and expanded. Two cupules were in Pit 2; a cob was in Pit 3.	1 2 3 4 5
Amaranthaceae		
Amaranthus	A minimum of 120 utricles are present, as well as six seeds.	1 2 3 4 5 6 7
Anacardiaceae		
Rhus trilobata type	One of the two stones was carbonized. Three fruits were unmodified.	1 2 4 5 7
Rhus radicans type	One of four stones was in Pit 5.	5 7
Asteraceae		
Artemesia dracunculus	12 heads are in Pit 1.	1
Helianthus annuus	18 whole achenes are present. Strips are in Pits 4, 5, and 6. Halves are in Pits 2 and 6.	2 4 5 6 7
Iva ambrosiaefolia	54 achenes are present.	1 2 3 4 5 6 7

Table A.6. Condition and Distribution of Plant Remains in Seven Pits* in Square D27, cont'd

Classification	Parts and Condition	Distribution** 1 2 3 4 5 6 7
Parthenium incanum	About 20 achenes were recovered.	1 4 5 6 7
Viguiera dentata type	60 achenes are present.	1 2 3 4 5 6 7
Berberidaceae		
Berberis	Only one stone was recovered.	5
Cactaceae		
Echinocactus horizonthalonius	Of 16 areoles bearing spines, 15 have burned spine bases.	2 3 4 5 6 7
Echinocereus pectinatus	Of five areoles, four show burned spine bases.	1 4
Mammillaria	One carbonized areole and spine from a nipple is present.	4
Platyopuntia	Of 17 seeds, two appear carbonized.	1 2 3 4 5 6 7
Capparidaceae		
Cleome	Only a single seed was recovered.	6
Chenopodiaceae		
Atriplex canescens	Of 87 fruits, only five do not have their wings or bracts eroded away.	1 2 3 4 5 6 7
Chenopodium	One seed in Pit 3 is carbonized.	3 4 5 6 7
Cheno-am	Of over a thousand seeds, 563 came from Pit 7. Some seeds in Pits 2, 3, and 4 were burned.	2 3 4 5 6 7
Cucurbitaceae		
Cucurbita foetidissima	A max. of 3 seeds were recovered from a single pit. Fruit fragments were in Pits 3, 4, and 7.	1 3 4 5 7
Fabaceae		
Prosopis glandulosa	In total, approximately 266 endocarps were recovered. Only one carbonized seed was found in Pits 1, 3, 4, and 5.	1 2 3 4 5 6 7
Phaseolus vulgaris	180 beans, mostly type C 11. See Table 2.4.	1
Fagaceae		
Quercus	Splintered acorn epidermis was present as well as some proximal scar tissue normally attached to the acorn cup in Pit 1.	1 4
Lamiaceae		
Salvia reflexa	The calyx type comes from a single pit.	1
Nyctaginaceae		
Allionia incarnata	One fruit came from Pit 6.	6
Mirabilis multiflora	Minced root fragments weigh .62 g. Carbonized pieces came from Pits 1, 3, 5, and 6.	1 2 3 4 5 6 7
Portulacaceae		
Portulaca seed	Three seeds came from Pit 7.	7
Zygophyllaceae		
Kallstroemia	One split mericarp segment was carbonized in Pit 4.	4
Larrea tridentata	Two fruits came from Pit 1 and one from Pit 6.	1 6 7

*See Table 1.3 for catalog numbers of the pits.

**Sample volume is 120 mL

Appendix B.1
High Rolls Cave: Content of Excavation Units and Features

Flotation samples from High Rolls Cave (LA114103) are presented by excavation units (Excavation Unit) and then by features (F) in ascending order. Each listing is prefaced by remarks on location, context, and radiocarbon date if available. The general level of preservation and signs of disturbance are presented and, where appropriate, notes on incomplete sorting are provided. Items are uncarbonized unless indicated to the contrary. Centimeters below surface (cmbs) and meters below datum (mbd) are abbreviated. The use of cf. indicates a lesser level of identification created by poorly preserved or broken specimens. The capsules that hold small plant parts have a 1 ml capacity.

Samples are cross-referenced by geographic grouping in Table 3.10 and indexed by Field Sample Number (FS) in Table B 1.1. The analysis of six flotation samples from thermal features by Teresa M. Fresquez is summarized in Table B 1.2. Table B 1.3 contains the carbonized content of nine thermal features analyzed by the author. The text accompanying each feature description includes the classification and description of uncarbonized items omitted from Table B 1.3. The collection of flowers, pollen, and seed by mice or rodents is most evident in FS 67 (the mouse pantry) from East Cluster B. The same sample contains unique information about seeds recovered in the heavy fraction. See Appendix B.2 for the basis of identification of selected items and a description of unknowns.

FS 70, EXCAVATION UNIT 4

Stratum 1, 0-10 cmbs, East Cluster B, sorted November 8, 2001.

Finely shredded grass stems and vegetal material dominate the largest size fraction followed by numerous grass stems 2 mm or less in diameter and 5 cm or less long. Minced coriaceous oak type leaves and charcoal are present.

Gymnosperms

Pinaceae
> *Pinus* type needles
> *Pinus edulis* type nutshell half: uncarbonized
> *P. edulis* type needles: 2

Cupressaceae
> *Juniperus* seed: 3, uncarbonized. One 6 mm long 3 mm broad and one very small

Monocotyledonous Flowering Plants

Poaceae
> Poaceae florets and grains: 5, carbonized, poorly preserved, size of *Eragrostis*
> *Eragrostis* type spikelet segments: 3 nerved lemma without awns, palea brownish
> *Eragrostis* type spikelet: 1 fire singed with one caryopsis within
> cf *Eragrostis* grains: 9 carbonized, 1 uncarbonized

Paniceae floret: 1 uncarbonized grain removed and entry hole evident
Sporobolus florets with grain: 5 uncarbonized
Sporobolus grain present: uncarbonized
Stipa type floret (not *S. neomexicana*): 1
Unknown with awned lemma: 6 florets uncarbonized

Dicotyledonous Flowering Plants

Asteraceae
Chrysothamnus type head with involucral bracts: 1, uncarbonized
Chrysothamnus type achenes: 5 uncarbonized, with pappus
Unknown achenes of same type: 2
Unknown head with graduated, hyaline involucral bracts 2.5 mm long on interior

Berberidaceae
Berberis cf *fremontii* leaf: 1 barbed, evergreen 14 mm long

Chenopodiaceae
cheno-am embryos: 12 uncarbonized, brown, but lack coat
cheno-am seed coats: 3 carbonized

Fagaceae
Quercus acorn scar from nutshell: 1 uncarbonized
Quercus type leaf fragments
Quercus gambelii leaf: 1 immature

Rutaceae
Ptelea fruit: 1 with eroded margins
cf Solanaceae seed fragment uncarbonized, porous surface

Unknowns
Angiosperm type A unknown seed: 16 uncarbonized
Dicotyledon anthers: 7 uncarbonized, without pollen

Animal
Rodent fecal pellets 3 mm by 10 mm, plus fragments

FS 139, EXCAVATION UNIT 4

Stratum 2, 50 cmbs, 11.65 to 11.81 mbd. East Cluster B, sorted March 9, 2002; Radiocarbon dated 3000 ± 60 B.P.

The 4 mm screen has many fine grass stems (1 mm or less diameter) and abundant macerated or finely shredded fiber from grass or another source tangled together. Included are short, narrow segments of *Yucca*, split and longitudinally shredded herbaceous stems, pinyon pine needles, coriaceous leaves of oak, Wright's silk tassel, and cornhusk fragments. The largest twig is 3 mm diameter. Only the venation remains of many dicotyledonous leaves. Very little is identifiable below the 4 mm screen in size.

Gymnosperms

Pinaceae

Pinus staminate cone 3 mm long with bracts at base
Pinus edulis type needles are mostly single: 31
        The three needle fascicles have the basal membrane missing.
cf *Pinus edulis* type nut shell fragment, carbonized

Cupressaceae
    Juniperus scale leaves (rare)

Monocotyledonous Flowering Plants

Poaceae
    Andropogoneae 2 spikelet pairs (one sessile, one pediceled)
    Eragrostis inflorescence segment
    Paniceae florets: 2
    cf *Zea mays* husk fragments, some burned; veins are widely spaced
    Zea mays cob shanks: 2 with base of husks attached; one is singed by fire
    cf *Zea mays* cupule, carbonized, extremely compressed

Dicotyledonous Flowering Plants

Anacardiaceae
    Rhus trilobata type stone: 1
    Rhus trilobata type fruits: 2, one immature

Asteraceae
    Ambrosia confertiflora achene: 1
    Gnaphalium type leaf: 1
    Iva ambrosioides achene: 1, coat black and smooth
    head of involucral bracts:1

Brassicaceae
    Erysimum capitatum type long narrow pod segment attached to disc-like area by a short stipe

Cactaceae
    Platyopuntia seed burned on one face and embryo excavated from it; narrow rim

Chenopodiaceae
    Cheno-am seeds: 6, one lacks coat
    Cheno-am seed coat halves: 2

Fabaceae
    Prosopis endocarp with seed missing
    Vicia (?) bean

Fagaceae
    Quercus acorn: 1, but edges jagged and empty
    Quercus acorn strips: 2
    Quercus type leaves with rounded and pointed lobes

Garryaceae
    Garrya wrightii type leaves

Unknowns

> Unknown Angiosperm Type A: 2
> Unknowns: 3 types described in Appendix B.2

Animal

> fecal pellets of rodents
> wood rat type: a cluster of 2 or more on some membranous substance 10 mm and 12 mm long and
> > 3 mm and 4 mm broad; another two, 8 mm by 3 mm; other fragments
>
> mouse type: 3, black, 4 and 5 mm long, about 2 mm broad
> rabbit type(?) flattened spheroid, 8 mm diameter 5 mm thick
> Animal tissue: thin, dried pieces of tissue—similar to jerky but light brown.
> Insect parts

FS 67, EXCAVATION UNIT 5, *THE MOUSE PANTRY*

Stratum 3, 11.72 mbd. East Cluster B, sorted February 12, 2002.

Grass stems, herbaceous stems, and even pine needles (at times to the very tip) were all longitudinally shredded. Uprooted grasses were shredded to the root base. All pieces were bent or shredded in segments 4 cm to 9 cm long. Stiff strips of *Yucca* leaf were reduced to 5 cm in width and 4 cm in length. The fibrous mass held a scatter of smooth edged charcoal of all sizes and mouse type fecal pellets, as well as the plant parts listed.

The vegetal mass was subject to wetting and drying because of the condition of pine needle fascicles and some cheno-am seeds. The thin, brown membranous covering on the base of the pinyon pine needle fascicle was often missing although the structure beneath as well as the needles were preserved. No cheno-am seeds showed signs of sprouting. Some weedy cheno-ams need light in order to sprout, so this moisture did not necessarily come after the seeds lost their viability. Many cheno-am seed coats had cracked and partially exfoliated from the remainder of the seed. Numerous cheno-ams lack seed coats.

The mouse pantry sample has many examples of rodent foraging. Limited evidence of human activity takes the form of carbonized or parched plant material and several identifications that indicate the plant material originated well beyond the normal foraging range of mice. While the deposit is in Stratum 3, the content may be Stratum 2 in age. Unlike the remainder of flotation, both the light and the heavy fraction were fully analyzed.

Light Fraction of Flotation

Gymnosperms

Pinaceae

> *Pinus* type terminal buds of branches: 8
> *Pinus* type male cone scales with pollen sac, some open: 10
> *Pinus* cone scale apophysis: 6, two with tip raised above matrix are of the pinyon type
> *Pinus edulis* type needles and needle fascicles number greater than 10, sample retained
> *Pinus edulis* type young needle fascicles less than 2 cm long: 8
> *Pinus cembroides* type needles: 4
> *Pinus* young twigs (with closely spaced nodes) and some with scale leaves intact; one with apical bud present but no needles. A set of 16 even younger twigs with needle fascicles evidently removed.
> *Pinus edulis* type nut shell fragments

Cupressaceae

> *Juniperus* branches with scale leaves
> *Juniperus monosperma* type uncarbonized seed fully rounded 5 mm long, hole at distal end.
> cf *Juniperus* seed fragments

Monocotyledonous Flowering Plants

Agavaceae

>*Yucca baccata* type seeds: 10, though some apparently immature. All seeds rather small, about 9 mm long where complete. The rim is missing or obscure on four seeds. Two fragmentary seeds could be carbonized.

Poaceae

>*Bouteloua* spikelets: 12, all with keeled lemmas
>*Bouteloua eriopoda* spikelet: 1
>*Elymus/Agropyron* complex: 6 florets, with grain removed. One flat rachis segment has several florets.
>Paniceae spikelets and florets: 18, all but two have fertile lemma and palea sculptured as in *Setaria macrostachya*.
>*Sporobolus* golden yellow grains with darkened embryos
>*Sporobolus gigantea* type: 18
>*Sporobolus* spp: 20
>Sporobous airoides type brown grains: 2
>*Sporobolus* spp. florets with grain: 5
>*Stipa neomexicana* awn segment, a hairy callus, splintered lemma with hairy callus, and three to five splintered lemmas that lack pubesence
>Unknown spikelet with flattened rachis segment: 1

Dicotyledonous Flowering Plants

Amaranthaceae

>*Amaranthus* spp. Two utricle caps and three bases; the latter have an extra long bract projecting. One cap resembles *Amaranthus cruentus*. Uncarbonized seed.

Anacardiaceae

>*Rhus trilobata* type stone
>*Rhus trilobata* type female flowers and an array of very young to mature fruits
>*Rhus trilobata* type axis of infloresence

Asteraceae

>*Ambrosia confertiflora*: 1 fruit or achene
>cf *Artemisia dracunculus* involucral bracts, empty heads
>cf *Chrysothamnus* heads with few involucral bracts which are narrow, graduated, some gland tipped.
>*Gnaphalium* type leaves, shredded, twisted
>*Iva ambrosiaefolia* type achenes: 9 total; three are warty, immature
>Heliantheae type disc flowers; floral tube with 5 fused petals 5 mm long, inferior expanded ovary. At least l0 are intact. Many specimens eaten down to the expanded ovary. Heads with chaffy bracts that would correspond to the flowers are absent.
>*Verbesina encelioides* type: 4 achenes
>A. *Helianthus* type glabrous achenes: 12, see Appendix B.2 for description
>B. *Helianthus* type glabrous achenes: 5, see Appendix B.2 for description
>*Viguiera dentata* type(?) hairy achenes: 31, see Appendix B.2 for description
>*Viguiera/Helianthus* achenes: 7, with high shoulders 4.5 mm to 5 mm long and 2 mm wide, hairy mottled outer coat
>*Viguiera/Helianthus* achenes: 30, see Appendix B 2 for description
>*Viguiera/Helianthus* achene fragments longitudinally split into strips

Boraginaceae
>*Lappula* nutlet and fragments of glandular hairy leaves that possibly belong with the genus.

Cactaceae
>Platyopuntia seed: 7, but only one is complete. The remainder have been entered from one flat side and the embryo removed.
>*Echinocereus* seed with embryo missing.

Chenopodiaceae
>*Chenopodium* seeds; some covered with fine, granular but papery membrane and enclosed with a farinaceous pericarp.
>cheno-am seeds greater than 100 both carbonized and uncarbonized. See preface.

Cucurbitaceae
>*Cucurbita foetidissima* type seeds: 3, one split along suture lines

Fabaceae
>*Prosopis* endocarps: 12; four were entered from the flat face to remove seed; six were split along the carpel juncture and have seed missing; two endocarps were immature.

Lamiaceae
>*Salvia* type nutlets: 7
>*Salvia* type: One shredded calyx with 2 immature nutlets with gland dots at the distal ends between the ribs.

Nyctaginaceae
>*Allionia* type (?) fruits: 2

Polygonaceae: one three winged achene, eroded

Solanaceae
>*Nicotiana* type crumpled leaf.

Animal: ant heads, beetle bodies, other insects
>wood rat fecal pellet fragment: 1, 4 mm by 9 mm
>mouse size fecal pellets: 24, 1.5 mm to 2.5 mm by 3.5 mm to 5 mm

Heavy Fraction of Flotation

Gymnosperms

Pinaceae
>*Pinus edulis* nutshell fragments fill 1.5 capsules

Cupressaceae
>*Juniperus* seeds: 4, plus fragments

Monocotyledonous Flowering Plants

Agavaceae
>*Yucca baccata* type: 4 seeds

Poaceae

Unidentified grains: 8, many dark. *Bouteloua* and *Eragrostis* present perhaps. Needs more study
Sporobolus giganteus type grain: 79
Sporobolus spp. grain: 410
Sporobolus airoides type darkened grains 9
Paniceae: 2 smooth lemmas from fertile florets
Zea mays kernel fragments: 2

Dicotyledonous Flowering Plants

Anacardiaceae

Rhus trilobata type stones: 11, one with a jagged hole
Rhus trilobata type stone fragments fill 2 capsules

Asteraceae

Gnaphalium type leaf with tomentum on one surface only
cf *Helianthus* type longitudinal strips of achene coat about 4.5 mm long
Unknown achene: 1
Viguiera/Helianthus type achenes: 23, see Appendix B 2 for description

Cactaceae

Platyopuntia type seeds: 14 whole, one of which is carbonized
Platyopuntia seed halves: 8 plus fragments, all devoid of embryos
spine 7 mm long, 1 mm broad, part of epidermis missing; tip may be eroded

Chenopodiaceae

cheno-ams: over 100, some without coats
Chenopodium present

Cucurbitaceae

Cucurbita foetidissima type of seed: part of a longitudinally split half of one seed

Fabaceae

Prosopis endocarps: 4, no seeds within

Fagaceae

Quercus acorn strip and 1/4 of inner cap

Portulacaceae

Portulaca type seed: 1

Solanaceae

One eroded seed half, epidermis absent

Animal

fecal pellets: 11, mouse-size, see Appendix Table B 2.2
bone fragments

Stone: red, also tiny fossil shells, fossil coral

Lithics: chips from manufacturing

FS 557, Excavation Unit 10

Stratum 2, 19 cmbs, 11.25 to 11.35 mbd. East Cluster A, sorted August 28, 2001.

FS 557 was investigated as a dry sample that was screened and sorted but not subject to flotation. The first two liters were screened and treated as a unit, then the remaining sediment. All material retained by the 0.5 mm screen and larger was examined. The 4 mm screen had *Yucca* type fibers shredded with little epidermis intact and small pieces of charcoal. Oak leaves, though incomplete, were preserved. The 0.5 mm screen had *Iva* and cheno-ams. The 1 mm screen had various bracts. The remainder of the plant material was typically recovered in the 2 mm and 4 mm screens. Many of the plant remains recovered (both burned and unburned) exhibited internal crystalline formation. Apparently some time following occupation the cave became increasingly damp or periodically wet.

The diversity of plants and almost all cheno-ams are in the first two liters screened. This condition suggests that the vibrations induced in transport resulted in granular movement to the top of the sample bag (Jaeger and Nagel 1997).

Gymnosperms

Pinaceae
>*Pinus edulis* type cone scale fragment, carbonized, see Appendix B.2 for description
>*Pinus* male cone
>*Pinus* needles bent, chewed
>*P. edulis* type nut shell fragments

Cupressaceae
>*Juniperus* seed: 3, entire with crystals on surface; one entire but nipped open at proximal end, plus two different halves
>*Juniperus* branches with scale leaves

Monocotyledonous Flowering Plants

Agavaceae

>*Dasylirion* fruit with crystals on it
>cf.*Yucca* shredded leaf fibers with crystals

Poaceae
>unknown caryopsis keeled, 1.3 mm by 0.6 mm
>floret, awned
>*Bouteloua* spikelet: 2, one in poor condition with crystals, another smashed
>*Elymus/Agropyron* complex type spikelet, with crystals
>*Eragrostis* type inflorescence
>*Stipa neomexicana* awn segment
>*Zea mays* embryo consists of coleoptile and central area, carbonized. 2.7 mm long, probably fully mature

Dicotyledonous Flowering Plants

Anacardiaceae

>*Rhus trilobata* type stone, empty fruit coat, uncarbonized globular fruit 6 mm diameter with crystals within fruit. Collar-like caylxes on short pedicels. One collar is 3 mm diameter.

Asteraceae
>> involucral bracts, heads
>> *Viguiera* type achenes: 2, both carbonized, one 2 by 3 mm, one smaller
>> *Iva ambrosiaefolia* type achenes: 2, one has smooth coat, one is warty

Berberidaceae
>> *Berberis* leaflet 1, barbed coriaceous, about 2 cm long; three barbs per side

Cactaceae
>> Platyopuntia type seed, whole; crystals on the surface
>> *Echinocereus* type seed fragment with orfice

Chenopodiaceae
>> *Chenopodium* seeds present, some carbonized
>> cheno-am seeds: greater than 100 seeds. Some uncarbonized cheno-ams have lost the seed coat, others have seed coat peeled back; some seeds are carbonized. Many seed coats were split along natural suture lines. One has a crystalline knob.

Fabaceae
>> pod segment unknown
>> *Prosopis* endocarps: 3. Crystals on the surface of two. One endocarp incomplete. One had strip removed for access to seed. No seed present.

Fagaceae
>> *Quercus* acorn with crystals, 1.5 cm by 1.5 cm, proximal end decapitated
>> *Quercus* type leaf fragments

Garryaceae
>> *Garrya wrightii* type leaves

Solanaceae
>> *Nicotiana trigonophylla* type leaf. See Appendix B.2. A second leaf of the same type as the first is 6 mm wide and has been rolled from the apex so that the petiole is exposed, forming a small, flattened package 6 mm by 5 mm.

Unknowns
>> unknown flower with crystal, bracts, Angiosperm type A seed

Animal
>> wood rat type fecal pellets 8: 3 mm by 8 mm, 3 mm by 6 mm, 3 mm by 7 mm

FS 557 B, Last batch from the bottom of the bag sieved 11/05/01

Gymnosperms

Pinaceae

>> *Pinus ponderosa* bark scale
>> *P. edulis* type needle fascicle
>> *P. edulis* type nut shell fragments
>> *Pinus* cf *edulis* cone scale apophysis: 2

Cupressaceae
>   *Juniperus* scale leaves, twigs
>   *Juniperus* seed 5 fragments
>   *Juniperus* seed half carbonized 5.5 mm broad, 5 mm long

Monocotyledonous Flowering Plants

Agavaceae
>   *Dasylirion* fruit carpel half, split apart
>   cf Agavaceae/Liliaceae: two seed fragments paper thin at least 1 cm long with expanded raised margin

Poaceae
>   *Bouteloua* spikelet: 1, crushed
>   *Stipa neomexicana* Four splintered lemma are hairless, as well as the callus which is retained on the base of three lemmas. The lemmas are normally pubescent and the callus very hairy. These hairs can be removed by fire.

Dicotyledonous Flowering Plants

Anacardiaceae
>   *Rhus trilobata* type fruit: 6 were glossy, wrinkled, hairy with the stone inside. Four were flat and immature; one cut in two, black.
>   *Rhus trilobata* type: Two fruit pedicels 0.5 mm diameter, stalk 8 mm long that expanded to a 4 mm diameter collar or cup. One has a dark resinous amorphous fruit in it about 4 mm long.

Cactaceae
>   Opuntia: 2 clusters of glochids, uncarbonized.
>   Platyopuntia seeds: 5. Four lack rim and embryo. One lacks rim but is intact.

Chenopodiaceae
>   Cheno-ams: 2 seeds carbonized, 1 uncarbonized

Animal
>   wood rat type fecal pellets: 9, about 8 mm long, uncarbonized

FS 187, EXCAVATION UNIT 12

Stratum 2, 46 cmbs, 11.3 to 11.5 mbd. Concentrated burned area in East Cluster A, 2 liters, sorted April 10, 2002; Sample radiocarbon dated 2220 ± 50 B.P. but may be questionable.

The sample consists of charcoal 1 cm or less in diameter with sharp fractures. The sample comes from above Feature 2.

Gymnosperms
Pinaceae
>   *Pinus edulis* type needle: 2, carbonized
>   *P. edulis* type nutshell fragments: 2, uncarbonized

Cupressaceae
>   *Juniperus* seed, uncertain if carbonized
>   *Juniperus* scale leaves, uncarbonized

Monocotyledonous Flowering Plants

Agavaceae

>   *Yucca baccata* type seed: 7, plus fragments, carbonized

Poaceae

>   cf. *Elymus/Agropyron* complex 1 grain, carbonized
>   *Sporobolus* grain 8 uncarbonized, some dark: 1 carbonized
>   *Stipa neomexicana* callus tip: 17, carbonized
>   *S. neomexicana* portion of lemma near awn, 20 carbonized
>   *S. neomexicana* awn base: 33, carbonized
>   *S. neomexicana* awn fragments: uncounted, carbonized
>   cf. *Zea mays* embryo and scutellum: 2, carbonized; measure 1.5 mm and 1 mm long
>   cf *Zea mays* coleoptile, carbonized 2.5 mm long

Typhaceae

>   Typha seed: 1, brown .75 mm long and 0.2 mm wide, truncated at one end

Dicotyledonous Flowering Plants

Asteraceae

>   cf *Artemisia dracunculus* achenes: 15, carbonized. One flower and one base of head uncarbonized.
>   *Iva ambrosioides* achenes: 2. One black and smooth, one black and abraded.

Amaranthaceae

>   *Amaranthus* seeds: 3 carbonized, oval in plan view

Cactaceae

>   Platyopuntia seed: 1, uncarbonized, split at top and embryo missing

Chenopodiaceae

>   *Chenopodium* seed: 2 carbonized, 2 uncarbonized
>   Cheno-am seed: 7, uncarbonized and greater than 18, carbonized

Fabaceae

>   *Prosopis* seed with portion of endocarp: 1, carbonized
>   *Prosopis* endocarp: 2, uncarbonized, split open?

Solanaceae

>   *Nicotiana* seed: 1, carbonized, 0.9 mm by 0.65 mm

Animal

>   bird feather fragment 1, uncarbonized
>   wood rat fecal pellet: 1, carbonized, 10 mm long
>   animal hair patch: 2 fragments, carbonized

FS 208, EXCAVATION UNIT 13

Stratum 2, 15 to 36 cmbs, 11.46 to 11.53 mbd. East Cluster A, 2 liters, sorted December 28, 2001.

FS 208 is from an ash area above matted organic material and radiocarbon dated 2910 ± 40 B.P. A projectile point is associated with the deposit. Evidently cold ash was deposited in this area, which then became the recipient of residues from parching and winnowing. The preservation appears as good as the best samples from Fresnal Shelter. Winnowing of *Chenopodium* and *Amaranthus*, of dropseed grass and false tarragon seed is evident from the chaff present as well as the actual seed. Since some seed is burned and some is not, processing by winnowing and by parching is represented. Some amaranth and cheno-am seed coats had cracked and partially exfoliated from the remainder of the seed. A few of the seeds lacked seed coats entirely. An alteration of wet and dry conditions must have taken place in FS 208 as in FS 67, where numerous cheno-ams lack the seed coat. Only two mouse fecal pellets were observed.

All items larger than 4 mm screen were examined. A 20 ml sample of plant material from the 2 mm and 4 mm screen was analyzed, but actually includes smaller material. In addition about 7 ml from the 0.5 mm screen were scanned for amaranth utricle caps.

Gymnosperms

Pinaceae

> *Pinus* cone scale stripped from very tip of cone
> *Pinus* cone scale apophysis from tip of cone
> *Pinus edulis* type needles and needle fascicles
> *P. edulis* type nut: one plus fragments

Cupressaceae

> *Juniperus monosperma* type 2 berries
> *Juniperus monosperma* type seed, 1, carbonized, 5.5 mm long, D shaped cross section
> *Juniperus monosperma* type seeds: 2, uncarbonized seeds fully rounded 6 mm long
> *J. pachyphloea* type seeds: 2, carbonized
> *Juniperus* branches with scale leaves

Monocotyledonous Flowering Plants

Agavaceae

> *Yucca baccata* type seeds: 27, apparently uncarbonized

Poaceae

> unknown, cf *Elymus* spikelet with flattened rachis segment: 1
> *Bouteloua* spikelets 6, all fertile florets with keeled lemmas
> *Bouteloua* eriopoda type spikelet: 1
> *Sporobolus* yellowish grain with darkened embryo; numerous florets
> *Stipa neomexicana* broken awn segments
> Of splintered lemma segments: two units are carbonized and five apparently uncarbonized, but only
>> two have callus hairs intact. Lack of callus hairs probably due to singing by fire.

Dicotyledonous Flowering Plants

Amaranthaceae

> *Amaranthus* utricle caps and bases present
> *Amaranthus* spp. seeds carbonized and uncarbonized. Four uncarbonized oval seeds have coats peeled back and appear thin when compared to *Chenopodium* coats.
> *Amaranthus cruentus* utricle caps: 10, isolated from a sample of 23

Anacardiaceae

> cf. *Rhus trilobata* type stone: 4 fruits, and 1 flowering stalk

Asteraceae

    Helianthus/Viguiera type achenes: 2, see Appendix B 2 for description
    Artemisia dracunculus achenes, involucral bracts, empty heads
    Artemisia dracunculus carbonized achenes
    Iva ambrosiaefolia type achenes: 15, half are warty

Cactaceae

    Platyopuntia seed: 1, carbonized
    Platyopuntia stem epidermis fragment, glochids present

Chenopodiaceae

    Atriplex canescens fruit uncarbonized, whole
    Chenopodium seeds
    cheno-am seeds carbonized and uncarbonized

Fabaceae

    Prosopis endocarps: 24 mature, 7 immature, all uncarbonized

Portulacaceae

    Portulaca seeds: 5

Zygophyllaceae

    Larrea tridentata: half of a hairy fruit

Animal

    mouse type fecal pellets: 2, 2.5 mm by 6 mm
    fur fragment

FS 742, Excavation Unit 27

South half, Stratum 2, Layer 1, 23 cmbs, 11.10 to 11.12 mbd. East Cluster A, sorted March 12, 2002.

In the 4 mm screen only 1/8 to 1/4 of the material appeared macerated. The bulk of leaves were crumbled or crushed in small fragments, but about 1/8 were whole or nearly so and potentially could be identified. Among them are very small Gambel oak leaves and coriaceous leaves of Wright's silk tassel. Some leaves have decayed until only the veins are left. Some charcoal is present. *Yucca* was not obvious. No pine needles are in the 4 mm screen, although they appear in low numbers in smaller sized screens. Insect parts are numerous. This sample contains a tobacco type leaf, of special interest when initially observed because of its superficially fragile nature and the other leaves that have been rolled. One cheno-am has a colorless coat.

    All but the 0.5 mm screen size were fully analyzed. From one of two envelopes from the 0.5 mm screen, 15 ml were analyzed.

Gymnosperms

Pinaceae immature cone scale tip

Cupressaceae

    Juniperus seed 4 mm long, hole at broad end

Monocotyledonous Flowering Plants

Poaceae

Andropogoneae 1 spikelet pair (one sessile, one pediceled)
Elymus/Agropyron complex type florets: one looks abraded or threshed
Possible grass grain unknown 1.9 mm long with acute ends, but no visible embryo

Dicotyledonous Flowering Plants

Anacardiaceae

Rhus trilobata type stone: 1, cracked open, worn

Asteraceae

family level:Various involucral bracts and heads, one involucral head with graduated striate phyllaries.
disc flower: 1, with fimbriate pappus and hairy ovary
Chrysothamnus type achenes: 15, with capillary bristles
Chrysothamnus type involucral heads: 9
cf *Chrysothamnus* achene

Boraginaceae

Lappula redowskii type nutlet: 1

Brassicaceae

Lepidium type seed: 1, with folded embryo .1 mm long, dark but uncarbonized and plump. Similar to
FS 853 and FS 597.

Cactaceae

Platyopuntia seed: 1, narrow rim, 3 mm diameter, embryo removed from one side
Echinocereus type seed coat fragment

Chenopodiaceae

Atriplex canescens type fruit: 1, with wings incompletely eroded leaving veins
Chenopodium seeds: 3
Cheno-am seeds 13: one has a light, tannish coat

Fagaceae

Quercus gambellii leaf: 1, small and immature

Garryaceae

Garrya wrightii type leaves present

Rutaceae

Ptelea fruit: 1

Solanaceae

1 seed with epidermis eroded leaving network, 2.1 mm diameter
cf *Chamaesaracha* seed: 1
cf *Nicotiana* corollas with united floral tube, 2. See FS 795 for similar corolla
Nicotiana trigonophylla flower: 1
Nicotiana trigonophylla type leaf: 3 and fragments, see Appendix B.2 and for others, FSs 853 and 557.
Seven additional leaves bear signs of manipulation. See Appendix B.2

Unknown

> Unknown angiosperm A type seed. 7 examples saved.
> Dicot anther, longitudinally open: a single sample retained
> Dicot bract or modified leaf tissue with scalloped edges, dense hairs on one surface. Net veins coalesce where modified leaf may have attached. About 2 cm diameter

Animal

> tissue: thin, brittle like jerky
> feather fragment
> snails: 3 vertical and 1 horizonal coil
> 10 pupal(?) cases, tan with a dark blunt end, analagous to a shuttle cock. See Appendix B.2 *Abies* for a revised identification
> insect legs, 2 capsules
> beetle wings, 2 capsules

FS 795, EXCAVATION UNIT 27

South half, Stratum 2, layer 2, 28 cmbs, 11.12 to11.25 mbd, East Cluster A, sorted March 14, 2002; Radiocarbon dated 3120 ± 40 B.P.

There is some charcoal with sharp edges along with other carbonized plant material that may be related in age. Many leaves of dicotyledons are decayed until only veins remain, grass stems seem bent every cm, and macerated stem material creates a fuzz. Rodent fecal pellets are present. Some uncarbonized items like the mesquite endocarp may have been transported by a wood rat. Dropseed (*Sporobolus*) only survives as a grain-coat in instances. The smallest screen size commonly has Asteraceae disc flowers and cheno-ams.

All but the 0.5 mm screen were fully analyzed. A fraction (15 ml) of the 0.5 mm screen was scanned and only selected identified items were saved. For example, *Sporobolus* florets and cheno-ams remain in the original sample.

Gymnosperms

Pinaceae

> *Pinus* cone scales: 2, rodent shredded
> *Pinus edulis* type cone scale: 1, carbonized
> *P. edulis* type nutshell: 1, gnawed open. Additional fragments

Cupressaceae

> *Juniperus monosperma* type seed: 2 dull, tan, fully rounded surface
> *Juniperus* pachyphloea seed: 4, reflective brown surface
> *Juniperus* scale leaves

Monocotyledonous Flowering Plants

Agavaceae

> *Yucca baccata* type seed: 1, uncarbonized and degraded
> *Yucca baccata* type seed: 1, carbonized seed and a fragment.\

Poaceae

> *Bouteloua* : spikelet 1, fertile floret keeled
> Paniceae 1 spikelet and 3 fertile florets. One fertile floret is color of milk chocolate

Sporobolus grains: 10, but some are just grain coats
Sporobolus florets were present but not removed from sample
Zea mays cupule: 1, with tough glumes free from remainder of cob, uncarbonized

Dicotyledonous Flowering Plants

Amaranthaceae
    Amaranthus seed: 2, oval in plan view

Anacardiaceae
    Rhus trilobata type in various stages from blossom to mature fruits
    Rhus trilobata type stones broken open and whole

Apiaceae
    1 mericarp carbonized, 2 mm long

Asteraceae
    head with equal length involucral bracts, brown, transparent
    small disc flowers abundant in 0.5 mm screen content
    Iva ambrosioides achenes: 10 black coats partially worn
    Verbesina encelioides achene: 1

Cactaceae
    Platyopuntia seeds: 10, five have begun to disintegrate from the micropyle, located where the rim on
        the seed narrows. Here the rim begins to detatch as well as the two faces of the seed. No dark
        lining is visible on the interior. Yet another seed that has been gnawed thru on the side exhibits
        the dark (carbonized?) interior. All the seeds have a dark brown surface.

Chenopodiaceae
    Chenopodium seed: some burned, some not burned. Some of unburned ones still have their perianth
        One of burned ones has the endosperm missing. Missing endosperm may mean the seeds
        were infested from storage before they were parched, similar to FS 853.
    Cheno-ams: Some cheno-ams have visible burned interiors, suggesting human introduction. Others
        have totally lost their coats and their interiors remain. Another showed a coat that has uplifted
        and peeled back, as with water damage.

Fabaceae
    Prosopis endocarps: 5 1/2. Only one seed enclosed

Fagaceae
    Quercus acorn: 1, immature
    Quercus leaf lobes of *Q. gambelii* type present

Lamiaceae
    1 nutlet, shiny brown, 2 mm long

Rosaceae
    Fallugia paradoxa type leaf fragments: 2

Solanaceae
    1 seed with degraded coat, 2 mm maximum diameter
    cf. *Nicotiana*: tubular corolla 1, 16 mm long, poor condition
    See FS 742 also

Zygophyllaceae
> *Kallstroemia* (unbroken) mericarps: 2 plus fragment

Unknowns
> Angiosperm type A seed

Animal
> Feather fragments 2, split shafts
> fecal pellets
> wood rat type, carbonized 4 mm by 10 mm
> wood rat type, uncarbonized
> Insect parts 1 capsule, including beetles
> Snails: 2 flat coiled, 6 vertical coiled

FS 805, EXCAVATION UNIT 27

South half, Stratum 2, Layer 3, 34 cmbs, 11.19 to 11.27 mbd. East Cluster A, sorted March 8, 2002.

The 4 mm screen contains small pieces of charcoal and cave spalls and a thumb-sized piece of uncarbonized highly shredded material. Some of the shredded strands are kinky as if it had been part of a woven plastic or nylon material. Because of the apparently modern contaminant, the unburned material and its source is suspect. Material uncarbonized unless otherwise indicated.

Gymnosperms

Pinaceae
> *Pinus edulis* nut shell fragments

Cupressaceae
> *Juniperus* Two split halves of seed with embryo missing and two fragments

Monocotyledonous Flowering Plants

Agavaceae
> *Yucca baccata* type seed and fragment, both carbonized

Poaceae
> Paniceae: 1 empty lemma
> *Sporobolus* grain uncarbonized
> *Stipa neomexicana* burned awn segment
> cf *Zea mays* cob cross section fragments, uncarbonized. Tough pair of glumes at tached to one segment
>> of a cob.

Dicotyledonous Flowering Plants

Asteraceae
> Iva ambrosiodes achene coat fragment

Anacardiaceae
> *Rhus trilobata* type stone: 1

Rhus trilobata type immature fruit: 6

Cactaceae
Platyopuntia seed: 1

Chenopodiaceae
Chenopodium at least one
cheno-ams: frequent, one with coat partly peeled back
cheno-ams halves of coats: 2

cf Solanaceae 1 fragment of degraded seed

Unknown
1 microfossil, 1 mm by 0.75 mm

Animal
Insect Parts
Bone 2 pieces, 1 segment burned

FS 1256, EXCAVATION UNIT 33

Stratum 3, 11.92 mbd. East Cluster B, sorted March 5, 2002.

The material in the 4 mm and 2 mm screens was all finely shredded fiber that needed to be torn apart with a tweezer and dissecting needle to see if other material was entangled in it. There was a tiny cluster of sky-blue fibers in the mass. Only the smallest seeds seem to have survived in any quantity. Some of the dropseed grass consisted of only the coats of the grain. I found no fecal pellets, but fine shredding may be the remains of a rodent nest. The woolly *Gnaphalium* leaves that also were in FS 67 add to that impression.

Gymnosperms

Cupressaceae
Juniperus scale leaves bleached white: 5

Poaceae
Sporobolus grains: 3

Dicotyledonous Flowering Plants

Asteraceae
cf *Artemisia dracunculus* achene
Gnaphalium type leaf
Iva ambrosiaefolia type achenes: 5. Some black coats are eroded down to tan layer
Unknown disc flower

Cactaceae
Platyopuntia type seed: 1

Chenopodiaceae
Chenopodium
Cheno-ams: 4

Solanaceae
    Nicotiana rustica type seeds: 9, measurements in Appendix B.2 include these seeds as well as 40 from FS 853.

Unknowns
    1 seed

FS 773, EXCAVATION UNIT 63

Stratum 2, Layer 3, 15 cmbs, 11.30 mbd. East Cluster A, sorted March 5, August and September 2002; Radiocarbon dated 2890 ± 60 B.P.

One can see the veined network of former leaves and the rachis from the infloresence of dropseed grass. Grass stems are finely shredded while other stems are bent every 2 cm and tangled with wiry stems. Pinyon needles are only occasional. Flecks (1-2 mm) of charcoal are scattered. The mixture attracts every size of plant debris in the 4 mm screen and must be examined at 25-power to catch the smallest items. The deposit looks well worked by mice. Wooly *Gnaphalium* leaves are present as in FS 67.

About 5 ml of the 4 mm fraction was sorted with tweezers and dissecting needle very slowly. The remainder was torn apart manually to locate large objects. The material held by the 2 mm and 0.5 mm screens was fully examined and all but 20 ml in the 1 mm screen. Amaranth utricle bases were retained by both the 4 mm and the 1 mm screen. The diagnostic amaranth utricle caps were abundant in the 0.5 mm screen. Amaranth seed with a thin seed coat were removed. Examples of cheno-am seeds and *Iva* achenes retrieved. The 4 mm screen sample may have amaranth or other small items of interest if sorted in greater detail.

Gymnosperms

Pinaceae
    Pinus twig segments: 4
    Pinus cone scales: 2
    Pinus apophysis: 3
    Pinus edulis type cone scale: 1
    Pinus edulis type needles: 5
    Pinus edulis type nutshell fragments

Cupressaceae
    Juniperus scale leaves

Monocotyledonous Flowering Plants

Agavaaceae
    Yucca baccata type seeds: 4, three uncarbonized, one carbonized

Cyperaceae
    Scirpus type achene: 1

Poaceae
    Bouteloua eriopoda spikelet: 1
    Bouteloua spikelets: 20, fertile florets with keeled lemmas. Four were hairy on keel nerve.
    Elymus complex head segment, floret
    Paniceae fertile florets: 2

Paniceae: *Setaria macrostachya* type fertile florets: 22

Setaria macrostachya spikelet: 1

Sporobolus grains: 13

Sporobolus florets: 4

Sporobolus airoides type floret: 4. one brown grain within floret is 0.75 mm long

Sporobolus panicle branches bare of florets

Stipa neomexicana awn segments: 7; callus tip: 1, carbonized; splintered lemmas that lack pubescence: 4, dark brown

Unknown florets: 12

Unknown grain: 3

Dicotyledonous Flowering Plants

Amaranthaceae

Amaranthus seeds: 43. Thirty-eight have seed coat parted enough to see they are very thin and one is thick by contrast. Seeds are 1 mm to 1.25 mm long.

Amaranthus spp. utricle caps: 0.5 ml unclassified. Some have two styles instead of three. Some have styles that diverge and many are erect as in A. *powellii*.

Amaranthus spp. recurved tepals with utricle bases, unclassified: 4

Amaranthus cruentus type utricle caps: 1/4 ml sent to S. Lentz for dating 8/4/02

Amaranthus cruentus type utricle caps .33 ml sent to S. Lentz for dating 9/30/02

Amaranthus cruentus type utricle caps: 0.1 ml retained 9/30/02

Both lots of 9/30/02 and *A.cruentus* caps in FS 208 were more rigorously identified, for the author became more aware that *A. powellii* was a source of confusion. See Appendix B.2 Taxonomic Notes.

Amaranthus cruentus type utricle bases and tepals: 36

Amaranthus hybridus type utricle caps: 4

Amaranthus torreyi type utricle bases and tepals: 8: caps: 4

Amaranthus powellii type utricle bases with tepals: 10 segregated but an additional 0.5 ml also separated, but may have small additons of other *Amaranthus* spp. in it. The 0.5 ml of utricle caps may be primarily *A. powellii* but with admixtures of other unknown species.

Anacardiaceae

Rhus trilobata type fruit: 1, mature; 1 immature

Rhus trilobata type stones: 6 and a fragment

Apiaceae

mericarp: 1, 2 mm long

Asteraceae

Artemisia dracunculus type achenes: 5, one carbonized

Gnaphalium: 1 leaf segment

Heliantheae disc flower: 1

Helianthus/*Viguiera* type: 4 achenes, one is high shouldered and dark; 2 achene strips

Iva ambrosioides achene: 10 examples removed, six have warty transverse ridges

Verbesina encelioides achenes: 15

Unknown achenes: 2

Unknown warty achenes: 84

Unknown disc flowers: 2

Cactaceae

Opuntia type areole: 2

Platyopuntia type seeds: 4

Chenopodiaceae
Chenopodium seeds with perianth: 9
Noted one *Chenopodium* where the coat is broken and peeled back as in FS 67
Cheno-am seeds: 11. All are circular in planar view, all but one are light brown. They could be amaranth. Two cheno-ams lack coats entirely, as is FS 208.

Ericaceae
Arctostaphylos uva-ursi type seeds: 19, three darkened by fire, 1 carbonized

Fabaceae
Prosopis endocarps: 27 endocarps with seed absent and 10 endocarps with seed enclosed
cf. *Prosopis* seeds: 2, carbonized
cf a Mimosoideae seed: 1, small

Fagaceae
Quercus type leaf fragments

Garryaceae
Garrya wrightii type leaves: 3, minimum

Lamiaceae
Salvia nutlet: 1

Nyctaginaceae (?)
Allionia (?) fruits: 5
Allionia (?) seed: 1

Portulacaceae
Portulaca seed: 34
Portulaca circumsissile capsule cap: 17
Portulaca capsule base: 7

Rosaceae
Fallugia paradoxa leaf fragment: 1, carbonized

Zygophyllaceae
Kallstroemia fruit: 1, with cut apex
Kallstroemia mericarp 1, split along sutures, interior absent
Centrosperm unknown 0.5 mm diameter, plump, black: 11, many carbonized

Dicotyledon embryos: 8

Animal
pupal (?) case dark on one end as in FS 742. See Appendix B.2 *Abies* for a revised identification,
insect cases crescentic, folded: 3
bird feather fragments: 3
wood rat fecal pellet: 1, 9 mm long
mouse fecal pellets: 6 plus fragments. 1 pellet 5 mm long

FS 853, EXCAVATION **U**NIT **88**

Stratum 2, Layer 1, 11.12 to 11.16 mbd. Intermediate between E. Cluster A and C, sorted March 16, 2002; Radio-carbon dated 2860 ± 40 B.P.

The 4 mm screen had a variety *ponderosa* pine bark scales, as well as shredded materials, two segments of *Yucca* with frayed tips, skeletonized leaves, and a scattering of charcoal. From the 2 mm screen come dicot leaves that have partly disintegrated.

All screen sizes were analyzed. When the 0.5 mm screen (full of fine fluff) was sorted, unknown Angiosperm type A seeds and cheno-am seeds were left in the residue unless the condition of the seeds conveyed important information. With all the decay evident, the retention of Unknown A dicot leaf, as in FS 742, seems a paradox, unless it belongs to tobacco, which might be decay resistant. (This apparently was the case; see Solanaceae.)

Gymnosperms

Pinaceae
> *Pinus edulis* needles: 3 retained as representative (uncommon)
> *Pinus edulis* type seed: 1
> *Pinus edulis* type seed fragments: 3, each represent 1/3 of a nut
> *Pinus ponderosa* bark scales: 10, one is burned

Cupressaceae
> *Juniperus* scale leaves
> *Juniperus* seed: 2. One whole, uncarbonized and one with embryo removed from broad end

Monocotyledonous Flowering Plants

Agavaceae
> *Yucca baccata* type seed: 4; one is a domed seed, two are typical flat seeds, and a fourth is a seed rind
>> fragment.

Poaceae
> *Eragrostis* grains: 2
> Paniceae fertile florets: 2
> *Sporobolus*: 8 grains. Some are whole, some are empty seed coats. They range from 0.50 to 1.00 mm
>> long.
> Poaceae unknown grain: 1

Typhaceae
> Typha type seed: 1

Dicotyledonous Flowering Plants

Amaranthaceae
> *Amaranthus* seeds are present. Some of coats are peeled back. Five look thin and fragile compared to *Chenopodium* coats. Perhaps these represent A. *cruentus*.
> *Amaranthus cruentus* utricle cap: 1

Anacardiaceae
> *Rhus trilobata* type stones: a half, plus one fragment

Asteraceae

    Artemesia dracunculus type achene: 1, 0.9 mm long, long strips, uncarbonized
    Chrysothamnus type achene with pappus of white bristles
    Helianthus/Viguiera: 1 mottled achene with high shoulders 6 mm long, 2.4 mm wide
    Helianthus/Viguiera 6 black achenes with high shoulders 2.5 mm long, some split
    Iva ambrosioides type achenes: 8; only two are warty
    Unknown achene: 1, very warty, tan, 2.4 mm long
    Achene without coat: 2 mm long, in shape of a cultivated shelled sunflower achene

Brassicaceae

    Lepidium type carbonized seed: 1; 1.5 mm long, folded embryo; similar to FS 742

Cactaceae

    Echinocereus type seeds: 2
    Platyopuntia seeds: 5 nearly whole plus 2 fragments; one is a darker brown, with a reflective surface,
        three have breaks near the micropyle, showing the darkened embryo. One fragment has the
        embryo missing, but one can see a dark area on interior of seed. Seeds were possibly parched.
    cf. *Cylindropuntia* seed: 1; surface layer has pulled back along one edge

Chenopodiaceae

    Atriplex canescens: fruit: 1, wings eroded away; four sided but two opposite sides are broader
    Chenopodium seeds carbonized: 3
    Cheno-am seeds: Two uncarbonized seeds are missing the seed coats entirely. Six have their seeds
        coats exfoliated so that a very thin seed coat is visible. These may be of the cultivated
        amaranth.
    Cheno-am seeds. Some burned and unburned seeds have endosperm missing. There is one roasted
        larva. Evidently seed was stored and insect damage resulted.
    Unknowns: 2 burned seeds in this lot are not cheno-ams.

Fabaceae

    Prosopis endocarp, split, seed missing
    Prosopis seed: 1, seed very flat, dark, degraded

Lamiaceae

    nutlet, shiny brown, two flattened faces at 90 degree angle, 2 mm long

Portulacaceae

    Portulaca seeds: 3

Rosaceae

    Fallugia paradoxa leaves finely divided into narrow segments, margins in-rolled

Solanaceae

    Nicotiana rustica type seeds: 254; some have only coats present
    One seed is carbonized. Two seeds appear parched. Some have seed interiors are shrunken from their
        coat. See Appendix B.2 for measurements. Two hundred fourteen seeds were sent to Stephen
        C. Lentz August 4, 2002 for radiocarbon dating. Sample dated 2860 ± 40 B.P.
    Nicotiana trigonophylla type leaf: See Appendix B 2 for description. Other leaves are in FS 742 and
        FS 557.

Unknowns

    centrosperm seeds: 4, 0.5 mm diameter
    Angiosperm A type unknown seed: 8 examples selected for retention
    microfossil: 4

Animal

> Insect parts, half capsule ant heads, tiny eggshell
> roasted larva: 1
> Two pupal (?) cases with dark blunt end, look like a shuttle-cock or dark bullet piece at one end. FS
>> 742 has ten like these. See Appendix B.2 for a revised identification to *Abies*.
> Fecal pellets:2
> The fibrous pellets are nearly lacking in solids.
> Two mouse type pellets are 2 mm by 4 mm and 2 mm by 3 mm.
> Two wood rat type segments: each 3 mm in diameter and 3 mm and 4 mm long,
> respectively. They might well belong together—making a pellet about 7 mm long.

Mollusca

> l horizontally coiled and one vertically coiled snail shell

FEATURE 1 (FS 60) PIT, EXCAVATION UNIT 5

Stratum 3, 73 cmbs, 11.75 to 11.85 mbd, East Cluster B, 2 liters; Radiocarbon dated 3080 ± 50 B.P.

Small, shallow circular pit excavated into sterile soil. Associated charcoal stain and burned area probably represents hearth fill of a simple, unlined hearth. See Appendix Table B 1.3 for identification of most carbonized remains.

Monocotyledonous Flowering Plants

Agavaceae

> cf *Yucca* vascular bundle segments, carbonized; 0.1 mm diameter with raphides

Poaceae

> *Sporobolus* floret with grain within
> Poaceae stem base: 1, carbonized

Dicotyledonous Flowering Plants

Chenopodiaceae

> Cheno ams and *Chenopodium*: 10, carbonized

FEATURE 2 (FS 80) THERMAL PIT, EXCAVATION UNIT 11

Stratum 2, Layer 1, 58 cmbs, 11.60 to 11.69 mbd. East Cluster A, 2 liters, sorted January 2, 2002; Radiocarbon dated 2850 ± 50 B.P.

Simple unlined oval hearth excavated into sterile soil. Depositional history indicates times when feature was left open or cleaned out and then filled with wind blown sand.

Monocotyledonous Flowering Plants

Agavaceae

> *Yucca baccata* type seed fragment: 2, carbonized

Poaceae

> cf. Poaceae grain: 1, carbonized, 1.5mm by 5.28 mm, hollow

Dicotyledonous Flowering Plants

Chenopodiaceae
Cheno-am: 1, with embryo, endosperm
Chenopodium seed coat halves: 2, perhaps parched

Unknowns
Angiosperm type A unknown seed: 1, carbonized

FEATURE 3 (FS 175), PIT, EAST HALF, EXCAVATION UNIT 4

Stratum 3. 60 cmbs, East Cluster B, sorted December 2, 2001; Radiocarbon dated by bone collagen to 2970 ± 40 B.P.

Oval pit excavated into sterile soil below Stratum 3. Deteriorated wood lined several parts of the perimeter, and may have lined it fully. It is unlikely to have been a thermal feature, but it may have been filled with redeposited ash.

Gymnosperms

Pinaceae
Pinus edulis type cone scale tip: 5 carbonized
P. edulis type nut coat fragment: 3 carbonized, 1 uncarbonized
Pinus cone scale tips: 2, carbonized

Monocotyledonous Flowering Plants

Agavaceae
Yucca baccata type seed: 1 carbonized, also 5 fragments carbonized. The seed contains the linear embryo impression.

Poaceae
Paniceae (*Setaria macrostachya* type) floret with grain: 1, looks parched but not carbonized; it has a brown lemma and a darker palea, cracked on the lemma, 2.5 mm long.
Stipa neomexicana awn segment: 1, carbonized
cf Poaceae grains: 4, carbonized, lacks features

Dicotyledonous Flowering Plants

Anacardiaceae
Rhus fruit coat: 1, carbonized

Asteraaceae
cf *Artemisia dracunculus* achene: 2, carbonized; more remain in residual fraction

Cactaceae
Platyopuntia type seed: 2, carbonized, narrow rim
Platyopuntia type stem fragment 1, carbonized

Chenopodiaceae
Cheno-am embryo/endosperm: greater than 8, uncarbonized
Cheno-am seed: 4, carbonized
Chenopodium seed: 2, carbonized

Malvaceae
  Sphaeralcea type seed: 1, carbonized

Portulacaceae
  Portulaca seed: 2, carbonized

Unknowns
  Angiosperm unknown type A seed: 2, uncarbonized

FEATURE 5 (FS 293), PIT, EXCAVATION UNIT 34

Stratum 2, layer 2, 30 to 34cmbs, 11.98 to 12.02 mbd. East Cluster B, 2 liters, sorted December 31, 2001; Radiocarbon dated 2990 ± 40 B.P.

Shallow basin-shaped oval pit excavated into sterile substrate. Excavator thought that the fill might have been used to level a depression in the cave floor.

Gymnosperms

Pinaceae
  P. edulis type nut fragments: 5, with fresh breaks
  P. edulis type nut: 1 whole nut
  Pinus cone scale tips 2, uncarbonized
  Pinus young cones: 2, uncarbonized

Cupressaceae
  Juniperus branch with scale leaves: 1, colorless
  Juniperus monosperma type seed: 1, uncarbonized

Monocotyledonous Flowering Plants

Poaceae
  Andropogoneae spikelet pair: 1
  Bouteloua spikelets: 3, with keeled, hairy fertile lemmas, uncarbonized
  Eragrostis grains: 49, uncarbonized (embryo is half length of grain) and carbonized
  Paniceae floret: 1, uncarbonized
  Sporobolus grains 2 uncarbonized, yellowish with dark embryos
  Poaceae unkown florets: 16

Dicotyledonous Flowering Plants

Asteraceae
  Iva ambrosiaefolia achene: 1, black, smooth; uncarbonized?
  cf *Helianthus/ Viguiera* achene: 1, split open, 4.25 mm long, 1.5 mm thick, 2 mm broad. Tan with
    black beneath coat.

Cactaceae
  Platyopuntia type seed: 2 uncarbonized, one is a furry half

Chenopodiaceae
  Atriplex canescens fruit: 1, good condition

Animal

    Insect parts, various
    bone 1, uncarbonized
    wood rat fecal pellets 10, about 8 mm long
    rodent or insect fecal pellets ½ capsule, some cf mouse

FEATURE 5 (FS 293), PIT , EXCAVATION UNIT 34

Stratum 2, Layer 2, 30-34 cmbs, 11.98-12.02 mbd. East Cluster B, 2 liters. Analyzed by Teresa M. Fresquez.

See Appendix Table B 1.2 for content.

FEATURE 6 (FS267), THERMAL PIT, EXCAVATION UNIT 33

Stratum 2, layer 1, bottom half of feature, 52 cmbs, 11.87-11.95 mbd, East Cluster B; Flotation radiocarbon dated 2850 ± 70 B.P. Analyzed by Teresa M. Fresquez.

Feature was a small pit filled with ash, charcoal, and artifacts. Organic flooring abuts its east edge. Botanical form indicates burned mesquite seeds were present. See Appendix Table B 1.2 for content.

FEATURE 7 (FS 273), PIT, SOUTH HALF, EXCAVATION UNIT 12 AND 31

45 to 49 cmbs, 11.55 to 11.99 mbd. East Cluster A. Sorted January 27, 2002.

Feature 7 is a shallow burned lens of soil with charcoal. Although radiocarbon dated to 3360 ± 40 B.P., the date is thought to be too early.

All screen sizes were fully sorted except the 0.5 mm screen. A minimum of one hour was devoted to scanning the 0.5 mm screen.

Gymnosperms

Cupressaceae

    Juniperus seed fragments, carbonized, represent at least 3 seeds
    Juniperus leaves: 4, carbonized

Monocotyledonous Flowering Plants

Poaceae

    cf Poaceae grains: 2, carbonized

Dicotyledonous Flowering Plants

Asteraceae

    cf *Artemisia dracunculus* seed: 31, carbonized. Only 0.5 mm long, wrinkled coats, many hollow

Cactaceeae

    Platyopuntia embryo: 1, carbonized

Malvaceae
> *Sphaeralcea* seeds: 29, carbonized, 2 mm long, 1.7 mm broad
> *Sphaeralcea* seeds: 7, carbonized, only 1.5 mm long

Unknown
> Angiosperm unknown A seed: 16, carbonized

Animal
> bone
> Insect parts

FEATURE 8 (FS 307), THERMAL AREA, EXCAVATION UNIT 16

Stratum 2, layer 1, 30 to 37 cmbs. West Cluster, 2 liters, sorted January 24, 2002; Radiocarbon dated 2880 ± 70 B.P.

Feature 8 is a shallow basin shaped hearth excavated into sterile soil. Organic flooring materials are present south and west of the feature. The radiocarbon date is at variance with the ash pit (Feature 9).

The 2 mm and 4 mm screen packets lacked flotation and may have been used for the radiocarbon date. The 0.5 mm screen sample was scanned for content, but items were left in the sample. See Appendix Table B 1.3 for carbonized plant identifications.

Unknowns
> *Artemisia dracunculus* type linear leaves, carbonized
> Angiosperm Unknown A: present, uncarbonized
> Unknown dicot seed
> Unknown matrix: 1, carbonized, very irregular parenchyma pattern; reexamine
> Unknown exocarp or nutshell fragments: 10, carbonized. They are variable in thickness. Not sure if they are pinyon.
> Unknown seed (?): 1, carbonized, 1 mm diameter, orbicular

FEATURE 9 (FS 310), ASH PIT, EXCAVATION UNIT 37

Stratum 2, level 3, 15 to 20 cmbs. West Cluster, sorted Jan. 7, 2002; Radiocarbon dated at 3010 ± 40 B.P.

The pit was apparently use to redeposit ash from a thermal feature. The radiocarbon date is at variance with the nearby thermal Feature 8. See Appendix Table B 1.3 for carbonized plant identifications.

FEATURE 11A (FS 263), THERMAL AREA, EXCAVATION UNIT 12

Stratum 3, 40 cmbs, 11.50 to 11.56 mbd, East Cluster A; Flotation 11a dated 3100 ± 60 B.P.

This large thermal feature is 13 cm deep (11.37 to 11.50 mbd) excavated into gravelly silt which was culturally sterile. To the south a charcoal stained utilized surface is associated with the top of the feature and articulates with the rim of the pit. The first inferred use of the feature is associated with Layer 1, which apparently articulates with Stratum 3. After a period of disuse, Layer II of moderately thick ash and charcoal begins and relates to Stratum 2, with temporally related Features 3, 5, 10, and 21. See Appendix Table B 1.3 for carbonized plant identifications.

Dicotyledonous Flowering Plants

Chenopodiaceae
    Chenopodium seeds greater than 45, carbonized. Not all removed from sample
Unknowns
    Unknown epidermis: 1 fragment, carbonized, rolled
    Unknown cone scale or fruit shell fragment, carbonized

FEATURE 11B (FS 782) THERMAL AREA, EXCAVATION UNIT 63

Stratum 2, Layer 3, 13 cmbs. East Cluster A, sorted April 2, 2002.

Radiocarbon dated 2940 ± 60 B.P. See Appendix Table B 1.3 for carbonized plant identifications.

Gymnosperms

Pinaceae
    Pinus edulis type nutshell fragments: 15+, uncarbonized

Monocotyledonous Flowering Plants

Agavaceae
    Yucca seed: 4 plus fragments, carbonized

Poaceae
    Sporobolus grain: 1, carbonized?
    Sporobolus grain: 1, uncarbonized

Dicotyledonous Flowering Plants

Amaranthaceae
    Amaranthus seed: 4, carbonized; one has coat raised

Asteraceae
    Iva ambrosiaefolia inner tan seed coat: 1, uncarbonized

Cactaceae
    Echinocereus seed coat half, black
    Platyopuntia type seed: 4, uncarbonized; embryo missing, micropyle end split open

Fabaceae
    Prosopis endocarp: 1, uncarbonized

Unknown
    Angiosperm type A seed: 2 uncarbonized
    Microfossil: 1, transparent .75mm diam, spherical, longitudinal lines to poles

Animal
    Animal skin (?) present
    Insect ant head: 2 uncarbonized

FEATURE 13 (FS 597), SOUTH HALF OF THERMAL AREA, EXCAVATION UNIT 58

Stratum 3, part of Layer II, 20 cmbs, 11.39 mbd, West Cluster, 2 liters, sorted March 30, 2002; Radiocarbon dated 2880 ± 60 B.P.

The hearth was the central thermal feature in the western part of the cave in Excavation Units 58, 59, 60, 80, and 81, with a depth of 22 cm (11.18 to 11.40 mbd). See Appendix Table B 1.3 for carbonized plant identifications.

Monocotyledonous Flowering Plants

Poaceae
> *Sporobolus* grain: 1, uncarbonized

Unknown Angiosperm type A: 1, uncarbonized, eroded until full of holes

FEATURE 13 (FS 586) NORTH HALF OF THERMAL AREA, EXCAVATION UNIT 58

Part of Layer I, 11.25 to 11.30 mbd West Cluster, 2 liters, sorted March 28, 2002.

See Appendix Table B 1.3 for carbonized plant identifications.

Gymnosperms

Cupressaceae
> *Juniperus* scale leaves 1 cluster carbonized; 1 cluster uncarbonized

Monocotyledonous Flowering Plants

Poaceae
> Unknown grains: 2, 0.75 mm long, embryo half of length; 1 parched?

Dicotyledonous Flowering Plants

Chenopodiaceae
> Cheno-am seed: 4, uncarbonized and lack seed coat; one embryo darkened

Unknown
> seeds fragments: 3, carbonized; one may be a legume: long, narrow, thin

Animal
> ant head 1, uncarbonized

FEATURE 14 (FS 568) PIT OR THERMAL PIT, EXCAVATION UNIT 80

20 cmbs, 11.16 to 11.29 mbd, contiguous with Feature 13 to south. West Cluster, 2 liters; Radiocarbon dated 3200 ± 60 B.P. but is questionable.

Analyzed by Teresa M. Fresquez. See Appendix Table B 1.2 for content.

FEATURE 15 (FS 630) PIT, EXCAVATION UNIT 83

Stratum 3, 11.08 to 11.16 mbd West Cluster, Radiocarbon dated 3130 ± 40 B.P. Analyzed by Teresa M. Fresquez. See Appendix Table B 1.2 for content.

FEATURE 18 (FS 934) THERMAL AREA, EXCAVATION UNIT 109 AND L34

Stratum 2, Layer 2, 38 cmbs, East Cluster C, 2 liters, sorted January 15, 2002; The feature was radiocarbon dated 2970 ± 40 B.P.

Feature was seen as a stain with a concentration of charcoal overlying a layer of cemented ash, limestone, and/or gypsum.

Gymnosperms

Juniperus branchlet: 1, uncarbonized; tan
The remainder of sample is charcoal

FEATURE 18 (FS 935) EXCAVATION UNIT 134

Stratum 2, Layer 2, 38 cmbs, East Cluster C, 2 liters; Radiocarbon dated 2970 ± 40 B.P. Analyzed by Teresa M. Fresquez. See Appendix Table B 1.2 for content.

FEATURE 19 (FS 964) THERMAL AREA, EXCAVATION UNIT 108

Stratum 2, Layer 2, 48 cmbs, 10.24 mbd, East Cluster C, 2 liters obtained from fire- hardened soil beneath the feature, sorted January 16, 2002.

Burned soil, charcoal, and fire-cracked rock compose this thermal feature that was 22 cm deep (11.20 to 11.42 mbd) and irregular in shape. The radiocarbon date is pending. See Appendix Table B 1.3 for carbonized plant identifications.

FEATURE 22 (FS 1063) THERMAL PIT, EXCAVATION UNIT 69

Stratum 3, 11.50 mbd , 3 cm. below Stratum 3, East Cluster B, full cut, sorted January 9, 2002; Radiocarbon dated corn shanks and husk from feature: 2840 ± 40 B.P.

A shallow saucer-shaped pit, 3 cm deep (11.43 to 11.45 mbd) was excavated into sterile ceiling spall fill.

All but the 0.5 mm screen content was fully sorted. A minimum of one hour was devoted to sorting the 0.5 mm sceen content. See Appendix Table B 1.3 for carbonized plant identifications.

Gymnosperms

Pinaceae

Pinus edulis type seed coat fragment, uncarbonized

Cupressaceae

Juniperus branchlet: uncarbonized, tan

Monocotyledonous Flowering Plants

Poaceae
> *Sporobolus* grain: 2, uncarbonized

Dicotyledonous Flowering Plants

Anacardiaceae
> *Rhus trilobata* type fruit coat: 4 uncarbonized, wrinkled, waxy, about 5 mm diameter
> *Rhus trilobata* type collared calyx and pedicel base: 1, carbonized, 2.5 mm diameter

Cactaceae
> Platyopuntia type seed: 1, uncarbonized, incomplete, eroded fuzzy margins

Chenopodiaceae
> Cheno-ams seeds or seed interiors: 10, carbonized
> Cheno-am seed interior only, coats absent: greater than 250. Lightly parched if at all; brown to tan.

FEATURE 23 (FS 1075) THERMAL AREA, EXCAVATION UNIT 69

Stratum 2, Layer 3, 36 cmbs, 11.45 mbd., East Cluster B, sorted January 6, 2002; Radiocarbon dated 3020 ± 60 BP.

Thermal area was irregularly shaped and excavated into sterile soil. The ash and limestone-gypsum fill had substantial quantities of charcoal but was highly compacted nevertheless. The feature was 11 cm deep (11.30 to 11.41 mbd) and held five pieces of fire-cracked rock. See Appendix Table B 1.3 for carbonized plant identifications.

Gymnosperms

Pinaceae
> *Pinus edulis* type needle segment: 1, uncarbonized
> *Pinus ponderosa* bark scales: 6, uncarbonized

Monocotyledonous Flowering Plants

Agavaceae
> *Yucca baccata* type seed: 1, uncarbonized

Dicotyledonous Flowering Plants

Anacardiaceae
> *Rhus trilobata* type fruit: 1, carbonized, 3.5 mm diameter
> *Rhus trilobata* type immature fruit: 2, carbonized, 1.5 and 2 mm diameter

Cactaceae
> Platyopuntia type seed: 1, uncarbonized, furry

Chenopodiaceae
> *Chenopodium* identifiable seeds: greater than 3, carbonized. 1.5 mm to 2 mm diameter

Fagaceae
> *Quercus* acorn: 1 strip plus an acorn cut in cross section

Feature 24 (FS 1093) Thermal Pit, Excavation Unit 105

36 cmbs, West Cluster, 2 liters. Radiocarbon dated 3090 ± 40 B.P. Flotation analyzed by Teresa M. Fresquez.

A substantial amount of faunal material was recovered from the feature. See Appendix Table B 1.2 for content.

Table B.1.1 List of Flotation Samples from High Rolls Cave Arranged by Field Sample Number				
Field Sample	Feature*	Location	Excavation Unit	Stratum/Layer
FS 60	1	E. Cluster B	5	3
FS 67		E. Cluster B	5	3
FS 70		E. Cluster B	4	1
FS 80	2*	E. Cluster A	11	2/1
FS 139		E. Cluster B	4	2
FS 175	3	E Cluster B	4	3
FS 187		E. Cluster A	12	2
FS 208		E. Cluster A	13	2
FS 263	11*	E. Cluster A	12	2/3
FS 267**	6*	E. Cluster B	33	2/1
FS 273	7	E. Cluster A	12.31	
FS 293**	5	E. Cluster B	34	2/2
FS 293	5	E.Cluster B	34	2/2
FS 307	8*	West Cluster	16	2/1
FS 310	9	West Cluster	37	2/3
FS 557		E. Cluster A	10	2
FS 568**	14	West Cluster	80	
FS 586	13*	West Cluster	58	
FS 597	13*	West Cluster	58	
FS 630**	15	West Cluster	83	5
FS 742		E. Cluster A	27	2/1
FS 773		E. Cluster A	63	2/3
FS 782	11*	E. Cluster A	63	2/3
FS 795		E. Cluster A	27	2/2
FS 805		E. Cluster A	27	2/3
FS 853		Between A and C 88	2/1	
FS 934	18*	E. Cluster C	109,134	2
FS 935**	18*	E. Cluster C	134	2/2
FS 964	19*	E. Cluster C	109	2/2
FS 1063	22*	E. Cluster B	69	
FS 1075	23*	E. Cluster B	69	2/3
FS 1093**	24*	West Cluster	105	
FS 1256		E. Cluster B	33	3

* Thermal Feature; unmarked features are pits
** Analyzed by Teresa M. Fresquez

Table B.1.2. Six Flotation Samples Analyzed by Teresa M. Frezquez

	F 5 FS 293	F 6 FS 267	F 14 FS 568	F 15 FS 630	F 18 FS 935	F 24 FS 1093
Gymnosperms						
Pinaceae						
Pinus cone scale	x*		x*		x*	
P. edulis nut shell	x	x				
Cupressaceae						
Juniperus	2		7*			
Juniperus twigs	x	x	x			
Monocotyledonous Plants						
Agavaceae						
Yucca fiber	x					
Yucca		36*	6*		3*	
Poaceae						
Bouteloua	6					
Oryzopsis hymenoides		1*				
Sporobolus		6				
Zea mays husk	x*					
Poaceae	23	4				
Dicotyledonous Plants						
Amaranthaceae						
Amaranthus		1*, 1				
Anacardiaceae						
Rhus seed or fruit		1*				1*
Cactaceae						
Platyopuntia			1*			
Chenopodiaceae						
Chenopodium		10*, 41	50+*	14*	9*	100+*
Cheno-ams					1*	
Fagaceae						
Quercus leaves	x					
Portulacaceae						
Portulaca		10				
Solanaceae						
Nicotiana		10*, 8				
Unidentified						
Unidentified seed					4	
Unknown taxon 91		3				
Nut shell		1*				

*Indicates carbonized remains; numbers refer to seeds or fruits; all other plant parts are specified

Table B.1.3. Carbonizede Flotation Samples Analyzed by Vorsila L. Bohrer

	F 1	F 8	F 9	F 11a	F 11b	F 13	F 13	F 19	F 23
	FS 60	FS 307	FS 310	FS 263	FS 782	FS 586	FS 597	FS 964	FS 1075
Gymnosperms									
Pinaceae									
Pinus cone scale			3		1	1			
P. edulis cone scale					1	1			
P. edulis nut shell			x						
P. edulis needle	1		1						1
Cupressaceae									
Juniperus seed		3	1+		1+				
Juniperus scale, leaves, twig	2				1	1			
Monocotyledonous Plants									
Agavaceae (seed)									
Yucca baccata type	2		1	1	4+	1+			1+
Poaceae									
Elymus/Agropyron grain									
Sporobolus grain	1								1
Stipa neomexicana									
lemma apex					23				
callus tip		1			40				
awn segment	2	x		1	> 20				
Zea mays embryo, cupules					x*	5		1	
Dicotyledonous Plants									
Amaranthaceae									
Amaranthus seed					4				
Anacardiaceae									
Rhus trilobata									
stone				1+	x				

Table B.1.3. Carbonizede Flotation Samples Analyzed by Vorsila L. Bohrer, cont'd

	F 1 FS 60	F 8 FS 307	F 9 FS 310	F 11a FS 263	F 11b FS 782	F 13 FS 586	F 13 FS 597	F 19 FS 964	F 23 FS 1075
floral axis					1				
fruit mature									1
fruit immature									1
Asteraceae (achenes)									
Artemisia dracunculus	40	x		4	18	5	3	2	
Iva ambrosiaefolia								1	
Viguiera/Helianthus								2	1
Brassicaceae									
Lepidium							1		
Cactaceae									
Platyopuntia type seed				1+	2				
Chenopodiaceae (seed)									
Chenopodium	x		6	>45	9	2	4	4	>3
Chenopodium no coat									275
Cheno-ams	x	x	5	x	40	19	50	8	x
Fabaceae									
Prosopis seed					1				
Malvaceae (seed)									
Sphaeralcea	2								
Nyctaginaceae									
Boerhavia wrightii fruit									1
Portulacaceae									
Portulacaseed	1								

* See Appendix B.2 for further description; +fragments, > greater than, x present

Appendix B.2

Taxonomic Notes

While classifying plant remains, certain taxonomic observations and measurements made helped determine the basis for identifications. In addition, plant materials that were of a doubtful nature or unknown deserved description.

Abbreviations for Excavation Units (EU) and Field Sample (FS) are used. Unless a taxon is designated as carbonized, it is safe to assume it is uncarbonized. When the word type appends the identification, the specimen resembles the genus or species given, but it may also represent other taxa. If such an archaeological seed were mixed in with the taxon named it would be difficult to know which to retrieve. We know seeds of two or more genera can look alike. Moreover, comparative seed collections are not extensive enough to say with certainty that the seed morphology of a species is unique to that species. The use of the abbreviation cf indicates a lesser level of identification created by poorly preserved or broken specimens.

GYMNOSPERMS

Pinaceae

Abies: Specimens (FS 742, FS 773, and FS 853) described as pupal (?) cases with one end closed, blunt, dark with remainder thin, transparent, and hyaline. They resemble a miniature badminton shuttlecock in shape. In 2004 the lateral shoots of Abies concolor were examined for the sheath covering the swollen terminal bud just prior to needle emergence and were found to be closely comparable.

Pinus cembroides type needle segments less than 5 cm long, imbedded in a two-warp sandal (FS 1177) with longitudinal indentations that suggest more than two needles per fasicle.
Pinus cembroides type nut is supposed to have thicker shells, but comparative material to make a distinction from P. edulis is lacking.

Pinus edulis type needle segments. D-shaped in cross section, a shape that allows for two needles per fascicle, typically less than 5 cm long.

Pinus edulis type cone scale tip, carbonized. In FS 60 it is irregularly quadrangular, lacks prickle, and has an apophysis raised from the scale, as in Adams (1980: 26). In FS 557 the carbonized cone scale fragment has no prickle, is semi-quadrangular, and has a raised apophysis wtih crystals on one *Pinus edulis* type cone scale fragment.

Cupressaceae

Juniperus monosperma has one seed, rarely two. Seed is circular or D-shaped in cross-section. Feature 11b has a rounded carbonized seed with a hole.

Juniperus pachyphyloea has four to five seeds per cone or berry. Seed shape is modified by the number of seeds in the berry. Seed may have two longitudinal flat faces.

Monocotyledonous Flowering Plants

Agavaceae or Liliaceae

Unknown (FS 557B): Paper thin seed fragment that is at least a centimeter long with an expanded raised margin.

Yucca baccata type seeds are thick, black, and of a fleshy fruited type of yucca. Carbonized in FS 60, FS 80, and FS 263. FS 60 seed (8 mm by 8 mm by 1.5 mm) is fissured on both sides and has a central cylindrical embryo. Another is 5 mm by 7 mm with parallel fissures. FS 80 is similar but shows a cast of a cylindrical embryo within endosperm. One seed has fissures on one face that coalesce to a central point. FS 264 (Feature 11a) shows central cylindrical embryo, parallel fissures on surface.

Poaceae

Elymus/Agropyron complex (FS 263): One grain, 3.25 mm long, depressed nerve the length of the grain; embryo on the opposite side evident by a burned depression 0.5 mm long; apex of grain blunt. The other grain was fragmentary and more distorted. It could be the same grain type, but larger. See Bohrer (1987: 82) for range of characteristics in complex.

Elymus/Agropyron complex (FS 187): Grain carbonized, swollen with long central nerve on side opposite to embryo, 2.5 mm incomplete length and 0.75 mm broad.

Bouteloua eriopoda (FS 67): One floret. Fertile lemma not keeled, in-rolled, obscuring palea, rudiments reduced to three long bristles, rachilla segment about half the length of the fertile segment (Musil 1963: 43).

Bouteloua spp. Other types are present but I find them less distinctive. FS 67 has a number of fertile lemmas sharply keeled on the back.

Eragrostis type (FS 70): Uncarbonized spikelet segments have three-nerved lemmas without awns and a brownish hyaline palea. Uncarbonized grain has embryo occupying half the length of the grain in FS 293. Five carbonized grains (FS 70) have the embryo 2/5 to ½ the length of the grain. When uncarbonized, the grain is somewhat keeled on the embryo side, but this aspect sharpens with carbonization. One tip of a spikelet segment is carbonized. Three uncarbonized grains measure 0.5 mm wide and 0.8 mm to 0.9 mm long. See Bohrer (1987: 83-84) for desciption.

Setaria macrostachya type fertile florets in FS 773 compare well to vouchered seed specimens of the same identification. Both the fertile lemma and palea have fine transverse sculpturing. This is also true of FS 67 of 11 fertile florets.

Sporobolus type grains: FS 70 has five uncarbonized florets with one nerved lemmas and strongly laterally compressed grain as per Gould (1951: 220). One grain is darker near the embryo.

Measurements were made upon four grains each of two different collections of *S. airoides, S. contractus, S. cryptandrus, and S. giganteus*. My own modern specimens of *S. giganteus* grain length ranges between 1.25 mm to 1.50 mm. They might be confused with my own *S. airoides* that also have the same range, but the grains of *S. airoides* are a dark brown. One collection of *S. cryptandrus* was consistently 0.75 mm long and another collection ranged from 1 mm to 1.2 mm. *S. contractus* ranged from 0.75 to 1 mm. While the smaller grains cannot be distinguished from size, the upper limits of the yellowish, larger grain appear to be typical of *S. giganteus*.

Sporobolus type yellowish grain with a darkened embryo in FS 67 falls into two lengths: 1.5 mm and 0.75 mm. The longer grains compare to the size of giant dropseed, *S. giganteus* (Gould 1951: 224). Two dark brown grains 1 mm long are *S. airoides*. In the heavy fraction of FS 67 there are nine Sporobolus airoides type darkened grains, eight small, one large.

Sporobolus airoides type grain FS 773 and FS 208 each have a brown grain within a floret. The FS 773 grain is 0.75 mm long. Because they are within the floret, the grain probably cannot be toasted brown without the chaff being marked also. *Sporobolus* type in FS 208. Two grains each within a translucent lemma and palea have darkened embryos and are otherwise yellowish. Grains are 1 mm long within 2 mm long lemmas. Three other loose grains measure 0.75 mm long, with darkened embryos and golden bodies, like a drop of oil in the sunlight. One grain within a floret looks brown and is of the *Sporobolus airoides* type. This is a selected set of observations from an abundance of chaff of this genus.

Stipa neomexicana type twisted awn base. FS 60 and FS 263 are carbonized. The more complete specimens recovered in Fresnal Shelter allowed the identification of smaller fragments at High Rolls Cave. The twisted awn base of the large terminal awn is characteristic of the genus (Gould 1951: 245).

Stipa neomexicana type FS 557 awn segment 1 mm diameter appears "2-ply Z twist." Four splintered lemma are hairless, as well as the callus which is retained on the base of three lemmas. The lemmas are normally pubescent and the callus very hairy. These hairs can be removed by fire.

Stipa (FS 70): uncarbonized floret, of another species than S. neomexicana. Lemma enclosing grain 5 mm long, 1 mm wide with base of apical awn twisted. The callus and first glume are hairy.

Zea mays The interior of a corn kernel can be divided into the starchy portion or endosperm and the embryo, rich in oil. When a kernel is charred, the two portions may separate from each other. My five modern samples of excised embryos from both chapalote and commercial (mature) corn measure 4.5 mm in length. This serves as a comparative standard, for at High Rolls Cave the embryo portion is preserved carbonized in some samples.

FS 67: Several tan epidermal layers are visible on a kernel fragment, 4.5 mm long.

FS 187: Two carbonized undersized embryos with shield (scutellum), 1.5 mm and 1 mm long. The entire embryo and the shield shaped portion in back of it (the scutellum) has been retained. The whole embryo is only 1 mm long, and the whole structure, including the scutellum is 1.5 mm. It is accompanied by a slightly smaller embryo and scutellum 1 mm long.

FS 557: Carbonized upper embryo half (coleoptile) and central area 2.7 mm long, probably fully mature.

FS 782 (Feature 11b): *Zea mays* embryo with scutellum: 2 carbonized, one 1.25 mm long, the other 1.50 mm. *Zea mays* embryo upper half (the coleoptile, plus the central portion) carbonized. 1.5 mm long. Immature corn roasted? *Zea mays* cupules/cob: 2 to 3, carbonized, poor condition. Some cob parts cling to cupules. *Zea mays* kernels carbonized, poor condition. Some cob clings to them. Can see structure.

A well preserved embryo and scutellum of the same size as the one in FS 187 was recovered as well as the upper half of another maize embryo—the coleoptile, plus the central portion measures 1.5 mm. This contrasts with the same portion of the embryo preserved in FS 557 that measured 2.7 mm in length, which would make the whole embryo close to the modern mature equivalent of 4.5 mm in length. I believe the ultra-small carbonized embryos came from immature (or small kernelled) maize that was roasted at High Rolls Cave.

Unknown Poaceae

FS 293 (Feature 5): 16 florets, uncarbonized. Grain is deep brown; 2.5 mm by .5 mm long with embryo somewhat over 1/3 the length. The lemma is awned. The palea exceeds the lemma by 1 mm or is equal to it. It is translucent.

FS 80: One carbonized grain 1.5 mm by 5.2 mm, hollow
FS 557: Uncarbonized grain 1.5 mm long, 0.6 mm broad, keeled, blunt distal end, pointed proximal end.

FS 557: Floret with acute lemma 3.5 mm long with 3 nerves and awn 3.5 mm in length, palea strongly keeled with central nerve.

FS 70: Six empty florets, uncarbonized. Awned lemma 0.5 mm wide, 3.5 mm long, awn as long or longer than lemma. Compare *Elymus glaucus* lemma in Musil 1963.

Typhaceae

FS 187: Typha seed. One, brown, 0.75 mm long, 0.2 mm wide, truncate at one end, roughened coat, uncarbonized.

FS 853: Typha seed: One 1.2 mm long, At truncate end, in depression, is nipple like protrubance, uncarbonized.

DICOTYLEDONOUS FLOWERING PLANTS

Amaranthaceae

Most smooth coated seeds of *Amaranthus* and *Chenopodium* appear circular in planar view, but sometimes a few amaranth seeds will be oval. It is these relatively infrequent seeds that were identified as amaranth.

Identifying prehistoric amaranth cultigens, even when reproductive parts (utricle caps and bases) are preserved, can be difficult. Cultivars have been selected for their numerous seeds and ease of threshing. Seeds remain small, and seed coloration does not necessarily differ from the wild species. Irritation of the hands during threshing has been reduced by shorter bracts and tepals. At High Rolls Cave the infloresence has separated into empty utricle caps and bases. Each must be compared to one or two scale drawings of species based on herbarium specimens published in a monograph resulting from the study of plant species grown under a uniform set of environmental conditions (Sauer 1950).

Cultivated species can show introgression with other cultivated species or with their wild relatives. The degree to which the environment affects variability is unknown. Thus when examining utricle caps and bases it is hard to know if (1) cultivated plants may bear a polyglot mixture of utricle caps and bases derived from introgression of cultivated and wild amaranth species, (2) if additional environmental variability is present, or (3) if wild species (e.g., *A. hybridus, A. powellii*) were also collected and have wound up in the threshed mixture. Potentially all three conditions might occur at the same time. The modern Fresnal environment has *A. hybridis* (Appendix A.2) and J. Sauer noted *A. powellii and A. torreyi* present in archaeological amaranth from Fresnal Shelter. Subsequently, I have noted the same species apparently present in High Rolls Cave in FS 773.

Amaranthus cruentus identification criteria in FS 773: "The utricle cap is unique among all the amaranth species I have seen, being contracted into a narrow tower below the bases of the style branches: the style-branches are slender and erect." (Sauer 1950: 601). In his 1967 revision, Sauer describes the erect style branches as the only distinctive utricle cap trait of *A. cruentus*. Complicating this assessment is a more recent description of *A. powellii* that indicates that the style branches are erect (Correll and Johnson 1970: 559). My own comparative material supports this description. In order to isolate examples of utricle caps of *A. cruentus* I have defined Sauer's narrow tower as less than 1/3 the diameter of the utricle cap. If, in addition, the style branches are erect, I have identified the specimen as *A. cruentus*. In reality, such utricle caps belong to the common race grown in Guatemala today, rather than the Mexican race.

FS 773 *Amaranthus* sp. possible cultivar. Seeds are slightly ovoid in planar view and 1 mm or more in diameter and have a portion of their seed coat raised. The seed coats are extremely thin when compared to the *Chenopodium* seed coat thickness. A thin seed coat is characteristic of a cultivated species as it promotes uniform early germination. One seed coat of *Amaranthus* contrasts in thickness.

FS 773 *Amaranthus cruentus* Eight utricle caps with slender, erect style branches that conform to this species were initially isolated from 30 utricle caps.

Amaranthus cruentus type utricle caps: 1/4 ml sent to S. Lentz for dating 8/4/02

Amaranthus cruentus type utricle caps 0.33 ml sent to S. Lentz for dating 9/30/02

Amaranthus cruentus type utricle caps: 0.1 ml retained 9/30/02

Both lots of 9/30/02 and *A.cruentus* caps in FS 208 were more rigorously identified, for I became more aware that A. powellii was a source of confusion.

Amaranthus cruentus type utricle bases with tepals. Tepals do not exceed the (projected) utricle cap. Note that A. hybridis (Martin and Hutchins 1980: 632) and A. hypochondriacus also apparently share this trait.

Amaranthus torreyi type utricle bases with tepals: The tepals are recurved, spatulate, obtuse, and single-nerved.

Amaranthus utricle bases unclassified: with recurved tepals that are not spatulate and have a single nerve. No examples of recurved spatuate tepals with branched nerves diagnostic for A. palmeri were noted in FS 773 or FS 208.

Amaranthus hybridus type utricle caps: These four resemble the tropical race described by Sauer (1950: 610), where the utricle cap tapers gradually and is not constricted into a definite tower.

Amaranthus powellii type utricle bases and tepals: straight tepals exceed the utricle cap in length and are mucronate on the tips. Ten were isolated but another capsule may have additional species as part of it.

FS 208 *Amaranthus cruentus* Ten utricle caps with style branches erect mounted on a narrow tower were isolated from a total of 23 and can be ascribed to A. *cruentus* . Thirty-eight other utricle caps do not conform to this identification, though some may be of this species. There are 43 utricle bases with straight long tepals and two utricle bases with recurved tepals that belong to uncultivated species.

Anacardiaceae

Rhus in FS 557 was classified first as *Lycium* type. When FS 67 showed a whole series of ages of *Rhus trilobata* type fruit from flower to maturity, the material in FS 557 fitted into the continuum demonstrated in FS 67.

FS 557 *Rhus trilobata* type. A 3 mm diameter collar or cup mounted on a pedicel, uncarbonized.

FS 557 *Rhus trilobata* type uncarbonized globular fruit 6 mm diameter with campanulate caylx and short pedicel. Crystals lie within fruit.

FS 557B Two fruit pedicels 0.5 mm diameter, stalks 8 mm long that expands to a 4 mm diameter collar or cup. One has a dark resinous amorphous fruit in it about 4 mm long.

FS 1075 *Rhus trilobata* type, formerly Lycium type. Two carbonized berries with campanulate calyces, one 1.5 mm in diameter and the other 3.5 mm in diameter. The neck of the larger berry is somewhat narrowed near the calyx. FS 1063 has a carbonized collared rim 2.5 mm in diameter surrounding the pedicel that could belong to this genus.

Asteraceae

FS 67 *Ambrosia confertiflora*. One fruit with inward bent spines on upper 2/3 of the body, 3.5 mm long including spines. Also FS 139.

FS 208 *Artemesia dracunculus* type achenes, carbonized. One carbonized achene 0.5 mm long, 0.175 diameter. Another carbonized achene has a small ring at distal end where tubular flower might have attached. Uncarbonized achenes 1.5 mm long with longitudinal striations. Tubular flowers each separate. Phyllaries of heads with very broad scarious margins, glabrous, longest 1.5 mm, in two distinct size classes; the very short ones are on the outside.

FS 60 *Artemesia dracunculus* type carbonized achenes: 40. Range from 0.5 mm to 0.75 mm long.

FS 536 (Feature 13) *Artemesia dracunculus* type: 5 carbonized achenes; 1 mm long, ovoid, swollen

FS 597 (Feature 13) *Artemesia dracunculus* type 3 carbonized achenes, 0.75 mm long. Smallest has longitudinal striations visible.

FS 80 *Artemesia dracunculus* type achenes: size and shape conform, but lacks striations.

FS 782 (Feature 11b): Two of the 18 carbonized achenes are well preserved with a visible apical knob. They measure 0.75 mm and 1.5 mm in length, respectively.

FS 70 *Chrysothamnus* type. One head of involucral bracts uncarbonized, coriaceous; bracts appear aligned vertically in 4 rows or cross-like in planar view.

FS 742 *Chrysothamnus* type head with bracts in distinct vertical ranks, keeled with spreading tips.

FS 742 cf *Chrysothamnus* achene, linear with about 10 ribs, 4.2 mm long

FS 67 (Light fraction) *Helianthus A* type glabrous achenes: 12 mottled brown and tan with inner dark (black) layer 4.5 mm to 5 mm long, 1.7 mm to 2 mm broad. Distal end has sloping shoulders.

Helianthus B type glabrous achenes: 5. One has a cracked coat in several places and partly burned on shoulder 4.5 mm by 2.5 mm; another possibly burned. The three are 5 mm long 3 mm wide. All appear plumper and more robust than those specimens in A.

FS 67 (Light fraction) *Viguiera dentata* type (?) hairy achenes: 31, commonly from 2.5 mm to 3 mm long, 1 mm to 1.5 mm broad with high shoulders; some show mottled surface. One achene, 2.5 mm by 1.25 mm, retains a pappus of short, scarious scales.

FS 67 (Light fraction) *Viguiera/Helianthus* type achenes: 30, with evidence of hairs near the shoulders. Shoulders neither truncate nor high, but not as sloping as in *Helianthus A* examples. They are 4.5 mm to 5 mm long 2 mm to 2.25 mm broad.

FS 67 (Heavy fraction) *Viguiera/Helianthus* type achenes: 23, high shouldered, mottled, some hairy about 1.4 mm wide, 3 mm long, with some variance in size and degradation.

FS 208 *Helianthus/Viguiera* type achenes: 2 hairy, mottled flattened achenes one 3.5 mm long and 1.5 mm broad; another 3 mm long and 1.25 mm broad.

FS l075 (Feature 23) *Helianthus/Viguiera* , One carbonized achene 2.25 mm long, 1.5 mm broad with slight hook at proximal end
FS 557 *Helianthus/Viguiera* , two carbonized achenes 3 mm long and 2 mm broad

FS 964 (Feature 19) *Helianthus/Viguiera* , one carbonized achene 1.8 mm long and 0.4 mm broad with vestiges of longitudinal stripes. Another carbonized 2 mm long, 0.75 mm thick, 1 mm broad, blunt proximal end.

FS 964 *Helianthus/Viguiera* , one carbonized achene 2.0 mm long and 1 mm broad, 0.75 mm thick, blunt at proximal end.

FS 67 Unknown achene: 1, mottled black and tan, pointed, 3.5 mm long, 0.5 mm wide, quadrangular at distal end. Pappus of 2 to 3 short, tan scales on each side.

FS 70 unknown head with graduated, hyaline involucral bracts 2.5 mm long on interior.

F.S 70 Two unknown uncarbonized achenes 2.5 mm long, 0.5 mm wide, black, flat with two white stringy margins.

Berberidaceae

FS 557 *Berberis* Barbed coriaceous leaflet about 2 cm long, with three barbs per side

FS 70 *Berberis fremontii* type leaflet about 14 mm long

Brassicaceae

This is the only large family with folded embryos and lacking significant amounts of endosperm (Martin and Barkley 1961: 162). Provisionally I am calling the ones whose seed contours show the embryo is bent or folded of the Lepidium type, though they might belong to another member of the family. Seeds measuring about l mm long with a folded embryo were encountered in FS 742, FS 853, and FS 597, Feature 13. The latter was in a thermal area and the carbonized seed was only 0.75 mm long. An additional carbonized seed l.5 mm long was in FS 853. The seed in FS 742 apparently was not carbonized, but dark nevertheless and plumper than expected for Lepidium, but about 1 mm long.

FS 139 *Erysimum capitatum* type shows a long narrow pod segment still attached to disc-like area by a short stipe.

Cactaceae

FS 175 Platyopuntia stem or joint fragment, 3 mm by 5 mm, consists of carbonized parenchyma with flattened vascular strands between.

FS 557 Opuntia, two clusters of glochids surrounded by tissue. Glochids are diagnostic for the genus.
FS 853 cf. *Cylindropuntia* (?) One seed is lens shaped, 3.3 mm diameter and very symmetrical. Surface layer has pulled back along one edge.

FS 67 *Echinocereus* seed: 1.8 mm maximum length, black, bumpy, embryo missing.

Fabaceaeae

FS 139 cf *Vicia* (?) bean 6 mm long, white surface covered with small bumps, long hilum as in vetch.

FS 853 *Prosopis* seed: 1, bears a U-shaped mark in its central face. Seed very flat, dark, degraded.

Ericaceae

FS 773 *Arctostaphylos uva-ursi* seeds: 19, dark brown 3.5 mm to 4 mm long. Three to five seeds per fruit estimated. The seeds resemble a wedge shaped segment of an apple cut longitudinally through the center. The exterior of the seeds are slightly depressed or bumpy.

Lamiaceae

FS 795 and FS 853: Shiny brown nutlets were 2 mm long. Each had two joined, flattened faces forming a 90-degree angle.

Malvaceae

Sphaeralcea from Feature 1 (FS 60), Feature 3 (FS 175), and Feature 7 (FS 273). Feature 7 had 29 carbonized seeds. The seeds were 2 mm long and 1.7 mm broad on the flattened face. While sharp angles are lacking, the three dimensional view is comparable to a longitudinally cut wedge of apple. Seven additional carbonized seeds in FS 273 were only 1.5 mm long and had sharper angles along the margins of the wedge.

Nyctaginaceae

FS 1075 *Boerhavia wrightii* type fruit, one carbonized, 2.5 mm long, hollow, 4 flanges at narrow end. There is only one species in Sacramento Mountains like this (Hutchins 1974).

FS 67 and FS 773 fruits provisionally placed with *Allionia*. Shape and size of fruit resembles *Allionia*, but involuted margins are thick and corky. FS 67 is 5 mm by 2 mm.

Rosaceae

FS 795 *Fallugia paradoxa* leaf fragments have a linear-dissected leaf with in-rolled margins.

Solanaceae

FS 742 cf.*Chamaesaracha.* One seed (1.75 mm by 1.85 mm) is flattened, dark, with raised epidermal reticulum that becomes finer near the hilum. Eroded.

FS 742 Solanaceae unknown. Seed is 2.1 mm diameter, flattened, with epidermis eroded until it appears to have a porous network. Additional seeds in FS 67, FS 70, and FS 805 are fragmentary but of this general nature.

Nicotiana rustica type seeds were recovered in FS 187, FS 853, and FS 1256. Rather than morphology, recent identifications have relied on seed size. Seeds larger than 1.0 mm in length or 8.0 in width are N. rustica. Seeds between 0.7 mm to 1.0 mm in length and 0.50 mm and 0.8 mm in width likely represent N. attenuata or N. rustica (Adams and Toll 2000: 145).

FS 187 has a carbonized seed that measures 0.9 mm by 0.65 mm. A series of six depressions across the length result from a coarse reticulum covering the seed.

FS 853 contains 254 seeds. The interior of some of the seed is shrunken from the coat, revealing it as translucent. Some seeds have only the translucent coats. Some seeds are carbonized.

FS 1256 has nine seeds. The nine seeds from this lot and 40 seeds from FS 853 were measured. They range from 0.85 mm to 1.05 mm in length, with a mean of 1 mm and a standard deviation of 0.076. For width they range from 0.70 mm to 0.90 mm, with a mean of 0.78 and standard deviation of 0.073.

Nicotiana trigonophylla type leaves were recovered in FS 742, FS 557, and FS 853. They resemble leaves of *Nicotiana trigonophylla* shown in Figure 16(i) in Goodspeed 1954.

Loose leaves

FS 742 *Nicotiana trigonophylla* type leaf: Sample contains three leaves and fragments. Oblanceolate, herbaceous leaf narrows gradually toward the base. One leaf, truncated near the petiole, measures about 1.5 cm long, 0.5 cm maximum width. The basal portion of two partial leaves seems to have petioles that extend about a cm, once the leaf tapering terminates. The crushed blade portion of one of the latter has enough volume that it might have been larger than the other leaves and fragments observed.

FS 557 *Nicotiana trigonophylla* type leaf. Sample has a complete oblanceolate leaf 0.4 cm broad and 2.5 cm long, The leaf surface is disrupted by small blisters as in another fragment in the lot. None of the fine white speckling is evident.

FS 853 *Nicotiana trigonophylla* type leaf. Sample has a leaf whose apex is truncated, but is 1 cm wide and about 3 cm long. The blade merges very gradually into the point of attachment. Fine white granular speckles are visible on the leaf from both sides at 32 power magnification. Leaf hairs are long, appressed, and extremely rare.

Manipulated leaves

Seven additional leaves in FS 742 bear signs of manipulation Three are rolled starting from the petiole, two are rolled beginning at the tip of the leaf, and two remain undetermined. One of the latter seems to be rolled from a longitudinal strip of leaf blade, as one margin is intact and another torn.

Width: One of the three rolled starting from the petiole is 7 mm wide. One of the two rolled from the tip but with an irregular twist is also 7 mm wide. I could not determine the width of the remaining rolled leaves.

Texture: Two of the three leaves rolled starting with the petiole and the one torn leaf rollhave fine white specks that seem to be part of the leaf. The other rolls have either smooth leaves or ones that have fine broken blisters on them.

A second leaf in FS 557 of the same type as the above is 6 mm wide and has been rolled from the apex so that the petiole is exposed, forming a small, flattened package 6 mm by 5 mm.

If the leaves are tobacco, then the oblanceolate shape of the leaves in the basal rosette would fit either *N. plumbaginifolia* or *N. trigonophylla*. But the leaf of *N. plumbaginifolia* is described as hispid, a botanical term defined as rough with stiff or bristly hairs (Correll and Johston 1970: 1753). Since there are very few hairs on the leaf at all, the leaves better conform to the range of variation described for *N. trigonophylla*. At the same time, the known range of variation in cultivated *N. rustica* might encompass oblanceolate leaves, possibly within the variety *pumila*. The blade is described as oblong-elliptic or ovate-elliptic with the apex very obtuse to distinctly acute (Winter 2000: 99). While the leaves at High Rolls Cave appear quite small, this may be brought about by differential destruction of larger leaves. However *N. rustica* leaf blades are relatively short as well, being only 10 cm to 15 cm long (Winter 2000: 97).

The corollas in the subgenus Rustica and the section Trigonophyllae of subgenus Petunioides all have a short and distinct tube proper and a throat several times longer, obconic to clavate (Goospeed 1954: 75). However, the most complete corolla (in FS 742 a) has most characteristics that conform to *N. trigonophylla*. See Appendix Table B.2.1.

FS 742 cf *Nicotiana*. Three sympetalous corollas as follows:

a. corolla with limb, enclosed filaments and stigma. The floral tube 5 mm long, 1.5 mm diameter, tomentose interior throat, 7 mm long limb divisions distinct, obtuse trichomes located in folds near distal throat are of two types: gland tipped or capitate and branched

b. corolla lacking limbs and part of throat, but 4 filaments of stamens extend beyond remnant throat. From distal end of filaments to base is 13 mm. The floral tube 5 mm long, 1.5 mm diameter.

c. corolla consists of remnant throat and limb only, 8 mm long. Two (?) anthers still attached to filaments.

FS 795 cf *Nicotiana*: One sympetalous corolla, 16 mm long, in poor condition. Floral tube is 1 mm long, 1.3 mm diameter and may have been longer, very distinct. Throat 15 mm long, 3 mm wide. Limb absent; 4 filaments visible. Similar corollas were recovered in FS 742.

Portulacaceae

Portulaca (FS 60) carbonized has rounded spine tips.

Unknowns

FS 557 Angiosperm type A seed: 1 mm long, brown irregular in shape, shiny surface, tesselate.

FS 139 Angiosperm Type A: 2 brown tesselate seeds. Largest 1 mm by 0.5 mm. Point of attachment must be sessile because it appears as a ripped hole. The micropyle is visible. The seed narrows to a tip of a wedge at the point of attachment.

FS 70 Angiosperm type A uncarbonized seed, 16.

FS 80 Angiosperm type A carbonized seed, 1.7 mm long. FS 293 has 7 with brown, hard surface. Common in many samples. When it erodes it is full of tiny pores.

Dicotyledonous Flowering Plant Unknowns

FS 557 B Dicotyledonous pediceled fruit stalk 0.5 mm diameter expands to 4 mm diameter cup with visible net veins. One of two has a dark resinous amorphous fruit within, about 4 mm long, uncarbonized.

Dicotyledonous seed, dark and oblong 4 mm by 2.5 mm by 2.5 mm, split of 2 cotyledons visible

FS 586 Unknown seeds, fragments: 3, carbonized. One may be a legume: long, narrow thin.
FS 175 Feature 3 possible dried fruit. Brown but apparently not carbonized, crystals on surface. 9 mm long, 3 mm deep. Appears as longitudianal slice from an apple, slightly concave on skin side.

FS 139 Unknown fragment superficially resembling walnut but porous exterior and ligneous striped interior negates the identification. Another piece might be husk.
Unknown stem segment with opposite decurrent attached spines

Unknown seeds: 2, one smashed, one plump ovoid, about 5 mm long. The structure at point of attachment reminds me of a Cucurbit but it is too short or squat for *C. foetidissima*.

FS 263 Unknown cone scale or fruit shell fragment, carbonized. Converging lines on interior face may indicate *Cucurbita* shell fragment

FS 307 Unknown seed: 1, carbonized, 2.7 mm long, 1.25 mm broad, with one end blunt and rounded and the other end pointed, cucurbitaceous in appearance.

FS 1256 Unknown single seed, black, lanceolate, flattened, 1.8 mm long

Microfossil Unknown

Unknown microfossil: FS 853 is 0.8 mm diameter, 1 mm long, globular, transparent. Major ribs reach from pole to pole, about 10. Smaller transverse cross ribs between major ones. Similar ones were recovered in FS 782 and FS 805, and only observed in several more samples.

FS 805: Microfossil: 1, white, beaded, hollow, 0.75 x 1 mm

FS 782 Microfossil: 1, transparent 0.75 mm diameter, spherical, longitudinal lines to poles.

Table B.2.1. Comparison of Corollas of *N. trigonophylla*, *N. rustica* (Goodspeed 1954), and Corolla FS 742a

Characteristic	*N. trigonophylla*	FS 742a	*N. rustica*
corolla length exclusive of limb	12 to 23 mm	13 mm	12 to 17 mm**
length of tube proper*	3 to 6 mm	5 mm	3 mm
width of tube proper	2 to 4 mm	1.5mm	2 mm
tomentum in tube proper	present	present	
length of throat	2 to 3 x tube l.	< 2x tube	3x tube l
shape of throat	a bit wider than tube	6 to 8 mm wide	

*Tube proper is defined as the narrowest basal portion of the tubular part (Goodspeed 1954:75)
**puberlent on exterior

Table B.2.2. Typical Measurements of Rodent Fecal Pellets

	Mouse	Pack rat
FS 67	1.5 to 2.5 mm by 3.5 to 5 mm	
FS 70		3 mm by 10 mm
FS 139	2 by 4-5 mm	
		3 to 4mm by 10 to 12mm
FS 208	2.5 by 6 mm	
FS 293	8 mm	
FS 557		3 mm by 8 mm
		3 mm by 6 mm
		3 mm by 7 mm

Appendix B.3

Chronology

Table B.3.1. Chronology of Radiocarbon Dated Charred Material Associated with Flotation from Features

Beta Lab No.*	FS dated/ Float FS	Cluster	Provenience Feature	EU	Stratum/ Layer	Age BP	Cal 2 Sigma BC
154634	263/263	A	11a	12	3	3100±60	1650 to 1405
164067	631/630	West	15	83		3130±40	1530 to 410
164078	1096/1093	West	24	105	3?	3090±40	1500 to 1360
149362	58/60	B	1	5	3	3080±50	1490 to 1270
149378	177/175	B	3	4	3	2970±40	1420 to 1250
164062	310/310	West	9	37	3/3	3010±40	1420 to 1250
164077	1076/1705	B	23	69	2/3	3020±60	1440 to 1130
164063	321/293	B	5	34	2/2	2990±40	1440 to 1200
164069	779/782	A	11b	63	2/3	2940±60	1400 to 1030
164072	931/934	C	18	109,134	2	2970±40	1380 to 1110
164066	592/586,597	West	13	58	3	2880±60	1320 to 960
							1360 to 1360
164061	306/307	West	8	36,37	2/1	2880±70	1310 to 910
172110	1300/1063	B	22	69	3	2840±40	1210 to 970
164059	270/267	B	6	16	2/1	2850±70	1300 to 900
154633	246/80	A	2	11	2/1	2850±50	1290 to 905
doubtful	or unknown	chronology					
164060	274/273	A	7	12,31		3360±40	1870 to 1840
164065	572/568	West	14	80		3200±60	1680 to 410
undated	964	C	19	108	2?		

* Beta Analytic Laboratory

Table B.3.2. Chronology of Radiocarbon Dated Charred Material Associated with Flotation from Excavation Units and Undated Interpolated Samples

Beta Lab No.*	FS dated/ Float FS	Cluster	Provenience EU	Stratum/Layer	cmbs	Age BP	Cal 2 Sigma BC
	1256	B	33	3			
	805	A	27	2/3	34		
164070	797/795	A	27	2/2	25	3120±40	1500 to 1360 &1360 to 1320
149368	98/96**	A	27		29	3070±70	1520 to 1210
149373	137/139	B	4	2	50	3000±60	1420 to 1110
	67	B	5	3			
149380	209/208	A	13	2	15-36	2910±40	1300 to 1030
	557	A	10	2			
164068	770/773	A	63	2/3	15	2890±60	1310 to 940
	742	A	27	2/1	23		
172106	853/853	A	88	2/1	†	2860±40	1200 to 940
149379	188/187	A	12	2	46	2220±50	380 to 80
	70	B	4	1	0-10		

* Beta Analytical Laboratory
**Sample 96 is pollen
† Depth not recorded by excavator

Beta Lab No.*	FS	Provenience Cluster	EU	Sample Type	Age BP	Cal 2 Sigma BC/AD
				Table B.3.3.Radiocarbon Dated Cultigens from Excavation Units in Stratum 2		
172104	773	A	63	*Amaranthus cruentus* capsules**	2640±40	1110 to 900 BC
172106	853	A/C	88	*Nicotiana rustica* type seeds**	2860±40	1200 to 940 BC
172110	1300	B	69	*Zea mays* shank, husk**	2880±40	1210 to 970 BC
172103	139A	B	4	*Zea mays* shank, husk**	2060±50	420 to 360 BC
149374	146A	B	4	*Zea mays* cobs	1820±80?	AD 260 to 290 & AD 320 to 640
156043	745	A	69	*Zea mays* cob	1600±70	AD 10 to 340
115845	1030	B	69	*Zea mays* cob	1560±50	AD 80 to 340
158044	977	B	69	*Zea mays* kernels	1520±50	AD 140 to 1410
158041	688	A	27	*Zea mays* cob	1510±90	AD 480 to 520 & AD 70 to 460
158040	695	A	86	*Zea mays* cob	1510±90	AD 30 to 450
158042	738	A	86	*Zea mays* cob	1510±90	AD 70 to 420
149375	146B	B	4	*Zea mays* cob	1320±80	AD 260 to 290

* Beta Analytical Laboratory
** TAMS radiocarbon analysis

Appendix B.4

Pollen Concentrations of Insect- and Non-Arboreal Wind-pollinated Plants from High Rolls Cave (LA 114103), Their Relation to Flotation, and Their Significance

Richard Holloway (2002) has created a fine reconstruction of the general environmental setting at High Rolls Cave during occupation through the use of arboreal pollen. My objective is to highlight potential ethnobotanical pollen and to discuss the possible reasons for it. I have used pollen concentrations provided by Holloway in his text, but have otherwise used data from his Tables 3, 5, and 6.

Flowers are normally pollinated by the wind or through insect vectors. Flowers lacking conspicuous petals tend to produce numerous small pollen grains adapted for wind transport over long distances. Examples of wind-pollinated plants include trees (pines, junipers, and walnut); shrubs such as saltbush (*Atriplex*), sagebrush (*Artemesia*) and Mormon Tea (*Ephedra*); and herbaceous plants like cattail (*Typha*), the grasses (Poaceae), and ragweeds (*Ambrosia, Franseria, Iva*). Conspicuous flowers bear few, relatively large and heavy pollen grains adapted to insect transport. Trees like mesquite and willow bear flowers with nectar glands that attract insects. Other insect-pollinated plants include sunflowers (*Helianthus*), chamisa or rabbitbrush (*Chrysothamnus*), wild celery (*Cymopteris*), and cacti (Cactaceae). Because species adapted to wind pollination disperse such abundant pollen, recognition of humans as a factor in pollen deposition is difficult. Since insect-pollinated plants are not expected to grow within the confines of High Rolls Cave, their presence even in small amounts deserves discussion.

POLLEN CONCENTRATION

Although wind served as an initial major distributor of pollen and a gradient of concentration can be demonstrated from the front to the rear of the cave (Holloway 2002), other factors may have influenced their final distribution and concentration. Almost all of the types of non-arboreal pollen are present in concentrations at least as high as 31,000 grains per gram although concentrations reach as high as 158,760 grains per gram (FS 252). Exceptionally low pollen concentrations include samples from thermal features where oxidizing conditions once prevailed. It is less clear if there are special depositional conditions toward the rear of the cave that have selectively reduced pollen (see Table B.4.1).

Because the organic deposits appear condensed by decay, the pollen should increase in concentration. Any tunnels previously formed by rodents might have collapsed with the stratigraphic compaction and obscured passages that might have once carried water-suspended pollen. Pollen concentrations expressed per gram and per cc are not strictly comparable, but two canal sediment samples from the middle Gila River of Arizona considered of a highly organic content are of interest. One sample contained the maximum pollen concentration recovered, 162,419 grains per cc, and the next two highest concentrations with 52,885 grains per cc and 45,509 grains per cc were from canal sediments believed deposited from slow, low-energy water flows (Adams and others 2002: 41). Water could have been one factor in creating high pollen concentrations in some samples at High Rolls Cave.

The location of human activity toward the front of the cave where pollen density would be the highest naturally tends to confound interpretation, including clues concerning the role humans had in pollen introduction. The variance of pollen taxa concentrations between samples is high, especially when samples are placed to approximate their original position

(Table B.4.2). However, the depth of each sample varies. In order to shorten the tables I have omitted three features that contain minimal ethnobotanical pollen categories (see Table B.4.1).

Despite problems, pollen analytical results suggest that many samples from excavation units appear intact. In some excavation units the pollen sample shows normally wind-pollinated types accompanied by a long tail of insect-pollinated types that have historic ethnobotanical use (Table B.4.2). Certain areas apparently were the focus of human activity. If pollen aggregates had been recorded frequently, a technique used in many other studies to help identify ethnobotanical usage (Bohrer l981, Gish 1991), or if more paired pollen and flotation samples from the same level were secured, they might help identify plant usage.

WIND-POLLINATED CATEGORIES

Grass Family (Poaceae)

The high concentrations of grass pollen (Table B.4.2.) noted beneath samples of organic material matted in dense layers suggested grass pollen originated from that source or otherwise was introduced by the inhabitant brushing against pollinating grass before entering the cave (Holloway 2002). While such activity undoubtedly contributed to the high pollen concentration values, the harvesting of several species of dropseed grass (*Sporobolus* spp.) would add to the pollen concentration. Dropseed grass grain was widespread in Stratum 2 and in all probability the grains are under represented in flotation (Chapter 4). Experimental pollen washes of the grain of alkali sacaton (*Sporobolus airoides*) reveal they serve as carriers for the pollen (Bohrer 1972). The continuously maturing floral cluster (indeterminate inflorescence with both blooms and grains) is a factor in accumulating pollen during grain harvest. It is less clear if the mechanism of pollen transfer might work in a similar manner for rye grass, lovegrass, New Mexico feather grass, and panic grass.

Aster Family (Asteraceae)

Artemesia

Holloway (2002: 20) predicted the culturally introduced nature of the normally wind-borne pollen based on a concentration likely produced from the pollen on clothing and footgear. A significant additional source was revealed after the completion of flotation analysis. False tarragon (*Artemesia dracunculus*) carbonized seed (achenes) were recovered from five features (Table 6.1) where human activity was concentrated. In the physical structure of the *Artemesia* floral head, the seed formed from the ray flowers remain packed tightly against old pollen units until threshed free, a process apt to release the retained pollen also.

Low spine Asteraceae

The Low Spine pollen type is represented by both ragweed (*Ambrosia*) and *Iva ambrosioides* in the flotation sample. The seed (achenes) of the latter species are scattered in small amounts throughout the cave, but lack evidence of processing. Some seed has smooth black coats while immature ones have tan, corky ridges. This may well indicate that younger pollen bearing structures were also introduced into the cave and contributed to the high concentration of pollen. In other words, though the plant is technically wind-pollinated, it is probable that the whole plant was brought into the cave by human or animal vectors.

High spine Asteraceae

The high spine pollen comes from flowers that are actually insect-pollinated, but because pollen deposition frequently seems as concentrated as wind-pollinated types in High Rolls Cave, I have inserted it with the wind-pollinated members of the family for comparison (Table B.4.2.). Sunflower (*Helianthus*), goldeneye (*Viguiera*), and *Encelia farinosa* have seeds or achenes in flotation samples; many are hairy. Members of this group have pollen-bearing stamens that are perched on the maturing ovary. When the ovary is covered with hairs the mature fruit or achene can retain pollen (Bohrer 1981b: 136). Some seeds bear marks of parching indicative of human consumption, but rodents were active in their harvest too (Chapter 4).

Even flowers and buds normally pollinated by insects may be carried by rodents (Bohrer 1981b: 135). *The mouse pantry* sample (FS 67) indicates that goldeneye and sunflowers achenes were harvested and floral tubes were eaten. The apparent complexity involving the arrival of high spine pollen illustrates that no single method of pollen transport fully excludes the possibility of another (Bohrer 1981b: 135).

Cheno-ams

Carbonized and uncarbonized seeds that represent mixtures of *Chenopodium* and *Amaranthus* are recovered throughout the deposits (Chapter 4). The wind-borne pollen of saltbush, goosefoot, and amaranth or pigweed is so similar that it is grouped in the cheno-am pollen category. Experimental pollen washes of seeds of both Amaranth and *Chenopodium* reveal cheno-am pollen (Bohrer 1972: 26). Pollen-laden blossoms toward the stem tip apparently drift upon mature seeds lower down (indeterminate inflorescence). Thus when seeds are beaten into a basket, ample pollen is collected as well. It seems more than likely that the high density of cheno-am pollen results at least in part from enrichment by the subsistence choices of the inhabitants. Holloway describes sample FS 1172 with a large amount of clumped cheno-am grains, 51 grains per gram. Unfortunately, this is the only sample when observations on pollen aggregates are recorded and thus comparisons are lacking.

Ephedra (Mormon Tea)

Mormon Tea, a wind-pollinated shrub, shows less variable pollen concentration than most wind-pollinated types. Still, some spikes in concentration are noteworthy, and may indicate human usage. The stems have been widely used for tea (Hodgson 2001: 12).

Zea mays (Maize)

When unusually large, maize pollen can be identified by its size alone. However, at High Rolls Cave Holloway (2002) used the distinctive morphology of the relatively small maize pollen for recognition. Even though husks enclose the ear from pollination to maturity, pollen can be washed from the husked ear, probably because humans transfer the pollen that accumulated on the husk exterior to the kernelled cob by husking (Bohrer 1972: 25-26). Mice are fond of loose maize kernels and can carry them in their cheek pouches and cache the kernels (Chapter 3). We do not know to what degree mice may be responsible for distributing the maize pollen record. The maize pollen near the back wall of the cave in three samples (Table B.4.2.) might be the result of their activity.

The distribution of maize pollen provides a far broader record of use than is evident from flotation (Chapter 4). All seven of the sampled excavation units from East Clusters A and B and Excavation Unit 59 in the West Cluster (Table B.4.2.) contain maize pollen. In addition, East Cluster B Feature 5 (FS 350) and Feature 6 (FS 286) have a unique record of maize pollen, as does FS 1053, just outside of East Cluster B.

When pairs of pollen and flotation samples taken from the same location (feature and level) are analyzed, the recovery of maize in both suggests little movement from their point of (original?) deposition. Because paired samples were rarely obtained, we have only two good examples.

(1) Excavation Unit 12, East Cluster A (FS 187) retained a carbonized maize embryo (46 cmbs) while pollen was recovered in the same excavation unit and at the same depth (FS 265). The radiocarbon date (FS 188, Beta Analytic 149379, 200 ± 50 B.C.) might provide a reasonable approximation of its age.

(2) Excavation Unit 69 (East Cluster B) is one where pollen (FS 1024) and a cob (FS 1030, Beta Analytic 158045, A.D. 220 ±50) in the same unit and depth (Stratum 2, Level 2, 32 cmbs) may have been recovered where deposited. The youngest date for Feature 22 is 1360 ± 50 B.C. (Beta Analytic 164075). The cob, complete with kernels with some pollen clinging, could have been introduced above the feature by a rodent.

Typha (Cattail)

Cattail pollen from High Rolls Cave remains in relatively large tetrads that are heavy enough to limit wind transport. Tetrads have been recovered in a sample from the West Cluster (Excavation Unit 59, FS 1006) in an unusually high concentration in association with a series of insect-pollinated types that also suggest, independently, human introduction. In addition, eight other pollen samples contain concentrations of cattail pollen (Table B.4.2.). Cattail pollen gives a high rate of energy return in relation to the energy cost in harvesting it (Table 7.1).

Cyperaceae (Sedge Family)

Pollen of the sedge family is relatively rare at High Rolls Cave and seems limited to East Cluster B (Table B.4.2.), which may be near the source of the pollen.

INSECT-POLLINATED FLOWERS

When insect-pollinated floral concentrations are charted in Table B.4.2; instead of the pollen being evenly distributed in excavation units, certain ones form isolated "tails" in the columns of concentrations. It is these samples in particular that may have been used by the inhabitants. Suspicions are further reinforced when related material is recovered from flotation. Many plant families have pollen-bearing structures in close proximity to the developing fruit. If that fruit has a rough or irregular surface some of the old pollen is apt to be left clinging to the mature fruit. A factor complicating interpretations of humanly introduced insect-pollinated plants comes from the consumption of floral parts by mice and rodents, as indicated earlier for sunflowers. Rodents have scattered their droppings over so many excavation units that I would expect a more general distribution of insect-pollinated types to result, as is apparently the case with sunflower (High Spine pollen category). There is always the risk that a pollen-filled anther was included accidentally in a sediment sample analyzed for pollen.

Apiaceae (Parsley Family)

The parsley family offers a flat landing platform of multiple flowers that makes pollination by insects efficient. In the southwestern United States, wild celery (*Cymopteris* spp) grows in rocky areas of juniper grasslands or among pinyons sometime between March and May (Dunmire and Tierney 1995: 193). It is used as an early green and herbal flavoring. Still other genera grow amidst ponderosa pines and along moist stream banks at higher elevations later in the season. Some have medicinal uses. Flotation samples from East Cluster A (FS 773 and FS 795) contain very small fruits from this family. The pollen record in East Cluster A (FS 776 and FS 96) and in Excavation Unit 33 in East Cluster B suggests human exploitation (Table B.4.2.). The recovery of the pollen in a coprolite (494-2) indicates internal consumption.

Brassicaceae (Mustard Family)

East Cluster A (FS 776), East Cluster B (FS 1024), and the West Cluster (FS 1006) have high concentrations of pollen (above 400 grains per gram, Table B.4.2). In addition, four coprolites found in disturbed back dirt contain the pollen. Three children's coprolites (494-2, 494-3, 494-4) have the pollen concentrations from 20 grains per gram to 32 grains per gram and that of an adult (107-1) has 48 grains per gram. Mustard seed from flotation appears in the West Cluster Feature 13, a thermal area that extends to where pollen was recovered in FS 1006. Seed is in East Cluster A (FS 742 and FS 853). The pollen evidence reinforces conclusions concerning human usage from flotation.

Cactaceae (Cactus Family)

Cholla cactus pollen (*Cylindropuntia*, FS 437, FS 521, and FS 551) comes from the back-of-cave Excavation Units 217, 242, and 258, and from two coprolites as single grains (494-2, 494-3). The remote location of the former suggests it might have once been part of human fecal composition or transmitted on cactus joints by wood rats.

Presumably the non-Opuntia or Cactaceae pollen category might include the hedgehog cactus (*Echinocereus*) and the barrel cactus from lower elevations (*Echinocactus*). Field Sample 525 had 75 grains per gram of non-Opuntia pollen as well as maize and other types that could be humanly introduced near the rear wall of the cave (Excavation Unit 252). East Cluster A (FS 235) has 48 grains per gram of cactus pollen. The isolated and low pollen concentration, the presence of only hedgehog cactus seeds in FS 742 and Feature 11b, and the lack of burned spine bases indicative of roasting the stems of cacti all combine to suggest utilization of the fruit, and this not very frequently.

Cucurbitaceae (Squash Famlily)

Pollen from the squash family occurs in FS 437 and FS 521 from the back of the cave (Excavation Unit 217 and 242) with 14 and 29 grains per gram respectively. The pollen is so large and heavy that accidental wind transport is impossible. While no cultivated squash came from flotation, the seed of buffalo gourd (*Cucurbita foetidissima* type) was in the mouse pantry sample (FS 67) in East Cluster B. The pollen bearing flowers are separate from the ones that bear fruit, though some extra pollen is apt to cling on a dried female flower at the tip of a developing fruit. Because bitter cucurbitacin needs to be washed from the seed prior to consumption, the role of humans in transporting the fruits to the cave is apparent. Not so apparent is how the pollen reached the rear of the cave.

Ericaceae (Heather Family)

Pollen in the heather family was recovered from East Cluster A (FS 264). Because only one species in this family is anticipated in the Sacramento Mountains, the family can be narrowed to bearberry or kinnikennik (*Arctostaphylos uva-ursi*). Actual bearberry fruits were in East Cluster A (FS 773, Chapter 4). Contemporary smoking of the leaves and the use of the fruits as food are sufficiently different to create doubt as to why the plant was obtained.

Eriogonum (Buckwheat)

Pollen of wild buckwheat is concentrated in East Cluster A (FS 264 and FS 776), in East Cluster B (FS 1024), and in the West Cluster (FS 1006) (see Table B.4.2). Four fecal samples from children have the pollen, one in concentrations of 116 grains per gram (494-5). Low amounts of the pollen are in three of six samples from the back wall of the cave (Table B.4.2), perhaps due to rodents.

Fabaceae (Legume Family)

The legumes are such a large and diverse plant family that only its presence can be noted from the pollen.

Lamiaceae (Mint Family)

Family level pollen identifications derive from East Cluster B (FS 1024) and the West Cluster (FS 106) (see Table B.4.2). Salvia type nutlets suggest rodent introductions (Chapter 4). It is otherwise difficult to suggest the vectors of the plant parts.

Portulacaceae (Purslane Family)

A concentration of pollen was recovered in one of the coprolites from a child (494-4) suggesting the consumption of greens at the earliest flowering stage. The seed was apparently utilized during Stratum 2 and Stratum 3 times (Chapter 4).

Prosopis (Mesquite)

When mesquite grows in the immediate environment of an archaeological site, it is difficult to know if the pollen simply was introduced on firewood or if some other ethnobotanical use is implied. Under such circumstances it takes an unusual context of recovery or a high concentration of the pollen to isolate ethnobotanical use. At High Rolls Cave, the trees grow sufficiently distant that incidental entry of pollen from firewood seems far less likely than on the pods. When fallen pods are gathered beneath mesquite trees it would also be from the same place where expended pollen rich flowers had fallen earlier. The pollen is distributed in 10 excavation units while mesquite pod endocarps are found in eight excavation units. Granting that disbursement of mesquite pods between excavation units of the cave may have been aided by wood rats, the overlap of only two excavation units (12 and 27) which had both pods and pollen may also indicate its potential importance to people. Optimal foraging studies indicate mesquite is a high ranked dietary component (Table 7.1). Mesquite pollen in one of the fecal samples from a child has a concentration of 72 grains per gram (494-2).

Rhamnaceae (Buck-thorn Family)

Wild lilac (*Ceanothus fendleri*) is a shrub of the pine forests browsed by deer. Its frequency is promoted by fires (Huisinga and others 2005, Table 1). Crucillo or lotebush (*Condalia*) with its edible berries belongs to this family. Perhaps the wood of a member of this family was used, or maybe the crucillo fruits were eaten. Whatever its use, it is part of the pollen signature of this Archaic people. Evidence is restricted to East Clusters A and B only (Table B.4.2). Pollen is present also in a child's fecal sample, 133 grains per gram.

Rosaceae (Rose Family)

Concentrations of rose family pollen are found in eight excavation units in East Clusters A and B and in three excavation units in the West Cluster (Table B.4.2). Apache plume, chokecherry, mountain mahogany, and perhaps a wild rose would all be available in the local flora. Pollen from the family was recovered in three fecal samples (107-1, 494-3, 494-5) in concentrations of 97 grains per gram, 177 grains per gram, and 167 grains per gram, suggesting the unknown plant part was edible. Chokecherry might bear residual pollen upon its fruit.

Salix (Willow)

Concentrations of willow pollen are found in all excavation units sampled in East Cluster A, East Cluster B, and the West Cluster (Table B.3.2). The highest concentrations are in East Cluster A at 1,157 grains per gram (FS 264) and in the West Cluster at 1,108 grains per gram (FS 1006). The willow pollen in the latter sample joins a long list of insect-pollinated types present that collectively suggests human use. Nothing recovered in flotation indicates the manner of use of willow. However the catkins can be eaten (Rea 1997: 195) and the new spring growth of willows is inherently more pliable when employed in making coiled baskets and trays, while the bark and stems have been long recognized for their medicinal value (Dunmire and Tierney 1995: 108-110).

Solanaceae (Potato Family)

Pollen from the potato family was small and within the size range of groundcherry (*Physalis*) or nightshade (*Solanum*). It was found in highest concentration (1,260 grains per gram) in Feature 2 in East Cluster A. It is recovered in the West Cluster in Feature 14 and in Excavation Unit 59 adjacent to it, as well as two samples from the back of the cave (FS 521 and FS 525). No pollen from the family was found in the five coprolite samples, yet the pollen does tend to be found in samples with other insect-pollinated types that suggest human use (Table B.4.2). Some unidentifiable highly degraded seeds belonging to this family were recovered in flotation. While there may be economic or medicinal uses, the matter would benefit from better resolution. No pollen samples derive from the Excavation Unit 27 at a depth where tobacco seed was found.

Sphaeralcea (Globemallow)

A high concentration of pollen in a child's coprolite (494-4: 1,987 grains per gram) indicates consumption. Charred globemallow seeds appear in Features 1, 3, and 7, all in contexts that appear early (Chapter 4). Pollen deposited on threshed seed prepared for consumption, or perhaps nibbled flowers might account for the concentration.

SUMMARY

While certain floral structures are adapted for wind pollination and others for insect pollination, pollen transported into High Rolls Cave also bears a relationship to the ethnobotanical priorities of the people occupying the cave, the percolation of water, the foraging of rodents, and to the weedy, disturbed-ground flora (cheno-ams, low-spine aster family) fostered by human activity in the immediate area. Our understanding is only fragmentary, but important.

What would otherwise be tentative flotation evidence of early seasonal use of the mustard and carrot families becomes much more convincing with additional concentrations of pollen across the cave and pollen in four coprolites. Similarly, the indications for the early use of maize based on flotation is relatively limited. The much broader distribution of maize pollen in excavation units (seven of seven units investigated in East Clusters A and B) indicates a much greater usage than would be known otherwise. Instead of a single instance of bearberry (*Arctostaphylos uva-ursi*) use, an additional one is apparent with the recovery of a pollen tetrad from the family to which bearberry belongs. From purslane seed and its capsule caps in flotation we only conclude that purslane seed was collected. Recovery of purslane pollen residues from an early flowering stage extends knowledge of the parts of the plant utilized. The known distribution of mesquite in excavation units doubles to 16 when the pollen record is included. Because roasting is not part of preparing the pods for eating, the probable decay of mesquite residue leaves the flotation record under-represented. The expanded distribution lends more credence to its possible importance. The recovery of cattail pollen in high concentrations tags this species for dietary use while its high rank in return for energy expended mark it along with mesquite as another item of dietary importance. An assumption of low rate of use of cholla and wild gourd from the rarity of flotation evidence is also supported by the low incidence of pollen.

The pollen record is unique in leaving a record of use of willow (*Salix*) and buck-thorn (*Rhamnaceae*). As helpful as the pollen record is, it lacks a few genera that might be discernable as pollen but are known only through flotation: *Celtis*, *Garrya*, *Nicotiana*, *Ptelea*, and *Rhus*. In the end, both pollen and flotation studies provide unique and valuable information on the early Archaic lifeways in High Rolls Cave.

Table B.4.1. Pollen samples with low concentration values from High Rolls Cave

Field Sample	Excavation Unit	Description	Pollen Concentration**	Pollen Sum
447	217	Rear of cave	7,891	507
663	103	South of W. Cluster	6,421	566
1172	106	South of W. Cluster	11,513	217
606	F 13*	Thermal pit	12,232	675
1074	F 23	Thermal pit	15,843	451
569	F 14*	Thermal pit	1,426	28
1095	F 24*	Thermal pit	6,565	124
1097	F 24*	Thermal pit	5,556	107

*Feature omitted from Table B.4.2

**Grains per gram

Table B.4.2. Pollen concentration* distribution of non-arboreal wind and insect pollinated plants from High Rolls Cave excavation units

	East Cluster A						East Cluster B			
Excavation Unit	30	12	12	12	27	64	33	33	69	F23
Field Sample No.	235	265	266	264	96	776	252	286	1024	1074
Centimeters Below Surface	12	46	47	48	26	15	44	56	32	36
Pollen Sum	669	722	550	597	422	1158	490	665	788	451
Pollen Concentration*	108,378	61,560	99,000	138,000	136,000	130,275	158,760	33,665	73,366	15,874
Wind Pollinated Types										
Poaceae	13,446	3,581	2,160	4,166	5,508	11,925	11,664	7,644	3,445	175
Aster Family										
Artemisia	24,624	2,984	26,829	29,391	78,732	13,838	26,244	1,620	3,352	386
Low Spine	19,116	2,302	5,580	5,091	9,720	4,950	4,536	962	4,655	421
High Spine	810	1,791	2,160	1,851	2,268	5,175	5,832	203	3,352	281
Cheno-am	39,204	2,473	8,100	8,331	28,836	9,450	45,684	658	4,934	1,543
Ephedra	486	72	334	249	35	1,463	1,620	658	1,397	70
Zea mays	486	92	180	89	451	113	0	101	27	0
Typha	162	0	51	231	23	450	0	0	0	0
Cyperaceae	0	0	0	0	0	113	0	0	93	0
Insect Pollinated Types										
Apiaceae	0	0	0	0	23	26	324	0	0	0
Brassicaceae	0	0	0	0	0	563	0	0	466	0
Eriogonum	0	6	0	694	0	338	0	51	186	0
Prosopis	648	72	308	106	35	3,488	1620	304	279	0
Rhamnaceae	0	85	0	0	0	26	324	51	0	0
Rosaceae	162	85	0	23	0	1,575	648	51	372	70
Salix	324	171	540	1,157	972	1,013	324	152	70	70
Solanaceae	0	0	1,260	0	12	113	0	0	0	0

*Concentration is expressed in grains per gram

Table B.4.2. Pollen concentration* distribution of non-arboreal wind and insect pollinated plants from High Rolls Cave excavation units, cont'd

Excavation Unit	West Cluster			South of West Cluster			Back Wall of Cave		
Excavation Unit	57	59	16	103	105	106	217	242	257
Field Sample No.	613	1,006	303	663	1,147	1,172	437	521	525
Centimeters Below Surface	20	20	73-80	25	42	10	16	17	17
Pollen Sum	603	625	589	566	196	226	567	1,111	574
Pollen Concentration*	50,878	67,500	68,155	6,421	31,129	11,513	7,891	32,605	43,050
Wind Pollinated Types									
Poaceae	4,472	1,404	1,967	125	476	408	125	176	2,400
Aster Family									
Artemisia	2,025	4,536	23,953	68	1,112	458	43	235	1,725
Low Spine	2,025	4,860	1,967	113	1,271	4,087	640	998	3,975
High Spine	1,603	2,484	2,083	136	159	153	264	646	1,875
Cheno-am	5,653	18,648	15,274	488	13,341	4,330	585	2,172	3,450
Ephedra	506	216	231	91	159	102	264	675	900
Zea mays	0	56	0	0	0	0	2	29	75
Typha	18	2,592	463	0	0	0	0	0	75
Insect Pollinated Types									
Apiaceae	0	0	0	0	0	0	14	0	0
Brassicaceae	169	1,296	0	0	159	0	0	0	0
Eriogonum	0	216	0	3	0	0	14	29	0
Prosopis	0	108	579	0	0	0	0	0	75
Rhamnaceae	0	0	0	0	0	0	0	0	0
Rosaceae	169	216	116	0	0	0	14	8	0
Salix	84	1,108	1,041	0	0	51	0	147	0
Solanaceae	84	216	0	0	0	0	0	29	300

*Concentration is expressed in grains per gram

References Cited

Adams, Karen R.
  1984 Evidence of Wood Dwelling Termites in Archaeological Sites in the Southwestern United States. *Journal of Ethnobiology* 4(1): 29-43.

Adams, Karen R., and Vorsila L. Bohrer
  1998 Archaeobotanical Indicators of Seasonality: Examples from Arid Southwestern United States. In *Seasonality and Sedentism*, edited by Thomas R. Rocek and Ofer Bar Yosef, pp. 129-141. Peabody Museum Bulletin 6. Cambridge: Peabody Museum of Archaeology and Ethnology, Harvard University.

Adams, Karen R., and Mollie S. Toll
  2000 Tobacco Use, Ecology and Manipulation in the Prehistoric and Historic Southwestern United States. In *Tobacco Use by Native North Americans*, edited by Joseph C. Winter, pp. 143-170. Norman: University of Oklahoma Press.

Adams, Karen R., Susan J. Smith, and Manuel R. Palacios-Fest
  2002 *Pollen and Micro-Invertebrates from Modern Earthen Canals and Other Fluvial Environments along the Middle Gila River, Central Arizona.* Gila River Indian Community Anthropological Research Papers No. 1. Sacaton, Arizona: Cultural Resource Management Program, Gila River Indian Community.

Adams, Karen R., Joe D. Stewart, and Stuart Baldwin
  2002 Pottery Paint and Other Uses of Rocky Mountain Beeweed (Cleome serrulata Pursh) in the Southwestern United States: Ethnographic Data, Archaeological Record, and Elemental Composition. *Kiva* 67 (4): 339-362.

Adovasio, James, and Gary F. Fry
  1976 Prehistoric Psychotropic Drug Use in Northeastern Mexico and Trans-Pecos Texas. *Economic Botany* 30(1): 94-96.

Agogino, George A., and Sherwin Feinhandler
  1957 Amaranth Seeds from a San Jose Site in New Mexico. *Texas Journal of Science* 9(2): 154-156.

Agogino, George A., and Jim Hester
  1958 Comments on a San Jose Radiocarbon Date. *American Antiquity* 24(2): 187-188.

Akins, Nancy J.
  2002 Archaic Animal Subsistence in Fresnal Canyon. MS, Office of Archaeological Studies, Museum of New Mexico, Santa Fe.

Aldon, Carl F., and George Garcia
  1972 Vegetation Changes as a Result of Soil Ripping on the Rio Puerco in New Mexico. *Journal of Range Management* 25(5): 381-383.

Aldous, Alfred E., and Homer L. Shantz
  1924 Types of Vegetation in the Semi-arid Portion of the United States and Their Economic Significance. *Journal of Agricultural Research* 28(2): 99-127.

Alexander, Hubert G. and Paul Reiter
  1935 *Report on the Excavation of Jemez Cave*. Monographs of the School of American Research 4. Santa Fe: School of American Research Press.

Allan, William C.
  1973 General Description of the Basketry from Fresnal Shelter. In *Technical Manual*, pp. 403-406. Human Systems Research, Tularosa, New Mexico.

Altschul, Siri von Reis
  1973 *Drugs and Foods from Little-Known Plants*. Cambridge: Harvard University Press.

Applegarth, John M.
  1979 Environmental Implications of Herpetofaunal Remains from Archaeological Sites West of Carlsbad, New Mexico. In *Biological Investigations in the Guadalupe Mountain National Park, Texas*, edited by Hugh H. Genoways and Robert J. Baker, pp.159-167. National Park Service Proceedings and Transactions No.4. Washington, National Park Service.

Asch, David L., and Nancy Asch
  1978 The Economic Potential of Iva annua and its Prehistoric Importance in the Lower Illinois Valley. In *The Nature and Status of Ethnobotany*, edited by Richard I Ford, pp. 301-341. University of Michigan Museum of Anthropology Anthropological Papers No. 67. Ann Arbor: University of Michigan.

Barkley, T. M. (editor)
  1986 *Flora of the Great Plains*. Lawrence: University Press of Kansas.

Basehart, Harry W.
  1973 Mescalero Apache Subsistence Patterns. In *Technical Manual, 1973: Survey of the Tularosa Basin*, pp. 145-181. Tularosa, New Mexico: Human Systems Research.

Beals, Ralph L.
  1932 *The Comparative Ethnology of Northern Mexico before 1750*. Ibero-Americana, Vol. 2. Berkeley: University of California.

Bean, Lowell John, and Katherine S. Saubel
  1972 *Temalpakh*. Morongo Indian Reservation, California: Malki Museum Press.

Beatley, Janice C.
  1974 Phenological Events and Their Environmental Triggers in Mojave Desert Ecosystems. *Ecology* 55 (4): 856-863.

Bell, Willis H., and Edward F. Castetter
  1937 *The Utilization of Mesquite and Screwbean by the Aborigines in the American Southwest*. University of

New Mexico Bulletin 314, Biological Series 5(2). Albuquerque: University of New Mexico Press.

1941 *The Utilization of Yucca, Sotol, and Beargrass by the Aborigines in the American Southwest.* University of New Mexico Bulletin 372, Biological Series 5(5). Albuquerque: University of New Mexico Press.

Benson, Lyman, and Robert A. Darrow
1954 *Trees and Shrubs of the Southwestern Deserts.* Tucson: University of Arizona Press.

Blair, Terrence C., Jeffrey S. Clark, and Stephen G. Wells
1990 Quaternary Continental Stratigraphy, Landscape Evolution, and its Application to Archaeology: Jarilla Piedmont and Tularosa Graben Floor, White Sands Missile Range, New Mexico. *Geological Society of America Bulletin* 102(6): 749-759.

Bohrer, Vorsila L.
1962 Nature and Interpretation of Plant Materials from Tonto National Monument. In *Archaeological Studies at Tonto National Monument, Arizona*, edited by Louis R. Caywood, pp. 78-114. Southwestern Monuments Association Technical Series Vol.2. Gila Pueblo, Globe, Arizona.

1972 Paleoecology of the Hay Hollow Site, Arizona. *Fieldiana Anthropology* 65(1): 1-30.

1975a The Prehistoric and Historic Role of the Cool Season Grasses in the Southwest. *Economic Botany* 29(3): 199-207.

1975b Recognition and Interpretation of Prehistoric Remains of Mirabilis multiflora (Nyctaginaceae) in the Sacramento Mountains of New Mexico. *Bulletin of the Torrey Botanical Club* 102(1): 21-25.

1975c The Role of Seasonality in the Annual Harvest of Native Food Plants in the Puerco Valley, Northwest of Albuquerque, New Mexico. *New Mexico Academy of Science Bulletin* 15(2): 3.

1978 Plants That Have Become Locally Extinct in the Southwest. *New Mexico Journal of Science* 18(2): 10-19.

1981a The Research Potential of Plant Remains from Fresnal Shelter, and Archaic Site in south-central New Mexico. In *The Research Potential of Anthropological Museum Collections*, edited by Anne-Marie Cantwell, James B. Griffin, and Nan A. Rothschild, pp. 387-392. Annals of the New York Academy of Sciences 376.

1981b Methods of Recognizing Pollen from Cultural Activity in Archaeological Sites. *Kiva* 46(3): 135-142.

1983 The Tale of the Burnt Bush (Rhus trilobata). *Desert Plants* 5(3): 122-124.

1987 The Plant Remains from La Ciudad, A Hohokam Site in Phoenix. In *Specialized Studies in the Economy, Environment and Culture of La Ciudad, Part III*, edited by JoAnn E. Kisselburg, Glen. Rice, Brenda Shears, and Frank E. Bayham, pp. 64-202. Anthropological Field Studies 20. Tempe: Arizona State University.

1994 Appendix B: The Plant Remains from the Wind Canyon Site in the Eagle Mountains of Western Texas. In *Data Recovery Excavations at the Wind Canyon Site, 41HZ119, Hudspeth County, Texas*, by Margaret H. Hines, Steve A. Tomka, and Karl W. Kibler, pp.169-180. Reports of Investigations No. 99. Austin: Prewitt and Associates.

Bohrer, Vorsila L., and Karen R. Adams
1977 *Ethnobotanical Techniques and Approaches at Salmon Ruin, New Mexico.* San Juan Valley Archaeological Project Technical Series 2. Contributions in Anthropology 8(1). Portales: Eastern New Mexico University.

Breternitz, David A
1960 Orme Ranch Cave, NA 6656. *Plateau* 33(2): 26-39.

Briuer, Frederick L.
1977 *Plant and Animal Remains from Caves and Rock Shelters of Chevelon Canyon Arizona: Methods for Isolating Cultural Depositional Processes.* Doctoral dissertation, University of California, Los Angeles. Ann Arbor: University Microfilms.

Brooks, Richard H., Lawrence Kaplan, Hugh C. Cutler, and Thomas W. Whitaker
1962 Plant Material from a Cave on the Rio Zape, Durango, Mexico. *American Antiquity* 27(3): 356-369.

Brown, David E. (editor)
1982 Biotic Communities of the American Southwest-United States and Mexico. *Desert Plants* 4(1-4).

Bryant, Vaughn M.
1974 Prehistoric Diet in Southwest Texas: The Coprolite Evidence. *American Antiquity* 39(3): 407-420.

Buffington, Lee C., and Carlton H. Herbel
1965 Vegetational Changes on a Semidesert Grassland Range from 1858-1963. *Ecological Monographs* 35(2): 139-164.

Bukasov, Sergei M.
1930 *The Cultivated Plants of Mexico, Guatemala, and Columbia.* Bulletin of Applied Botany, Genetics, and Plant Breeding, pp. 261-273, 47th Supplement. Leningrad.

Bunzel, Ruth
1932 *Zuni Ritual Poetry.* Forty-seventh Annual Report of the Bureau of American Ethnology, pp. 611-1108. Washington, D.C.: Smithsonian Institution.

Bye, Robert A., Jr.
1979 Hallucinogenic Plants of the Tarahumara. *Journal of Ethnopharmacology* 1(1): 23-48.

1972 Ethnobotany of the Southern Paiute Indians in the 1870s: With a Note on the Early Ethnobotanical Contributions of Dr. Edward Palmer. In *Great Basin Cultural Ecology, A Symposium,* edited by Don D. Fowler, pp.87-104. Publications in the Social Sciences 8. Reno: Desert Research Institute.

Cable, Dwight R.
1979 *Ecology of Arizona Cottontop.* Forest Service, Rocky Mountain Forest and Range Experiment Station Research Paper RM 209. Fort Collins: Rocky Mountain Forest and Range Experiment Station, Forest Service, United States Department of Agriculture.

Callen, Eric O.
1965 Food Habits of Some Pre-Columbian Mexican Indians. *Economic Botany* 19 (4): 335-343.

1967 Analysis of the Tehuacan Coprolites. In *The Prehistory of the Tehuacan Valley, Vol. 1: Environment and Subsistence*, edited by Douglas S. Byers, pp. 261-289. Austin: University of Texas.

Cameron, Catherine
1973 An Analysis of the "Low Muscle Mass" Bone Fragments in Relation to Hearth Areas at Fresnal Shelter. In *Technical Manual*, pp. 398-401. Tularosa, New Mexico: Human Systems Research, Tularosa.

Carpenter, Thorne M., and Morris Steggerda
1939 The Food of the Present-Day Navajo Indians of New Mexico and Arizona. *Journal of Nutrition* 18(3): 297-305.

Castetter, Edward F.
1935 *Uncultivated Native Plants Used as Sources of Food*. University of New Mexico Bulletin 266 Biological Series 4(1). Albuquerque: University of New Mexico.

Castetter, Edward F., and Willis H. Bell
1951 *Yuman Indian Agriculture: Primitive Subsistence on the Lower Colorado and Gila Rivers*. Albuquerque: University of New Mexico Press.

Castetter, Edward F., and Morris E. Opler
1936 *Ethnobiology of the Chiricahua and Mescalero Apache*. University of New Mexico Bulletin Biological Series 4(5). University of New Mexico, Albuquerque.

Castetter, Edward F. and Ruth M. Underhill
1935 *The Ethnobiology of the Papago Indians*. University of New Mexico Bulletin 275 Biological Series 4(3). Albuquerque: University of New Mexico.

Castetter, Edward F., Willis H. Bell, and Alan R. Grove
1938 *The Early Utilization and Distribution of Agave in the American Southwest*. University of New Mexico Bulletin 335 Biological Series 5(4). Albuquerque: University of New Mexico.

Chamberlin, Ralph V.
1964[1911] *The Ethnobotany of the Gosiute Indians of Utah*. Memoirs of the American Anthropological Association, Vol. 2(Part 5): 331-405. New Work: Krause Reprint Corporation.

Chapline, W.R.
1919 *Production of Goats on Far Western Ranges*. Farmer's Bulletin 749. Washington, D.C.: United States Department of Agriculture.

Coffin, Edwin F.
1932 *Archaeological Exploration of a Rock Shelter in Brewster County, Texas*. Indian Notes and Monographs 48. New York: Museum of the American Indian.

Corbusier, William F.
1886 The Apache-Yumas and the Apache-Mohaves. *American Antiquarian* 8(5,6).

Correll, Donovan S. and Marshall.C. Johnston
1970 *Manual of the Vascular Plants of Texas*. Renner, Texas: Texas Research Foundation.

Curtin, Leonora Scott Muse
1947 *Healing Herbs of the Rio Grande*. Santa Fe: Laboratory of Anthropology, University of New Mexico.

1968 *Preparation of Sacred Corn Meal in the Rio Grande Pueblos.* Southwest Museum Leaflets 32: 3-15.

Cushing, Frank
1920 *Zuni Breadstuff.* Indian Notes and Monographs 8. New York: Museum of the American Indian, Heye Foundation.

Cutler, Hugh C.
1952 A Preliminary Survey of the Plant Remains from Tularosa Cave. In *Mogollon Cultural Continuity and Change: The Stratigraphic Analysis of Tularosa and Cordova Caves*, by Paul Sidney Martin, John.B. Rinaldo, Elaine Bluhm, Hugh C. Cutler, and Roger Grange, Jr., pp. 461-479. Fieldiana: Anthropology 40. Chicago Natural History Museum.

Dayton, William A.
1931 *Important Western Browse Plants.* United States Department of Agriculture Miscellaneous Publication 101. Washington, D.C.: United States Department of Agriculture.

Dering, Phil
1999 Earth-Oven Plant Processing in Archaic Period Economies: An Example from a Semi-Arid Savannah in South-Central North America. *American Antiquity* 64(4): 659-674.

Doebley, John F.
1984 "Seeds" of Wild Grasses: A Major Food of Southwestern Indians. *Economic Botany* 38(1): 52-64.

Doleman, William H., Richard C. Chapman, Ronald L. Stauber and June. Piper (editors)
1992 *Landscape Archaeology in the Southern Tularosa Basin, Vol. 3: Archaeological Distributions and Prehistoric Human Ecology.* Albuquerque: Office of Contract Archaeology. University of New Mexico.

Doleman William H., and Peter L. Eidenbach
1992 Strategic Perspectives on Small Sites and Human Landscapes in the Tularosa Basin: A Review of Existing Models. In *Landscape Archaeology in the Southern Tularosa Basin, Vol. 3: Archaeological Distributions and Prehistoric Human Ecology*, edited by William H. Doleman, Richard C. Chapman, Ronlad L. Stauber and June Piper, pp.13-20. Albuquerque: Office of Contract Archaeology, University of New Mexico.

Doleman William H., and Marilyn K Swift
1991 Geomorphological and Environmental Context of Cultural Remains. In *Landscape Archaeology of the Southern Tularosa Basin, Vol. 2:Testing, Excavation, and Analysis*, edited by William Doleman, Richard C. Chapman, Jeanne Schutt, Marilyn K. Swift and K. D. Morrison, pp. 17-47. Albuquerque: Office of Contract Archaeology, University of New Mexico.

Dunmire, William T., and Gail D. Tierney
1995 *Wild Plants of the Pueblo Province.* Santa Fe: Museum of New Mexico Press.

Dutton, Bertha P.
1962 *Happy People: The Huichol Indians.* Santa Fe: Museum of New Mexico Press.

Eidenbach, Peter, and Mark Wimberly
1980 *Archaeological Reconnaissance in White Sands National Monument.* Tularosa, New Mexico : Human Systems Research.

Elmore, Francis H.
1943 *Ethnobotany of the Navajo.* University of New Mexico and the School of American Research Monograph Series Vol. 1(7). Albuquerque: University of New Mexico Press.

Emerson, Fred W.
1935 An Ecological Reconnaissance in the White Sands, New Mexico. *Ecology* 16: 226-233.

Felger, Richard S.
1977 Mesquite in Indian Cultures in Southwestern North America. In *Mesquite, Its Biology in Two Desert Ecosystems,* edited by Beryl B. Simpson, pp. 150-176. U.S. and International Biome Project Synthesis Series 4. Straudsburg, Pennsylvania: Dowden, Hutchinson, and Ross.

Fish, Suzanne K., Paul R. Fish, Charles H. Miksicek, and John Madsen
1985 Prehistoric Agave Cultivation in Southern Arizona. *Desert Plants* 7(2): 100, 107-112.

Fowler, Catherine S.
1976 The Processing of Rice Grass by Great Basin Indians. *Mentzelia* 2: 2-4.

Fowler, Don D., and Catherine S. Fowler (editors)
1971 *Anthropology of the Numa: John Wesley Powell's Manuscripts on the Numic Peoples of Western North America 1868-1880.* Smithsonian Contributions to Anthropology 14. Washington, D.C.: Smithsonian Institution.

Fry, Gary F.
1977 *Analysis of Prehistoric Coprolites from Utah.* University of Utah Anthropological Papers 97. Salt Lake City: University of Utah.

Gallagher, Marsha V.
1977 *Contemporary Ethnobotany Among the Apache of the Clarkdale, Arizona Area Coconino and Prescott National Forests.* U.S.D.A. Forest Service Report 14. Albuquerque : Southwestern Region, United States Department of Agriculture.

Gardner, John L.
1951 Vegetation of the Creosote Bush Area of the Rio Grande Valley in New Mexico. *Ecological Monographs* 21(4): 379-403.

Gasser, Robert E
1982a Hohokam Use of Desert Plant Foods. *Desert Plants* 3(4): 216-234.

1982b Anasazi Diet. In *The Specialists' Volume: Biocultural Analysis,* compiled by Robert E. Gasser, pp.8-95. Coronado Project Archaeological Investigations, Salt River Project. MNA Research Paper 23, Coronado Series 4. Flagstaff: Museum of Northern Arizona.

Gifford, Edward W.
1932 The Southeastern Yavapai. *University of California Publications in American Archaeology and Ethnology* 29: 177-252. Berkeley: University of California.

1933 The Cocopa. *University of California Publications in American Archaeology and Ethnology* 31(5): 257-333. Berkeley: University of California.

1936 The Northeastern and Western Yavapai. *University of California Publications in American Archaeology and Ethnology* 34:247-354. Berkeley: University of California.

1940 Culture Element Distributions XIII. Apache-Pueblo. *Anthropological Records* 4(1): 1-207.

Gifford, James C.
1980 *Archaeological Explorations in Caves of the Point of Pines Region.* Anthropological Papers of the University of Arizona No. 36. Tucson: University of Arizona Press.

Gifford-Gonzalez, Diane P., David.P. Damrosch, Debra R. Damrosch, John Pryor, and Robert L. Thunen
1985 The Third Dimension in Site Structure. An Experiment in Trampling and Vertical Dispersal. *American Antiquity* 50(4): 803-818.

Gish, Jannifer
1991 Current Perceptions, Recent Discoveries, and Future Directions in Hohokam Palynology. *Kiva* 56(3): 237-254.

Goodspeed, Thomas H.
1954 *The Genus Nicotiana: Origins, Relationships, and Evolution of its Species in the Light of Their Distribution, Morphology, and Genetics.* Chronica Botanica Vol.16. Waltham, Massachusetts: PUBLISHER.

Goodwin, Grenville
1935 The Social Divisions and Economic Life of the Western Apache. *American Anthropologist* 37(1): 55-64.

Gould, Frank W.
1951 *Grasses of Southwestern United States.* University of Arizona Bulletin 22(1), Biological Science Bulletin 7. Tucson: University of Arizona.

Guest, Evan
1933 *Notes on the Plants and Plant Products with Their Colloquial Names in Iraq.* Iraq Department of Agriculture Bulletin 27. Baghdad: Iraq Department of Agriculture.

Hall, Gordon
1973 Infant Burial: Fresnal Shelter. In *Technical Manual 197: Survey of the Tularosa Basin*, pp.386-395. High Rolls, New Mexico: Human Systems Research.

Hall, Robert L.
1974 Appendix C: Plant Remains from the Escalante Ruin Group. In *Excavations in the Escalante Ruin Group, Southern Arizona*, by David E. Doyel, pp 203-210. Arizona State Museum Archaeological Series 37. Tucson: Arizona State Museum, University of Arizona.

Hamilton, J. William, III, and Kenneth E.F. Watt
1970 Refuging. *Annual Review of Ecology and Systematics* 1: 263-286.

Hard, Robert J., and John R. Roney
1998 A Massive Terraced Village Complex in Chihuahua, Mexico, 3000 Years Before Present. *Science* 279: 1661-1664.

Harlan, Jack R.
1975 *Crops and Man.* Madison: American Society of Agronomy and Crop Science Society of America.

Harrington, Harold D.
    1967 *Edible Native Plants of the Rocky Mountains*. Albuquerque: University of New Mexico Press.

Havard, Valery
    1896 Drink Plants of the North American Indian. *Bulletin of the Torrey Botanical Club* 23(2): 33-46.

Hickey, Wayne C., and H. W.Springfield
    1966 Alkali Sacaton: Its Merits for Forage and Cover. *Journal of Range Management* 19(2): 71-74.

Hill, Kim, and A. Magdalena Hurtado
    1989 Hunter-Gatherers of the New World. *American Scientist* 77(5): 437-443.

Hines Margaret H., Steve A. Tomka, and Karl W. Kibler
    1994 *Data Recovery Excavations at the Wind Canyon Site, 41HZ119, Hudspeth County, Texas*. Reports of Investigations No. 99. Austin: Prewitt and Associates.

Hitchcock, Albert S.
    1950 *Manual of the Grasses of the United States*. Second edition. United States Department of Agriculture Miscellaneous Publication 200. Wasington, D.C.: United States Department of Agriculture.

Hodgson, Wendy
    2001 *Food Plants of the Sonoran Desert*. Tucson: University of Arizona Press.

Hofman, Albert
    1972 Ergot--A Rich Source of Pharmacologically Active Substances. In *Plants in the Development of Modern Medicine*, edited by Tony Swain, pp.234-260. Cambridge: Harvard University Press.

Holden, William C.
    1937 Excavation of Murrah Cave. *Bulletin of the Texas Archaeological and Paleontological Society* 9: 48-73.

Holloway, Richard
    l983 Diet and Medicinal Plant Usage of a Late Archaic Population from Culberson County, Texas. *Bulletin of the Texas Archaeological Society* 54: 319-329.

    2002 Pollen Analysis of Samples from LA 114l03, High Rolls Cave, Otero County, New Mexico. Quaternary Services Technical Report Series Number 2002-14, February 2002. MS, Office of Archaeological Studies, Museum of New Mexico, Santa Fe.

Hubbell, D.S., and J.L. Gardner
    1944 Some Edaphic and Ecological Effects of Water Spreading on Rangelands. *Ecology* 25(1): 27-44.

Huckell, Bruce B.
    1995 Of *Marshes and Maize: Preceramic Agricultural Settlements in the Cienega Valley, Southeastern Arizona*. Anthropological Papers of the University of Arizona No. 59. Tucson: University of Arizona Press.

Huckell, Lisa W.
    l995 Farming and Foraging in the Cienega Valley. In O*f Marshes and Maize: Preceramic Agricultural Settlements in the Cienega Valley, Southeastern Arizona*, by Bruce B. Huckell, pp. 74-97. Anthropological Papers of the University of Arizona No. 59. Tucson: University of Arizona Press.

Huisinga, Kristin D., Daniel C. Laughlin, Peter Z. Fule, Judith D. Springer, and Christopher M. McGlone
 2005 Effects of an Intense Prescribed Fire on Understory Vegetation in a Mixed Conifer Forest. *Journal of the Torrey Botanical Society* 132(5): 590-601.

Human Systems Research
 1972 Tentative List of Mammals Identified on the Western Sacramento Mountain Slope. In *Training Bulletin*. Albuquerque: Human Systems Research.

 1973 *Technical Manual, 1973:Survey of the Tularosa Basin*. High Rolls, New Mexico: Human Systems Research.

Hunt, Alice
 1960 *Archaeology of the Death Valley Salt Pan, California*. Anthropological Papers of the University of Utah 47. Salt Lake City: University of Utah.

Hutchins, Charles R.
 1974 *The Flora of the White Mountain Area, Southern Lincoln and Northern Otero Counties, New Mexico*. Privately published, Albuquerque.

Hyland, D.C., and James Adovasio
 2000 The Mexican Connection: A Study of Sociotechnical Change in Perishable Manufacture and Food Production in Prehistoric New Mexico. In *Beyond Cloth and Cordage: Archaeological Textile Research in the Americas*, edited by Penelope B. Drooker and Laurie D. Webster, pp. 141-159. Salt Lake City: University of Utah Press.

Irwin-Williams, Cynthia
 1973 *The Oshara Tradition: Origins of Anasazi Culture*. Contributions in Anthropology 5 (1). Portales, New Mexico: Eastern New Mexico University.

 1979 Post-Pleistocene Archaeology, 7000-2000 B.C. In *Southwest*, edited by Alfonso Ortiz, pp. 31-42. In Handbook of the North American Indians, Vol. 9, William C. Sturtevant, general editor. Washington, D.C.: Smithsonian Institution.

Jaeger, Heinrich M., and Sidney R. Nagel
 1997 Dynamics of Granular Material. *American Scientist* 85 (6): 540-545.

Jaynes, Richard A., and K.T. Harper
 1978 Patterns of Natural Revegetation in Arid Southeastern Utah. *Journal of Range Management* 31(6): 407-411.

Jennings, Jesse D.
 1980 *Cowboy Cave*. University of Utah Anthropological Papers 104. Salt Lake City, University of Utah.

Jones, Kevin T.
 1983 [1981] Optimal foragers: Aboriginal Resource Choice in the Great Basin. Paper presented at the Annual Meeting of the Society of American Archaeology, San Diego, 1981. In *The Archaeology of Monitor Valley 1: Epistemology*, by David Hurst Thomas, pp. 65. Anthropological Papers of the American Museum of Natural History Vol.58, Part 1. New York: American Museum of Natural History.

Jones, Kevin T., and David B. Madsen
 1989 Calculating Cost of Resource Transportation: A Great Basin Example. *Current Anthropology* 30 (4): 529-534.

Jones, Robert C.
1990 Technological Analysis of a Lithic Sample, Fresnal Rock Shelter, South-Central New Mexico. Unpublished Master's Thesis, Department of Anthropology, Eastern New Mexico University, Portales.

Jones, Volney H.
1931 The Ethnobotany of the Isleta Indians. Unpublished Master's Thesis, Department of Biology, University of New Mexico, Albuquerque.

1938 An Ancient Indian Food Plant. *El Palacio* 44(5,6): 41-53.

1941 The Nature and Status of Ethnobotany. *Chronica Botanica* 6(10): 219-221.

Jones, Volney H., and Robert L. Fonner
1954 Plant Materials from Sites in the Durango and La Plata Areas, Colorado. In *Basket Maker II Sites Near Durango, Colorado*, edited by Earl H. Morris and Robert F. Burgh, pp. 93-115. Carnegie Institution of Washington Publication 604. Washington D.C.: Carnegie Institution.

Kaplan, Lawrence
1956 The Cultivated Beans of the Prehistoric Southwest. *Annals of the Missouri Botanical Garden* 43(2): 189-251.

1963 Archaeoethnobotany of Cordova Cave, New Mexico. *Economic Botany* 17(4): 350-359.

1965 Beans of Wetherill Mesa. *American Antiquity* 31(2/2): 153-155.

Kearney, Thomas H., and Robert H. Peebles
1960 *Arizona Flora*. Berkeley: University of California.

1942 *Flowering Plants and Ferns of Arizona*. United States Department of Agriculture Miscellaneous Publications 423. Washington, D.C.: United States Department of Agriculture.

Keegan, William F.
1986 The Optimal Foraging Analysis of Horticultural Production. *American Anthropologist* 88(1): 92-107.

Kelley, William H.
1977 *Cocopa Ethnography*. Anthropological Papers of the University of Arizona No. 29. Tucson: University of Arizona Press.

Kelly, Isabel T.
1932 Ethnography of the Surprise Valley Paiute. *University of California Publications in American Archaeology and Ethnology* 31:67-210. Berkeley: University of California.

1939 *Southern Paiute Shamanism*. University of California Anthropological Records 2(4). Berkeley: University of California.

1964 *Southern Paiute Ethnography*. University of Utah Anthropological Papers No. 69. Salt Lake City: University of Utah.

Kelly, Robert L.
1998 Foraging and Sedentism. In *Seasonality and Sedentism: Archaeological Perspectives from Old and New*

World Sites, edited by T.R. Rocek and Osef Bar-Yosef, pp. 9-23. Peabody Museum Bulletin No. 6. Cambridge: Peabody Museum of Archaeology and Ethnology, Harvard University.

1995 *The Foraging Spectrum.* Washington, D.C.: Smithsonian Institution Press.

Kelrick, Michael I., and James A. Macmahon
1985 Nutritional and Physical Attributes of Seeds of Some Common Sagebrush-Steppe Plants: Some Implications for Ecological Theory and Management. *Journal of Range Management* 38 (1): 65-69.

Kennedy, John G.
1996 *Tarahumara of the Sierra Madre.* Pacific Grove, California: Asilomar Press.

Kirpatrick, David T., and Richard I. Ford
1977 Basketmaker Food Plants of the Cimarron District, Northeastern New Mexico. *Kiva* 42(3,4): 257-267.

Kroeber, Alfred L. (editor)
1935 *Walapai Ethnography.* Memoirs of the American Anthropological Association No. 42. Menasha, Wisconsin: American Anthropological Association.

Lamb, Samuel H.
1971 *Woody Plants of New Mexico and Their Value to Wildlife.* New Mexico Department of Game and Fish Bulletin 14. Santa Fe: New Mexico Department of Game and Fish.

Lambert, Sherman
1980 Structure and Dynamics of Forest Tree Communities of the Sacramento Mountains. Unpublished Master's Thesis, Department of Biological Sciences, University of Texas, El Paso.

Lancaster, Mark, Richard Storey, and Nathan W. Bower
1983 Nutritional Evaluation of Buffalo Gourd: Elemental Analysis of Seed. *Economic Botany* 37(3): 306-309.

Lange, Charles H.
1968 [1959] *Cochiti, A New Mexico Pueblo, Past and Present.* Carbondale: Arcturus Books Edition. Southern Illinois University Press.

Lanner, Ronald M.
1981 *The Pinyon Pine: A Natural and Cultural History.* Reno, University of Nevada Press.

Lehmer, Donald J.
1948 *The Jornada Branch of the Mogollon.* University of Arizona Social Science Bulletin No. 17. Tucson: University of Arizona.

Lentz, David L.
1984 Utah Juniper (Juniperus osteosperma) Cones and Seeds from Salmon Ruin, New Mexico. *Journal of Ethnobiology* 4(2): 191-200.

Lentz, Stephen C.
2006 *High Rolls Cave" Insectos, Burritos, Y Frajos, Archaic Subsistence in Southern New Mexico. Excavations at LA 114103, Otero County, New Mexico.* MS Archaeology Notes 345. Santa Fe: Office of Archaeological Studies, Department of Cultural Affairs.

Leopold. A. Carl, and Robert Ardrey
1972 Toxic Substances in Plants and the food Habits of Early Man. *Science* 176: 512-514.

Linskens, H.F., and W. Jorde
1997 Pollen as Food and Medicine-A Review. *Economic Botany* 51(1): 78-87.

Little Elbert L., and Robert S.Campbell
1943 Flora of the Jornada Experimental Range, New Mexico. *The American Midland Naturalist* 30(3): 626-670.

Lumholtz, Carl
1900 *Symbolism of the Huichol Indians.* Memoirs of the American Museum of Natural History 3:1-228.

1973[1902] *Unknown Mexico, Vol.2.* Charles Scribner's Sons, New York. Facsimile edition. Glorieta, New Mexico: Rio Grande Press.

MacMahon, James A.
1988 Warm Deserts. In *North American Terrestrial Vegetation,* edited by Michael G. Barbour and William Dwight Billings, pp.232-264. New York: Cambridge University Press.

Maker, H.J., Phillip S. Derr, and James U. Anderson
1972 *Soil Associations and Land Classification for Irrigation, Otero County.* New Mexico State University Agricultural Experiment Station Report 238. Las Cruces: Nex Mexico State University..

Maker, H.J., H.E. Dregne, V.G. Link, and James U. Anderson
1974 *Soils of New Mexico.* New Mexico State University Agricultural Experiment Station Research Report 285. Las Cruces: Nex Mexico State University.

Marshall, Michael P.
1973 Background Information on the Jornada Culture Area. In *Technical Manual, 1973: Survey of the Tularosa Basin*, pp.49-119. Tularosa, New Mexico: Human Systems Research.

Martin, William C., and Charles R. Hutchins
1980 *A Flora of New Mexico.* Germany: J. Cramer.

McBrinn, Maxine
2005 S*ocial Identities Among Archaic Mobile Hunters and Gatherers in the American Southwest.* Arizona State Museum Archaeological Series 197. Tucson: Arizona State Museum, University of Arizona.

McDaniel, Kirk C., and J.A.Tideman
1981 Sheep Use on Mountain Winter Range in New Mexico. *Journal of Range Management* 34(2): 102-104.

McNally, Elizabeth
1996 Variation in Flaked Stone Tool Assemblages at Lower Stanton Ruin and Fresnal Shelter, South-Central New Mexico. Unpublished Master's Thesis, Department of Anthropology, Eastern New Mexico University, Portales.

Mehringer, Peter
1967 Pollen Analysis of the Tule Springs Area, Nevada. In *Pleistocene Studies in Southern Nevada,* edited

by M. Wormington and D. Ellils, pp. 130-200. Anthropological Paper No. 13. Carson City: Nevada State Museum.

Meinzer, Oscar E.
1927 *Plants as Indicators of Ground Water.* United States Geological Survey Water Supply Paper 577. Washington, D.C.: United States Government Printing Office.

Meinzer, Oscar E., and R.F. Hare
1915 *Geology and Water Resources of Tularosa Basin.* U.S Geological Survey Water Supply Paper 343. Washington, D.C.: United States Government Printing Office.

Merchant, Janet D.
2002a Fresnal Rock Shelter Sandals: Descriptive Analysis and Chronological Placement. Unpublished Master's Thesis, Department of Anthropology, Eastern New Mexico University, Portales

2002b High Rolls Sandals. MS, Office of Archaeological Studies, Museum of New Mexico, Santa Fe.

Merrill, William L.
1978 Thinking and Drinking: A Raramuri Interpretation. In *Nature and Status of Ethnobotany*, edited by Richard Ford, pp. 101-117. Anthropological Papers No. 67. Ann Arbor: Museum of Anthropology, University of Michigan.

Miller, Myles R., and Nancy A. Kenmatsu
2004 Prehistory of the Jornada Mogollon and Eastern Trans-Pecos Regions of West Texas. In *The Prehistory of Texas*, edited by Timothy K. Perttula, pp. 204-265. College Station, Texas: Texas A&M University.

Moots, Rita E.
1990 Technological Analysis of a Cordage Sample, from Fresnal Rock Shelter, South-Central New Mexico. Unpublished Master's Thesis, Department of Anthropology, Eastern New Mexico University, Portales.

Morris, Earl H., and Robert F. Burgh
1954 *Basket Maker II Sites Near Durango,Colorado.* Carnegie Institution of Washington Publication 604. Washington, D.C.: Carnegie Institution.

Musil, Albina F.
1963 *Identification of Crop and Weed Seeds.* U.S. Department of Agriculture Handbook 219. Washington, D.C.: United States Department of Agriculture.

Nabhan, Gary P.
1985 *Gathering the Desert.* Tucson: University of Arizona Press.

Nequatewa, Edmund
1943 Some Hopi Recipes for the Preparation of Plant Food. *Plateau* 16(1): 18-20.

Niederberger, Christine
1979 Early Sedentary Economy in the Basin of Mexico. *Science* 203(4376): 131-142.

Nusbaum, Jesse L.
1922 *A Basket-Maker Cave in Kane County, Utah.* Indian Notes and Monographs Miscellaneous Series 29, edited by Frederick W. Hodge. New York: Museum of the American Indian.

Palmer, Edward
  1878 Plants Used by the Indians of the United States. *American Naturalist* 12(9): 593-606, 646- 655.

Pearce, J. E., and A.T. Jackson
  l933 *A Prehistoric Rock Shelter in Val Verde County, Texas.* Anthropological Papers of the University of Texas 1(3). Austin: University of Texas.
Pearce, Thomas M. (editor)
  1965 *New Mexico Place Names.* Albuquerque: University of New Mexico Press.

Pennington, Campbell W.
  1963 *The Tarahumar of Mexico.* Salt Lake City: University of Utah Press.

Phelps, Alan L.
  1968 A Recovery of Purslane Seeds in an Archaeological Context. *The Artifact* 6(4): 1-9.

Polyak, Victor J., and Yemane Asmerom
  2001 Late Holocene Climate and Cultural Changes in the Southwestern United States. *Science* 294: 148-151.

Provenza, Frederick D.
  2003 Twenty-five Years of Paradox in Plant-Herbivore Interactions and "Sustainable" Grazing Management. *Rangelands* 25(6): 4-15.

Pulliam, H. Ronald
  1981 On Predicting Human Diets. *Journal of Ethnobiology* 1(1): 61-68.

Pyke, G.H., H.R. Pulliam, and E.L.Charnov
  1977 Optimal Foraging: A Selective Review of Theory and Tests. *The Quarterly Review of Biology* 52(2): 137-154.

Rea, Amadeo
  1997 *The Desert's Green Edge: Ethnobotany of the Pima of the Gila River.* Tucson: University of Arizona Press.

Reagan, Albert B.
  1929 Plants Used by the White Mountain Apache Indians of Arizona. *Wisconsin Archaeologist* 8 (4): 143-161.

Roalson, Eric H. and Kelly Allred
  1995 *A Working Index of New Mexico Vascular Plant Names.* New Mexico State University
  Agricultural Experiment Station Research Report 702. Las Cruces: New Mexico State University.

Robbins, Wilfred W., John P. Harrington, and Barbara Freire-Marreco
  1916 *Ethnobotany of the Tewa Indians.* Bureau of American Ethnology Bulletin 55. Washinton, D.C.: Smithsonian Institution.

Roberts, Frank H. H.
  1930 Recent Archaeological Developments in the Vicinity of El Paso, Texas. *Smithsonian Miscellaneous Collections* 81(7): 1-14. Washington, D.C.: Smithsonian Institution.

Robertson, Joseph H.
1977 The Autecology of Oryzopsis hymenoides. *Mentzelia* 2: 18-21, 25-26.

Roney, John R.
1985 Prehistory of the Guadalupe Mountains. Unpublished Master's Thesis, Department of Anthropology, Eastern New Mexico University, Portales.

Rothrock, Joseph T.
1878 *Reports on the Botanical Collections Made in Portions of Nevada, Utah, California, Colorado, New Mexico and Arizona During the Years 1871-1875.* Report Upon U.S. Geographical Surveys West of the 100th Meridian 6. Washington, D.C.: United States Government Printing Office.

Russell, Frank
1908 *The Pima Indians.* Bureau of American Ethnology 26th Annual Report (1904-1905). Washington, D.C.: Smithsonian Institution.

Russell, Paul
1968 Folsom Complex near Orogrande, New Mexico. *The Artifact 6(2).*

Sauer, Jonathan D.
1967 The Grain Amaranths and Their Relatives: A Revised Taxonomic and Geographic Survey. *Annals of the Missouri Botanical Garden* 54: 103-137.

1950a Amaranths as Dye Plants Among the Pueblo Peoples. *Southwestern Journal of Anthropology* 6(4): 412-415.

1950b The Grain Amaranths: A Survey of their History and Classification. *Annals of the Missouri Botanical Garden* 37(4): 561-632.

Schoener, Thomas W.
1971 Theory of Feeding Strategies. *Annual Review of Ecology and Systematic*s 2: 369-404.

Schultes, Richard E. and Albert Hofman
1980 *The Botany and Chemistry of Hallucinogens.* Second Edition. Springfield: Charles C. Thomas.

1979 *Plants of the Gods.* New York: McGraw-Hill.

Shields, Laura
1956 Zonation of Vegetation in the Tularosa Basin, New Mexico. *Southwestern Naturalist* 1(2): 49-68.

Silko, Leslie Marmon
1987 Landscape, History, and the Pueblo Imagination. In *On Nature-Nuture, Landscape, and Natural History,* edited by Daniel Halpern, pp. 83-94. San Francisco: North Point Press.

Simms, Steven R.
1987 *Behavioral Ecology and Hunter-Gatherer Foraging.* B.A.R. International Series 381. Oxford: B.A.R.

Simpson, Beryl B. (editor)
1977 *Mesquite, Its Biology in Two Desert Ecosystems.* U.S. and International Biome Project Synthesis Series 4. Straudsburg, Pennsylvania : Dowden, Hutchinson and Ross.

Sims, Phillip L.
1988 Grasslands. In *North American Terrestrial Vegetation*, edited by Michael G. Barbour and William D. Billings, pp.266-286. New York: Cambridge University Press.

Smith, C. Earle.
1950 Prehistoric Plant Remains from Bat Cave. *Botanical Museum Leafltets*, Harvard University 14 (7): 157-180.
1967 Plant Remains. In *The Prehistory of the Tehuacan Valley 1: Environment and Subsistence*, edited by Douglas S. Byer, pp 220-255. Austin: University of Texas.

Smith, Eric Alden
1983 Anthropological Applications of Optimal Foraging Theory: A Critical Review. *Current Anthropology* 24(5): 625-651.

Sobolik, Kristin D.
1988 Diet Change in the Lower Pecos: Analysis of Baker Cave Coprolites. *Bulletin of the Texas Archaeological Society* 59: 111-127.

Sparkman, Philip S.
1908 The Culture of the Luiseno Indians. *University of California Publications in American Archaeology and Ethnology* 8(4): 187-234.

Spencer, Donald A., and Alice Spencer
1941 Food Habits of the White-throated Woodrat in Arizona. *Journal of Mammology* 22(3): 280-284.

Spoerl, Patricia M.
1981 Mogollon Utilization of the Sacramento Mountains of South-Central New Mexico. Paper presented at the Second Jornada Mongollon Conference, Portales, New Mexico.

Standley, Paul C.
1912 *Some Useful Plants of New Mexico*. Smithsonian Institution Annual Report for 1911: 447-462. Washington, D.C.: Smithsonian Institution.

Steggerda, Morris and Ruth Eckardt
1941 Navajo Foods and Their Preparation. *Journal of the American Dietetic Association* 17(3): 217-225.

Stevenson, Matilda C.
1915 *Ethnobotany of the Zuni*. Bureau of American Ethnology 30th Annual Report (1908-1909). Washington, D.C: Smithsonian Institution.

1904 *The Zuni Indians*. Bureau of American Ethnology 23rd Annual Report (1901-1902). Washington, D.C.: Smithsonian Institution.

Steward, Julian H.
1933 Ethnography of the Owens Valley Paiute. *University of California Publications in American Archaeology and Ethnography* 33(3): 233-350.

1938 *Basin-Plateau Aboriginal Socio-Political Groups*. Bureau of American Ethnology Bulletin 120. Washington, D.C.: Smithsonian Institution.

Stiger, Mark
    1979 Mesa Verde Subsistence Patterns from Basketmaker to Pueblo III. *Kiva* 44(2): 133-144.

Stuart, David E., and Rory P. Gauthier
    1981 *Prehistoric New Mexico Background for Survey.* Sant Fe: State Planning Division, Historic Preservation Bureau.

Stubbs, Stanley S., and W.illiam S. Stallings. Jr.
    1953 *The Excavation of Pindi Pueblo, New Mexico.* Monographs of the School of American Research and the Laboratory of Anthropology 18. Santa Fe: School of American Research.

Swank, George
    1932 The Ethnobotany of Acoma and Laguna. Unpublished Master's Thesis. Department of Biology, University of New Mexico, Albuquerque.

Swift, Marilyn K., Kathleen Morrison, and William H. Doleman (editors)
    1991 Mitigated Sites. In *Landscape Archaeology of the Southern Tularosa Basin, Vol. 2: Testing, Excavation and Analysis*, edited by William H. Doleman, Richard C. Chapman, Jeanne Schutt, Marilyn K. Swift, and Kathleen D. Morrison (spell out names), pp. 49-189. Albuquerque: Office of Contract Archaeology,. University of New Mexico.

Tagg, Martyn D.
    1996 Early Cultigens from Fresnal Shelter, Southeastern New Mexico. *American Antiquity* 61(2): 311-324.

Thomas, David Hurst
    1983a *The Archaeology of Monitor Valley 1: Epistemology.* Anthropological Papers of the American Museum of Natural History 58 (Part 1). New York: American Museum of Natural History.

    1983b *The Archaeology of Monitor Valley 2: Gatecliff Shelter.* Anthropological Papers of the American Museum of Natural History 59 (Part 1), pp. 1-552. New York: American Museum of Natural History.

Toll, Mollie S.
    1983 Changing Patterns of Plant Utilization for Food and Fuel: Evidence from Flotation and Macrobotanical Remains. In *Economy and Interaction Along the Lower Chaco River*, edited by Patrick Hogan and Joseph C. Winter, pp. 331-350. Albuquerque: Office of Contract Archaeology and Maxwell Museum of Anthropology, University of New Mexico.

    1998 *Botanical Analyses at the High Rolls Cave: LA114103, in the Sacramento Mountains, N.M. (N.M. Project 41.6381).* Ethnobotany Lab Technical Series No.63. MS, Museum of New Mexico, Office of Archaeological Studies, Santa Fe.

Toll, Mollie S., and Anne C. Cully
    1994 Archaic Subsistence and Seasonal Occupation Flow in Northwest New Mexico. In *Archaic Hunter Gatherer Archaeology in the American Southwest*, edited by Bradley J. Vierra, pp. 103-120. Contributions in Anthropology 13(1). Portales, New Mexico: Eastern New Mexico University.

Train, Percy, James R. Henrichs, and W. Andrew Archer
    1941 *Medicinal Uses of Plants by Indian Tribes of Nevada.* Contributions Toward a Flora of Nevada No.33 (mimeographed). Washington, D.C.: United States Department of Agriculture, Bureau of Plant Industry, Division of Plant Exploration and Introduction.

Trigg, Heather B., Richard I. Ford, John G.Moore, and Louise D. Jessop
1994 Coprolite Evidence for Prehistoric Foodstuffs, Condiments, and Medicines. In *Eating on the Wild Side*, edited by Nina L. Etkin, pp.210-223. Tucson: University of Arizona Press.

United States Department of Agriculture (U.S.D.A.)
1937 *Range Plant Handbook*. United States Department of Agriculture Forest Service. Washington, D.C.: U.S. Government Printing Office.

1974 *Seeds of Woody Plants in the United States*. Washington, D.C.: United States Department of Agriculture Handbook 450.

1976 *Soils and Vegetation Inventory of White Sands Missile Range*. Portland, Oregon: United States Department of Agriculture Natural Resources Conservation Service (Soil Conservation Service), West Region.

Van Devender, Thomas R., Julio L. Betancourt, and Mark Wimberly
1984 Biogeographic Implications of a Packrat Midden Sequence from the Sacramento Mountains, South Central New Mexico. *Quaternary Research* 22(3): 344-360.

Vander Wall, Stephen B.
1990 *Food Hoarding in Animals*. Chicago: University of Chicago Press.

Vestal, Paul A.
1952 *Ethnobotany of the Ramah Navaho*. Papers of the Peabody Museum of American Archaeology and Ethnology 40(4). Cambridge: Harvard University.

Wallen, Deborah R., and John A. Ludwig
1978 Energy Dynamics of Vegetative and Reproductive Growth in Spanish Bayonet (Yucca baccata Torr.) *The Southwestern Naturalist* 23(3): 409-422.

Weber, Steven A., and P. David Seaman (editors)
1985 *Havasupai Habitat*. Tucson: University of Arizona Press.

Wells, Philip
1976 Vegetational History from Woodrat Middens. *Quaternary Research* 6(2): 223-248.

Wetterstrom, Wilma
1986 *Food, Diet, and Population at Prehistoric Arroyo Hondo*. Arroyo Hondo Archaeological Series 6. Santa Fe: School of American Research Press.

Wheat, Margaret M.
1967 *Survival Arts of the Primitive Paiute*. Reno: University of Nevada Press.

White, Leslie
1942 *Pueblo of Santa Ana*. American Anthropological Association Memoir 60. Menasha, Wisconsin: American Anthropological Association.

Wiens, John A.
1976 Population Responses to Patchy Environments. *Annual Review of Ecolotgy and Systematics* 7: 81-120.

Wills III, Wert H.
  1988 *Early Prehistoric Agriculture in the American Southwest*. Santa Fe: School of American Research.

Wimberly, Mark L., and Peter L. Eidenbach
  1981 Preliminary Analysis of Faunal Remains from Fresnal Shelter, New Mexico: Evidence of Differential Butchering Practices During the Archaic Period. *The Artifact 19* (3,4): 21-40.

  1977 *Futures Past: The Research Prospectus*. Human Systems Research, Tularosa, New Mexico.

Wimberly, Mark L., and Alan Rogers
  1977 Archaeological Survey Three Rivers Drainage New Mexico. *The Artifact 15*:1-472.

Winter, Joseph C (editor)
  2000 *Tobacco Use by Native North Americans*. Norman: University of Oklahoma Press.

Winterhalder, Bruce
  1981 Optimal Foraging Strategies and Hunter-Gatherer Research in Anthropology: Theory and Models. In *Hunter-Gatherer Foraging Strategies*, edited by Bruce Winterhalder and Eric Alden Smith, pp. 13-35. Chicago: University of Chicago Press.

Wooton, E. O., and Paul C. Standley
  1912 *The Grasses and Grass-Like Plants of New Mexico*. Agricultural Experiment Station Bulletin 81. Las Cruces, New Mexico: New Mexico State University.

  1915 *Flora of New Mexico*. Contributions from the U. S. National Herbarium 19. Washington, D.C.: U.S. National Museum, Smithsonian Institution.

Writers Program of the Work Projects Administration
  1940 *New Mexico: A Guide to the Colorful State*. American Guide Series. New York: Hasting House.

Wyman, Leland C., and Stuart K. Harris
  1941 *Navajo Indian Medical Ethnobotany*. University of New Mexico Bulletin Anthropological Series 3(5). Albuquerque: University of New Mexico Press.

  1951 *Ethnobotany of the Kayenta Navajo*. University of New Mexico Publications in Biology 5. Albuquerque: University of New Mexico Press.

Yanovsky, Elias
  1936 *Food Plants of the North American Indians*. U.S.D.A. Miscellaneous Publication 237. Washington, D.C.: United States Department of Agriculture.

York, John C., and William A. Dick-Peddie
  1969 Vegetation Changes in Southern New Mexico During the Past Hundred Years. In *Arid Lands in Perspective*, edited by William G. McGinnies and Bram J. Goldmen, pp. 157-166. Tucson: University of Arizona Press.

Zauderer, Jeffrey
  1975 A Survey of Typical Antelope House Quids. *Kiva* 41(1): 65-70.

Zigmond, Maurice
  1981 *Kawaisu Ethnobotany*. Salt Lake City: University of Utah Press.